£10

THE
LANCASHIRE
NOBBY

The Annan Presentation Model. (Dumfries Museums, Nithsdale District Council)

THE
LANCASHIRE NOBBY

NICK MILLER

AMBERLEY

First published 2009

Amberley Publishing Plc
Cirencester Road, Chalford,
Stroud, Gloucestershire, GL6 8PE

www.amberley-books.com

British Library Cataloguing in Publication Data.
A catalogue record for this book is available from the British Library.

ISBN 978 1 84868 490 4

Typesetting and Origination by Diagraf (www.diagraf.net)
Printed in Great Britain

Contents

Plates

ILLUSTRATIONS

Introduction

The objective of this book is to set down the origins and development of the Lancashire nobby; to describe the way these vessels were worked under sail, and the communities that used them. It attempts to record the one or two-man cutter rigged trawlers from the Irish Sea coast of mainland Britain. Their builders and owners called them 'nobbies', 'half-deckers', 'prawners', 'smacks', 'shanking' or 'trawl boats', and they were called Morecambe Bay 'prawners' by authors and journalists. This study has grown out of researches undertaken to facilitate the rebuild to original condition of the author's nobby, *Nora* LR 59. The term nobby is also used for a standing lug-rigged herring drifter from the Isle of Man, of which some were commissioned by the Irish Congested Districts Board of 1891 for use in Connemara. The Manx nobby has a different bloodline and mode of fishing, sharing only its name with the Lancashire nobby. Although the nobby took well to motors, and some motor nobbies were built, this work concentrates on the period of the sailing trawl boats.

The nobby's range, as shown on the map of the Irish Sea (fig. 1) extended from Annan to Aberystwyth when fishing, although yachtsmen have cruised converted nobbies all round the British coast. They were the workhorses of a longshore and near-water industry, fishing for cod, flatfish, herring, mackerel, sprats, whitebait, and pink and brown shrimp, whilst also serving as pleasure boats at holiday resorts. They conducted the fishery with beam trawl, drift net, stow net, and occasionally with long line, hand line and oyster dredge. Some boats stayed within a tide's sail of their mooring, whilst others followed their quarry to other ports. This book concentrates on the sailing era, up to the 1920s. Nobbies took well to engines, but the economics of fishing and boat building meant that few nobbies were built after the Second World War.

Thanks go to the many people who shared their memories and explained details. Most thanks go to Keith Willacy, who gave access to his notes and sketches, and to Maurice Evans and Cdr Gil Mayes for sharing their researches. Maurice Evans has provided much of the information identifying the builders and owners of the nobbies mentioned herein. Thanks go to Ben Holmes who opened doors in Fleetwood, the Duddon and Annan, and to Alfred Crossfield who shared his memories. Thanks go to Tom Willacy of Annan, Len Lloyd for locating original sources and nobbies to be drawn around Southport, and to Edward Sharkey and Percy Dunbavand of Runcorn. Thanks also go to the North Western and North Wales Sea Fisheries Committee, Lancaster Maritime and Dumfries Museums, and the Public Record offices on the Cumbria, Lancashire, and Welsh coasts for access to the material used here. The archive sources included the records of the surviving fisherman's mutual insurance organisations, town directories, early Ordnance Survey maps, *Yachting Monthly*, *The North Lonsdale Magazine*, and photographic collections.

The author and Mr L.J. Lloyd measured the boats' lines that have been recorded, with the exception of those of *Provider*. The models were measured thanks to the courtesy of the Science Museum, South Kensington, and the Botanic Gardens Museum at Churchtown, Southport. Some of the lines plans are lodged with the Mersey Maritime Museum, whilst the lines, construction, and outfit plans of *Nora* are also lodged with both the Science and National Maritime Museums.

Where values have been quoted, they have also been converted to £.np (New Pence) at 2005 values using data from the National Statistics website, www.statistics.gov.uk, and Twigger (1999). These 2005 values appear in parentheses following the original values.

This book tries to set out a true record of the workhorses of a regional industry: it is a story occasionally distorted by the romance of the most yacht-like of the British fishing craft. Many nobbies do now survive as yachts, and a few yachts are now claimed to have been trawlers – a phenomenon of the current interest in vintage working boats, which conspires to make the field-worker's life difficult.

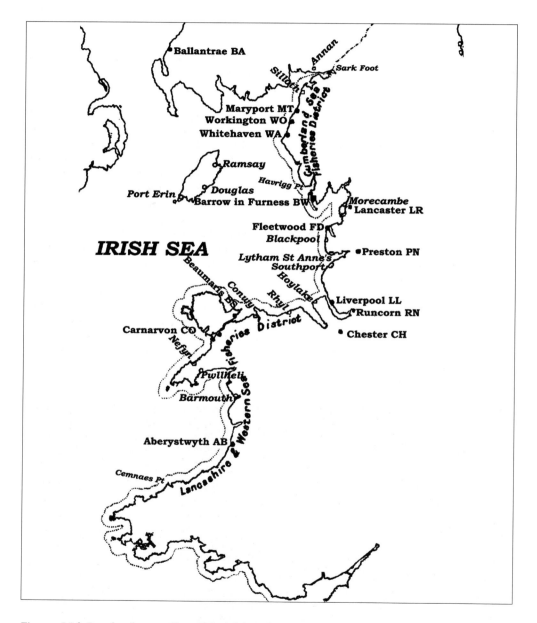

Fig. 1. Irish Sea sketch map. (from F.G. Aflalo, *The Sea Fishing Industry of England and Wales*)

Chapter 1

Origins

The earliest documentary evidence for trawl boats found in the nobby's history dates from 1800, in a lecture given by Mr M.N. Hosker of Southport drawing on local sources. However the word 'trawling' was also used to describe the use of longlines, so we cannot be sure whether these boats were trawling with a net. There are records of the fishing industry going much further back. A reference discusses the ownership of the fishing rights at North Meols back to 1086. Thomas de Multon granted rights for fishing with a boat at Ellenfoot to the Abbey of Holm Cultram in the thirteenth century. In 1382 there is reference to legislation to prohibit the denial of access for fishermen setting their nets in the sea. Records show that herring were supplied by George Wright of Melles (Meols, Southport) in 1594, whilst in 1614 the inventory of the estate of the Rector of North Meols included sixteen yards of sailcloth. In 1636 Reverend Richard James, fellow of Corpus Christi, Oxford, while on tour met with a Meales fisherman who was 'Wading for ye soles ... – which the last morning tides had stayed in nets, or did at anchor ride upon his hooks'. In addition to sole he caught rayes, fluke, cod, whiting and place [sic]. Neither of these techniques involves trawling, using instead kettles or stake nets and longlining.

The waters along the nobby coast must have been very prolific up until the beginning of the nineteenth century, as Eija Kennerley (1982) recorded that both cod and herring were caught in the fixed traps called baulks in 1813. Jack Mount told the *Visitor*, one of the Morecambe newspapers, that his great-grandfather drowned, lost in fog, when tending fixed herring nets on Middleton Sands in around 1800. Prodigious quantities of mackerel were taken at North Meols in 1703, and on 4 of August 1728, 30,000 herring were taken at Hale on the Mersey.

Plate 1. Morecambe model of *c.*1870, profile. (Courtesy of Lancaster City Museums)

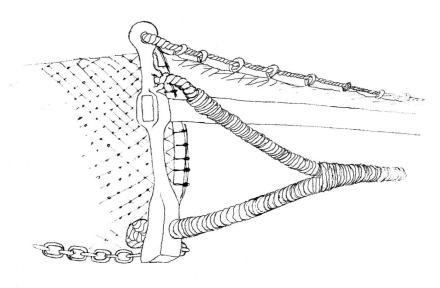

Fig. 2 Beam trawl head, Scheveningen, after E.W. Cooke, 1860.

The first mention of a beam-trawl like engine is from 1376, when oyster dredgers were complaining of the use for the past seven years of a 'wondyrchoun', as it destroyed the ground over which it worked. Davies (1958) reports that the wondyrchoun was described as 'three fathom long and ten men's' feet wide, and that it had a beam ten feet long, at the end of which were two frames formed like a colerake, that a leaded rope weighted with a great many stones was fixed on the lower part of the net between the two frames, and that another rope was fixed with nails on the upper part of the beam, so that the fish entering the space between the beam and the lower net were caught. The net had maskes of the length and breadth of two men's thumbs'. The only part of this description requiring any further explanation is that of the trawl head. A colerake was a scraper used to remove un-burnt coals and ashes from bread ovens. The Museum of Welsh Life has an early version, an L-shaped iron on a haft. The earliest form of trawl head is believed to be the 'Barking' pattern, which is shaped like a stirrup. However as stirrups came to Britain in the ninth century the use of 'colerake' as a descriptor in the fourteenth century implies that the Barking pattern had not then been developed, and that the first trawl irons were L-shaped. This is supported by a painting by E.W. Cooke in the Guildhall Art Gallery, London, of Dutch pinks at Scheveningen, executed in 1860. The pink in the foreground has a beam trawl stowed on her rail. The head of this trawl is an iron stanchion with a heavy square base, pierced for the lower part of a two-part end to the aft bridle. The upper part of the bridle was bent to a ring above the beam, so that they both kept the stanchion upright when under tension. Fig. 2 is a line drawing based on this painting that illustrates the trawl iron, bridle, head and footrope. This group of Danish fishermen may have continued to use this ancient form of beam trawl into the nineteenth century, so preserving the design of trawl iron used on the wondyrchoun. However there is a difference, in that the back of the net is carried above the beam from the top of the stanchions, rather than being nailed to it.

There were mentions of trawling in Essex in 1377 and 1566. Acts of Parliament from the seventeenth century were passed to regulate trawl-net mesh size, at which time trawling was also carried out in Devon's inshore waters. This industry developed so that the *Sherborne Mercury* was able to advertise the sale of thirteen trawl boats and gear in its edition of 11 December 1764. There were also references to a fleet at Brixham of seventy-six decked sloops in 1785; this had increased to ninety by 1791. Holdsworth (1874)

Plate 2. Morecambe model
of *c*.1870, deck. (Courtesy of
Lancaster City Museums)

implies that trawling could have been common in the Lancashire fishery for many years, so
the technique may have been used earlier than 1800. There is a specific reference in 1800
to a fleet of thirteen trawl boats in Hosker's sources, but we have found no evidence for
when trawling began in Lancashire.

Edgar March (1970) refers to trawlers supplying Liverpool from the North Meols Bank
at the end of the eighteenth century. This is confirmed by the image of a schooner, the
Wherry *Isabel* dragging a trawl on a commemorative bowl dated *c*.1760. Brockbanks,
the Lancaster shipbuilder, launched a 34-ton smack named *Otter* in 1803 to supply the
Lancaster markets, but Kennerley (1982) reports no mention of her mode of fishing. She
will have been about 50ft long, with a of 13ft 8in beam. The trawl boat *Greyhound* started
landing fish at Lancaster in 1838. The sources continue to establish the existence of fishing
with boats at Poulton and Southport, alongside references to baulks, without specifying
the craft's size or the method used. It should be remembered that although there has always
been a demand for fish, especially salt cod, herring, kippers and red herring, as a durable,
transportable and relatively cheap source of protein, there would also have been a steady
demand for fish in the strong Catholic population of Lancashire for their Friday meal.

Whilst the size of the markets in the big coastal towns and cities made the use of big
trawlers a viable proposition, smaller coastal towns and villages could only sustain a
fishery large enough to feed the number of dwellings that could be serviced in a day's walk.
The only exception to this was where a resident was wealthy enough to set up a curing or
smoke house to preserve herring – this is known to have occurred at several villages on
the Welsh, Lancashire, and Cumbrian coasts. The Welsh ports and Southport used herring
boats crewed by half-a-dozen men, whilst at Allonby in Cumbria wherries were employed.
Small-scale fishing supplying a local market could be carried out using fish baulks, stake
nets, and trotlines without recourse to boats. However, as townships grew and holidays
including sea bathing began to grow in popularity during the eighteenth century (see later
chapters), additional demand encouraged investment in boats and fishing gear that yielded
bigger catches to feed the larger markets.

The development of seaside holidays began with the belief that a dip in the sea was of
medicinal benefit. Medical practitioners were discussing the benefits of sea bathing in print
around 1700. Mill workers and mechanics would come to seaside towns and villages for
a weekend visit when there were big tides. Initially their local carriers and shopkeepers

Plate 3. Morecambe
model of *c.*1870, stern.
(Courtesy of Lancaster
City Museums)

provided transport to the coast in delivery carts as an alternative to walking. As the factory
system of cotton manufacture developed in Lancashire and West Yorkshire, providing
employment for all of the family including the young teenage children of the household,
family incomes increased to allow holidays of a week's duration to be enjoyed. This
broadened the market and opportunities for boatmen at the Lancashire coastal towns. This
growth experienced an almost stepwise increase when the railway network allowed three
developments to drive a greater demand for fish. They allowed easier access to seaside
holidays for the workers in industrial towns, as well as allowing the businessmen to bring
their families to new dormitory towns at the seaside, and allowed the fish to be sent inland
to the big markets of the inland cities. There was also an additional feedback loop creating
a demand for shrimp once the railways and higher wages of the mill workers allowed them
to holiday at towns were shrimp were available as a delicacy. Having enjoyed them when
on holiday, there grew a demand in the hometowns' markets for shrimp all the year round.
Blackpool and Morecambe's growth as resorts outstripped the development of many other
seaside towns due to the higher earnings of the mill workers in the Lancashire mill towns.
The policies and aspirations of the landowners who sponsored the development of the other
resorts also affected the type of visitor and resident, which affected the development of the
opportunities for the fishing community. This will be discussed in the following chapters.
The cotton industry began to decline in the 1920s, which is just after the timeframe of this
book, but may be of relevance as the rate of building of new nobbies also began to decline
in the '30s, when the decline in the cotton towns really began to bite.

In searching for the origins of the nobby some guidance can be taken from the
terminology used to identify the boats. Elmer (1973) lists the names as 'nobby' from
Morecambe round to mid-Wales, and variously as 'prawner', 'shrimper', 'half decker', and
'smack' to the north. There was the inevitable exception at St Anne's and Lytham were the
term smack survived. It is likely that 'nobby' is a colloquialism as the officials of the Sea
Fisheries Committees on our coast refer to the smaller second-class boats as 'shrimpers' or
'shrimp trawlers', and the larger type as 'prawners'. There are two possible explanations
of the change from the generic term 'smack' to the name 'nobby'.

One possible explanation for the term reflects the evolution of the fishing craft on our
coast. Edgar March (1970) talks of trawlers, called smacks, originally built as cutters being
converted to ketch rig from 1830 through to 1880. It follows that when Fleetwood was

Plate 4. Nobby in Ulverston Channel. (*The North Lonsdale Magazine* 1894)

Plate 5. Nobby from astern. (*The North Lonsdale Magazine* 1894)

Plate 6. Abandoned lute-sterned nobby. (*The North Lonsdale Magazine* 1900)

Plate 7. Nobbies in
Walney Channel.
(Collection of A. Lockett)

being set up from 1838 to 1842, all of the smacks used on our coast may well have been cutters, although by this time the Manx had given up their cutter rig herring boats for the dandy with a lug mizzen. The Manx adopted the lug mizzen from the Cornish herring luggers.

According to *A History of Furness* (Richardson 1880), Mr Richard Ashburner, (who joined his brother William at Barrow-in-Furness) had been building coasters and small fishing boats at Greenodd from about 1830 to 1850. The fishing boats were reputedly for Fleetwood owners. Ashburners' Barrow-in-Furness shipyard built coasters for the iron-ore trade and also built three 'trolling' boats. One was the Fleetwood ketch-rigged smack *Gratitude* FD 156, built in 1858 as a trading flat, being lengthened and re-rigged in 1880; the others were *Ebenezer*, and *Champion* FD 67 of 1853. Mr William Ashburner ran his Barrow-in-Furness shipyard from 1847.

As ketch-rigged smacks were coming in by 1850, and were building at Fleetwood by 1866, it will have been necessary to distinguish between the new larger boats and the smaller cutters that became the nobby. Similarly small cutters were adopted at Hoylake when the full-size ketch-rigged smacks became inconvenient to use as the Hoyle Lake sanded up around about 1880 to 1890. The *English Dialect Dictionary* of 1898 states that the word 'nobby' refers to 'smallness' in many of its usages: e.g. a lump of material, the head, a child's nose, and through middle England a colt. Taking this with the continued use of 'smack' for the cutters at Maryport, where we have found no evidence for large ketch-rigged trawlers but a big herring fishery attracting Manx nobbies, it is possible that the small cutters were called nobbies to distinguish them from the big ketches.

The northern ports also used more descriptive names. Barrow-in-Furness uses 'half-decker', as does Fleetwood on occasion. 'Prawner', 'shrimper', 'smack', and 'half-decker' seem to be used without pattern north of Barrow-in-Furness. Morecambe, and the builders at Arnside and Freckleton, also use 'trawl boat', whilst Ulverston and Duddon fishermen can only remember using the name 'prawner'. South of Morecambe the term 'nobby' is usual, although 'smack' and 'shanking boat' were recorded at Lytham. This derives from the shrimp shank used by the cart-fishermen, and used to describe the shrimp trawl at Fleetwood, Lytham, and Southport. The coasts from Fleetwood to mid-Wales were used to the big Fleetwood and Hoylake smacks, and the mid-Wales ports were also used to the Milford Haven fleet. The northern part of the nobby's range was exposed to the Manx fleet of drifters, with only Whitehaven having big trawlers. Lytham seems to be a rule unto itself with its terminology, as they alone do not use the word 'nog', using the more universal term 'timberhead'. If it were not for the use of 'smack' at Lytham, this would tend to support

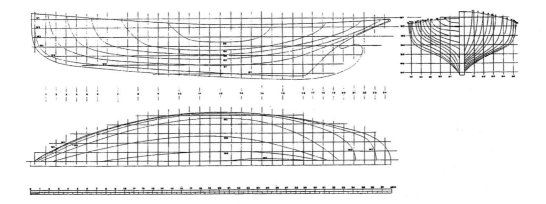

Fig. 3. Lines, Southport nobby of 1880.

the premise that the use of 'nobby' in the south refers to a small cutter-rigged trawler, to differentiate from the big smacks.

Alternatively both the *Oxford English Dictionary* and the *English Dialect Dictionary* list nobby as being of a rich man, a nob or toff, or 'smart', and give it a wide distribution. The *Vocabulary of the Anglo-Manx Dialect* quotes the first Manx nobby in 1884 receiving its name because it was 'a rale nobby little thing'. The Lancashire nobby may have received its name in the same way, as a smart trawl boat. Determining when is difficult, as the written word is rarely recorded the fisherman's dialect. The earliest record we have comes from the newspaper reports of the Hoylake Regatta of 1889. Hoylake fishermen were changing over from big first-class smacks to second-class trawl boats and shrimpers around this time, so a name to differentiate a second-class boat from first-class smacks was needed. The reports of the regattas in the Dee and Mersey at this time did not use the term nobby, so it appears to have been peculiar to Hoylake, and may well have spread from there.

The boats from which the nobby evolved were first mentioned at Southport in the source used by W.T. Bulpit, in the eighteenth century. Four boats moved from Banks to Fleetwood in 1842, encouraged by the railway company, four years after Sir Hesketh Fleetwood laid out the new town. The fishing families of Baxter and Leadbetter moved to Fleetwood in that year. Four more boats moved round from Marshside in the following year. There is no dated description of the Southport form of cutter earlier than *c.*1880, the lines of which appear as Fig. 3. Edgar March (1970) described a hull similar to the photograph of an old Fleetwood nobby published by Robert Simper (1979) photographed by Francis Frith, and to the Annan trawl boat of *c.*1880 whose lines are reproduced as Fig. 4. There are photographs of Lytham boats and Blackpool beach boats that may give an indication of the form of older Southport boats. They are clench-built, flat-floored craft with a moderate round to the forefoot and a short, shallow, squarish elliptical counter. Their lines (Fig. 5) are derived from the excellent photograph of two craft laid up on the crest of the Double Stanner at Lytham taken in 1892 published by Haley (1995).

A report in the *Lancaster Gazette* of 7 November 1840 indicated the wide extent that the fishing communities up and down the coast were in contact with each other, the *Gazette* reported:

Man drowned – We understand that a Southport fisherman was drowned at Poulton, by falling out of his boat last Saturday.

The boat shed of Francis John Crossfield produced its first boat at Arnside in 1838, forming part of the second strand of the rope that when laid up together with the strand formed by the southern boats produced the Lancashire nobby. The earliest description of the Morecambe boats of 1854 is from a descendant of the fishing community at Annan. The four Poulton fishermen, James Baxter, John Holmes, William Woodman, and Mr Woodhouse, set this community up at Kenizels, Waterfoot, at Annan. The nobbies are described as 30-35ft long, half decked, square sterned, and clench built. The four Poulton men were herring drifting off Maryport when caught in a gale and driven up the Solway Firth. After sheltering at Waterfoot they tried their luck in the Firth before returning home. Their good catch made them decide to return to Annan with their families.

This record also gives some idea of the strength of the craft existing in the 1850s. The documentation of the arrival of the Morecambe fishermen at Annan is also strong evidence for the widespread use of trawling as an established technique from before the mid-nineteenth century. The Annan community that was set up when the Poulton fishermen took shelter there was enlarged when other Poulton families followed them, including the Willacys.

The description 'square-sterned' must be questioned, as by 1871 a Poulton fisherman was throwing away a fine model of a clench-built cutter with a stern-like a square tuck, now in the collection of Lancaster Maritime Museum. Three views of the model appear as Plates 1, 2 & 3. Her rig and deck layout is reminiscent of a large cutter, with pin-rails at the bowsprit bitts and shrouds. This model, and Holdsworth's (1874) publication of an engraving of a sloop-rigged beam trawler with a similar stern from Morecambe Bay suggests that 'square-sterned' described a square tuck or square counter, rather than the modern usage indicating a transom stern. The engraving that is copied in Fig. 6 is from an original drawing by Holdsworth from his own observations. The reason for this proposal is that for a model to be discarded in 1871, it will have been built in about 1850 or 1860. This is at about the same time that the Morecambe fishermen took square-sterned boats to Annan. Chapelle (1951) documents Bermuda cutters with the same stern. Chapelle refers to the counter as a 'square tuck' and states that the form was common in both America and Great Britain in the early nineteenth century. The term 'tuck' survives at Morecambe in the local term for the bulkhead at the sternpost, and in the hollow shape in this area of the hull. Local usage of the term 'main stern' for the bulkhead at the sternpost also supports the proposition of a square tuck stern as the original form.

The *Peggy*, named after her owner George Quayle's mother, was launched into Castletown harbour in 1791. She worked many years at trade and smuggling until she became too well known. Although she is now referred to as a yacht, and did take part in a regatta on Windermere, she may be a sole survivor of the Irish Sea Wherry, a general-purpose shalop or schooner employed in the herring fishing as a carrier, and both commercial and illicit trade. Whilst many Manx wherries were double-ended with a round stern (a common hull form in the Irish Sea), the existence of *Peggy* and records of square tuck-sterned shallops built by Brocklebank's at Whitehaven and similar vessels being used as ferries on the Mersey (Mannering et al, 1997) indicate that the square tuck stern may have outnumbered the round stern form. The wherries of the Irish Sea coast that have the square tuck stern confirm the earlier existence of this form of stern that is proposed for the cutter rigged trawl boats on both shores of Morecambe Bay.

The North Lonsdale Magazine published three photographs from 1894 to 1900, copied here as Plates 4, 5 & 6. They are all sloops with a square tuck stern, the last of which was old and tatty enough to have been abandoned. She must have been forty to fifty years old then, which again dates the square tuck stern to about 1850 and the Annan adventure. These photographs were taken along the north shore of the Bay at or above Ulverston, so they could have been built at Greenodd or Ulverston. Deck details, especially the bowsprit heel chock, do indicate a common practice both to the north and south coast of the Bay. The bowsprit on the sailing model, the Annan model whose photograph forms the frontispiece, and *The North Lonsdale Magazine* photograph, was housed in a transverse chock with an iron staple to retain its heel. The pump discharge is also visible; the plunge hole shows clearly in the middle of the thwart. The remains of the discharge trough are visible on the top of the thwart and the port in the shear strake can just be seen. Plate 7 records a square tuck stern amongst more modern nobbies in Walney Channel. The lines plan of the square tuck-sterned form, Fig. 7, was recreated by carving a model that captured all of the information from all of these photographs. This model was then measured to take off its lines.

The proposal that the Morecambe nobby had a square tuck stern before 1850 also gives a more reasonable timescale for the evolution of the elliptical counter at Annan and Morecambe by 1880. It seems unlikely that the hull form could evolve from transom to counter in thirty years, although a sudden adoption of a yacht-style counter could have occurred. The nobby's evolution from a square tuck-stern is also indirectly supported by the process known to have taken place with both the lute-sterned Hastings luggers and the Essex smacks. The last known surviving square tuck-sterned smack is the 35ft *Mary*. She is believed to have been built at Burnham-on-Crouch in 1850.

The change to an elliptical counter by the Bay fishermen was probably due to their familiarity with the Fleetwood and Southport boats. The report of the drowning accident of 1840 confirms this possibility. The Crossfields and their customers were also familiar with the local yachts, sailing as hired hands, and may well have adopted yacht sterns. Dixon Kemp (1878) records that in 1872 the Windermere yachtsmen tried rule-cheating by immersing the counter. The rules were changed in 1881, by which time the Windermere yachts sported long elliptical counters. William Crossfield designed the *Bonita*, as the *White Rose*, in 1880. As her lines (Fig. 8) show she has the fully developed shrimping nobbies' counter on the older form hull with the upright sternpost and straight floors. The counters designed by the Crossfields tended to be deeper than the older southern boats, so they may have been more heavily influenced by the Windermere yachts. The counter stern allowed for a sweeter run with more lift in a seaway than a square tuck. The twin drives of competitiveness and safety would have ensured its adoption. The shrimpers working the channels of the bay retained their shoal draft whilst now having the same general form as the bigger Fleetwood and Southport nobbies.

Having reached the point when the two disparate forms have evolved towards each other, it is appropriate to use Commander Eric McKee's method to classify the two original types, as set out in Chapter 10 and Appendix VII of his *Working Boats* (1983). The Southport nobbies were 'unrelated grades' in continuous but limited distribution. If the origin of the Poulton nobby included the Greenodd and Ulverston fishing boats, they will have been continuous but limited unrelated grades. With time it will be shown that the nobby evolved into an unrelated grade with continuous and extended distribution.

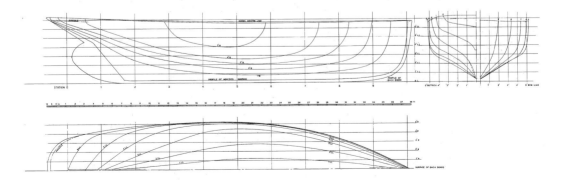

Fig. 4. Lines, Annan model of 1880.

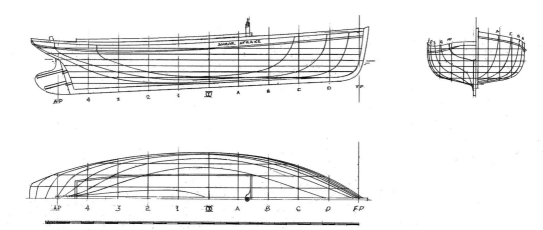

Fig. 5. Lines, Lytham smack.

Subsequent chapters of this book will record that the Lancashire Nobby hull form was used for a variety of craft. At Morecambe the form was used for pleasure boats and for one or more volunteer lifeboats. The pleasure boats were of two types: smaller open craft with standing lugsails, and shoal-drafted nobbies known as 'Bay boats' at Morecambe. William Stoba at Fleetwood applied the form to larger craft, including two Bristol Channel pilot skiffs and a ketch-rigged smack.

There is one other form that needs to be discussed even though it is hardly within the remit of this work. These are the pond yachts made by the fishermen. Reference has already been made to the Morecambe pond yacht of pre-1871; a later model belongs to the collections of Lancaster Maritime Museum and a model named *Joy* at the Botanic Gardens Museum, Southport. It is likely that pond yachts of this form were also made and sailed at Barrow and at Fleetwood. In order for a pond yacht to sail it needs to be deeper drafted in proportion to its full-size prototypes, and have a larger rudders. It may also have greater freeboard. This is apparent in both surviving models. The greater freeboard creates a feature of both models that may help to differentiate a pond yacht from a model of an actual boat. Nobby counters are built with a straight-horn timber; however, a large freeboard combined with a straight horn would pull the counter out to an inordinate length. The pond yacht builders have compromised by carving a spoon-shaped counter with a curving horn timber. The Southport model has also been outfitted as if it was a fishing nobby, although the bowsprit fittings and mainsheet screw eye of the pond yacht have been retained. The model was owned by a John Wignall of Shellfield Road, Marshside, who was not a fishing nobby owner in his own right.

Fig. 6. Morecambe
nobby *c.*1870. (E.W.H.
Holdsworth, *Deep
Sea Fishing & Fishing
Boats*)

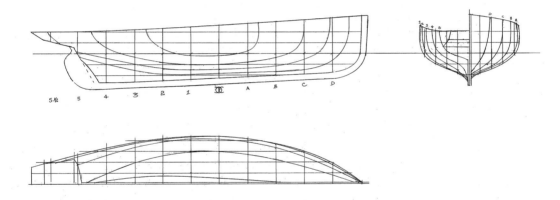

Fig. 7. Lines of lute-sterned nobby.

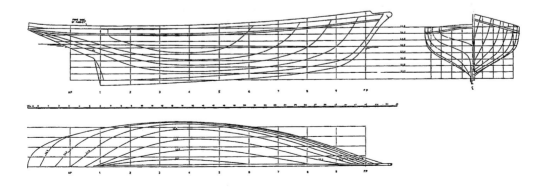

Fig. 8. *Bonita* lines.

Chapter 2

Fishing Techniques

Because use tends to define the tool, it is appropriate to discuss how the nobby was worked. The nobby was primarily a trawl boat; however, she has been worked as a stowboater, herring drifter, mackerel boat, and used to set longlines. As a sailing trawler, dependant on unreliable and uncontrollable wind and tide, her crew had to adopt techniques to suit the conditions as they were found. There were two methods, each with its regional variant. When there was insufficient wind the nobby was set to broadside, using the power of the tide. When there was sufficient wind and enough sea room, the nobby could use the drive of the sails to drag the trawl. As the nobbies could not make a sufficiently fast or consistent speed through the water to keep otterboards apart, they all used some form of beam trawl until marine engines became sufficiently powerful to allow otterboards to work. This chapter describes the most commonly used techniques as used at Morecambe. The chapters on the fishing ports set out their local variations.

Nobbies trawled for three target fish, flatfish, sprawn and shrimp, but with gear tailored to suit each fish. The shrimp gear varied from place to place, but the fish and prawn trawls were all based on beam trawls with conventional trawl irons. It is appropriate to give a clearer definition of the nature of the catch. The shrimp were the common brown shrimp *Crangon vulgaris*. The sprawn were the pink shrimp *Pandalus montagui*, sometimes known as Aesop's prawn, and was not either of the common prawn *Leander serratus* or *Leander sequilla*. The term sprawn was coined because when the Morecambe men first found them they thought that they were a hybrid bred from *Crangon vulgaris* and *Leander serratus*, and coined a mixed name. Neither of the Leander prawns was taken in trawls, although

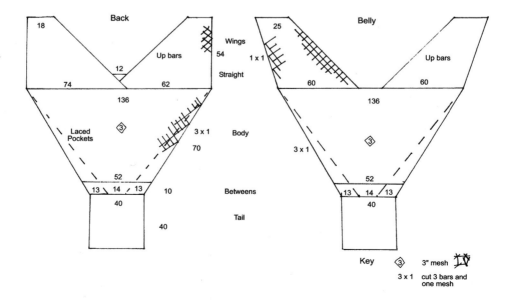

Fig. 9. Mesh count, backless fluke trawl. (Courtesy E. Nicholson)

the Sea Fisheries officers and reports persisted in calling *Pandalus montagui* and the bigger nobbies that fished for them 'prawns' and 'prawners'.

The nobbies were provided with sets of gear comprising two beams and nets for shrimp. Sprawn and fluke gear was heavier, so only one trawl was carried. The descriptions are based on notes made by Keith Willacy and from Dick Woodhouse's memoirs (Woodhouse 1979). The trawls were sized to suit the length of the hull, with a stern trawl that could stow from the front of the shrouds to the counter, and a bow trawl that could stow on the foredeck, from behind the shrouds to the stem. A 31ft shrimping nobby like the author's *Nora* LR 59 at Morecambe would have fished a 17ft stern trawl and a 10ft bow trawl. Dick Woodhouse, who as a member of the Morecambe sprawning fleet, used bigger boats of about 36ft, used an 18-20ft beam aft and one of 16ft on the bow. The fluke trawl was assembled with heavy gear, and the shrimp trawls were much lighter, until the industry began to turn down, and the gear was simplified by using the same beam and changing the net. By this time the nobbies were trawling under power, which allowed both the simplification to be made and the abandonment of the bow trawl.

All of the nets were made from cotton, the net lofts using machine-knitted sheet net. The net was prepared for use by oiling, after the net was sewn together and the ringing braided on to the head, belly, and tail ends. Side cords were not normally used as the process of sewing the back to the belly caught up three or four meshes of the selvages. The ringing were larger meshes braided on to shrimp and sprawn nets as a transition between the small meshes and the back and ground ropes. The net was dressed by being sprinkled with a boiled oil, red lead and red ochre mixture from a spouted ladle. This mix was boiled up in an old Dutch pot. The net was then dried completely for several weeks until 'sharp'. It was then taken to the promenade, to the Green Street landing, and the head was tied to the railings, drawn out to its intended width. The tail was drawn out and stretched with a tackle tied to a stake driven into the sand by the slipway. The net was left for a further two or three weeks to stretch, and to allow the excess oil to be washed off. It was then taken home to dry again. When the net was completely dry it could be rolled up and stored until needed. If it was not completely dry the middle of the rolled net might be reduced to char by spontaneous combustion.

Rigging the net was started by sewing a back cord to the back and a stoving rope to the curve of the belly. Light cord was sewn to the heads of the belly wings. The heads of the belly wings were lashed to the back of the irons, the stoving rope was attached to the foot rope (using the appropriate method for each net), and the back was lashed to the beam. All nets were originally cut full-backed, until either Jack Mount or Percy 'Pop' Baxter cut a backless net in the 1920s. Jack claimed credit in an interview in the Morecambe *Visitor*, whilst Pop was given credit by Dick Woodhouse. Keith Willacy suggests that shrimp trawls were always cut full-backed, but Mr Nicholson's book has backless shrimp nets from 1952. The innovation came in because the backs of the cotton nets always rotted first – a net may have had three backs knitted in before the belly wore out. Backless nets had a whipped eye in the back cord at the end of the wings, and four or five floats threaded on in the cover. The backless back was made fuller than the full-backed trawl so that it would rise higher when fishing. When rigging the net, care was taken to ensure that the net towed from its back. This was to ensure that the footrope dropped into any hollows in the path of the trawl. The sloping back to the trawl irons helped to guarantee this, since the head of the back leads the foot of the net. This also ensured that the back covered the footrope, so that as the fish jumped they were covered by net. Fig. 9 illustrates the mesh count for a backless fluke trawl worked out from Mr Nicholson's workbook.

The trawl irons were originally hand-forged, of only three components. They differed from the more usual design of iron only in that the bridle attachment was to a long staple, instead of an eye. This was thought to allow the bridles to settle high or low on the iron as required. Fig. 10 illustrates the iron.

The beam at Morecambe was ash in two pieces, shaped to fit a square socket on the top of the iron. The ash saplings were selected with a bend, so that when scarfed and fitted to

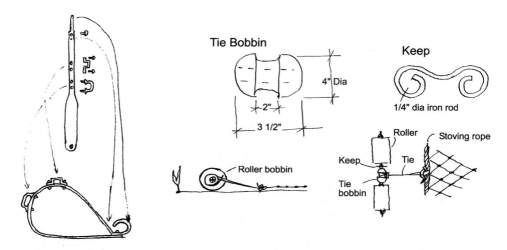

Above left: Fig. 10. Morecambe trawl head.

Above right: Fig. 11. Rigging on a sprawn net.

the irons they rose in an arch. The curve was set to match the curve of the deck edge for when the net was boarded and stowed. The butt ends were joined with a scarf, which was shaped with an adze (called a foot axe at Morecambe) and secured with one bolt and rope lashings. Apart from squaring the ends of the beam where it was to fit the cap socket on the irons, the beam was not dressed and the bark was left on. Other ports used greenheart or made the beams in three pieces.

A set of sprawn trawl-iron heads weighed 60lb (27kg) on a sprawner and 40lb (18kg) on a shrimper. They stood between 18 and 24in high (45-60cm), and were fitted to a beam of about 19-20ft length. Our sources can only remember sprawn gear with bobbins on the ground gear, so we do not know how the footrope was made before 1928, when bobbins were adopted. The gear was rigged with a chain footrope on to which the bobbins were threaded. The bobbins were turned on a lathe to 12in diameter and 10in long, bored with a hole to pass the $3/_8$in ground chain. As the bobbins near the end irons rolled obliquely over the ground they wore down until 6in in diameter, when they were replaced. The ground gear was assembled with a roller bobbin in the middle of the foot chain, and then came a 4in diameter tie bobbin, turned out of oak, and shaped like a bull's eye. Next came an iron stopper, an S- or spectacle-shaped piece of ¼in iron rod fitted into the chain to stop the bobbins bunching up. Then came a roller bobbin, tie bobbin and stopper until the chain was filled, using progressively smaller rollers (see Fig. 11 for a sketch of these components). A length of chain with a large end-link, used to recover the footrope, was put in near the bow (left hand) end of the assembly. The ground chain was fitted to the irons by being passed through the eye at the toe of the iron, and then being secured by wrapping several turns around the back of the iron. It was rigged so that the net was said to have a 4ft draught. Plate 8 records an excellent view of a trawl stowed on the side deck of Blowney Baxter's nobby *Peggy*. The trawl iron and the size of the bobbins can clearly be seen. Part of the day's catch of shrimp is being poured into a barrel from a net washer, whilst the next batch of shrimp is being sorted through in the riddle.

The net was made with seventy meshes to the yard in the wings, eighty-five in the body, and ninety meshes to the yard in the tail. The mesh count of a fairly typical sprawn trawl is illustrated by Fig. 12. Shrimp trawls used the same mesh sizes but were braided from thinner twine. Because the sprawn net was exposed to rougher usage, side cords were fitted by some of the fishermen, and pressed leather rubbers were sewn on to the belly and tail to protect from chafe, instead of net rubbers. The stoving rope was attached to the

Plate 8. Jack (Blowney) Baxter on *Peggy*. (Courtesy of Lancaster City Museums)

ground gear with pressed leather ties. These were about ¾in wide and 14-18in long. The ridges in the pressed leather guided the knife when cutting them out. The tie was cut to form an eye at one end; this end was passed round the tie bobbin, and the tie was passed through the eye and pulled tight. The other end was passed through a lay of the stoving rope and tied in a form of sheet bend. The sketch Fig. 13 illustrates the knot. The ties were left long if the net was not to be used on extremely rough ground, or when used on shrimping grounds when the same gear was used for all modes of fishing. If the net was to be used on very rough ground a length of junk rope, called the fishing rope, was put on the ties by passing them through the lay of the fishing rope. The ties were then put into the stoving rope, and pulled up tight so that the fishing rope rubbed on the roller bobbins. As the rollers turned they lifted the belly of the net off of the ground and saved it from chafe. The tail tie was doubled and attached 8in up one selvage, it was simply wrapped around the bunched up tail three or four times and tied with a slipped half hitch.

Dick Woodhouse recorded the size of the trawl rope and bridles. His trawl rope was one 100yd of 36-strand manila. This was just under 2¼in circumference, of 2t breaking load. The bridles were each 40yd of 10-thread rope on a big nobby and 8-thread rope on a shrimper (1⅞in and 1¾in circumference). At Morecambe the bridles and rope were tarred, but it is recorded that the warp was greased at Fleetwood.

Because sprawning grounds ripped nets and broke the gear, sprawners carried additional equipment. A grapnel was stowed under the ballast boards in the pump bay, to drag for lost gear in case the trawl rope parted. A spare beam end was carried to fish broken beams, until the broken end could be replaced, and pieces of netting called spechings were carried to be laced into torn nets.

The shrimp gear was much lighter, with irons weighing only 25-30lb (11-14kg) a pair, standing 10-12in (25-30cm) high. The stern beams were the same length as the sprawning

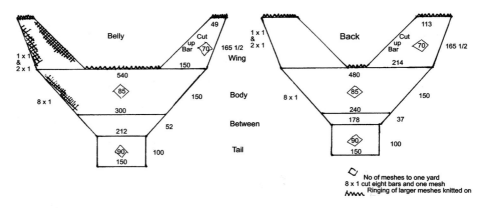

Fig. 12. Mesh count, backless sprawn trawl. (Courtesy E. Nicholson)

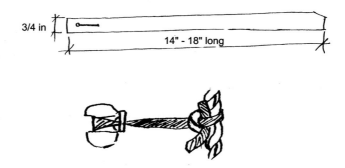

Fig. 13. Stoving rope knot.

beam, but the net was only 24-30ft from beam to tail. The bow net was also shorter in proportion. The beam was thinner at 4in diameter at the scarf and 2in diameter at the iron, so that one could easily pick up both shrimp beams and irons together. The ground chain was $^3/_{16}$in long-link chain, with 2ft 6in draught, attached to the stoving rope every foot, so that it was just in advance of the net when fishing. The net was protected from chafe with net rubbers under the belly, and pressed leather or sheet rubber under the tail. The tail tie was rigged the same as on the sprawn trawl, although the tail used to be laced like a fish trawl. Fig. 14 records the mesh count for a full backed shrimp trawl, and Fig. 15 that of a backless trawl.

One modification to the shrimp and sprawn trawl, used after the days of sail, was the fitting of a veil. This was a piece of net fitted between the back and belly of the trawl, intended to direct any fish that entered the net down and out of an opening in the belly, before they entered the cod. The shrimp or sprawn passed through the meshes of the veil to be caught in the cod. Not everyone used it as it sometimes caused the net to sand up. The Sea Fisheries committee, specifically in the Lancashire and Western District, made every effort to prevent shrimp and prawn trawls killing immature flatfish by limiting the length of the trawl and banning pockets – the short trawl and lack of pockets allowed fish to swim back out of the net's mouth.

The fluke trawl had iron ends that weighed 35-40lb a pair (16-18kg) on a 25-30ft beam; the net measured 450-45ft from beam to tail, braided or cut from net with 3½in bar (90 mm). The fluke trawls at Morecambe were rigged with pockets, but not with a flapper. Many flatfish, especially dab, swim forward when in the trawl: if the net had pockets dab would work forward into the pockets rather than out of the net. The belly of the trawl

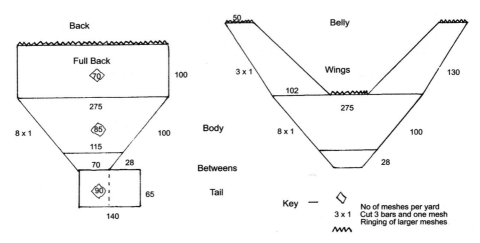

Fig. 14. Mesh count, shrimp trawl. (Courtesy E. Nicholson)

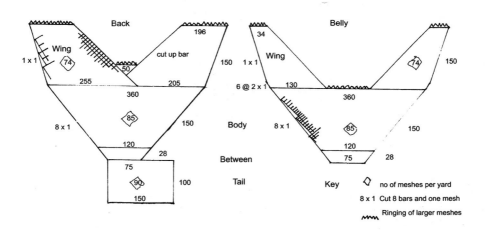

Fig. 15. Mesh count, backless shrimp trawl. (Courtesy E. Nicholson)

was protected from chafe with rubbers of net. The tail tie was tied in to one selvage and was used to lace the cod end closed, finishing with a slipped half hitch. Some fishermen fitted a tail chain, of about fifteen to twenty links, to ensure that the net would not turn inside out when being shot or hauled. The back cord on a fluke trawl had five to six yarns per strand (1½in circumference); the stoving rope had ten to twelve yarns per strand (2in circumference).

The ground rope was originally wire or fibre rope woulded round with junk rope and fastened with staples, or rope lapped round with light chain. The rope wouldings would have protected the foot rope from wear, and would have picked up mud and sand which would have weighted it down better to keep the ground. Keith Willacy stated that each type of ground gear was meant for its own particular type of bottom. By 1928 the Lancashire and Western Sea Fisheries Committee recorded that bobbins were in use. These would have been used in Morecambe (where our informant Keith Willacy fished) and Fleetwood for sprawning, but later as the gear evolved together, they were used on all trawls on the Morecambe grounds. Some fishermen fitted a lazy decky, this was to aid lifting the cod end, especially if made heavy by sanding. This gear was rigged by sewing a sail hank on to the each side of the net at the selvage where the tail was laced to the betweens. A rope

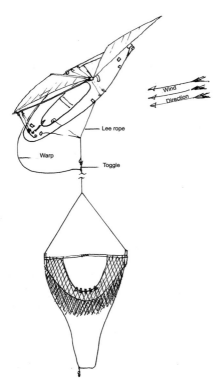

Fig. 16. Lee rope-rigged.

was reeved through these; one end made with an eye splice, through which the other end was passed before being bent on to the forward iron. The rope was made long enough and stopped off at the eye with marline, so that it would not restrict the net. If it was necessary to use it the fish tackle was hooked in and hauled until the marline broke. The running eye closed on the net that could then be lifted by the fish tackle.

The nobby required additional gear to work. One or two 12ft ash sweeps were carried to move the nobby in the calms and to sound for depth. Morecambe nobbies rowed against the mid nog, whilst Fleetwood boats had oarlocks to go into sockets in the coamings. A lead line was also carried. Shrimpers and sprawners also carried the tallegoram (shrimp boiler), standing in a wooden tray to contain the ashes, a supply of coal and a hammer to break it up, a shovel, a bucket to fill the Dutch pot and damp down the ashes, and rock salt to make the brine for rough shrimps. Hampers, half apple barrels, netting sacks known as washers, a net lader (ladle) for lifting the cooked shrimp or sprawn out of the Dutch pot, sacks for bagging the shrimp, and riddles for sorting the catch prior to boiling were required. The riddle was known as a three-penny riddle, because it was made to pass three old pennies, the byelaw defines this as spaces 7mm by 76mm between the wires. Three penny and a farthing, and three penny and a halfpenny riddles were also carried for sorting cobs from the smaller shrimps. The body of the riddle measured 18in internal diameter by 4in deep. The hamper in the collection of the Fleetwood Maritime Museum measures 18 x 24in at the top, 15in deep and 13 x 19in inside the bottom.

Trawling could be carried out either by broadsiding or by dragging under sail. Keith Willacy told the author that shrimpers like *Nora* were fitted with a mid-nog for fluke trawling, this may have been to allow the nobby to broadside with only one trawl. The choice between broadsiding and dragging under sail would have depended on the direction of the wind. The shrimp grounds and some of the flatfish marks were in the channels of the estuaries, which further restricted the ability of the nobby to sail. Broadsiding would have been the only practical way to trawl on all but the rarest of occasions. The trawl was always towed in the direction of the tidal current, so the nobby could be sailed with the wind with or across, but not over, the tide. The speed could be controlled by dropping or scandalising sails, or if the nobby was going too slowly by using only the stern trawl when broadsiding. Extra speed over the ground could be won by using water sails. These were the head sails hung from an oar over the stern and from the bowsprit, with a 56lb packing weight tied to their heads. It is also suggested by some that centreboards were also used to give more grip to the nobby when broadsiding. *Edith Nora*, now *Day Star*, is a centre boarder.

Morecambe men always fished from the port-side deck for preference, so when shooting the trawl the gear will have been made ready with the trawl rope coiled down on t' foc's'le. If dragging under sail, it would have been easiest to shoot on the starboard tack. When ready to shoot the fisherman checked the tail tie and then threw the tail over into the water. The nobby's movement pulled the net overboard until held by the beam. The net's drag pulled the nobby's head round to port. The fisherman then went to the bow iron and allowed the boat to come round to 45 degrees of the desired track. He then threw the end of the beam over and walked back with the bridle until he could take a couple of turns round the port stern nog. The nobby gybed onto the port tack whilst this was happening. The tiller was then lashed to port, the aft, starboard iron is shot, and both bridles were taken off their respective nogs. Both bridles were then paid out until the beam went under the water. The fisherman then brought the bridles together and used the drag of the trawl to steer the nobby. If he wanted to go to starboard he threw a turn round the starboard stern nog as he paid the trawl out. When the trawl was settled on the bottom to the fisherman's satisfaction, the fisherman put a holding turn on the nog, and went forward to secure the trawl to the bow nog.

Because the nobby was moving slowly in relation to the water the rudder was ineffective, so the boat was steered by controlling the position of the trawl rope tension. Depending on the wind direction the trawl rope could be placed behind one of the stern nogs or controlled by a springer, a rope secured to the nog, passed round the trawl rope and belayed to a cleat or pin in the cockpit. So far the same methods were used for fluke, shrimp and sprawn; however, if the nobby would not settle on the port tack it was necessary to tow from starboard. When shrimping or trawling for fluke, a rig called the lee rope (some called it the windward rope) was used. This was in two parts, a short length with a bull's eye called the toggle, and a long length belayed to the starboard bow or mid-nog with a hook in its aft end. This was stowed coiled around the base of the stern nog. It was used by belaying the toggle to the trawl rope with a rolling hitch, and hooking the long end in to the bull's eye. The springer was passed around the lee rope and belayed before the fisherman went forward and paid out the trawl rope from the bow nog until the weight came on the lee rope. This gear is illustrated in Fig. 16.

Because of the greater risk of fasteners when sprawning, the gear differed slightly. The trawl rope was assembled from 30yd lengths shackled together. If it was necessary to pass the trawl to starboard the rope was held on the starboard aft nog, and split at a shackle. The coil end was passed outboard around the stem under the bowsprit, and taken aft outside all, to be re-shackled to the trawl end. The turns were then taken off of the stern nog and the nobby settled down to trawl. Should the trawl come fast on a snag the springer was let fly and the nobby allowed to swing round to lay head to the net. This was a rare occurrence when shrimping or fish trawling in the channels, but if it did occur when the lee rope was in use, some smart boat handling was needed. The stern was swung across to bring the rope back onto the port side; the fisherman then had to hurry forward to haul in the main rope and take the load off of the lee rope. With the lee rope cleared and the nobby lying head to the trawl rope, attempts could then be made to lift the trawl over the snag.

When it was time to haul the nobby was prepared by reducing sail and the rope was put behind the port stern nog. If on the lee rope the rope was pulled hand tight and secured to the port bow nog. The lee rope was then paid out from the starboard bow or mid-nog until the toggle could be freed off. The lee rope was then re-stowed. The main sheet was then taken in and the rope lifted off of the stern nog and allowed to go over the side. The

Plate 9. Hauling the trawl. (Courtesy of Lancaster City Museums)

bow should then swing to port; the tiller was lashed to port and the fisherman then went forward to haul the trawl. If sprawning on the starboard tack the nobby was prepared by taking the rope off of the starboard bow nog and securing it to the port bow nog. Then the procedure was the same except that the nobby was swung round to starboard, going right round until it lay to the port forward nog. This is why it was important to pass the rope under the bowsprit outside of everything and why working nobbies did not have bobstay or bowsprit shrouds. The boat was now laying with he head at about 30 degrees to the stream.

The trawl rope came in hand over hand, being coiled down on the foc's'le until a mark on the stern bridle came to hand. This was called the splitting mark, and was placed at a point one-and-a-half times the length of the beam up from the iron. The fisherman separated the bridles, jamming the stern bridle against the outside coaming with his foot; the bow bridle was then hauled away until the iron surfaced. The bow end was then secured to the midship nog, and the stern bridle carried aft and heaved in until the fisherman could pull the iron in so that its toe hooked on to the coaming. The stern bridle was made up on to the starboard stern nog and the tiller freed. The fisherman went forward as the nobby turned broadside to the tide and hauled in the bow bridle until he could hook the toe of the bow iron over the coaming. He then secured the bow bridle to the shroud iron. Aft again to lift the iron aboard – this allowed the bow iron to drop onto the deck. The stern iron was settled on to the counter and the beam and irons were now stowed against the outside coaming.

The footrope was then boarded, the heavy ground gear of the sprawn trawl being lifted by the headsail halyard or fish tackle (see Plate 9) and the net hauled by going down the selvages. The tail end would be boarded by hand, or tackled aboard using the headsail halyard if too heavy to lift by hand. If the tail must be tackled aboard the springer was passed around the tail and secured to the stern nog to prevent the halyard pulling the tail forward as it was lifted. The tail was untied and emptied, onto the ballast boards if fish trawling, or into hampers if fishing for shrimp or sprawn. The nobby was then sailed back to the top of the ground for another trawl, and the catch sorted. Under-sized fish, and rubbish like weed, starfish, empty shells, and water-logged wood and junk would have been shovelled overboard. The shrimp or sprawn would have been tipped from the hamper onto the cleaning deck in manageable quantities, to be riddled and sorted. The fisherman had to be aware of the weaver fish, whose dorsal fins have spines that give a painful and inflamed puncture wound. Big shrimps, called cobs, could be sorted to be marketed separately. The shrimp destined to be picked for market was cooked first, and then more rock salt was thrown into the pan to make stronger brine. This was used for the rough shrimp, as the extra salt preservative made picking difficult.

When broadsiding with one trawl, the net was shot as follows. The nobby was put across the tide with the net side up tide. The trawl was prepared to be shot by moving the stern trawl aft, with its aft end overhanging the counter, and the forward end aft of the shrouds. The trawl was shot by throwing the tail end over and paying out the net – this is where the tail chain was needed, as the boat was dead in the water. When all of the net was out the aft bridle was taken off of the nog. The bow iron was then thrown overboard, allowing the beam and stern iron to follow. The bridles were then taken in hand and the trawl was paid out using the midship nog, until the trawl was bottoming. The rope was then made up on the bow nog, and the springer passed round the rope. The nobby could be steered as it drove broadside by using the springer to bring the stern up, which made the nobby move sternwards, or by letting it fall off moving the nobby ahead. Fig. 17 illustrates the disposition of the gear. The trawl would have been hauled in the same way as if it had been dragging under sail.

When shrimping, if there was sufficient power in the tide both trawls were used. This was not possible on weak neap tides, or if a strong wind blew over the tide, slowing the nobby down. Three differing rigs have been described, all relating to the stern trawl. At Annan the rope was lead in around the stem. Keith describes it made off to the mid nog, and Dick Woodhouse had it secured under the thwart. All three used a springer on the stern rope to steer by. Tom Willacy

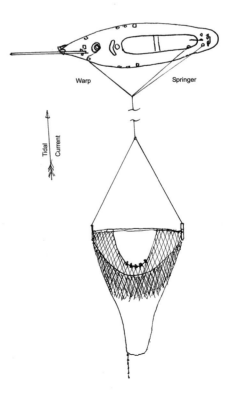

Fig. 17. Broadsiding a single trawl.

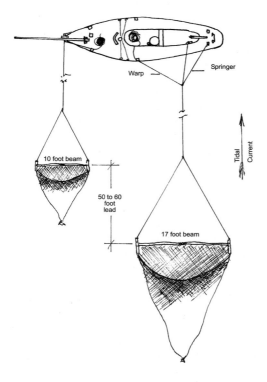

Fig. 18. Broadsiding two trawls.

at Annan remembered a springer on the bow trawl as well. The trawls were prepared to be shot by moving the stern trawl aft, with its aft end overhanging the counter, and the forward end aft of the shrouds, whilst the bow trawl was moved forward with its aft end ahead of the shrouds and the beam overhanging the coaming. The stern trawl rope was coiled down in the fore bay of the cockpit, and the bow rope on the foc's'le. The stern trawl was shot away as before, but secured either to the mid-nog, or under the thwart with enough rope paid out to give the bow trawl a 50-60ft lead. The bow trawl was then shot in a similar fashion, paying out round the bow nog; when it was bottomed satisfactorily it was secured and a bight put into the cheek block. If the cheek block was on the wrong side of the stem a short strop with a hook was secured around the stem head and the rope was put in the hook. The fisherman then went aft to open out the stern trawl by putting a springer on the hawser and hauling it aft (see Fig. 18). The springer was used to steer, as before; however, Dick Woodhouse did not speak of a springer, but opened the net out by putting the rope over a pin in the counter coaming.

Both Keith and Dick described different parts of the process of hauling the trawls, so this is a combination of their advice. The nobby was allowed to lie with her head slightly up tide to slow her down. The bow trawl was shortened up and the aft trawl freed from the counter (or its springer). The bow trawl was then hauled until the stern iron was put inside the rigging. The bridles were then hauled around the bow nog until the beam came aboard. With the net boarded, the stern trawl was hauled as previously described. If the wind allowed the nobby would then be sailed back up the mark, if not the nobby would anchor until the tide turned and then would broad side back the other way.

The shrimp shank was used by nobbies from both the north and south shores of the Ribble estuary. It was probably the universal shrimp trawl until fish beam trawls came into the area, to be scaled down to suit shrimp, and it now survives as cart or tractor shanking gear both in Morecambe Bay and on the Ribble sands. The Southport form was the more primitive model, whilst the Lytham and St Anne's version was part way along the line of development to the modern steel tube shanks. The beam was 10ft 6in long on the foot of the net, the original form used a withy hoop to lift the head, constrained by a stanchion in the centre of the beam to 1ft 8in height (see Fig. 19). The net was made with twenty score (400) meshes round the head. W.S. Wignall of Marshside described the construction of the later Southport shank. The beam was 2 x 2½in pitch pine, ballasted with iron straps on the front and top. Two-inch diameter sockets were attached to the ends to take the steam-bent ash sapling bows. The end bows were scarfed to a middle piece, with lashings to secure the scarf. The stanchion was ¾in iron with a ring at the top clasping the middle of the bow; its base was forked and opened out at right angles to the stanchion to be fixed to the front of the beam. The upper aft corner of the beam was bored through to take the ties to the net. This form of net requires a three-legged bridle, the middle leg going to the centre of the bow to make the frame stand up.

The Lytham shank was similar, 10ft 6in wide, and 1ft 6in high, but was made with an iron stanchion at each end, and a lighter, nicely tapered round beam to support the head. The Lytham beam will have been easier to repair, as there was no tricky steaming to do, but it was easier to rig the net on the Southport shank, which accounts for Southport fishermen's loyalty to their form. The Southport men worked four shanks: one boomed out over the bow, two from the nobby and one boomed out over the counter. The Lytham men used the nobby as if it was a cart. The cart shankers worked two shanks kept open by dragging them from the ends of a boom laid across the front of the cart. The Lytham nobbies used a spar called a boomer, laid across the front of the well. The trawl ropes came from the boomer ends, in through the stem to be turned up on the bow timberheads. Springers controlled both ropes. The shank may have been retained around the Ribble as it was found to suit some bottom conditions better than the beam trawl.

This chapter began with the words 'Because use tends to define the tool, it is appropriate to discuss how the nobby was worked'. We can now consider the drivers imposed by her main employment. The shrimpers worked in shallow water, fishing for a high-value perishable catch in amongst narrow channels. This required a fast, shallow-drafted, manoeuvrable hull. Shrimping gear was light, so could be worked by one man. This set the upper limit of hull size at about 31ft. Shoal draft required a beamy hull to provide form

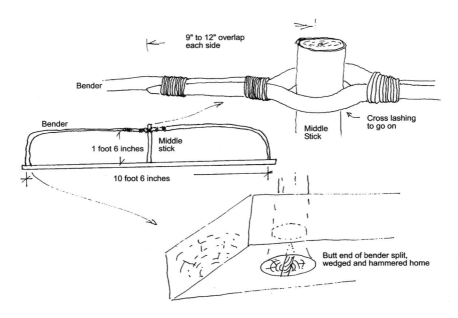

Fig. 19. The Southport shank. (after F.M. Davis, *An Account of the Fishing Gear of England and Wales*)

stability. The freeboard was kept low, in order to limit the height that the gear had to be lifted, which also required a stiff hull form. Wide side decks provided safety with the low freeboard, as well as stowage for the gear and a working area for sorting the catch. The prawn boats worked heavier gear in deeper water, so they were larger and deeper drafted, both they and the gear requiring a crew of two. The prawn nobbies from Morecambe were still limited by the depth of water at their moorings, whilst those from other ports could and did develop yet deeper draft hulls.

Manoeuvrability was necessary as the nobbies worked in channels amongst sand banks. It was provided by the cutter rig, and by the development of a raked sternpost and cut away forefoot. The cutter rig also allowed single-handed working, whilst the raked sternpost allowed both quicker turning and the production of a finer hull form which suited speed and low-weight, high-value catches.

The next most widespread method of fishing the nobby was drifting for herring. The Morecambe men fished out of Maryport, whilst nobbies replaced the local herring boats in those Welsh ports that provided sheltered moorings. A third hand joined the skipper for drift netting, as both shooting and hauling the net requires a hand on the foot and head ropes. In Wales the nobby set off in the evening, so that the fleet of thirty-five nets, each 30-40yd long were fished overnight. When shot the warp was bought to the mooring roller and the nobby set to lay head to the net. The net was rigged with the warp at its head; the foot was weighted with beach stones, tied in rag on the Welsh coast and with baked clay weights at Morecambe. They were made from clay gathered from the Red Bank at Carnforth, moulded and dried, before being carved to shape with a penknife and baked in the range.

Stowboating with the bogey net was actively pursued at Morecambe. None of our sources have described the gear that was used between 1915 and 1919, and as the gear used in the 1950s and '60s used galvanised steel scaffold poles, courlene net and polypropylene rope we can be sure that the earlier gear was different from that described here, if of similar proportions. Keith Willacy gave us the most detailed description of the gear and how it was worked, which we have supplemented from Dick Woodhouse's notes. The bogey gear required its own anchor and cable to hold the drag of a net 18ft wide and deep and 60yd long, in addition to the weight of the nobby. In 1915 the anchor weighed 1¾cwt (196lb – 89kg) and cost £2 10s (£134.04) from the blacksmith Armistead, the normal anchor weighed 35-50lb. Armistead also sold winches costing £1 6s (£71.78) that were bolted to the inner coaming, for operating the shutting up rope.

During the later phase of stowboating, from the 1950s, a 2cwt fisherman's anchor was shackled to 25-30fm of ⅜in or ½in chain, and provided with a buoy rope to its crown. The length was not too important but had to exceed 15fm. The upper end of the chain was shackled to a ring, large enough to take the shackle of the nobby's anchor rope (with a hard eye) and a shackle for the four bridles. Each bridle, which had soft eyes, went to the ends of the 18ft top and bottom beams (poles at Morecambe), to transmit the drag of the net to the anchor. Guy ropes from the ends of the upper pole supported the weight of the net, and a shutting-up rope ran from the middle of the lower pole, through a staple on the upper pole and up to the mooring roller. The side ropes of the net took the weight of the lower pole, unless the fisherman wanted to reduce the depth of the pole with the shutting-up chain. This was 4½fm of ¼in chain with a rope tail. One further strop was required, a riding strop long enough to support the top pole just under the water. The net itself was made from four mesh sizes, about 60yd long, tapering from the 18 x 18ft mouth to about 3ft diameter. The tail end was fitted with a tail end rope long enough to reach back to the nobby. An iron bowler (child's hoop) with a rope tail was used for cutting in the catch.

The mouth was 30ft of fish trawl net (85mm bar, 6in mesh), then came 10ft of herring net (20mm bar, 3in mesh), followed by 120ft of shrimp net (16mm or ½inmesh), the tail ends of 15-24ft of 5mm dock hose. Fig. 20 illustrates these proportions. The net was developed from the Tollesbury stownet described by Hervey Benham (1977) by reducing its gape and length. The mesh counts of the Morecambe net are not on record, but we can use mesh geometry and the recorded dimensions to recreate the probable mesh count. The

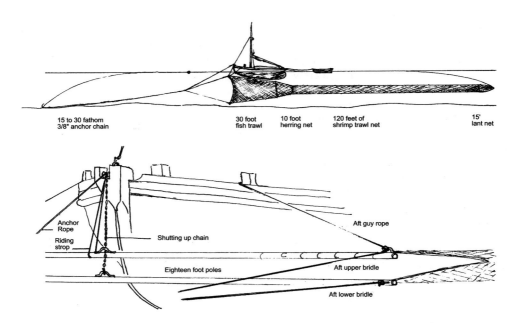

15 to 30 fathom
3/8" anchor chain

30 foot
fish trawl

10 foot
herring net

120 feet of
shrimp trawl net

15'
lant net

Anchor
Rope

Riding
strop

Shutting up chain

Eighteen foot poles

Aft guy rope

Aft upper bridle

Aft lower bridle

Fig. 20. Stowboating.

East Coast prototype tapered rapidly from the mouth to the enter; it also used smaller mesh in the forelint. By reducing the counts to allow for the changing dimensions we can propose the following mesh count. Four panels of 120 meshes, 10ft long, then taper from 120 meshes to 60 meshes of fish net over 20ft. The enter was laced on two meshes to one, so we get four panels of 120 meshes, tapering to 60 meshes of herring net over 10ft. The 120ft of shrimp net did not taper, and was also laced on two to one, so there will have been a tube of 480 meshes, followed by 400 meshes of lant-net dock hose.

When preparing for the whitebait season, from the end of February to mid-April, a season of about seven weeks, the nobby was put on the beach and her bottom was cleaned of snags. Anything that could catch or tear the net was removed or covered with tingles. A loop of cod line was fastened to a frame near to the coupling flange in the propeller shaft, so that it could be hooked over a bolt head to stop the propeller from windmilling and picking up the net. The trawling gear and tallegoram were put ashore and the stowboat anchor and poles were retrieved from under the landing stage where they were stored. The gear was put aboard with the poles laid along the port side deck, and the anchor stowed on the foc's'le, with the stock over the starboard side so that the arms laid flat. The anchor cable was assembled, but the bridles were coiled down on the net. The nobby proceeded to the grounds with the punt in tow, and a crew of two. The anchor buoy rope was bent to the anchor's crown, ensuring that it was long enough to show at all states of the day's tide, Dick Woodhouse used one at least as long as the anchor chain. When on the fishing mark, the anchor was dropped and the nobby allowed to fall back until the shackle between the chain and anchor rope was just outboard; the anchor buoy was then put over. The nobby was held on the anchor rope whilst the ends of the four bridles were brought forward out side the rigging and shackled in to the big link at the end of the anchor chain. The anchor rope was then paid out until the aft bridles (going to the port end of the two poles) began to come tight. Many nobbies had a mark in the anchor rope to indicate this point. The anchor rope was then turned up on the Samson post. The wise fishermen then paused and checked that everything was clear and free to run.

The bow guy rope was then bought forward, passed under the stem, and made up hand tight on the starboard bow nog. The stern guy was secured hand tight to the aft shroud above the upper dead eye. The shutting-up chain was bought forward, outside everything, put over the mooring roller and turned up on the capstan. The tail end was wrapped around the port stern nog, and with everything ready the nobby was given a sheer to starboard. The anchor rope was paid out, so that the tension came on the bridles, which pulled the poles and net overboard. Immediately the poles went into the water the sheer was taken off the nobby. The anchor rope was turned up on the Samson post when the poles were under the boat's stem. Again the anchor rope may have been marked to indicate this position. The poles were then lifted clear of the water on the shutting-up rope, and the riding strop was passed around the top pole. The two guys were made up to their respective bow nogs, hand tight, and the riding strop was adjusted to allow the top pole to lie just submerged under the forefoot. The shutting-up chain was then paid out to settle the lower pole at the desired depth and turned up on the capstan. The tail end was closed, tied to the stern line, and allowed to run overboard and away. The anchor rope was adjusted to ensure that the bridles were taking the drag of the net and then made up on the Samson post.

The crew then settled down to let the net fish the tide. If a big shoal hit the net, the shutting up rope would be used to reduce the mouth of the net; the net would be picked up just clear of the counter, and pulled aboard down each selvage until the cod end was reached. Two men could lift 10-15st aboard but any more would have required the mast tackle. In order to avoid crushing the delicate fish a heavy cod end was worked forward, and secured by a strap to the shroud iron or bow nog. The bowler was then passed up the cod from the back end, to divide the cod into manageable portions. If the fishing was light it was usual to leave the mouth of the net open and use the punt to lift the cod end and empty it whilst the net was still fishing. The crew could expect to fish for four to five hours, sometimes getting two tides in a day. The catch was sorted with the aid of a three-penny shrimp riddle to sieve out the bigger sprats, blebs (sea gooseberries) were separated out with a square mesh riddle that retained the bait and allowed the blebs to fall through. Shrimps are about the same size as the bait so had to be picked out by hand, as was the weed.

The net was hauled by first hauling the shutting-up chain until the poles were hard up to the mooring roller. The two guys were taken from their nogs and a couple of round turns put round the pole ends to keep them together. The bow guy was then passed under the nobby's bow and made up hand tight on the port nog. The stern guy was run out, outside the rigging and secured hand tight to the aft shroud. The riding strap was taken off the upper pole, passed round both poles, and hooked into the fish tackle, which was also set up hand tight. The shutting up chain was then slacked off, dropped from the mooring roller, and secured to the port bow nog with at least 2fm hanging overboard. The cod end was then retrieved, emptied, and wrapped round the port stern nog.

The anchor rope was transferred to the capstan and hauled until the mark was reached that indicated the length of the bridles from the bow to the aft end of the stowed poles. With this mark inboard the anchor cable was turned up, and the stern guy pulled aft to pull the poles around the stem to lie alongside the port bow. They were prevented from moving too far aft, from sinking, or coming too tight on the bow guy. The aft guy was then turned up on the stern port nog. The fish tackle was unhooked from the riding strop, passed aft under the shrouds, and hooked into the centre strop on one of the poles. The poles were then heaved up to about 3ft above the deck, and the tackle was belayed. The net was then pulled aboard and stowed on the port deck, the shutting-up chain being placed on top of the net under the middle of the pole's stowed position. The poles were then lowered away into their stowed position and secured by the guys. The anchor rope was heaved in until the shackle was just outboard, and was then turned up again. The bridles were then un-shackled, coiled up in their pairs and stowed, the forward pair forward and the aft pair aft.

The anchor chain was then hauled until it was up and down, and transferred from the capstan to the Samson post. The anchor buoy rope was bought on board, led round the aft side of the starboard bow nog. The anchor buoy rope was taken to the capstan and hauled in until the anchor broke out and came up to bring the crown level with the outside coaming. The slack anchor chain was pulled in by hand and secured to the Samson post to prevent its running back out. A tackle strop was put on the crown of the anchor and the fish tackle hooked on, to be hauled in on the capstan until the anchor was on the point of balance. The fish tackle was then gradually paid away as the anchor was drawn inboard and stowed with the stock left outboard. The bemel was secured to the nog with a lashing, the mast tackle was unhooked and stowed, and the anchor chain cleared from the mooring roller to clear it for the nobby's own mooring. The process of setting the net required care and skill to prevent the net becoming foul or damaged, but hauling could put the nobby at risk. The use of the fish tackle to lift the poles with the weight of the fore end of the net, and later the big stowboat anchor, reduced the stability of the nobby, so that on occasion quick and drastic action was required to avoid disaster.

Harry Allan told us that his son had worked out a method for setting the bogey net over the nobby's stern. Shooting away would be easier over the stern, but hauling may have been a struggle.

Two other methods were employed to take whitebait: the fly net and the set net. The set net was similar to the net of a shrimp trawl, staked out on the beach just below the low-tide mark, with its mouth facing the ebb tide. The head rope was fitted with floats to lift the back, the sides were stopped to light rods, and the foot pegged down to the beach. The tail was held down tide on the ebb with a stake to prevent the net becoming fouled on the flood; the net only fished the ebb. The fishermen tended the net with a punt, to prevent the whitebait from settling onto the sand and spoiling. The fly net was both ground and mid-water trawl, with a beam to support the head of the net, and 3ft stanchions fitted to conventional irons to hold the foot down. As a mid-water trawl it was towed at speed, and its depth was regulated by the amount of rope paid out. It was used around about the First World War to take sprats, and as an experiment during the 1960s looking for whitebait.

Nobbies also went longlining and mackerel fishing. The Southport men took their punt to tend the longlines, but there is no record of either Morecambe or Fleetwood men doing so. None of our sources have described the longline gear so we must assume that it was rigged and set conventionally, Fleetwood men used herring bait in the 1960s, but Morecambe was selling mussel for the longline fishery on the east coast, so it is most likely that they also used mussel, or small fish from the trawls when fishing for roker. It is apparent that the Fleetwood men laid the lines out straight, rather than in zigzags as the haddock lines on the Scottish east coat were laid.

Dick Woodhouse described the mackerel gear. The nobby fished four lines, each with one hook on a 2fm snood. The forward lines were boomed out on oars, and weighted with 4-4½lb leads, and the aft streamed from the counter with 3-4lb leads. The main lines were thick cotton shrimp trawl twine, or Fleetwood longline cord. The snood was attached to the main line with a brass swivel, attached to a piece of leather. The leather was about 1½in long, and was often cut from the lacing holes of a shoe. A hole at one end was threaded onto the main line, and a hole at the other accepted the swivel. Dick did not mention any form of lure to dress the hook, and mackerel have been known to take a bare hook if it glitters enough. The mackerel ground was off the mouth of the Duddon, a good sail away from Morecambe. The nobby was sailed slowly around the mark until the shoal was found, and then the work started, hauling lines and trying to keep the nobby within the shoal.

Chapter 3
Legislation of the Fishery

Mention has been made of the Lancashire and Western Sea Fisheries Committee. This committee was responsible for the southern part of the nobby's range. The Cumbrian coast was administered by its own committee, whilst the Scottish Office administered the Dumfries and Galloway part of the range. These English and Welsh committees were set up under the authority of an Act of Parliament, The Sea Fisheries Regulation Act of 1888. This act built on several earlier acts. The earlier act of most relevance was that of 1868 which provided for the registration of fishing boats, and the creation of the 3-mile limit as a British fishery, amongst other issues. It is useful to the researcher, in that it specified how the boats were to be marked, and that it required that the second-class boats placed their number before the Port Mark whilst the first- and third-class boats placed their number after. This convention was changed with the later act and so helps to classify and to date photographs of fishing boats. The numbers on a second-class boat were to be 10in high, of 1¾in breadth, painted on both side of the bow, and one-third larger each way on the sails. The vessel's name and port were to be painted in letters 3in high and ½in wide on the stern.

The committees set up under the Act of 1888 were the Cumberland Sea Fisheries District from Sark Foot to Haverigg Point, and the Lancashire Sea Fisheries Committee, whose district extended from Rhos Point, Colwyn Bay to Haverigg Point, later the Lancashire and Western Sea Fisheries District from Haverigg Point to Cemnaes Head. The committees managing these districts were empowered to enact byelaws to regulate or prohibit methods of fishing. These byelaws were to be ratified by the Board of Trade. They could appoint Fisheries Officers with power of search and seizure, and were obliged to provide statistics to the Board of Trade. Further acts of 1891 and 1894 consolidated these powers and provided more effective protection to shellfish. Aflalo (1904) reported that the system was not adopted around the Scottish coast on the grounds of local expenditure.

In 1882 responsibility for protecting Sea Fisheries in Scottish waters was given to the Fishery Board for Scotland. The board's responsibilities also included land-based inspection. The first vessel the board took over in 1885 was a former Royal Navy sailing cutter, *Vigilant*, which had worked for some years on protection tasks. Development of steam-powered trawlers and controls on various methods of fishing made it necessary to build up the protection and surveillance effort, and by 1909 the board's fleet included no fewer than five steam vessels. Lord Mackenzie reviewed the job of the service in 1923, and by the outbreak of the 1939-45 war the fleet had been increased to eight vessels, which included two small motorboats. In 1939 the functions of the Fishery Board were transferred to the Secretary of State for Scotland. The organisation is now called the Scottish Fisheries Protection Agency.

The Lancashire Sea Fisheries Committee was formed in 1890. It later amalgamated with the Western Region (North Wales) to form the Lancashire and Western Sea Fisheries District in 1900. Their minutes and superintendent's quarterly reports were printed in bound volumes, of which all but some of the earliest are preserved at the Lancaster headquarters of the committee. The Dee, out to a line from Hilbre Point to Point of Ayre continued in the control of a River Conservancy Board.

The Cumberland Sea Fisheries Committee was set up due to a resolution of the Cumberland County Council made at a meeting of 7 August 1889. The Cumbrian County Records Office preserves the minute books and associated correspondence and notes; they were not published in printed volumes in the manner of the Lancashire committee's minutes but survive in handwritten form. It was agreed that the district ran from the boundary of the Lancashire District to the junction of the River Sark and the River Esk, to the Burgh Marsh Point on the east and the 3-mile limit to the west. Throughout this chapter references to these committees are drawn from the quarterly reports and minute books cited in the References.

The byelaws extant in 1904 were set out by Aflalo (1904) are reproduced in Appendix I. Those applying directly to nobby fishermen from the Lancashire District were:

4. No person shall use in fishing for sea fish, other than shrimps, prawns, mackerel, herring, sparling, or garfish, any net having a mesh through which a square gauge of one and three-quarter inches, measured across each side of the square, or seven inches measured round the four sides, will not pass without pressure when the net is wet, provided that between the 1st day of June and the 15th day of November following, both inclusive, it shall be lawful to use a trawl net having a mesh through which a square gauge of one and a half inches, measured across each side of the square, or six inches measured round the four sides, will pass without pressure when the net is wet, on the seaward side of lines drawn within the following limits:—
(a) A line drawn straight from the south-western extremity of Haverigg Point, in Cumberland, to the north-western extremity of Walney Island;
(b) A line drawn straight from Walney lighthouse to the Wyre lighthouse;
(c) A line drawn straight from the 'Star Inn', South Shore, Blackpool, to the inner northwest seamark on Formby Point;
(d) A line drawn straight from the lifeboat-house at Formby to the Crosby lightship, and then straight to the Leasowe lighthouse, in the County of Chester.

5. No person shall use in fishing for sea fish other than shrimps or prawns, any trawl net except in accordance with the following regulations: —
(a) When the length of beam does not exceed eighteen feet between the trawl heads or irons, the circumference of the net shall be not less than fifty meshes.
(b) When the length of beam, measured as aforesaid, exceeds eighteen feet but does not exceed twenty-five feet, the circumference of the net shall not be less than sixty meshes.
(c) When the length of beam, measured as aforesaid, exceeds twenty-five feet, the circumference of the net shall be not less than eighty meshes.

10. No person shall use, in fishing for shrimps or prawns, any trawl net except in accordance with the following regulations: —
(a) When the length of beam between the trawl heads or irons does not exceed twenty feet, the circumference of the net shall be not less than one hundred and twenty meshes.
(b) When the length of beam, measured as aforesaid, exceeds twenty feet, the circumference of the net shall be not less than one hundred and forty meshes.
(c) The length of beam, measured as aforesaid, shall not exceed twenty-five feet.

In the Cumberland District the equivalent byelaws were the same, with these exceptions:

4. No person shall use, in fishing for sea fish other than [...] when the net is wet. Provided that between the 1st day of July and the 15th day of October following, both inclusive, to the west and south of a line drawn from Bow House Point, near Caerlaverock, on the Scotch side of the Firth to Skinburness on the English side, it shall be lawful to use a trawl net having a mesh through which a square gauge of 11 inches measured across each side of the square, or six inches measured round the four sides, will pass without pressure when the net is wet.

5. Between the 1st day of January and the 30th day of June following, both inclusive, no person shall use in fishing for sea fish any trawl net having a beam of greater length than thirty feet between the trawl heads or irons, or any trawl net from any vessel exceeding 15 tons gross register.

Nearly every byelaw affected the nobby fishery, the regulation of set nets and baulks ensuring that nobbies could also work where these fixed engines were rigged.

The Merchant Shipping Act of 1868 required that the name and port mark must be displayed in letters of at least 3in height. Holdsworth (1874) listed the following port marks on the nobby coast in 1872, with the number of Class II and III boats at each; Aflalo (1904) added one more port:

Port Mark	Port	2nd Class	3rd Class	Port Mark	Port	2nd Class	3rd Class
DS	Dumfries	No statistics		PN	Preston	46	
CL	Carlisle	18	1	LL	Liverpool	137	10
MT	Maryport	48	2	RN	Runcorn	33	17
WO	Workington	14		CH	Chester	No statistics	
WA	Whitehaven	15	34	BS	Beaumaris	58	68
BW	Barrow	Listed by Aflalo in 1904		CO	Caernarfon	115	36
LR	Lancaster	122	101	AB	Aberystwyth	6	75
FD	Fleetwood	27		CA	Cardigan	54	35

In the days before steam and motor, second-class boats were sailing vessels of less than 15t gross register and third-class boats were propelled by oar. The Welsh ports used an assortment of sailing herring boats, and the Morecambe mussel doggers and Lune whammel boats carry sail, so the second-class boats listed are not all nobbies, whilst the registrar was allowed discretion to allow small open boats with both oar and sail to be classed as third-class boats.

These acts and byelaws set the scene against which the Sea Fisheries Committees administered the fishery out to the 3-mile limit. An indication of the issues discussed by the committee was culled from the *Minutes and Quarterly Reports*. In May 1891 the Lancashire Sea Fisheries Superintendent set out the size of the industry in their division. The statistics are:

Northern Division

Shrimpers	67 boats
Trawlers	10
Mussel doggers	90
Stake nets	45,400yd
Hedge Baulks	11
Eel Nets	3
Fluke Draw nets	10
Cocklers	Total employed 550 men plus pickers

Central Division

Deep Sea Trawlers	65
2nd Class boats	186
Shrimp hose nets	972
Cart shankers	50, plus men working power nets
Baulk nets	7,800yd plus stake nets on Ainsdale beach for Herring and mackerel

Southern Division

Hoylake shrimpers	15
Tranmere ditto	17
New Ferry & Rock Ferry	17
New Brighton & Egremont	10
Dingle shrimpers	4

Cockle hole ditto	10		
Widnes ditto	7		
Runcorn ditto	6		
Garston ditto	5		
Speke ditto	4		
Ince ditto	2		
Formby ditto	1		
Hoylake 1st Class boats	37		
Liverpool	11		
Liverpool Steamers	6		
Stake nets, Fluke	6,200yd		
Mackerel	4,500yd		
Herring	3,960yd		
Shrimp hose nets	310		
Total employed	Shrimping		252
	Trawling		260
	Other methods		77

The debate continued during 1892 on the size of trawl mesh to be used in the Lancashire District. The committee wanted 7in, the Cheshire men 6in, whilst the Mersey men wanted 4-5in mesh in fluke trawls. The committee boat was used to try southern division grounds including Jordan Flats and Queens Bar, Rock and Horse Channels, and the Crosby Channel. The minutes of February 1893 recorded that the steamer '*John Fell*' was commissioned and named after the committee chairman. The committee discussed taking in the Cumberland District, and changes to the disposal of sturgeon. The meeting of May 1893 resolved to expend money on sea fish hatcheries and research, and that trawl beams of 30ft were to be restricted to south of Formby Head. The extension of the district into Wales was discussed but the resolution was withdrawn. Concern was expressed about the hawking of foreign shrimp of poor quality at Southport. The Southport Town Council were to be warned of the committee's concern.

There was a proposal placed before the committee in November 1893 to ban fishing from midnight Saturday to midnight Sunday, except for tending longlines. The representatives nominated by the Board of Trade for service on the committee for 1893 were mostly fishermen, but the committee also included men of high political or commercial stature. The names are listed in Appendix I.

The Cumberland Sea Fisheries Committee, at their meeting on 26 April 1893 agreed to meet with the Lancashire committee during the second week in May, to discuss sharing the cost of the steamer *John Fell*. They also discussed adopting Lancashire's byelaws, with suitable amendments. The meeting took place on 5 May in Preston. Agreement was reached, with the result that the committee recommended to the county council that a rate of one-fortieth of a penny in the pound be voted to raise about £150 (£11,713) to contribute to the cost of the steamer and officers to police the district. After meetings under the auspices of the county council on 7 November 1893, 31 May 1894, and 7 November 1894, the committee finally met at Whitehaven Town Hall. Those in attendance were: county council representatives – Mr Barratt, Mr Burnyeat, Mr J.C. Grainger, Mr Hine, Mr J. Musgrave, and Mr Vaughan. Representative of Eden Fisheries Board – J.H. Hodgson; West Cumberland Fisheries Board – R. Jefferson; appointed by Derwent Fisheries Board – G Falcon; appointed by the Board of Trade – H. Dixon, W. Little, G. Holmes, and L. Moore.

At meetings of 11 June and 16 July the Cumberland committee discussed the War Office proposal to site an artillery range at Whitehaven. In July and on 5 November they discussed and agreed the byelaws. The county council appointed committee's membership for 1896. They are also listed in Appendix I.

The Lancashire Sea Fisheries Committee agreed at a meeting of February 1894 that two bailiffs were to be stationed at Roa Island; £150 (£11,958) was voted to procure a sailing cutter to a design by G.L. Watson (to be named *Piel Castle*). The August 1894 meeting agreed to limit fishing to be practised under sail and oar only, unless hooking; they agreed no Sunday fishing, this to be resubmitted to Board of Trade who disagreed; they agreed that the upper limit on inshore trawlers to be 15t register. After discussion the committee dropped the Sunday fishing byelaw. They accepted a tender from John Gibson of £160 (£12,755) for building of the Barrow bailiff's boat *Piel Castle*; Gibson's were working on her during the October of 1894.

A problem was reported in the Lancashire District Quarterly Report of 31 December 1897 about the use of bought-in sheet net, braided with a knot that imparted a twist to the mesh, reducing the mesh aperture when fishing, although the gauge would still pass. The quarterly report of June 30 1898 notes that a prosecution took place due to the use of the 'Bridport knot' (the twisted knot of the bought-in netting). The bailiffs assisted the Western Sea Fisheries Committee policing the grounds off Aberystwyth.

At a meeting on 14 January 1897 the Cumberland Committee began to discuss bailiffs and how to use the SS *John Fell* off Cumberland. On 18 February they considered patrol boats and bailiffs for policing north of Maryport; the *John Fell* could not cover these grounds due to the shallow nature of the Solway. They agreed a vote of £100 (£8,048) for a sailing cutter and a Chief Inspector at Maryport at a salary of £130 (£10,463) and travelling expenses, to crew the cutter a captain at 30s (£120) a week, and second boatman of 27s (£108) a week. All uniforms and oilskins were to be provided by the committee. Mr George Holmes of Bowness (one of the Board of Trade appointees) applied and was appointed inspector.

It was reported on 8 April 1897 that, in response to the advert for a boat of 32ft length, a half-deck cutter of maximum draft not to exceed 4ft, the committee received offers from W. Baxter of 29 Clarence Street, Morecambe, price £65 (£5,230), described as 32 x 9ft, 4ft 8in depth and 3ft 9in draft, new built by William Crossfield in September 1896, ceiled throughout with hatches and 2t of ballast. William Wilson of Waterfoot Road, Annan, offered *Britannia* at 31ft 2in, by 9ft 3in beam with a 9cwt iron ballast keel. She was thought to be a slow boat, at a price of £62 10s (£5,030). T.L. Willacy of 61 Port Street Annan offered at a price of £58 (£4,670) a boat of 31ft 2½in by 9ft, which won third prize at an Annan regatta. Richard Woodhouse of 3 Gordon Terrace, Annan, offered a five-year-old boat for £50 (£4,025); Robert Woodhouse of 49 Cheapside, Morecambe, a boat built by Crossfield Brothers, Jan 13 1896 (selling the boat as he had had words with his brother and the boat is now too big for him, they were living aboard in Wales at the time). The boat was 38ft, 28ft keel, 10ft 9in beam and 5ft draft, and offered for £85 (£6,840). W. Wilson of Annan offered to build for £69 (£5,550) with an iron keel, but trimming kentledge extra at cost. J. Bell of 42 Port Street, Annan, offered to build at £80 10s (£6,480). It was believed that he built to the same form as the reputedly slow boat offered by William Wilson. The committee agreed to buy George Holmes's boat *Valkyrie* at £70 (£5,365). She was under two years old, larch on oak, galvanised iron fastened, 24ft of keel, 32ft 8in long, 9ft 2in beam, draft less than 4ft, with 12cwt on the keel and 3t inside, and was provided with iron legs, stove, mainsail, topsail, forestay sail and two jibs.

At the committee meeting of 20 May 1897 Vickers & Sons notified their wish to establish a gun range at Eskmeals. The committee appointed J.E. Routledge of Esk Street Silloth as Boatman, and Richard Haughton of Nicholson Street Annan as Second Boatman. On 13 January 1898 the committee considered and resolved to discontinue the use of the SS *John Fell*. At the meeting of 6 July they considered commissioning a four-man 20-ton Thames measurement cutter.

The Lancashire District Committee heard that the Bridport knot was no longer used in 1898. Their meeting of 15 May 1899 resolved that with the exception of shanker bows of 13ft length, no shrimping or prawning was to take place from June to 15 October on the Burbo Bank ground. The banning of shrimp trawls with iron heads and a beam was due to the large amount of fry and juvenile flatfish taken and killed in them. The Draft Order amalgamating the West and the Lancashire Sea Fisheries Districts was discussed. The minutes of 28 August 1899 recorded that the head bailiff of the southern division wrote requesting a pay rise. His letter reported that he had to police from Formby Point to Colwyn Bay, up to Runcorn Viaduct and all of the Dee, while there were 150 boats to police in the Mersey. He was obliged to live at New

Brighton, and as this was a holiday resort the rents were expensive at £31 (£2,495) per annum. The committee agreed to increase his salary to £124 (£9,980) p.a. (Note: it was recorded that all bailiffs received a new suit of clothes each second year, and a jersey each year).

The Cumberland committee held their AGM on 20 April 1899; they resolved to order the patrol boat for the south of their district from W.H. Holford of Gloucester for £475 (£38,230). She measured 49ft 10in on deck, 13ft beam, drew 7ft 8in of water, and was named *The Solway*. She was employed on patrol duties until 1907, with a crew of four. Her master was Luke Woodhouse of High Street, Maryport. The 1901 census described Luke Woodhouse as a 36-year-old 'Sea Fisheries Boatman'. From 1903 her master was John Edmondson Routledge, of 105 High Street, Maryport. On 20 of June 1907, the boat was transferred to ship chandler John Thomas Kee of 25 West Quay, Ramsey, Isle of Man. She is still in commission as the yacht *Carlotta* in British Columbia.

The quarterly report of 30 September 1899 reported that the inspector and boatmen had difficulty enforcing the Cumberland byelaws amongst the prawn fishermen. Trouble flared on 17 and 18 July 1899 when Henry Mount, Thomas Hodgson, Samuel Baxter, Joseph Parkinson, and John Mount of Morecambe, and James Wilson, Henry Wilson, Matthew Wilson, and George Woods of Fleetwood received a summons for taking soles in their prawn trawls, and on the 18th Henry Mount was charged with assault against Officer Haughton.

The Cumberland committee meeting of 22 January 1900 voted to order new sails for the cutter based at Silloth, commissioning the Wignall Brothers of Southport who quoted £7 19s (£620). On 19 July 1900 the committee gave consideration to harmonising the byelaws with the Scottish district. The inspector reported prosecutions against James Johnson, James Anderson, John Robinson and Thomas Rae of Annan, George Stephenson and Gunson Wood of Maryport, and Henry Mount and George Mount of Morecambe, all for taking berried lobsters.

The minutes of May 1900 record the first meeting of the Lancashire and Western Sea Fisheries Committee. They agreed to purchase a sailing boat for £200 (£15,620) for the northern division of the Welsh District. Later in the year there were problems with the southern men failing to letter and number their boats, one caught in Cardigan Bay was prosecuted. The committee agreed to purchase the cutter *Eric* of 19t for £185 (£14,445). She was stationed at Anglesey; Lytham's cutter was sent to Pwlhelli. The committee placed a centreboard cutter of 10t at Pwlhelli.

The meeting of 25 April 1901 discussed a letter from the University College of Wales, who were desirous of making Aberystwyth a centre for fishery investigation, offering laboratory facilities in return for finance to cover the salary of a Fisheries Expert. The manning of the districts of the joint region were reported to be as follows:

No. 1 District	Haverigg Point to the Ribble	3 bailiffs and a cutter at Piel 1 assistant bailiff at Morecambe 4 assistant bailiffs at Blackpool 1 assistant bailiff at Lytham.
No. 2 District	South bank of the Ribble to Rhos Point	3 bailiffs and a cutter at New Brighton 1 assistant bailiff at Southport.
No. 3 District	Rhos Point to Nefin Bay	3 bailiffs and a cutter.
No. 4 District	Nevin Bay to Cemnaes Head	2 bailiffs and a cutter at Pwlhelli 1 Bailiff at Aberystwyth.

At their meeting of July 1901, the Cumberland committee considered amendments to the byelaws to allow bunching of the tail of shrimp and prawn cod ends. This was in response to complaints from Annan fishermen, who claimed that their Morecambrian relatives were allowed to bunch instead of lacing the cod of the shrimp net, a great saving in time with ½in mesh. The report of 30 September 1901 stated that since 1897 when the byelaws were adopted there were two two-man boats at Maryport. There were now (1901) up to forty boats, twenty-four of which belong to Maryport. Some of these boats earned £16 a week (£1,235). During the last quarter of 1901, the inspector, George Holmes, conducted an experimental drag with a prawn trawl on grounds between Silloth Pier and Cote Lighthouse. One twenty-minute drag took 1st of fine plaice, 2qt of shrimp and 4,887 immature fish. They also heard reports of the landings of fish, which included 3t 7cwt of shrimp valued at £83 7s 8d (£6,438) and 50t 31cwt of prawn at £876 (£67,620) at the Cumbrian ports, whilst the railway at Annan exported 162t 19cwt of flounder at £1,955 (£150,960) and 200t 11cwt of shrimp at £4,055 11s 4d (£323,290) in the preceding year.

The Quarterly Report of March 1901, read to the Lancashire and Western District committee, stated that on occasion trawlers were taking seven- to ten-score pounds (200lb) of plaice in a tide. Shrimping was good to excellent with 200 quarts taken per boat per tide. There were seventy shrimpers working the Burbo Bank; fewer fry were caught in cold weather. Longlining was poor, steamers caught most fish before they came inshore. Trial hauls on the Blackpool closed ground took 1,000 fry per quart of shrimp. On 30 June 1901 there was discussion of mesh sizes, of six inches versus seven inches. There were 532 second-class boats, 470 third-class boats, and 746 shore fishermen working in the district. The limit of beam length of 45ft was agreed to be applied in the Western Region all year. The committee had sponsored a research station at Roa Island, at the southern mouth of Walney Channel, using the summer residence of one of Barrow's founding fathers, the iron master H.W. Schneider. They also inaugurated a school for the district's fishermen at the same facility. In 1901 Thomas Hardman and John Robert Wignall of Lytham and Richard Wright of Fleetwood attended the new school.

The joint committee voted expenditure of £40 (£3,058) on a new deck for *Eric*, and £10 (£764.50) for an alteration to the cutter *Rock Light* in March 1902. The first class of fishermen of 1902 selected to attend the school at Roa Island numbered fifteen, including men from Southport, Banks, St Anne's, Lytham, Fleetwood and Morecambe. Committee cutters were now posted at Fleetwood, New Brighton, Caernarfon, and Pwlhelli. The superintendent reported that most fish were in deep water outside of the three-mile limit. The Mersey's cutter was moved to New Quay. Robert Lathom of Crossens offered to tender for a new boat £189 (£14,450), and £61 (£4,660) for sails, rigging and ballast.

1902 saw the Cumberland committee discuss a close season for shrimp and prawn from 1 May to 31 July to protect immature fish as proposed by the inspector. The report of the quarter ending March saw eighty boats shrimping and prawning from Maryport to the Solway Viaduct, some twenty miles. They were broadsiding with two trawls of 18-19ft with a chain footrope. During the quarter ending 31 December 1901 further investigations of the prawn bye-catch were made, in the company of nineteen prawners; the contents of three trawls were counted. The catch after one hour drags were 40qt of prawn with 665 immature fish, 1qt of prawn with 309 immature fish, and 40qt of prawn with 1,135 immature fish. There were also twenty-one shrimp trawlers making three to five drags per day. The minutes of 23 October 1902 record that prawners were taking excellent hauls on the prawn ground between Pillar Fairway Buoy and Workington Pier, a distance of seven miles, making three to five drags per day of one to two hours' duration. During further trials, working over sixteen days during which the trawl was down for an aggregate time of thirteen hours ten minutes, the trawl took 15,076 small fish, 4 large soles, 236qt of prawn and 9qt of shrimp. More trials were conducted on 11 August in the presence of fifteen prawners. After a one-hour drag 1,337 fish were taken with 50qt of prawn, and after the net was down for forty-five minutes, 782 fish were taken with 40qt of prawn, later the same month there were twenty-six boats prawning.

During 1903 Robert Lamb Ashcroft Esq.; Bancroft Cooke, Esq.; Rev. Alfred Hamilton King, Birkenhead; Dr J.H. Lister; and Enoch Lewis came off the Lancashire and western joint committee to be replaced by W.E. Thorney, Esq. Ansdell, Lytham; William Dean, 15 Alexandra Road, Lytham; A.R. Rogerson, St Anne's Road West, St Anne's-on-Sea; S. Ashbrook, 56 Livingstone Road, Tranmere; and Thomas Davies, Westward Ho, Prussia Road, Hoylake. 1904 saw debates on two issues: the proposal to open the Blackpool closed ground from October to March, and to use 6in mesh all year. Both were rejected. The superintendent reported the value of shrimp and prawn landed from Rhyl to Morecambe to be:

	1895 £	1896 £	1897 £	1898 £	1899 £	1900 £	1901 £	1902 £	1903 £	1904 £
January	206	1,376	573	658	607	965	1,403	1,161	1,414	1,418
February		1,141	352	500	658	672	1,102	1,108	1,219	584
March	293	1,101	516	530	808	768	1,201	1,363	927	1,297
April	1,470	885	743	874	1,082	1,417	2,188	1,744	1,377	1,788
May	2,054	1,553	981	1,030	1,585	1,761	2,625	2,186	2,276	2,473
June	1,253	1,498	1,044	996	1,735	1,675	2,546	1,629	2,472	2,252
July	1,603	1,322	731	741	885	1,482	2,367	1,688	2,508	2,209
August	1,819	1,024	1,086	1,053	1,215	1,346	1,908	2,188	2,064	1,805
September	1,885	897	1,217	1,410	1,678	1,933	2,118	2,243	2,604	2,048
October	2,270	2,534	1,170	1,565	2,217	2,218	2,156	2,422	2,750	1,995
November	2,405	1,653	663	1,254	2,071	2,120	2,000	2,407	2,358	1,472
December	1,719	797	520	1,130	1,079	1,709	1,106	1,742	2,040	949
Totals	16,977	15,781	9,596	11,736	15,620	18,066	22,720	21,881	24,009	20,290
2005 Value (£m)	1.413	1.327	0.788	0.936	1.298	1.411	1.754	1.673	1.817	1.520

Mention was made in the minutes of March 1906 of two more patrol boats, as new sails were required for the cutters *Eric*, *John Fell* and *James Fletcher*. The superintendent reported on the growth of the industry in 1910

Year	Steam Trawlers	1st Class Sail	2nd Class Sail	3rd Class Sail
1892	8	118	487	220
1893	7	121	504	213
1894	9	116	515	205
1895	24	100	507	213
1896	29	102	514	214
1897	46	97	503	221
1898	48	93	505	202
1899	18	96	459	198
1900	19	95	422	214
1901	20	99	413	209
1902	23	105	391	203

The values of prawn and shrimps landed in entire region in the second quarter of 1909 and 1910 were 7,147cwt @ £6,628 (£473,540); and 5,087cwt @ £5,445 (£385,460). In 1911 the joint committee updated their fleet of cutters. A new Cutter for Fleetwood was tendered for by Crossfield Brothers for £216; she was delivered for £278 19s 3d (£19,566). The Pwlhelli cutter *Rock Light* was up for sale to go for £37 10s (£2,630); a faster cutter, *Alice*, was purchased second-hand for £130 (£9,118) for the station. Cutters were now at New Quay, Pwlhelli, Bangor, New Brighton and Fleetwood. The values of prawn and shrimps landed in entire region in the first quarter of 1910 and 1911 were 2,884cwt @ £3,643 (£257,890); and 2,704cwt @ £3,496 (£245,200). The committee were also considering procuring a fast motorboat, estimated at a cost of £1,300 (£91,180).

There was a need to consider how to regulate the emergent whitebait fishery in 1914. There was a request for permission to shrimp under motor (after a motor shrimper was launched at Boston, Lincolnshire), and to open the Blackpool closed ground until the year's end. The Piel and Barrow channels were closed to fishing, and it was decided to allow trawling with 6in mesh on the Blackpool closed ground from January to March inclusive. The values of prawn and shrimps landed in entire region in the second quarter of 1913 and 1914 were 8,802cwt @ £8,477 (£53,370), and 7,563cwt @ £7,426 (£50,629). The war continued to affect the district's inshore fishery. The minutes of 1915 recorded that 'In accordance with Admiralty instructions permits have been issued to certain boats fishing

	July 1903				March 1910			
	Nos of Boats	Nos of Men	Totals Boats	Men	Nos of Boats	Nos of Men	Totals Boats	Men
North Lancashire Division Haverigg Point to Ribble								
1st Class Sail	48	240			30	120		
2nd Class Sail	143	238			138	248		
3rd Class, part decked	4	4			7	14		
3rd Class open	139	179			149	278		
Steam	32	288			80	780		
Shore Fishermen		329	366	1,278		399	404	1839
South Lancashire Division Ribble to Rhos Point								
1st Class Sail	45	186			35	140		
2nd Class Sail	148	296			120	240		
3rd Class, part decked	30	36			46	50		
3rd Class open	36	36			5	5		
Steam	17	136			17	170		
Shore Fishermen		254	276	944		206	223	811
Caernarfonshire Division Rhos Point to Nevin								
1st Class Sail	7	28			9	28		
2nd Class Sail	28	61			26	60		
3rd Class, part decked								
3rd Class open	241	241			103	108		
Steam	1	4						
Shore Fishermen		68	277	402		225	138	421
Pwlhelli Division Nevin to Barmouth								
1st Class Sail	8	24			6	18		
2nd Class Sail	20	43			30	71		
3rd Class, part decked	23	46			29	58		
3rd Class open	75	75			95	100		
Motor					1	3		
Shore Fishermen		133	129	321		115	161	365
Aberdovey Division Barmouth to Aberystwyth								
1st Class Sail	6	23			5	15		
2nd Class Sail	25	50			20	49		
3rd Class, part decked	3	6						
3rd Class open	40	40			55	65		
Motor					2	6		
Shore Fishermen		60	74	179		52	82	187
New Quay Division Aberystwyth to Kemmaes Head								
1st Class Sail	2	7			2	6		
2nd Class Sail	4	9			6	12		
3rd Class, part decked	13	26			15	30		
3rd Class open	49	49			20	20		
Motor					2	4		
Shore Fishermen		70	68	161		60	45	132
			1,187	3,285			1,053	3,755

in certain parts of the district.' Security prevented the record of which boats were involved and where the grounds were located. The values of prawn and shrimps landed in entire region in the second quarter of 1915 were 5,937cwt @ £6,775 (£37,410). In the southern division many Mersey grounds were closed to all boats due to war effort, whilst areas off Point of Ayre and off the Foryd Point were closed to provide for rifle ranges. There were then twenty-four second-class boats at Pwlhelli, although thirteen were laid up, and eight crews had joined up.

Motor trawling was discussed again in 1917 and again in 1919. The committee had a motor put in the New Brighton cutter *Alice*. The *Piel Castle* was still in service. An enquiry showed that fishermen (thirty-six men) on the North Wales coast and at Morecambe were not in favour of motor trawling; however, second-class boats on Mersey were fitting motors (they could be used to go to and from the ground, but not when a net was down). Trawling under power was allowed under licence with 7in mesh in the Menai Straits and off Rhyl. Nicholas Parkinson, the spokesman for the Western District, petitioned for a byelaw to allow motor trawling in 1921. During the following year there was discussion of motor trawling off Conwy, and a meeting was called at which the Morecambe representatives put on record their opposition to motor trawling. The permission to trawl under power was extended, for fish only, up to the Mersey in late 1923. There was a report of a prosecution for trawling for shrimp under power during the summer of 1924; the debate and gathering of data continued, with a discussion on the pros and cons of motor trawling. The report of this discussion created the impression that few boats were as yet fitted with motors at Morecambe. The last quarter of the year indicated that the Morecambe nobby owners were engaged in having motors fitted. The Morecambe men then indicated that they were in favour of motors in early 1924.

The new byelaw permitting motor trawling was drafted and advertised by September 1925; by the end of the year most boats in the Lancashire and west district including nineteen Morecambe boats had fitted motors. There was a change of topic in the first quarter of 1926, when a limit was set on the length of the head rope on otter trawls to 36ft. This was linked to the topic of trawling under power, as a sailing smack cannot work otter trawls effectively. The district committee were concerned about the possibly damaging effects of bobbins on the sprawn on the Rossall grounds in their discussions of the third quarter of 1930. There was a discussion on the possibility of creating a closed season on shrimp and sprawn, the superintendent reported that the breeding seasons were from October to November and again from March to June for *Crangon vulgaris*, and from November to February for *Pandalus montagui*. The committee was considering limiting engine hp during 1932, and received a report on the type and power of engine currently installed in the Lancashire half of the district; the initiative was not accepted.

The Lancashire and Western District committee held a discussion of the byelaws in 1933. It was reported that the Morecambe men do not use the otter trawl. The committee set a limit on the length of the shrimp beam at 25ft. 1935 saw a discussion on freeing the Blackpool closed ground by repealing the relevant byelaw (Byelaw 13). Amos Willacy was consulted in his capacity as Secretary of the Trawler Co. on this topic. The repeal of byelaw was advertised in the third quarter of 1935 and opened on 27 November. 1936 saw reports of some of the district committee's other activities; their patrol boat, *Piel Castle*, had found sprawning grounds seventeen miles off Fleetwood, and cleared snags from off the Lune ground.

Piel Castle was a yacht-like cutter, with higher freeboard than a nobby and a moderately raked stem above the turn into the forefoot. She was sold to become the yacht *Trilby*, the 1919 *Lloyd's Register of Yachts* lists her as *Sheila*, with a yawl rig fitted in 1913. 1937 saw a continuation of the discussion on setting a limit on motor power, without result; however, a decision was reached to set it at 40hp in 1938, followed by a limit for trawling in the district to boats of less than 25t, 80ft length and 40hp. There were then twenty-nine sailing, and 303 second-class motorboats in the district. The shrimp trawl byelaw, Byelaw 8, was amended in 1945 to take account of the otter trawl, which was first commented on in the district in 1942; the net was confirmed at 25ft wide, with a depth of one-and-a-half times the width.

Chapter 4
Southport, Marshside and Crossens

As the earliest references to inshore fishing craft on the Lancashire coast are from the Southport area, it is appropriate to begin a consideration of the context in which the nobby worked in the Southport and district community. The coast in this area has been long subject to accretion, even before the modern efforts to reclaim farmland from the sand and marsh. Crossens and North Meols parish are the earlier settlements, Crossens being a contraction of the 1240 spelling Crosseness, or the Cross on the Ness. The ness was a boulder-clay knoll at the northeastern end of a bay extending to North Meols. Meols and its various spellings derive from the Old Norse *melr* meaning sand dune, a legacy of the settlements that occurred when the Norse were thrown out of Ireland in 902. There was also a double bay to the south, extending to Birkdale, the part nearest to Crossens being called North Meols bay, where in 1793 'a prodigious quantity of mackerel was taken'. The shore originally came to the churchyard of North Meols church, at the sea exit to the Otterpool stream. A wharf was found 12ft below the road at the entrance to the Churchtown Botanic Museum (Ashton 1920).

Ashton (1920) quotes the Rev. W.T. Bulpit's catalogue of sea defence banks in the Churchtown area, setting them out in the following sequence. Sugar Hillock on the landward side of Sunny Road, mid-way between Churchtown Station and St Cuthbert's church, was old in 1565 when a ship with a cargo of sugar and potatoes was wrecked there. The first sea bank (cop) in the Bulpit list started from near Pool Bridge, and formed the landward boundary of Bankfield Lane. The second cop approximately followed the line of the railway. The third, Nab's Cop, begins at Marshside Road near Baker's Lane. Dagerts Loan was made on the seaward side, and then Shellfield Road was made, opening onto the beach at Crossens. Rossall men's bank was building in 1809, erected by men from the Hesketh estates on the Wyre.

Ashton estimated the coastline in Elizabethan times, as it would have been when the Rev. Richard James was interviewing the Meols fisherman mentioned in the chapter 'Origins'. Ashton proposed that the beach approximated to the line of the railway from Churchtown to Hesketh Park Station, and then ran to seaward of Marlborough Road, Haweside Street, and Yellow House Lane. This would have marked the end of North Meols Bay. There was little evidence for Ashton to use south of here except for a fisherman's cottage built by Peter Hodges, that stood in 1709 near Jackson's Grove about 100yd landward of Lord Street West. By 1736 sand hills had formed, blown from the south, followed by a second range that had formed to seaward of 'the New Marsh', creating a valley with fresh water slacks. Lord Street was laid out to the landward of these to avoid the flooding that occurred as late as 1840 (Ashton 1920). Just to the south of the boundary with Birkdale a stream, called the Nile stream, drained onto the beach. This stream, until it was piped into a sewer, washed the sand blowing in from the south out to sea, thereby slowing accretion at Southport.

A record taken from the Hearth Tax Rolls of 1666 for the parish of North Meals, supplemented by data from 1673, lists the names of the householders (Bailey 1955). Many of these families were later to form the fishing community.

The householders of these villages worked the land and fished for their living, until weaving was introduced to the area. A Mr Hooton introduced handloom weaving of both cotton and silk in the mid-eighteenth century. This provided a cottage industry with cash income to supplement the living eked out from the land and sea. A slump in the market and the effects of the American Civil War destroyed the industry in the late nineteenth century, a period called 'The Cotton Famine' that damaged all of the cotton towns. Prior to its development as a resort the area that became Southport was known variously as Hawse Side, South Haws, and Haws Houses. The land was settled with a scattering of cottages; from 1733 to 1763 this community produced eighty-one births, and recorded forty-nine burials. Haws Side Lane served the community as a continuation of Roe Lane, part of it survives as Hawside Street (Bailey 1955).

Southport began as a sea-bathing resort due to the initiative of a Churchtown innkeeper, William 'Duke' Sutton. Duke Sutton kept the Bull Inn, which used to be three fishermen's cottages, and survives as the Hesketh Arms at Churchtown. There had been visitors to the area as the craze for bathing developed; visitors lodged in the cottage of the fisherman Peter Hodges in 1707 that Ashton used to justify his estimate of the coastline. The crowds discovered North Meols Bay later than they found Blackpool and Morecambe, but by 1790 the Churchtown inns and cottages were full in summer. The sea bathers were taken by cart from Churchtown through the valley of slacks between the haws and onto the beach to the north of the Nile Stream. There were no facilities, so the carts were driven into the tide to allow the bathers to enter the water. The visitors normally stayed only for the weekend, usually when there was a spring tide for easy access to the water, as the only purpose of the trip was to improve their health by bathing in sea water. Then William Sutton erected a beach hut in 1792, followed in 1798 by a hotel, named the South Pool Hotel after an eleven-fathom pool. Ashton casts doubt on the story that this pool justified the name Southport, but does record that the district was called 't' Poort' long before 1798 (Ashton 1920). The eleven-fathom pool has been identified by Bailey (1955) as an inlet in the banks some half-mile from the shore that was used by shipping as an anchorage. There are references to it from 1688 and 1710, but it had sanded up by 1776. The hotel bankrupted Sutton, and was nicknamed 'Duke's Folly'. The revellers at the hotel's house-warming party also named the Nile Stream, after Nelson's sea battle. The Nile Stream gave access at high tide to a pool where the local boats were anchored, opposite the site of the Prince of Wales Hotel (Ashton 1920). Bailey (1955) casts doubt on the size of the Nile stream. It may have been dug as a boundary ditch between Haws Houses and Birkdale, as it does not appear on maps predating 1736. It is of course possible that once the stream became established, wetter winters caused it to cut its bed deeper, allowing small boats to use it, whilst drier seasons will have reduced it to the size that Bailey describes. The larger scale Ordnance Survey of 1847 (Fig. 21) indicates a narrow stream crossed by footbridges.

The *Lancaster Gazette* of 18 January 1806 reported under SHIP NEWS Col. 5, LANCASTER:

One fishing boat with six men on board, belonging to North Meols, has been lost, and we understand the unfortunate sufferers have left large families.

The same news paper reported on 13 February 1808, SHIP NEWS Col. 5, LIVERPOOL Feb 10:

The loss of the American vessel, which was wrecked on the coast of North Meols, close to Southport, on the 28th of last month, mentioned in some papers, as wrecked near Bideford, was attended with the following circumstances: In the early part of the day she was seen by the fishermen on the shore dismasted, and in the greatest distress, the sea at this time running to high as to render it impossible for them to afford her any relief. She continued pitching for some time with great violence, and at length struck the ground. The shrieks of the two women on board were truly distressing. The fishermen now put off in their boats, and at the extreme hazard of their lives, succeeded in reaching the ship, and bringing away the whole of the crew, consisting of 22 men, and the two women in safety: the vessel afterwards went to pieces.

North Meals	1666	1673	Banks continued	1666	1673
Peter Bold, Esquire	P		John Brackfeild	P	P
Thomas Selby, Esquire	P		Richard Abraham	P	P
Robert Hesketh Esquire		P	William Bond		
Banks			Widdow Rymer		P
James Starkie, Rector	P	P	William Wright		P
Robert Rymer (Rimmer)	P	P	Edward Park	P	P
Thomas Ball	P	P	Richard Matthew	P	
John Ball	P		Widdow Matthew		P
Widdow Ball		P	William Wright	P	
John Rymer	P	P	Edward Wright		P
John Abraham	P	P	John Aspinall	P	P
Edmund Wright	P	P	John Matthew	P	
Crostens			Richard Wright		P
John Copeland	P		Richard Johnson	P	
Thomas Copeland		P	Nicholas Johnson		P
Thomas Thomason	P	P	Richard Richardson	P	P
James Blevin	P		Widdow Cowell		P
Thomas Blevin		P	Hugh Hodges	P	P
John Rymer	P		Thomas Bank	P	
Robert Rymer		P	Richard Johnson		P
Richard Breakers	P	P	Thomas Mathew		P
Richard Such	P		Barnabas Mathew		P
Edward Scarisbrick		P	Widdow Breakell		P
William Bradshaw	P		Robert Blundell		P
John Bundall	P	P	Richard Aughton		P
Richard Blevine	P	P	William Rimer		P
Peter Rymer	P	P	Thomas Blanke		P
Widdow Rymer	P		John Swift		P
John Rymer		P	Thomas Hodges	P	P
John Heaworth		P	John Haworth	P	P
George Allonson	P	P	Thomas Ball	P	P
John Haworth	P	P	John Ball	P	P
Nicholas Rymer		P	Widdow Ball		P
Robert Thompson	P	P	John Rymer	P	P
Widdow Mathew		P	Thomas Ball	P	P
Hugh Wignall	P	P	James Rymer	P	P
Widdow Bond	P		John Rymer		P
Robert Matthew	P		Edward Wright	P	
Widdow Matthew		P	Richard Wright		P
Peter Wright	P	P	John Richardson	P	P
Robert Wright	P	P	William Rimer		P
Nicholas Rymer	P		Thomas Rymer	P	P
Thomas Wright		P	Henry Dod		P
Henry Liniker	P		Robert Wright	P	P
John Liniker		P	John Wilkinson		P
Adam Bannester	P	P	Barnaby Ball	P	
Church Town			Widow Ball		P
Elizabeth Jumpe	P	P	William Bond	P	P
Robert Breakell	P	P	Widdow Bond		P
Edward Bradshaw	P	P	John Blundell		P
Hugh Hesketh	P	P	Thomas Rymer	P	P
Thomas Aughton	P	P	Henry Dod		P
Thomas Aspinall	P	P	William Orme	P	

Hugh Haworth	P	P	John Aughton	P	
William Rymer	P		Hugh Stevenson	P	P
William Breakell	P		John Blundell	P	P
William Breakel	P		Richard Rymer	P	P
Peter Such		P	Thomas Aindew	P	
John Jumpe	P	P	Thomas Rymer		P
William Blundell		P	Thomas Rimer, Junior		P
Henry Such		P	James Burch	P	P
James Such		P	John Rymer	P	P
Richard Charneley		P	Wigwam Belshaw	P	P
Robert Ball		P	William Rymer	P	P
John Hesketh		P	Hugh Matthew	P	P
Adam Charneley	P	P	Richard Rymer	P	P
John Dobson	P	P	Anne Rymer	P	
John Wright	P	P	Alice Rymer		P
John Ball	P	P	John Hewson	P	P
John Gillardson	P	P	Margaret Jump (widow)	P	P
Richard Ball	P	P	John Rymer	P	P
William Wilkinson	P	P	Gilbert Ryder	P	P
Richard Rymer	P	P	William Jump	P	P
John Rymer	P		John Aindow	P	P
Widdow Rymer		P	William Rymer	P	P
William Lant	P		Robert Jumpe	P	P
Widow Lant		P	James Wilkinson	P	P
Widdow Ball	P	P	James Gill		P
Robert Lant	P	P	John Richardson	P	P
Robert Wright	P	P	James Gill		P
Thomas Rimer		P	James Rymer		P
Richard Johnson		P	Henry Howorth		P
Bircdaile			Dorothy Rymer (widow)	P	P
James Belshaw	P	P	William Johnson	P	P
Thomas Rimer		P	Nicholas Rymer	P	P
				138	165

The name Southport was coming into official use around 1808. A visitor used the name in correspondence in 1809, in which year there were thirty-eight houses (Aughton 1988), and the first official record dates to a parish register in 1812, South Haws having been used until then (Bailey 1955). There were thirty-eight dwellings and a second inn, the Union, on the site of the Prince of Wales Hotel, by 1810. These properties were all set back from the slacks on the drier ground of the dunes, so that when the cart track was re-laid as Lords Street, named in honour of the two Lords of the Manor, the spacious proportions that grace Southport were created. Southport's growth continued apace, its permanent population growing from one hundred in 1809 to almost 10,000 in 1861. There were sufficient residents in 1812 to enable Southport to raise the cost of a lifeboat with its house and carriage by public subscription. The Liverpool Docks Trustees supported the organizing committee by also taking a subscription. The Southport Lifeboat Committee had not formed a crew, but made the boat available to anyone at hand to take it out. Unfortunately the local fishermen preferred to use their own boats on rescue service, so the lifeboat lay unused until 1817 when it was sold for £30 (£1,617). This sum was transferred to the Marine Fund (Lloyd 2000). This fund was formed to 'reward the inhabitants of this parish who save lives and property in cases of shipwreck'. Rothwell (1983) put this at 1817.

The *Lancaster Gazette* of the 2nd March 1816 printed the following report:

> *Distressing occurrence.* – On the 18th ult. four fishermen belonging to N. Meols, were drowned from one of their small boats, near South Port. This afflictive event has made four disconsolate widows and fourteen poor fatherless children! Those who knew their situation, can truly say, that their case deserves the tenderest sympathy. One of their wives was daily expecting her confinement at the time: her case peculiarly critical and distressing, until the 18th, when she was delivered of a fine boy. The body of her husband has not yet been found. A subscription has been opened for them in their immediate neighbourhood.

This, and a map surveyed in 1824 indicate that the place name 'Southport' was still evolving from two words. These two reports of accidents to boats with a crew of four and six probably relate to fishing longlines, or possibly herring drifting: trawling is less likely as it requires a smaller crew.

In 1825 the landlords, the Bold, Fleetwood, and Hesketh families, took a serious interest in the new resort, laying down planning standards for the quality of the new buildings, and setting out the governance of the sea bathing, segregating the ladies from the gentlemen by a 100yd width of beach. Bathing machines were kept to a proscribed area of beach, and boats were prevented from approaching within thirty yards, on pain of a five-shilling fine. The fishermen were also debarred from dirtying the beach with fish offal. The interests of these landowners caused the centre of Southport to develop into a more select residential and 'upper-class' resort, more aesthetic, and less crowded. A map surveyed in 1834, and dedicated to P.K. Fleetwood Esq., MP, and H.B. Houghton Esq., delineates the Nile Stream and identifies 'Duke's Folly' as the Original Hotel. The map describes the frequency of the coaches that served Southport, and includes a reference to the fast canal packets that plied the Leeds & Liverpool Canal, bringing passengers to Scarisbrick Bridge where carriages were available to complete the journey. The Original Hotel is no longer standing, its site being absorbed into the realignment and widening of Lord Street and Lord Street West; a hotel on Duke Street has commemorated Duke Sutton by adopting the name Duke's Folly.

A second lifeboat was funded in 1840, again with help from the Liverpool Docks trustees. The boat, the *Rescue*, was housed in a boathouse built on the foreshore where Coronation Walk ends. She was 30ft long, 8ft 3in beam, pulling ten oars double banked. This time a cox'n, Richard Rimmer, was appointed. A sub-cox'n and bowman were also appointed, but the Southport boat relied on volunteers for the rest of its crew. Richard Rimmer retired eight years later, to be replaced by William Rockliffe of Eastbank Street, who served for twenty-five years, passing, away in 1873.

The *Southport Visitor* of Saturday 24 August 1850 published a list of vessels wrecked and saved between Formby Point and Southport from 1815 to 1850. Those entries that state how the rescue was affected and are listed here.

1823 Brig J. FITZPATRICK, oats, crew all saved by the Southport boats, vessel lost.
1824 Brig WALLACE EDKIN, timber, crew all saved by the Southport boats, vessel lost.
1830 Brig LORD HORRILL, grain, crew all saved by Marshside boats, vessel saved.
1832 Brig COMMERCE, timber, crew all saved by Southport boats, vessel lost.
1833 DIANA, general cargo, crew all saved by Southport boats.
1840 Schooner LIBERTY, clay, crew all saved by the Southport lifeboat (the Rescue), vessel lost. Ship ANTILLES, assisted off Mad Wharf by Southport and Formby lifeboats.
1847 Sloop JANE and MARY, flags, crew saved by the Southport lifeboat, vessel lost. Schooner CERES, grain, crew saved by the Southport lifeboat, vessel lost. Barque HILLSBOROUGH, coals, crew saved by the Marshside boats, vessel lost. TRUE BLUE, general cargo, crew and vessel saved by the Southport lifeboat. Schooner BROMILOW, meal, crew and vessel saved by the Southport lifeboat.

1848 PERU, meal, crew and vessel saved by the Southport lifeboat. Sloop ALICE, stone, crew and vessel saved by the Southport lifeboat. Sloop J. CHRISTIAN, crew and vessel saved by the Southport lifeboat. Schooner COMMERCE, general cargo, vessel and cargo taken to Liverpool by the Southport lifeboat.

1850 Ship HOWARD, cotton, crew saved by the Southport lifeboat, vessel lost. Steamer PRINCE ARTHUR, passengers and crew saved by the Southport lifeboat, the two firemen threw themselves from the wreck and were drowned.

Southport agreed to accept an RNLI lifeboat in 1860, the new boathouse built under Coronation Walk Bridge housing the *Jessie Knowles* in 1861. She was followed in 1874 by the *Eliza Fearnley*, which served until the tragedy of the *Mexico* rescue of 9 December 1886. The *Eliza Fernley* launched with the sixty-year-old cox'n Charles Hodge, sixty-year-old sub-cox'n Ralph Peters, and John Jackson the Bowman with a volunteer crew of thirteen. Only two, John Jackson and volunteer Henry Robinson, survived the lifeboat's capsize (Aughton 1988).

The *News of the World* magazine, 19 December 1886, reported on the opening of the inquest, which was limited to the identification of those lost.

The sad disasters on the Lancashire seaboard have evoked widespread sympathy. Through General Ponsonby the Queen sent her condolence with the widows and families of the deceased and from all parts of the country messages offering help have been received at both Southport and St Anne's. The mayors of various Lancashire towns have opened subscription lists, and there has been a prompt and generous response. The inquest was opened at the Palace Hotel, Birkdale. The bodies of the St Anne's boat's crew were placed together – as were those of the Southport crew side by side. At one side of the stable where the bodies were laid were piled the lifebelts worn by the deceased. The inquest was attended by several gentlemen, including Captain Nepean, one of the Lifeboat Inspectors of the Government. John Lathom, of Lytham, said he identified the bodies of William Johnson, aged 35, a fisherman, and James Johnson, 45, fisherman, of Lytham. The first was the coxswain of the St Anne's boat and was single; the second, his brother, was married and had six children. Thomas Harrison identified the bodies of his brother James Harrison, 19, fisherman; James Dobson, 22, fisherman; and Thomas Parkinson, 28, slater. The first and third were volunteers, but Dobson was a member of the crew. Two of the crew, it seems, were tired, and the number being short, Harrison and Parkinson volunteered to go out. William Yates said he recognised the bodies of Michael Parkinson, 21, fisherman, Lytham, single; Charles Tims, 43, fisherman, married, leaving widow and three children; Reuben Tims, 30, fish dealer, Lytham, leaving widow and three children; and John Wignall, 20, fisherman, Lytham, single. James Parkinson, of Lytham, recognised the body of Nicholas Parkinson, his son, a fisherman, 22, single. Joseph Cartmel, Lytham, identified the bodies of Richard Fisher, 49, fisherman, Lytham, married, leaving a widow and four little children; and Oliver Hodson, 39, fisherman, single. Martha Tims recognised her husband, Charles Tims, 43, fisherman, St Anne's, leaving five children, the eldest being nine and the youngest fourteen months. Catherine Wright identified her father, Thomas Rigby, of Southport. She said that a cousin and the husbands of two sisters were among the drowned. Margaret Wright identified her brother, Thomas Spencer, fisherman, Southport, aged 47, who left a widow and son, aged 11. Henry Hodge identified his father, Henry Hodge, fish dealer, Southport, 43 years old, leaving widow and seven children; also recognised Charles Hodge, 60, the coxswain of the Southport boat, and who left a widow. Henry Robinson identified John Robinson, 25, and Richard Robinson, 19, of the Southport crew, his brothers, both single. Ralph Peters recognised Ralph Peters, 60, fisherman, Southport, his father, and Ben Peters, 24, fisherman, his brother. There were eight children left, the eldest 17 years of age. John Rigby identified Peter Wright, 24, of the Southport crew, his son-in-law. Peter Jackson recognised Thomas Jackson, fisherman, Southport, 27, and Timothy Rigby, who was a fisherman, 28 years of age, Southport, and the son of the first witness. Jackson left a wife and two children, and Rigby a wife and four children, the youngest being a week old. Timothy Rigby identified Harry Rigby, 27, fisherman, Southport, single. Mary Ann Jackson spoke to the identity of Peter Jackson, of Southport, her husband, aged 52. Amy Ball recognised her husband, John, a Southport fisherman, aged 26, who died at the Southport Infirmary on the previous night from exhaustion, and who left two children. This death made the total of fatalities twenty-eight. The Coroner said it would be well to adjourn the inquiry for a week, when further evidence would be presented.

This disaster left eleven widows and twenty-four fatherless children amongst the fishing community. A monument was erected on 28 June 1888 when a large lifeboat of new and improved principle, (presented by the Misses Macrae), and named *Edith and Annie* was placed at the Southport station.

The Southport community also lost three from their lifeboat crew when William Robinson, John Robinson, and Fred Rigby were drowned on service in 1899. Southport continued as a lifeboat station until 1925 (Lloyd 2000).

The fishing community responded to the opportunities offered by the holidaymakers. In addition to opening their homes as lodgings, and taking fish to feed them, they also provided pleasure boats for their entertainment. An advert in the Southport *Independent* of 1863 promoted the sixty-year-old Southport Sailing Company, offering excursions to Lytham and Blackpool. Thus the beginning of an organized pleasure boat service followed within a year or two of William Sutton's enterprise. There were seven pleasure boats in 1826, according to Glazebrook (1826), of 3-4t burden, capable of accommodating forty passengers. These were rigged with two masts (Lloyd 2000). An advert in 1862 listed ten pleasure boats. The Southport *Independent* advert of 1863 may have provided the historian J.H. Lawson Booth with part of his list of boats and their owners from that year (Lawson Booth 1949). This list includes the *Rescue* and four schooners. The *Catalogue and Guide to the Botanic Gardens Marine Collection* (Lloyd 2000) states that the Lifeboat *Rescue* was sold to be rigged as a schooner for use as a pleasure boat. It is likely that the schooners and a two-master named *Old Tar* were all similar to those pleasure boats used at Blackpool, and photographed in

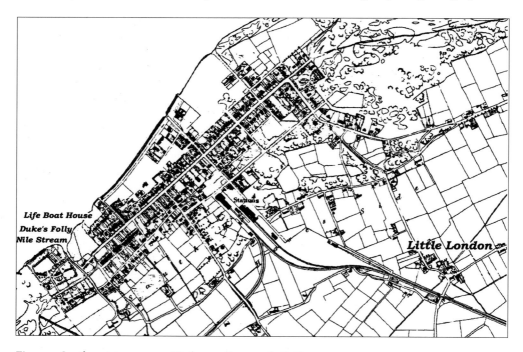

Fig. 21. Southport town map. (Ordnance Survey of 1848)

1866. Captain Rockliffe owned *Rescue*, Lawson Booth also lists a Capt. Bunker, Capt. Johnson, and two Capt. Rigbys. It is probable that the honorific 'Captain' indicates that these men all ran pleasure boats, or captain could be a nickname. Unfortunately the Southport community was not very imaginative in their nicknames, often using the same nickname for several men with the same family name. However, as none of the other owners were given nicknames in the list, on balance we may assume that the list does include nine pleasure boats, out of the total of twenty-nine craft (Lawson Booth 1949).

The list of probable pleasure boats includes:

Rescue	Schooner	Capt. Rockliffe
Manchester	Schooner	
Shearwater	Schooner	
True Blue	Schooner	
Volunteer	Schooner	
Triumph		Capt. Rigby
Sutton		Capt. Bunker
We Will Try It		Capt. Rigby
Who'd have Thought It		Capt Johnson

Old Tar was the last two-master at Southport, being mentioned in a list compiled by William Wignall (Lawson Booth 1949).

A list of boats repaired at the Freckleton yard of Peter Rawstrone includes five Bay boats from 1871 to 1874. These are:

Esther Ellen	Robert Rimmer	20 Sept 1871	A Little London address
Bay Boat	James Robinson & Co.	27 Nov 1871	
Ann Jane	Hugh 'John's' Wright	27 Feb 1872	
Mary	J. Rimmer	Late 1872	Major rebuild
Clipper	John 'Ball' Rigby	14 Feb 1874	

We do not know whether Rawstrone used the term Bay boat for a pleasure boat as at Morecambe in the late nineteenth and early twentieth centuries, but it is likely that it was a common term. *Clipper* reappears as a shanker in 1877 owned by Richard Wright, to be insured by him in 1884. They also worked on a yacht for Captain Baldwin of Southport in July to October 1878; this may have been a pleasure boat if the above proposition is correct.

Development continued apace: the promenade from Neville Street to Coronation Walk was commenced in 1834 after the Fleetwood-Hoghton map was published. The railway arrived in 1848, and as happened at all of the seaside resorts this accelerated growth. The improvement in communications allowed Southport to grow as a dormitory for Liverpool and Manchester middle classes when the railway connection to those metropolises was established in 1855. The care taken by the landowners in governing the style of development of Southport encouraged the wealthier industrialists to settle there. Whitsunday week in 1855 saw 40,000 visitors come to Southport. The *Southport Guide* of 1868 recorded 623 residents in 1848 growing to 1,097 in 1861. Southport may have started later than Blackpool, but overtook her becoming a municipal borough in 1867, nine years before Blackpool and thirty-five years before Morecambe. Her growth outstripped them, the 1871 census recording a permanent population of 21,451 compared with 6,100 at Blackpool and 3,005 at Morecambe. There was also a large influx of visitors during the season, so much so that there were the occasional epidemic, Walton (1978) referring to an outbreak of smallpox in 1876 damaging Southport's reputation amongst the trippers.

The fishing industry developed out of the communities that lived at Churchtown, Crossens and Banks, and as the cops were created the community of Marshside developed from about 1662 (Bailey 1955). There were also the fishing communities of Little Ireland, and Little London, but they came later. London Lane appeared on a map of 1736 (Ashton

1920); Little London was named on the 1847 edition of the OS, as a hamlet with an inn called the Anchor at the junction of London Lane and Tithe Barn Lane. There is a record contemporary with the 1736 map that states that shrimps were taken on the beach where Lord Street now stands (Ashton 1920). The men of Crossens and Banks may have laid their moorings in the gutters draining the water from the Marton Mere into which the New Pool ran, between Crossens and Banks, and those at Southport in the mouth of the Nile Stream. The Nile used to run across St Paul's Square under Nos 5 and 7 Lord Street West to the shore. It then ran northwest across the sand to empty into the hollow opposite Seabank Road. The map in *Slater's Directory* of 1887 gives St Paul's Square the name Nile Street. There are references to fishermen from 1709, three accidents resulting in fatalities being recorded in 1737, 1782, and 1799. These record the families of Hodge, Hodges, Howard, Barlow, Wright, Johnson, Blundell, and Ball. The fishing community was not large, with only thirteen trawlers in 1805 (Bailey 1955). Storm damage had reduced these to six by 1809. In the same year Glazebrook (1826) wrote of push netting for shrimp with a net with a deep bow pushed from the breast with a 7-8ft pole.

Storms in 1807 moved the banks and scoured a pool close to the beach opposite Neville Street, allowing the boatman to lay moorings and build a jetty. The lack of deep water close to both the beach and the open sea made the Neville Street pool most welcome, even though it was a two-mile walk along the shore from Marshside, with the tide's catch in a leap on your back. Records show that Southport fishermen saved the crew of the brig *James and Frederick* aground on Horse Bank in January 1825 (Rothwell 1983). It was these banks that gave shelter from the big seas that made moorings at Southport and Marshside viable. The fleet grew slowly in Southport's early days, with only eight trawl boats – five at Southport and three at Marshside – in 1826 (Bailey 1955). By 1840, when Fleetwood was being developed the silting of the Ribble shores, and the number of boats available at Banks caused the Leadbetters to consider hiring four of their boats out to Fleetwood. The next year these boats were replaced by the sale of five boats from Southport. There was also an emigration of families with maritime skills to Lytham at this time. Lawson Booth's list of 1863 includes a probable twenty trawl boats (Lawson Booth 1949).

Southport continued its development as a premier seaside resort by building a pier, opened in 1860. It was built over the Neville Street pool, and required the removal of the fishermen's jetty. The fishermen did well out of this development as the pier reached out to the deep water of the Bog Hole, which intruded from the southwest towards Southport across the Bug Breast. The fishermen could lay moorings on which they lay afloat at most states of the tide, using boarding punts from the end of the pier. The dredging works and placement of training walls in the upper Ribble was causing changes to the channels and banks at the mouth of the estuary by the 1860s, which would have made the pier a most welcome facility for the Crossens and Marshside men. As the estuary narrowed at Banks and Crossens, the gutter from the Marten Mere pumping station called Crossens Pool became narrower and longer, and less workable for moorings. The continual rise in the level of the sand caused concern to the Southport holiday interests, so in order to ensure that there was always some sea to be beside, a marine lake was created in 1867. This lake extended from Coronation Walk to just north of the pier; the lake was extended northward in 1892 to extend past Saunders Street nearly to Albany Road.

The Marshside community was well established by now, with the Wright family living on Shellfield Road and running a boat yard on Kirkham Road, the area originally named Dagerts Loan (Fig. 22). The boat builder Richard Wright, born in 1838, was called Peter's Dick. Richard must have been a popular Christian name as there were also Hutches Dick, Peggy's Dick, and Dicky Ewe. Peter's Dick married into the Marshside family Ball taking as his bride Mr Richard 'Bosses' Ball's daughter Bessy. Bosses, who may have given his name to Bosses Brow, on the south-west side of Marshside Road opposite Shellfield Road, was a boat builder. Peter's Dick gave up his family's trade of silk weaving, to join and then take over his father-in-law's business. This indicates the continuing importance of the weaving industry introduced to the area so many years before. A sail maker William Wignall had his

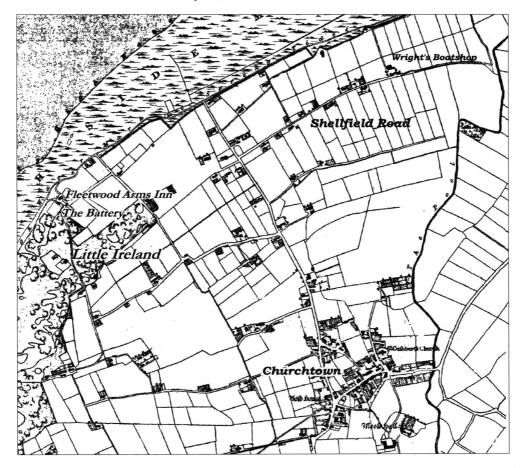

Fig. 22. Marshside map. (Ordnance Survey of 1848)

loft on Shellfield Road, and a ropewalk was set up close by. A group photograph, taken in 1905 at the boat shed, has three Wignalls, all sail makers, three Wrights and seven others mostly identified as boat yard employees. There were two other ropewalks also serving the Southport fleet: one lay alongside the lane that linked Little London Lane to what is now Manchester Road, on the same alignment as East Street.

As was common in many fishing communities, the Marshside men followed the Methodist church, but at Marshside they also embraced the Temperance movement. Peter's Dick was a leading light of this movement, and gave the use of his boat shed for meetings every Saturday. This *ad hoc* arrangement held until the community built the Temperance Hall on the corner of Shellfield and Kirkham Roads during 1864; it stands to this day. The lord of the manor, Rev. Charles Hesketh, granted them the land, and the society found the materials and provided the labour.

There were other boat builders in the area. A boat builder launched into the Nile, from a yard at the end of King Street, about where Trinity Hall was built. This yard survived until 1870, but as the Nile, which was piped into the main sewer by 1875, was so narrow they may have been building rowing boats for hire. Peter Rawstrone at Freckleton built, rebuilt, and repaired several Southport shankers. This included the purchase of cast iron keels of over 8cwt. One was purchased for the boat builder Richard Wright, for whom they made the mould and had the keel cast in 1873. The available records run from 1870, with the following Southport and Banks boats.

Entered on	Boat Name	Boat Type	Customer	Domicile
20 Sept 1871	*Esther Ellen*	Bay boat	Mr Robert Rimmer	Little London
27 Nov 1871		Bay boat	Mr Jas Robinson	Southport
27 Feb 1872	*Anne Jane*	Bay boat	Mr Hutch (John's) Wright	Southport
9 March 1872	*Morning Star*		Jas Spencer	Southport
April 1872		Bay boat		Southport
13 March 1873	*Clipper*	Bay boat	Mr Richard (Henry Cotty) Wright & John (Bull) Rigby	Southport
1 March 1873	*Marco Polo*		P. Jackson	Southport
28 June 1876	*Mary*	Shanking boat	John Rimmer	Southport
Jan 1877	*Anne Williams*	Yacht	James Spencer	Southport
1877		Yacht	Mr Hays	Southport
1 July 1878	*Ivanhoe*	Yacht		Southport
28 Sept 1878	*Maud*	Yacht	Capt Baldwin	Southport
22 Oct 1879	*Northern Light*		J. Spencer	Southport
27 Oct 1880	*Maggie*	Pleasure boat	Howard	Southport
Jan 1881	*Polly*	Shanking boat	Lawrence Abram	Banks
March 1881	*Onward*	Shanking boat		Long Lane, Banks
12 Aug 1881	*Clipper*	Shanking boat	Richard (Henry) Wright	Banks
12 Aug 1881	*Lizzie*	Shanking boat		Southport
20 Oct 1881	*Little Willie*			Southport
5 Dec 1881	*Chester*	Shanking boat		Southport
1881	*New boat*	Shanking boat	Benjamin Ball	Southport
14 Feb 1883	*Mary*	Shanking boat	John Rimmer	Southport
14 Feb 1883	*Little Willie*	Shanking boat		Southport
April 1883		Shanking boat	John Johnson	3 Shellfield Road, Marshside
29 Nov 1883		Shanking boat		Southport
15 Feb 1884	*New boat*	Shanking boat	John Ball	Marshside
23 April 1884	*Little Willie*			Southport
10 June 1884	*Northern Light*	Shanking boat	J. Spencer	Southport
July 1884	*Moon Light*	Shanking boat	Lawson	Southport
26 Aug 1884		Shanking boat	B. Ball	90 Virginny Street, Southport
August 1885	*New boat*	Shanking boat	W. Watkinson	Marshside
1885			Chas Rigby	Southport
3 Jan 1887		Shanking boat	Chas Rigby	Southport

There is a Virginia Street, which was probably B. Ball's address.

Lathom's also built for the fishing fleet, erecting their yard at Crossens Sluice, with a marine railway for launching and hauling the boats broadside up the bank to the yard's hard standing. This was on the triangle between Banks Road, before it becomes Ralph's Wife Lane, and the original outfall of Three Pool Waterway where it used to join the outfall from Crossens Sluice to become Crossens Pool (see map Fig. 23). Robert Lathom was working at Crossens Sluice during the 1890s, until the buildings caught fire in 1901. Peter's Dick's son Peter Wright took over at least part of the site for their larger building contracts. The move to Crossens will have been a godsend, as the build-up of the sand at Marshside, and the increase in size of the boats will have prevented any launches at Marshside. Robert Lathom set up a new yard at Hesketh Bank on the River Douglas. The Lancashire and Western Sea Fisheries Committee minutes of March 1903 records that Robert Lathom of Crossens tendered £189 (£14,306) for a new patrol boat, and £61 (£4,766.50) for sails, rigging and ballast.

John Crossfield's list from Crossfield Brothers and his own yard include twelve Southport nobbies. Crossfield's would have built more than these under Williams's management, but as no records survive from his part of the business a detailed search of the fishing boat registers will be necessary to identify more of their products. John Crossfield's list includes the following nobbies:

Rosebud X	12 Sept l893	R. Wright
Kathleen	31 March 1896	Robert Wright
Speedwell	19 Oct l896	John Wright
Kingfisher	22 Dec l896	Thomas Wright
Terror	21 Dec l897	R. 'Pop' Wright
Florence	10 Jan 1902	John Wright
Marjorie	22 Jul 1902	Wm. Wright
Ernest	18 Sep 1902	Thomas Wright
Frances Peel	17 Mar 1901	W.H. Watkinson
Ivy	9 Dec 1904	R.D. Robinson
Mary	21 Feb 1905	P.W. Rimmer
J.B.W.	22 Nov 1906	W. 'Wheel' Wright

As the Southport nobbies developed into big boats, of between 36ft and 45ft long, and about 5ft draught, so the Shellfield Road yard's output was taken on large 'trucks' to a ramp near the pier, some 2½ miles. Plate 10 illustrates the new *Snipe* on a truck at the start of the tow to the head of the slip. Only the Douglas yard now survives; the Crossens site is levelled, and the Marshside yard has been built over. Four builder's half models survive, all lift models. The oldest is an unnamed nobby of about 1880; then there is *Genesta*, registered LL 7 on 16/8/1886; *Sir George Pilkington*, registered LL 78 on 27/12/1900; and *Jenny*, registered LL 368 on 31/10/1902 (her lines appear as Fig. 24). The *Sir George Pilkington* was built by Peter Wright at the Shellfield Road yard, for R. Wright. She was named after Southport's MP, and the use of an iron keelson and ballast ingots moulded to fit their locations indicates that she was built to the highest standard. In addition to the lift models the *Sir George Pilkington* survives as a yacht, as did the Crossens-built *Wild Cherry* until she parted her moorings at Broomborough on the Mersey. Mr Leonard J. Lloyd measured *Wild Cherry*, and her lines are reproduced here as Fig. 25. *Wild Cherry* was built in January 1904 for John Jones of Connah's Quay.

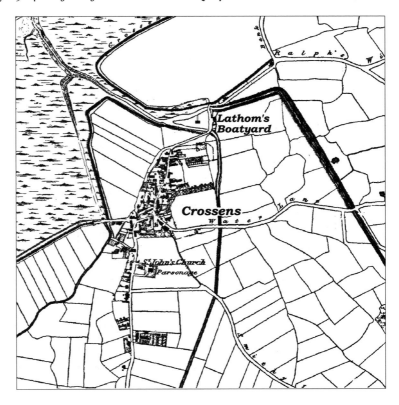

Fig. 23. Lathom's boatyard. (Ordnance Survey of 1848)

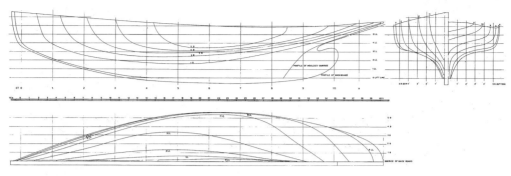

Above: Fig. 24. Lines of Southport nobby *Jenny*

Below: Fig. 25. Southport-built nobby *Wild Cherry*

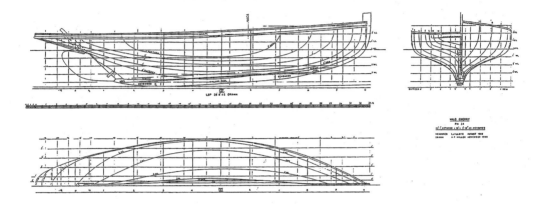

The fishing community set up The North Meols Fisherman's Provident Association with an inaugural meeting on 14 March 1877, a Wednesday. They met again at the Temperance Hall on the following Saturday, the 17th, to agree a structure to the committee. It was decided that the numbers of the representatives from the fishing communities were five for Southport, six for Marshside, and one from Banks to serve on the committee. The local rector, Rev. Charles Hesketh Knowlys, was elected the association chairman, and was credited by the community for establishing the association, with a testimonial in 1885. Mr Wm Baker of The School House, Churchtown, was elected secretary during the early years. The meetings were held in the rectory on Roe Lane, occasionally in the Churchtown National School, and in the Temperance Hall. The minutes, transcribed by Lawson Booth in 1949 are a valuable source, although unfortunately not as detailed as the Morecambe Insurance Book referred to later. It is not stated, but may be inferred from the transcript that the association was funded by members taking shares. However, non-members could also insure their boats with the fund, which commonly paid out two-thirds of the boat's value, and could advance loans for the purchase of new or replacement boats. There were at least fifty shares issued, whilst an additional five fishermen are mentioned in the minutes in the inaugural years.

The transcripts prepared by Lawson Booth (1949) include the names of boats and their owners from the minutes of the Southport Marine Fund. This list adds names of fishing families to that of Hodge that we know from 1709. There were Ball, Rigby, Abraham, and J. Wright Junior in 1838; R. Hodge, and J. Cotty Wright are listed in 1839; Rimmer and Jackson appear in 1840; Wignall in 1844; Bolton in 1847; and Leadbetter in 1848. This is the only reference to the Leadbetters in Lawson Booth's transcripts, which raises

Fig. 26. Southport map.

the question of whether all of the fishing Leadbetters migrated to Fleetwood as that haven developed. It is likely that the Hodge family remained near their first cottage home, as a Hodge was living on Lord Street in 1880. A Mr W. Robinson appears in the Marine Fund list in 1875, which then continues with three more boats in 1895, overlapping with the more enlightening Provident Association minutes (Lawson Booth 1949).

The records include the addresses of some of the fishermen in the lists in 1879 and 1880. Bolton and Johnson lived at Marshside, whilst Peters and Rimmer lived at Southport addresses. The Provident Association minutes abbreviated the Rimmer address, and Lawson Booth (1949), transcribed the abbreviation as 'Wm. St'. There is no street that abbreviates as 'Wm.' in existence now, but William Street was listed in the Southport Guide of 1868 between Boundary Street and South Bank Road; it was not listed in 1880. By coincidence there is a Rimmers Avenue, which if extended would link East Bank Street (1 on Fig. 26) to the old Boundary Lane. The Rimmers also lived on Canning Road, Blowick (5 on the map) at numbers 17, 19 and at another house whose number was not recorded (Lawson Booth 1949). The lists also include Baxter, Blundell, Caldwell, Evans, Gardiner, Halsall, Holdsworth, Howard, Lloyd, Southworth, Spencer, Sutton, Tornlinson, Wareing, and Watkinson.

The minutes of the Provident Association are very cryptic, but do provide some insights into the issues affecting the fishing community. The first topic to be recorded during 1879 was amalgamation with the Southport and Birkdale Provident Society. This was rejected, as the members did not wish to lose their identity as a fishermen's association. The association set upper and lower limits of £100 and £10 (£6,763-£676) on the values of the boats insured, the valuation to be agreed by the committee. The membership subscription was set at 5s (£16.91) in 1879. The first calls on the association were for 16s (£52.63) for damage to Thos Sutton's boat in 1882, and £10 (£727) for the loss of Richard Wright's boat *Clipper*, and £5 for Richard Hutch Weight's *Come* in 1885. As the rules paid out two-thirds of the value, these boats were valued at about £15 (£1,090) in the mid-1880s (Lawson Booth 1949). *Clipper* was at the Freckleton boat yard in 1873, for sixty-seven man-days' work costing £24 14s 3½d (£1,407.62). The records do not state what this work was, but this account probably represents a major rebuild. She was back at the yard three more times until 1881, when Richard (Henry) Wright had moved to Banks. We find *Great Annie* at £45 (£3,275), *Little Nellie* at £40 (£2,910), several at £35 (£2,546), and *Boozer*, LL 317, at £25 (£1,820) in 1885. *Little Nellie* appears in the *Fishing Registry* as LL 397 from 26/1/1888 until 26/10/1903 when she transferred to Preston.

The Provident Association records include a minute in 1885 that mentions the existence of a battery which was putting the lives of the trawler men and cocklers at risk by firing out over the banks, set up at the New Inn (Lawson Booth 1949). The 1881 *Slater's Directory* of Southport published an advertisement for Mr John Allen's Fleetwood Arms at Marshside. By the time the directory of 1887 was published it was renamed or rebuilt as the New Inn and acted as the clubhouse for the new golf club; it later reverted to the name Fleetwood Arms. The inn was sited just to the south of Bank Nook (15 on Fig. 26) on what became Fleetwood Road, and the battery was just to the south of the inn. There was a reference later in 1885 to the Irish cocklers; these could be members of the Little Ireland community that was located between the New Inn and Cockle Dick's Lane. Their cottages and school appear on the Ordnance Survey of 1889 and 1894. Richard Aughton, 'The Cockle King', gave his name to Cockle Dick's Lane (6 on the map, Fig. 26), which still exists on the Hesketh Golf Links. These links were built over the cleared site of Little Ireland (Bailey 1955). These sites appear on Fig. 22.

By 1889 the value of the boats was listed as £35 to £40 (£2,675 to £3,058); there is a mention of 'ballast boards' confirming the wide extent of the nobby's own terminology. The association committee was discussing the re-sighting of the Fog Bell, and the appointment of a bell ringer. The Fog Bell was erected as both a memorial and a safety device after seven Marshside shrimp power netters were drowned having become lost on the banks in thick fog on a rising tide. It was erected close to where the Marshside Primary School now stands, soon after the accident that occurred on 26 January 1869, and was later moved to its present site on Marshside Road (14 on Fig. 26). The August meeting of 1889 appointed John Latham to the post of Fog Bell Ringer at the rate of 5s (£19.11) per week. A minute of September of the same year establishes that the boats have iron ballast keels. The later Southport built boats were fitted with lead ballast keels (Lawson Booth 1949).

One of the duties carried out by the association committee, or its nominees, was to inspect both boats and their moorings. The minute of November 1890 sets out the work required to make the moorings good, the work to be completed within two weeks. In 1891 Thomas Wright's *Surprise*, registered LL 108 from 9/11/1889 until 1894, and J Rimmer's *Pollie* were insured at the value of £50 (£3,986). *Pollie* appears in the Freckleton accounts in 1881. The committee was also investigating the purchase of lifeboat trucks. These were four-wheeled bogies, the main wheels of which were five or more feet in diameter. These were probably wanted to launch and recover the nobbies back to the Shellfield Road boat yard. The photographs of the movement of *Snipe* from Shellfield Road to the Pier Ramp have her on a truck with main wheels of about 7ft diameter, and steering wheels of 4ft (Plate 10).

The Lancashire and Western Sea Fisheries District Committee minutes refer to Southport fishing techniques and the manner of pursuing the industry. The first specific reference states that in 1891 longlines were fished with between five to nine six-man boats from mid-October until early May. The minutes of May 1893 state that concern was expressed about the hawking of foreign shrimp of poor quality at Southport; the Southport Town Council are to be warned of the committee's concern. The lists of committee members also

Plate 10. *Snipe* on her truck, from the collection of W.S. Wignall. (Courtesy of Lancaster City Museums)

names Southport fishermen, with their place of residence: William Robinson, 135a Lord St Southport; John Ball, Marshside; and Lawrence Abraham, Banks served in 1893. The enquiry into the destruction of fry on the Burbo Bank included the information that the ground behind the Burbo Bank is mud, and unsuited to the Southport shank which can only fish a sand bottom (Lancashire and Western Sea Fisheries Committee 1891 et seq.).

Nicholas 'Manty' Wright and his crew John Wright got into difficulties in *Two Sisters* in 1891. *Two Sisters* LL 123, built in 1889, had stayed out over night when either dodging foul weather or seeking shelter in North Hollow when she bumped across Salthouse Bank. The crew showed distress signals at 10.00am, which were answered by the St Anne's boarding boat *Daniel Proctor* (Mayes 2000). The committee of 1892 was still concerned about the activities of the battery, which was still putting trawlers at risk by firing as they were passing. Two members' boats, *Violet* LL 212 and *Fleetwing* LL 198 were valued at £50 (£3,784) for insurance purposes. Both boats were registered in 1893, *Fleetwing* leaving the register in 1901, and *Violet* joining the Liverpool register on 4/8/1893, transferring to Conwy from 24/4/1903 until 26/4/1907 when she went to Aberystwyth.

Lawson Booth's transcripts (Lawson Booth 1949) of the association's paperwork continued until 1897, but the minutes maintained that cryptic style which frustrates the researcher. The transcripts give an insight into the size of the trawling community, and there is a note for 1900 that gives a 'census' of the fishing communities. There were 175 at Marshside, 100 at Crossens, and ninety at Southport, of this community eighty persons owned ninety boats (Lawson Booth 1949). As most of the Southport boats will have been crewed by two, there were about 180 trawling and 180 live cockling, power netting, cart shanking, and hawking the catch.

The minutes and lists combine to give a sample of the fishing families. They will not be complete as some of the boatmen will have remained independent, and there was only passing mention of those who fished without going afloat. The most prolific family were the Wright family; discounting possible duplicate references brings the seventy-three entries down to forty-two individuals for the period of the records of sixty-four years from 1838. The family favoured a small selection of Christian names: there were six different Johns, at least six Richards and Thomases, and there were three Williams, at least three Roberts, two Peters, a Nicholas and a Henry. Some nicknames were popular – John, Nicholas, Peter, Thomas, and William were all called 'Manty'. John, Peter, and Robert were called 'Cotty', and there were two 'Pens' and two 'Stems'. There were five Rimmers listed; J. and William Rimmer were nicknamed Willocks. The others were John 'Manty', Robert 'Bold', and Thomas 'Pluck' Rimmer (Lawson Booth 1949). Geoffrey Aughton of Glebe Lane Banks joined the Sea Fisheries Committee in 1898.

The creation of the Marine Lake provided an opportunity for the fishermen. A group was able to add to the pleasure boating activities, taking trippers out from the pier in the nobbies, by setting up 'The Southport Boating Company Limited' in 1899. The founding members were six residents of Shellfield Road, and one from Bank Nook. The business built and maintained for hire on the north part of the lake a fleet of up to nine small self-sail yachts. These were small, of necessity shoal-drafted boats, with a moulding beneath the shear strake, and a curved slightly raking stem. The company continued to trade until 1960 (Lloyd 2000).

The minutes of the Sea Fisheries meetings of 1899 (Lancashire and Western Sea Fisheries Committee 1891 et seq.) refer to line fishing in the central division, which included Southport. There was a report of two new boats coming to Southport in the summer of 1901; by the year's end one was launched at Southport and there were seven in build or on order. The Roa Island School, run by the research station of the Lancashire and Western Sea Fisheries Committee was attended by John Wright, 125 Shellfield Road, Southport; Robert Wright, 115 Shellfield Road (11 on the map Fig. 26), Southport; John Aughton, Glebe Lane, Banks; and Richard Abram, Glebe Lane, Banks in the spring of 1902. Robert Johnson, Marshside; Richard Robinson, 8 St Luke's Rd, Southport; Daniel Rigby, 18 St Luke's Rd; and Henry Wright, 29 St Luke's Rd, Southport (no. 7 on the map Fig. 26) attended the second class at Roa. The quarterly report to December 1902 recorded that seven second-class boats were new built for Southport, one was on the stocks, and four were on order. Shrimps were plentiful at the start of the quarter with 100-160qt per day taken from the Ribble to the Dee.

The British Association discussed the shrimping industry at a meeting of 1903. The section on Southport established that there were seventy two-man boats working from Southport, taking 30qt per day in the season. The paper also considered the by-catch of fish fry taken with the shrimp, reporting a pair of drags made on the Blackpool ground late in December 1893. One beam trawl (probably 18ft wide, although its size was not stated) took 22½qt and over 2,000 undersized fish, while two shanks (combined width of 21ft) took 21½qt, and under 9,000 fish. It was stated that this large number of fry of soles, plaice, cod, haddock, and whiting was a regular by-catch. The paper also recorded the structure of the Southport industry. The income from the catch was divided into five shares: two each for the crew, and one for the boat. When rigged for shrimp shanking the boat towed four shanks, the boat's share paying for two and the crew one each. The industry supported about 200 shrimpers, with seventy boats, there will have been sixty cart shankers and power netters working. The wives and children picked and potted the shrimp, which generated business for the local dairies supplying butter for potting and printers supplying labels and packaging.

The Lancashire and Western Sea Fisheries Superintendent reported (Lancashire and Western Sea Fisheries Committee 1891 et seq.) that up to March 1903 four boats were added to the Southport fleet. In the same period all boats were hampered by bad weather; however, second-class trawlers made landings of up to 25-score pounds (500lb) per day at Southport. The fishermen who attended the school at Roa Island in March were James Robinson, 89 Shakespeare Street (8 on the map); William Jackson, 22 Boundary Street (9); Thomas Wright, 62 Lethbridge Road (10 on the map); and John Wright, 116 Shellfield Road (11) Southport; and from March into April 1903 Lawrence Abram (Ned's), Long Lane, Banks; John Wareing (Stephen's), Long Lane, Banks; Richard Sharples, Long Lane, Banks; Richard Wright, 24 Lytham Road (12 on the map), Marshside; and Nicholas Wright (Selby), Lytham Road, Marshside. A map of Banks appears as Fig. 27. In 1905 H. Robinson, R. Rimmer, M. Johnson, H. (Hutch) Wright, J. Foster, and J. Wright all of Marshside, and R. Johnson, B. Abram, J. Bond, and W. Leadbetter all of Banks attended the school. In summer, twenty-two Southport boats went trawling in Tremadoc Bay; during the autumn Lytham and Southport trawl men were obliged to go musseling.

Aflalo (1904) recorded seventy boats in 1904, trawling from Southport and Marshside. He stated that the fleet were all no more than six years old, two-man boats, catching about 30qt a day through the season. 1906 saw J. Abram, J. (Bunger) Johnson, P. Brookfield, and J. Aughton, all of Banks, attend the Roa Island School (Lancashire and Western Sea

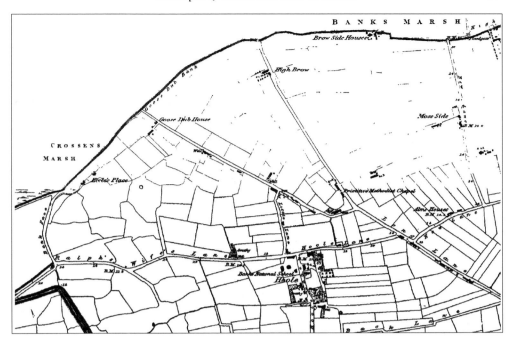

Fig. 27. Banks. (Ordnance Survey of 1848)

Fisheries Committee 1891 et seq.). A note taken in 1908 suggests that the fleet numbers had dropped to forty, all moored in the Bog Hole. Because of the strength of the tidal flow they normally worked from slack water to slack water, for safety in picking up their moorings under sail and the impossibility of stemming the tide in a rowing punt.

There were favoured grounds for shrimp in the channels of the Ribble estuary and up to Blackpool, whilst they trawled to the south for fish, shooting away at the Horse Bank Buoy. The note states that sole were the most valued fish and also comments that the trawl often picked up enough coal to feed both the house fires and the shrimp boiler. As will always be the case, some men were doing better than others, 'Fleetwood' Rimmer being one, as owner of three boats. The fishermen have always marketed their own fish, or used local dealers. There was dissatisfaction with this system due to the demand outstripping the supply, linked to the excellent reputation that Southport shrimps enjoyed. As there was a ready supply of cheap shrimp from the Continent, especially Holland, the dealers began to import Dutch shrimp, and market them as Southport caught. Aflalo (1904) commented on this. The fishermen knew that they were being undercut and that they could lose their reputation for quality, and attempted to persuade the dealers to pay a higher price for local caught shrimp and to stop marketing the imports as Southport shrimp. The fishermen's patience ran out in 1913. Direct action ensued when a dealer went to meet a consignment of shrimp from the train at Churchtown Station. The police records report that he was met by a 'shouting mob of fishermen', who pursued him at least a quarter of a mile to Larkfield Lane before tipping his shrimp into the ditch and spoiling them with paraffin. The fishermen attempted to intercept the next day's consignment, but were met at the station by twelve police constables and two mounted officers. This did not deter them, as when the dealer had loaded his cart and began to move away the fishermen surrounded him and his cart. The police waded in and battle was joined. The fourteen police managed to arrest twenty-nine fishermen, who were charged with wilful damage, obstruction, and assault. The fishing community with many supporters marched to the County Borough Court on the day of the trial, with a banner and placards. The magistrates imposed fines on the 'shouting mob', but sympathy for their cause was so high that a benefactor paid their fines.

During 1909 W. Leadbetter Jnr and Wm Bridge of Banks attended Roa Island. The superintendent reported that Southport boats had given up shrimping for summer, trawling for soles. Robert Brookfield, Bonds Lane; and John Abram, New Lane Place, Banks, attended the school during 1910. Richard Howard, 80 Lytham Road (12 on the map Fig. 26); Benjamin Wright, 7 St Luke's Road (7 on Fig. 26); John Wright, 16 Lytham Road; and William Wright, 23 Lytham Road, Southport, followed them in 1911, with the Banks fishermen John (John's) Abram, Long Lane; Richard Brookfield, Long Lane; Richard Abram, Ralph's Wife's Lane; and Thomas Abram Church Lane. More names of Southport fishermen can be found in the 1912 and 1913 school roll: Richard Ball, Charnley's Lane; James Johnson, New Lane Place; and Thomas (Edwards) Abram, Long Lane, Banks; William Wright, 88 Shellfield Road (11 on Fig. 26); Richard Sutton, Knob Hall Lane (13 on the map); Robert Ball, 73 Marshside Road; Thomas Howard, Bank Nook (no 15 on the map); Thomas Sutton, 56 Lytham Road; and James Wareing, Lytham Road, Marshside; John Wright, 17 St Luke's Road; and John Rigby, 31 St Luke's Road, Southport (Lancashire and Western Sea Fisheries Committee 1891 et seq.).

During 1913 Southport men were working Taylor's Bank and Crosby Channel. The classes continued in 1914, attended by Robert Johnson, Banks; and James Evans, Henry Wright, Richard Rigby, and William Wright, Southport; and in 1915 by Daniel Robinson, 25 St Luke's Road; Peter Sutton, 6 Shellfield Road; William (Bull) Wright, 75 Lytham Road; and William Wright, 54 Shellfield Road, Southport; and Jeffrey (Bens) Abram, Long Lane Banks. In 1916 thirty boats were noted trawling the Horse Channel. 1919 saw a longlining revival at Southport; the committee minutes of 1920 note that there are rumours of Dutch shrimps at Southport and that siltation is causing Southport boats to sell up. At this time Southport half-deckers experienced their best fishing in summer and autumn, so some lay-up over the winter, whilst the crews took up casual labour. In 1924 there was mention made of boats working from Crossens Pool (Lancashire and Western Sea Fisheries Committee 1891 et seq.).

The sanding up of the channels and gutters caused by the dumping of dredge spoil from the Mersey and Ribble, combined with the changes caused by the Ribble training walls, made the ascendancy of the big nobby short lived. *The Ivy*, new built in 1904 for Richard D. Robinson, was sold to St Anne's by 1906. The Southport community began to return to shoal draft forms as the grounds became shallow before the boats were driven away entirely. The loss of sheltered moorings and the ability to trawl the banks will have become acute from after the period 1915 to 1925. Although nobbies remained to be motorized, there had already been a migration of Southport fishermen to Lytham in the days of sail. The Marshside men went over to cart shanking, and the fishermen would have become unpopular in Southport itself as it promoted its holiday and superior residency image. The addresses of the nobby fishermen indicate that they lived away from those parts of Southport that were most likely to accommodate the holiday makers, so it is most likely that their wives were employed within the home processing the shrimp for market, rather than supplementing the income by running boarding houses. The industry did not form a co-operative as at Fleetwood and Morecambe probably as the industry was declining after the First World War, at the time when the northerly towns had more confidence in their industry.

Little evidence survives from before 1880 of the form of the nobbies. There are two examples from 1880 to 1885. The Botanic Gardens Museum collection (Lloyd 2000) has an unidentified builder's half model, and photographs of *Little Nellie* survive after her stranding in 1906. She was in for repairs at Peter Rawstrones in 1881 and insured by William Willocks Rimmer for £40 (£2,780) before 1885. The half model has an almost straight keel and rebate, with a moderate round in the forefoot turning into a vertical stem above the water line. There was moderate hollow in the garboards rising to an easy bilge carried fairly high. The model is 28$^5/_{16}$in, which at a probable ¾in to the foot scale would build at 37ft 9in by 11ft 3in and 4ft 8in draft. *Little Nellie* was of similar form, the only apparent difference being that her counter was less round in plan. Both nobbies had sufficient rake to the sternpost to place the head of the rudderstock well aft on the deck of the counter. During the next ten to fifteen years the Southport nobbies increased in size to 40-45 ft length, and the draught increased to over 5 ft. The form evolved towards a cut away forefoot and rockered keel with outside ballast. The evolution was achieved by changing the profile of the keel, from the nearly straight keel with drag, to a deeper curve. The sections were changed by keeping the bilge at the same height, and hollowing the garboards to fair them into the ballast keel. The effect was to add depth and area to the profile with little alteration to the canoe body. The evolutions continued to further cut away the forefoot and lengthen the counter. The later big Southport-built nobbies were fitted with lead keels, the only nobbies known to be built this way. Some of these nobbies, having been motorized and sold away to the Mersey, had their draft reduced by dropping the lead keel, when afloat, onto the foreshore. The deadwoods were then cut away, the keel bolts made good and the nobby began a new phase of her life. The discarded keels were abandoned to the mercies of scavengers who gradually nibbled away at them for beer money or a subsistence income in depressed times.

The lines of *Wild Cherry* from 1904 do not show any distinguishing form that may be attributed to her builder, Peter Wright at Crossens. She had a conventional 'U'-section iron ballast keel, moderately cut away profile, and conventional sections. The only unusual detail was the way that her rebate was worked on her sternpost. These details can be seen in her lines plan.

Mention has been made of the Little London and Little Ireland communities. Little London was the small area surrounding St Luke's and the southern end of Tithebarn Road. The Ordnance Survey of 1865 places it alongside the original rail track bed that ran between Hart Street and Forest Road. As the area was rebuilt the community moved to St Luke's road. This community tended to look further a field for their grounds, taking their trawlers round to the Cardigan Bay ports, marketing some fish at Aberystwyth and at the bigger trawling port of Milford Haven. They lived aboard their boats, or in lodgings at the Welsh ports they favoured for the season. Houldsworth (1874) reports that big trawlers from Southport were fishing the Cardigan Bay grounds, these may have been from the Little London community. The Little Ireland community no longer exists, as the cottages were cleared for the golf course at Fleetwood Road. We know of Irish cocklers from the Provident Association minutes, and it is apparent that the community existed on the fringes of the industry, working at cockling, perhaps power-netting for shrimp, and casual general labouring.

The nobbies were used for trawling, shrimp shanking and longlining. The trawl gear used for plaice and soles was a beam trawl, with 25 ft beam, and a rope ground rope wrapped with chain. The beam was in three pieces, and the net full backed. The big nobbies will have easily been powerful enough to broadside, or to drag a 25 ft trawl, the size of the gear was probably limited by the strength of the two-man crew. Cod and ray was taken on long lines, on herring bait. The Southport fishermen have no memory, nor spoken record of the six-man line boats of 1891, but could describe longlining from the nobby. The nobby was not used to work the line, the punt was towed out to the ground, and two of the three crew taken for longlining set the line from the punt. In common with the older North Sea longline cod fishery out of Barking, the punt would be used as a line turning boat. The line was under-run, by lifting the line, unhooking any fish, and re-baiting before the line went back over the punts other gunwale, as the punt worked along the line.

The shrimping methods were unique to Southport where they preferred the shank for shrimping, using a withy bow rather than the stanchions and top beam favoured for the shank elsewhere. Davis describes and sketches the earliest form of the shank (Davis 1958) made without any ironwork. The beam was the conventional boat shank of 10 ft 6 in in length. This was bored through at the mid-length and at each end to take the butt end of a 7 or 8 ft willow rod. The "middle stick" formed a stanchion, just over 1 ft 6 in high. The butt ends of the rods were split and driven through the beam, and then wedges were driven home in the splits to secure them into the beam. The end rods called 'benders' were bent over to form the bow and lashed to each other, one in front and one behind the middle

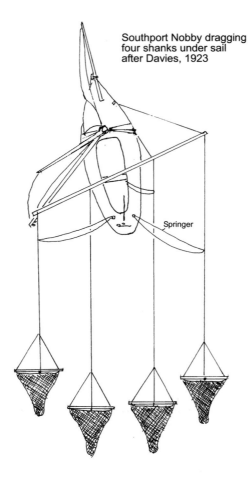

Southport Nobby dragging
four shanks under sail
after Davies, 1923

Springer

Fig. 28. Towing four shanks. (after
F.M. Davis, *An Account of the
Fishing Gear of England and Wales*)

stick. A cross lashing was then applied around benders and middle stick to hold all secure. Davis describes the net as follows: 'round netted, with the flat knot: braid tail 100/100 about 3 feet; continue 100/20 score, creasing twice every round; after this the last 3 feet or so should be braided 20 score/20 score. Then put in "nooks" as follows: divide the 20 score at the mouth into four sections, each of five score; alternate sections are then discontinued; the other sections are continued backwards and forwards in the usual manner, the last five meshes each side being dropped each round, until a blunt triangle is formed with the apex ten meshes across. These triangles are the "nooks".'

The towing bridles about 8ft long were made off to staples on the front of the beam and a tilt line ran from the top of the middle stick to the towing eye of the bridles. There was no mention of ballast to sink the beam, but iron straps may well have been nailed on the top surface of the beam. The later form of the shank used iron sockets on the end of a 2in by 2½in pitch pine beam, with an iron stanchion and ash bows in three parts. The 2in diameter sockets were attached to the beam-ends by ¾in by ⅝in straps. The stanchion was of ¾ bar, split and spread into a tee to be secured to the front of the beam, with an eye in the top for the middle bit of the bow, 1ft 3in high. Ballast straps of ⅝in iron were fitted, at ¾in wide on the front, and 1in wide on top.

The big Southport nobbies worked four shanks, no one now remembers how. E.J. March (1970) referred to the 'forward', 'tack', 'quarter', and 'hindmost', stating that the first and last were boomed out with a long pole. Davies provides a sketch plan of a nobby running or reaching with a long boomer across the aft end of the cockpit, streaming all four shanks (Davis 1958; see Fig. 28). The boomer would have had to be at least 33ft long to spread

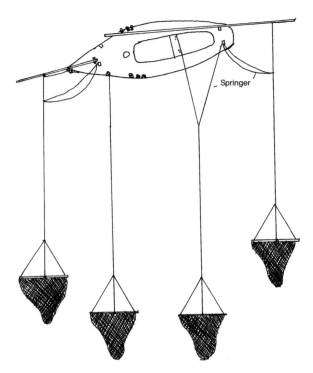

Fig. 29. Broadsiding with
four shanks.

four 10ft 6in shanks, more to allow for the beam of the boat between the middle two
ropes. The working of this set-up may have been as follows. With the nobby reaching
slowly forward, the windward outer shank rope was secured to the end of the boomer and
its springer passed. It was shot away and the boomer passed out board until the leeward
shank could be rigged to the leeward end of the boomer and its springer passed. This
would have been shot away before the boomer was passed across to allow the in board
shanks to be rigged and shot away. The inner shanks ropes would have been longer than
the outboard ones so that the outboard shanks could be retrieved ahead of and under the
inboard ropes. Davies' sketch is small, which probably is why he did not include springers,
nor indicate whether the trawl ropes were secured to the boomer, or ran forward to the
nogs on the nobby.

The broadsiding set up may have required two boomers, as March specified a long pole
for the forward and hindmost shanks; however, the jib outhaul on the bowsprits will have
served very well, allowing the boomer that Davies sketched, laid along the side deck and
over the counter, to serve for the hindmost shank. The probable method of shooting, using
the logic that we know worked for broadsiding with two trawls, may have been as follows.
The quarter shank would have been shot, with a springer rigged to the stern nog to open
it out from the tack shank. The tack shank would then be shot and towed from the bow
nog; the hindmost shank could then be rigged to the boomer, with a springer to allow it to
be retrieved, and shot away with a shorter rope than the quarter shank to ensure a lead.
Next the forward shank could be shot from the bow, secured to the Samson post or bow
nog, and hooked into the traveller on the bowsprit. With one crew member forward and
one aft, the shanks were probably shot in pairs, and would be opened out in pairs, to keep
the nobby broadside on to the tide. The outer pair would have been opened out to the
boomer end and to the bowsprit end, followed by opening out the tack and quarter, so that
the nobby was balanced and each shank covered fresh ground, it was probably necessary
to work both quarter and hindmost springers to steer the nobby, but again no information
has come down the eighty years since Southport nobbies relied on wind and tide to power
the drag to confirm or correct these proposals. Fig. 29 illustrates this layout.

The Southport power net was also unique in its construction, being very similar to the all-wood shank. Davies describes a construction with the bows wedged into a 6ft beam, and coming together to make a 2ft 6in high bow. They were lashed together, again with one bender passing behind and one in front of the staff, with an 18in overlap. The staff, of 8ft length, was fitted into an iron socket on the beam. The net was braided from No.12 cotton, shaped like a full backed trawl, but with the full back on the beam and the swept belly round the bow. The tail was 2ft 6in long, and then the body widened out to fit the 6ft beam, followed by 2ft 6in belly and wings. The net was pushed from the chest, so the socket and holes bored for the bows were set at an angle to keep the beam flat on the ground.

Dispensing with the iron socket, dispensing with the wedges in the butts of the benders and passing both benders in front of the staff simplified later power nets. Cord stays between the bow and the beam and a lashing at the bow stabilised the structure.

Mention has been made of the leap, a wickerwork basket used to carry the catch. This form of basket survived into the era of the photograph at Southport: examples are in the collection of the Fleetwood Maritime Museum, and the author has a copy of an engraving of a view of Piel in Walney Channel with power netters and their leaps on the foreshore. The leap was 20in wide and 12in front to back at its top, the base was a rectangle 16in by 9½in, and it measured 16in high. It was shaped like a flattened barrel with bellied back and sides. A pair of 12in ropes were tied in 11in up, at each side of the hollowed front surface, these went to each end of a 20in oak barrel stave. The leap was carried by putting the stave across the chest, just below the throat, with the ropes going outside the upper arms. The fishermen all used leaps, the power netters carrying them as they worked, whilst the boatmen carried them as they walked to and from the pier, until the tram service which reached Churchtown in 1878 was started and they were able to ride part of the way.

Chapter 5

St Anne's and Lytham

The title of this chapter recognises that there were originally two towns with differing fishing communities. We must record our gratitude to Cdr Gil Mayes who shared his research for the book *On a Broad Reach* (Mayes 2000). Much of the data about the fishing communities comes from this source. Lytham is the oldest township, but conversely the fishing community that lived where St Anne's now stands may have been older. Lytham developed at the gates of the Lytham Hall Park, home of the Clifton Family. It has been a semi-industrial port, with a shipyard at the mouth of the Liggard Brook, and a lightering and transhipment dock in the mouth of the Main Drain. This dock served vessels working into the Ribble, going into the River Douglas and the canal system, and served the hinterland of Lytham. The map of Lancashire surveyed in 1786 records a small community at the gates of John Clifton Esq.'s manor. The dock had been dug, but there was no real development. By the time of the Ordnance Survey of 1842 Lytham was now a town, and the Blackpool and Lytham railway was about to arrive, but the shipyard was not yet in evidence. Lytham continued to develop as a holiday resort, providing good hotels and accommodation for the well-to-do industrialists' families in the summer season.

The community of fishermen in the St Anne's area lived in the hamlets and cottages strung out on the lanes between Lytham, Squires Gate, and Little Marton, at the south end of Blackpool. This area is relatively new land: Speed's map of 1610 shows the coast to be about thousand yards further inland where St June's now stands. The land was built by the successive deposition of shingle banks (called stanners) of stone washed from the Blackpool cliffs, and wind-blown sand that originated from the Mersey. William Ashton (1920) reports that the outermost shingle bank formed from about 1813. The southeastern

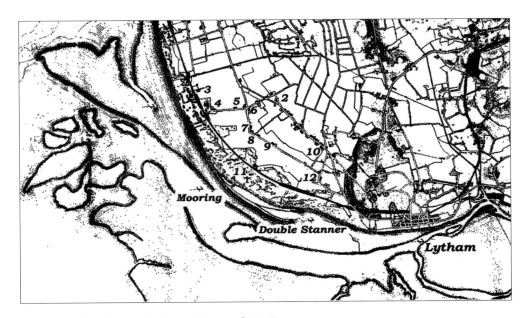

Fig. 30. St Anne's map. (Ordnance Survey of 1848)

end of the newest stanner, called the Double Stanner, divided to enclose a tidal stretch of foreshore near Ansdell on the map Fig. 30, now called Fairhaven. This provided sheltered and drying lay-up moorings for the cottagers' smacks in a natural harbour called Granny's Dock, until the Double Stanner was used for the foundation of the sea wall enclosing Fairhaven Lake. The sand hills and new land was named Lytham Common on the 1786 survey, a lane running parallel to the shore being called Common-side Lane. This and the lane called Hey Houses provided homes for most of the fishermen; the community that was to become Ansdell is not named on the earlier survey, but bears the name South Houses on the Ordnance Survey. After an urban bistrict boundary between St Anne's and Lytham was drawn in 1894, the South Houses found themselves in Lytham and became known as Commonside. J.D. Marshall (1974) records that Hey Houses was named after the hedged fields, as hey is Old English for hedge.

The fishing families from this area included:

No. on map		
1	Harrison	From Marton
2	Melling	From Melling Lane
3	Whiteside	At Cross Slack
4	Eaves	On Head Roo Gate Road; farm labourers and part time fishermen
5	Greaves	On Head Room Gate Road
6	John Singleton Snr	The corner of Head Room Gate and Leech Lane
7, 11, & 12	Cartmell	On Head Room Gate, Lighthouse Cottages, and at Commonside
8	Barrow	On Commonside Lane
9	John Singleton	On Commonside Lane
10	Richardson	The corner of Heyhouses and North Houses Lanes
[No number]	Ball	from Squires Gate

These are indicated on the map by being blocked in solid. William Cartmell, a farmer and publican, ran the Trawl Boat Inn on the corner of Heyhouses and North Houses Lane. He was related to Mrs Bailey of Baileys Hotel in Blackpool. Commonside also housed the Derbyshires, Fishers, Hodsons, and Johnsons. As St Anne's grew up it housed the Dobsons who were part-time fishermen, Hankinson, Harrisons, Hibbertson, Hodges, Tims, and the Bonney family from Lytham.

Some given names were very popular, Thomas and William being the most common. This may have engendered a tradition of nicknames; some were as obscure as one can find anywhere. There were Robert 'Skip' Harrison, a Thomas and a William 'Butler' Harrison, as well as William 'Ting' and 'Tiller' Harrison; Thomas Ball was called 'Skew'. Others had the more usual contractions like 'Ike', and 'Algy' for Alfred. There were in total some twenty-six families fishing at St Anne's although not all worked smacks, some relying on power netting and cockling for a living.

Photographic records indicate the common ancestry of the smacks with the Blackpool pleasure boats. Edgar March (1970) stated that the Lytham and St Anne's boats had rounder sections with little hollow. As most of the later nobbies came to the area second hand, March may have been referring to an older type. Photographs (Plate 11) show a clinker hull with a straight stem, rounded forefoot, and a short, squarish elliptical counter (Haley 1995). They are perhaps finer than the Blackpool beach boats, since they were not formed for beach work, which requires flatter floors and fuller ends. The deck layout is the same as that of the North Lonsdale square tuck-sterned nobby with low coamings and square-ended cockpit with a mast gate on the sailing beam, and the conventional cutter rig. One, the *Margaret* PN 40, has conventional outer coamings running round the counter, whilst the other has a head ledge across the counter in front of the rudderstock on which the outer coamings terminate. The photo of two smacks apparently laid up on the top of the Double Stanner also includes a shrimp shank set up for the photographer. The beam is 10ft 6in long, with 1ft 8in high iron stanchions to support the top beam. It is fitted with its three-legged bridle, but not rigged with a net. The fishermen stuck with the shrimp shank, working two from the smack, right the way up to the First World War, and changed over to a beam trawl if they were looking for flatfish.

The working moorings were laid in the deep channels under the shelter of the Salthouse (Salters) and Crusader Banks (Fig. 31). Crusader Bank was named after the East Indiaman *Crusader* of 584t, with a cargo valued at £100,000 (£6,513,000), wrecked there in 1839 (Bailey 1955). The Harrisons from Marton laid moorings off Cross Slack between the end of Division Lane and Head Room Gate Lane, where North Hollow, Nix Hollow, and North Channel meet behind Crusader Bank. The Mellings, and as St Anne's developed the St Anne's families, moored in the North Channel just south of the site of the pier, and the Heyhouses and Commonside men lay afloat in Granny's Bay, at the mouth of Granny's Dock. These men fished for shrimp in the channels of the Ribble estuary and on the Blackpool grounds, and for flatfish in the deeper water off the banks. Some of the men maintained pleasure boats. A photograph of 1866 shows two two-masted open beach boats in front of the Wellington Hotel, Blackpool. They both have the same small high counter as the St Anne's smacks but are completely open with four thwarts and side benches from stem to stern. Although the sails are stowed the masts are of schooner proportion with what appears to be a lug-footed foresail. A later photograph of the 1880s shows larger sloop-rigged pleasure boats, again completely open, with a short bumpkin for the forestay.

Blackpool provided the market supplied by this community, before the advent of the railways. The catch was taken to market by donkey, and hawked around the town and its pubs. This was after the boat's crew had to walk back home from the moorings, carrying the catch in a leap on their back. The Harrisons will have walked over two miles down Division lane, the Commonside Lane men had to walk about a half mile to the beach at Granny's Bay, but lived three miles further from their markets.

There were about twenty-six families fishing, some powering for shrimp, setting night lines (trots), and cockling on the banks opposite St Anne's; those with smacks fished the channels and into the deep water off the estuary. There is no record of boat builders, although a local supplier of boat gear seems to have been a smith at St Anne's. The

Plate 11. Lytham smacks. (from Haley Robert, *Lytham St Anne's a Pictorial History*)

fishermen went to Fleetwood for sails and bought their chandlery at the Grimsby Coal Salt and Tanning Co. They all braided their own nets until the net company opened in Fleetwood. After the advent of the railway, fish buyers were sending the catch to the Manchester markets.

The town of St Anne's was the idea of the estate manager of the Cliftons' estate, Mr James Fair. The land was surveyed in 1870, before building began in 1872 at Clifton Drive. The west end of Commonside Lane was renamed Church Road when the church of St Anne was built in 1872-3. Church Road served the cottages for the building workers that were started in 1874 and 1875. Members of the fishing families also found work on the building sites, when fishing was slack. Further momentum was created when a Rawtenstall businessman, Mr Elija Hargreaves, met with Thomas Fair, who had taken over from his father as the estate's land agent. This meeting resulted in the creation of the St Anne's on Sea Land and Building Company, in October 1874. This company leased an initial 82 acres from Clifton Estates; this later grew to 600 acres. The Land and Building Company issued its prospectus, drawing its subscriptions and directors from the industrialists of Rossendale. The prospectus set out their intention to create a resort with all of the natural advantages of Blackpool, whilst attracting a more 'select, better class' of visitor. The prospectus disparaged Blackpool, which was the resort that the Rossendale supporters of the St Anne's initiative were wont to use, by referring to its becoming a resort of excursionists, and its having unhealthy buildings, bad drainage, and fishermen's huts.

With the publication of the prospectus came the appointment of architects Messrs Maxwell & Tuke, followed in March 1875 by the laying of the foundation stone of St Anne's hotel by Master John Talbot Clifton, grandson of squire Colonel Talbot Clifton. By 1878 St Anne's became a separate local government entity, under a Local Board with one hundred houses, thirty cottages, and twenty-six farms within its boundaries. As with Southport, the ownership of the land by one family allowed the development of St Anne's to be properly planned, and to attract a more select resident, allowing fewer opportunities for the fishing families to exploit.

One notable development was the institution of the lifeboat station, set up in 1881. Its crew, and later its reserve crew, were drawn from the St Anne's area fishermen, with some Lytham fishermen and members of other trades required to make up the crew of often twelve oarsmen with coxswain, assistant cox'n and bowman. The chief inspector sent to assess the suitability of St Anne's found seventeen fishermen capable of manning the lifeboat, none of which lived closer than a mile from the beach at St Anne's. The town developed slowly, often with interruptions due to lack of capital caused by a slump in trade since 1860. It is possible that these problems caused the development company to neglect drainage with the sad result that typhoid broke out in 1883. The only recorded fatality was William 'Butler' Harrison, a fisherman and lifeboat cox'n living at Gasworks Cottages on the west side of the new town. During this period the town was developing in a very piecemeal fashion, mostly to the seaward side of the railway, with only seven roads laid out, and utilities like the slaughter house and gasworks standing isolated in the low sand hills and scrubby pasture. The new buildings were surrounded by grazing animals in summer, and blasted by windblown sand in winter (Mayes 2000).

In 1882 a decision was taken at Preston that would have a profound effect on the St Anne's fishing community. The Corporation of Preston put in train the process that would lead to the building of Preston's docks and the building of training walls and dredging that would change the channels in the estuary, and cause the silting up of the deep water channel, the North Channel in which the St Anne's men moored. By 1885 the new pier was completed, to be opened in June of that year, and the towns population had grown to 1,450; by 1901 there were 6,838 listed in the census roll. The pier was provided with an additional jetty that enabled the coastal steamer service to call at the town.

On a Broad Reach (Mayes 2000) records the hard life and sacrifices made by the fishing community. In December 1886, the barque *Mexico*, when outward-bound from Liverpool, was driven on to Trunk Hill Brow, Ainsdale beach, by a severe gale. The Lytham, the St

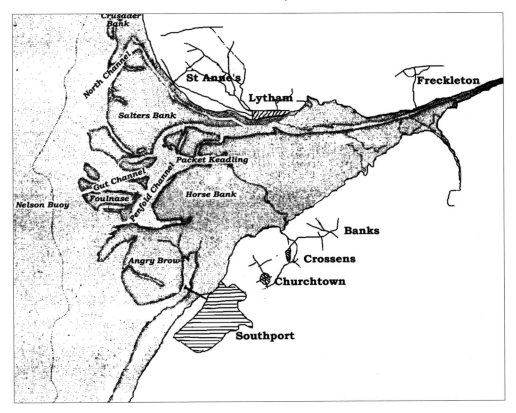

Fig. 31. The Ribble Estuary.

Anne's and the Southport lifeboats launched to attempt rescue. The Southport lifeboat, the *Eliza Fearnley*, capsized with the loss of all but two crew, and the St Anne's boat *Laura Janet* was lost with all thirteen of her crew. All but one of *Laura Janet's* crew were fishermen. The Board of Trade Enquiry findings could not attribute a cause for the loss of the *Laura Janet*, but to quote from the report:

> 'We regret to have to state that from evidence taken by us at St Anne's and Lytham, we find that the coxswain was physically unfit for the performance of so arduous and difficult a service, as he was ill with consumption, and was not expected by his medical man to last beyond the spring. Two or three of the others were not strong men, and one poor fellow had only had a basin of gruel all day prior to proceeding on this service. The honorary secretary of the branch states in his evidence with reference to this man – "I believe he" (Bonney) "stinted himself for the sake of his family. I don't think his privations lasted for more than a week or two; he showed no signs of it." We were privately informed that this man's children always appeared to be well clothed and fed, and that he only stinted himself for their sakes.'

The St Anne's branch committee was very conscious of the parlous finances of the members of their crews, and did everything that they could to ensure appropriate payments were made for launches and exercises. In the days of pulling and sailing lifeboats the society paid its crews, and would also pay pensions to retired crewmen or the crews dependants. The widows and dependants of the victims of this and other disasters were paid annuities funded by collections and subscriptions, the results of which were invested in Consols. The *Mexico* disaster left four widows and eighteen fatherless children amongst the fishing community.

The Ribble Navigation works continued to struggle on, amidst the need to submit new bills to Parliament for the borrowing of extra capital, and the opposition of organizations claiming to represent the ratepayers of Preston. In July 1889 the Board of Trade appointed a Ribble Navigation Commission, who purchased additional dredgers and hopper barges. These were to continue to extend the channel out along the Gut Channel. This and the training walls needed to maintain the navigable channel caused the North Channel to continue to silt up. A report on the buoyage of the channels had been presented in 1887; the Nelson buoy was replaced in 1890 by a converted bell boat buoy, and a similar float was placed in the entrance to the Penfold Channel. As a result of this initiative the Lytham Lighthouse became redundant, to be finally darkened in December 1890. There is a record that John Melling of Church Road took his shanker *Annie* PN 106 to the Freckleton boat yard in 1890, she received 211¾ man-hours of work including a 37ft spar for a mast. She was registered by John in 1882 and continued at St Anne's until her registry closed in 1906.

1890 saw the start of another development that affected some of the fishing community. Thomas Riley of Fleetwood leased the land between St Anne's and Ansdell that was to become Fairhaven. He and his son James set out to create a resort building on the developments of St Anne's that was to include pleasure gardens and a Marine Lake creation by reworking Granny's Dock and the Double Stanner. The Marine Lake was completed in August 1893. The lease of the land was sold to a new company, the Fairhaven Estate Company (1895) Ltd, after James died in 1893, and the undertaking became too much for Thomas Riley. The name Fairhaven was selected as a tribute to the Fair family, who as land agent to the Cliftons had such an important role in the creation of St Anne's. St Anne's Urban District Council took over from the local Board in 1894, and drove the development of the town forward, building an electricity power station, an abattoir, the fire station and a refuse incinerator, using gas from St Anne's gas works, and manufacturing lime mortar with the ash.

The records of the storm of October 1895 give us an insight into the grounds worked by the St Anne's men. The afternoon of Tuesday, 1 October, was fine with a light NW breeze, so that many of the St Anne's men decided to go round to Blackpool to fish the Blackpool grounds for a night's fishing. One of these was Thomas Harrison and his son John, trawling with *Wild Duck* PN 24, who passed *Jane and Alice* from Lytham when towing from the Nelson Buoy towards Blackpool; they were later seen to be running for shelter up North Hollow. Fortunately all of the St Anne's boats got home safely. There were other occasions when the St Anne's men were not so fortunate. On the Thursday, 18 January 1906, Isaac Dobson and his crew John William Harrison were working *Little Nellie* PN 36 in company with *Tern* PN 64 (crew Henry Melling and Robert Harrison). *Why Not* PN 25 (crew Skew Ball and Hugh Rimmer), and *Wild Duck* crewed this time by Nicholas Johnson and William Harrison. They were trawling near the 3fm line towards the Gut Channel Buoy. The weather worsened dramatically at about 12.30, about an hour and a half after the start of the flood. *Little Nellie* and *Tern* ran for home, whilst *Wild Duck* with her mainsail blown out was able to reach the Sand Pump *Maynard* in the Penfold Channel. *Maynard* towed her and several Lytham smacks back in to Lytham. Meanwhile the *Tern* sailed back to her mooring, and immediately alerted the lifeboat's honorary secretary to the need to launch. Unfortunately at about 2.30, under the eyes of those watching from the pier and on St Anne's promenade, *Little Nellie* was driven onto Salthouse Bank, to disappear under the breakers. The body of 36-year-old Ike Dobson was recovered on the following Sunday, but 27-year-old John William Harrison was never found.

The St Anne's men were fortunate that their moorings were in deep channels, as this allowed them to work larger nobbies, including the large 42ft Southport boat *The Ivy* PN 60 and the 39ft *Tartar* LL 40. This was not to last, as the channels underwent change due to the dredging and building of training walls. It was also alleged, but 'not proven', that the spoil from dredging both the Ribble and the Mersey washed straight back into the Ribble. This affected Southport as well, which prompted the gradual migrations of Southport families to Fleetwood and to Lytham. *The Ivy* and other bigger smacks were bought from Southport owners when they became unworkable for the Marshside and Crossens men. *The Ivy* was built by Crossfield Brothers in the Top Shop at Arnside for Richard D. Robinson of Southport, and finished on 4 December 1904. She came to St Anne's on 30 September 1905, being used to recover the hull of *Little Nellie* in 1906, and was sold on to Hoylake in 1907.

Yet another bill was required to allow Preston Corporation to extend the training walls to a point three miles west of Lytham pier. Two clauses were inserted into the bill of 1896 making provisions intended to encourage the outgoing tide to scour the North Channel. A return wall was to be constructed to direct the flow into North Channel, and the south wall was to curve nearer to Lytham. This return wall was completed by 1897, and by January 1900 the north wall had been extended to two miles west of the gap into the North Channel. Unfortunately the bulge towards Lytham was not constructed allowing siltation to occur in the channel. The material dredged to clear this was dumped on the Salter's Bank, and promptly washed into the North Channel. By 1903 the North Channel had shallowed, and Salter's Bank had flattened out so that the smacks, pleasure boats, cockle and mussel punts moored off St Anne's were denied the shelter from the WSW gales that they used to enjoy. The training walls were having their effect, and new channels were opening up. The New Road, which formed to the north of the new navigable channel, became a prolific shrimping ground much used by the Lytham and St Anne's men.

A further bill was enacted in 1905 to enable the training wall to be extended to the low-tide line. St Anne's won some concessions as the bill was being drafted, to have the bulge in the south wall built opposite Lytham, to have the middle and west end of the North Channel dredged, but at their expense, to have the east end of the North Channel dredged along the length of the return wall, and to have all spoil dumped at sea. The building work was eventually completed in 1913. A town guide for St Anne's of 1908 included a list of the fishing community:

Harrison, Robert, 43 Church Road
Harrison, T., 59 Church Road
Johnson, N., 53 Church Road
Melling, Harry, 61 Church Road
Rimmer, E., 68 Church Road
Rimmer, H., 35 Nelson Street
Rimmer, Thomas, 15 Nelson Street

Mayes (2000) records a launch of the St Anne's lifeboat to stand by the *The Ivy*, the *Oliver Williams* PN 57 and *Tern* in the autumn of 1907. This confirms that there was still water enough in the North Channel for the big *The Ivy* to moor at St Anne's, although this was her last year there. *The Ivy* was crewed by Thomas Ralli Hardman and Nicholas Johnson, *Oliver Williams* by Thomas and Edward Rimmer, and *Tern* by Henry Melling and Robert Harrison. *Oliver Williams* was owned at St Anne's from 1894, until she was broken up in 1915. By 1908 North Channel was so shallow that it dried out at low-water spring tides where the No.1 Lifeboat was moored, and the steamers were unable to use the pier jetty. This prompted St Anne's Urban District Council to seek tenders for the dredging that the 1905 act allowed. However, in 1910, after considerable to-ing and fro-ing, the council finally decided to defer the dredging on the North Channel due to its cost.

Boats were moving between Lytham and St Anne's during this period: *Penguin* PN 33 moved from Lytham to Nicholas Barrow's ownership at St Anne's, to be sold to John Bonney of 81 Clifton Street Lytham in December 1910; he sold her to Beaumaris in 1912. By 5 April 1913 Henry Melling had sold *Tern*, due to the lack of water in the North Channel, and bought a smaller nobby from Morecambe, which he registered as *Irene* PN 65 from 14/9/1917 until 4/6/1935 when she ceased fishing. Even though *Irene* drew less than *Tern*, she was not in daily use, and Henry Melling was also setting nightlines. *Tern* dates from 1893, and was first registered at Preston as PN 64 by Mr J.H. Bullock of

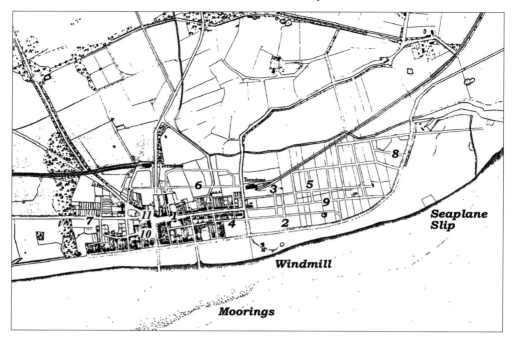

Fig. 32. Lytham street plan. (After Ordnance Survey of 1848)

Lytham in 1894. It is most probable that she was built as a yacht, as Mr Bullock raced her during the yachting season and employed a crew for fishing when she was not racing.

There is a mention (Mayes 2000) of hatch boards in relation to *Irene* when she required the assistance of the lifeboat. In 1923 Henry Melling had been shanking in North Road when the wind went round to the SE and had him embayed. The only option available was to anchor, but duress of weather parted *Irene*'s cable, and before a spare anchor could be bent on to the trawl rope *Irene* had gone aground. Henry Melling put the hatch boards on to the cockpit to limit the amount of water coming inboard. As the St Anne's lifeboat was being launched the gale went round into the SW, which allowed Henry Melling to set the foresail and sail off of the bank on the rising tide. When the lifeboat came up to the smack a crewman, Hugh Rimmer, jumped aboard the *Irene* to help the 55-year-old Henry Melling make sail for home. The records of the St Anne's lifeboat continue to give insight into the state of the channels, it was recorded that the lifeboat could only be launched for two hours either side of high tide in 1918. In 1919 the lack of water caused many of the demobilized fishermen to take up a mixed employment at labouring jobs, whilst powering for shrimp, cockling and setting nightlines.

The two towns of Lytham and St Anne's merged in 1927 to form a municipal borough; this was after discussion about a merger with Blackpool, which on several occasions seemed to drive the two towns apart rather than together.

As the estuary channels silted up and the bigger two-man smacks were sold away, or transferred to Lytham. The St Anne's men were limited to the smaller single-handed 25-30ft smacks, or gave up their boats and concentrated on powering for shrimps with a push net and setting trot lines for flatfish. There were only at most a dozen smacks working from St Anne's, and by the mid-1920s the siltation had driven away all but the *Irene*, the *Sunbeam* PN 10 owned by Robert Skip Harrison, and the *Playmate* PN 49 worked by Teddy and Hugh Boxer Rimmer. It was agreed in 1925 that the St Anne's lifeboat station be closed in September of that year. This was due to both the lack of water at St Anne's and to the lack of experienced fishermen to man the boat. These last three St Anne's smacks moved round to Lytham in 1927.

The Lytham fishing community included old Lytham families supplemented by the Southport families of Rimmer and Wignall. John William Wignall was nicknamed 'Dido', whilst another John Wignall lived on Clifton Sreet. The Lytham families included Anderson of St Johns Street; Birch and Bonney of Wharf and South Clifton Street, Derbyshire; Donnelly, and the two Thomas 'Ralli' Hardmans, father and son, of South Clifton Street (2 to 4 on the map Fig. 32). The Parkinsons, who included John William 'Squint' Parkinson, lived on East Cliffe, Westby Street (6 on Fig. 32) and Clifton Street (1 on the map); one of the Whitesides lived on Clifton Street; another, Thomas "Filter" Whiteside, served in the Lytham lifeboat crew as bowman in the attempted rescue of the crew of *Little Nellie*. There were Fisher of Church Road (7 on the map) and Commonside; and a Dobson family moved from St Anne's to Nelson Street (8 on the map). As can be seen from the map (Fig. 32) most of these streets are at the east end of the town. John Edmondson had the command of the lifeboat in 1863 (Mayes 2000). Some of the Southport families came to Lytham in the 1840s, as did the Clarkson family who came from Ulverston. Thomas Clarkson was Lytham lifeboat cox'n from 1878. James Parkinson was lost, though his brother in law William Bonney survived when James's *Waterwitch* capsized in North Channel off Crusader Bank in October 1864.

A sixteenth-century plan survives (Marshall 1974) setting out the layout of the Lytham township fields. The plan included the town, its parish church, Heyhouses, Lytham pool, and a monastery, which became the site of Lytham Hall. There is a record of storm damage at Lytham in 1717 that swept away 175 houses in the town (Rothwell 1983). As the eighteenth-century fashion for sea bathing attracted visitors to the coast, Lytham also developed, in a more restrained manner than Blackpool, providing bathing machines and select lodgings. The first hotel, The Wheatsheaf, was built on the corner of Clifton Street and Dicconson Terrace in 1794 (No.1 on the map Fig. 32). The Cliftons ensured that Lytham's growth was somewhat more gracious during the Regency and Victorian eras, a restraint that was echoed in St Anne's. The town guide of 1850 was advertising Lytham as a fine watering place with clean flat sands, bathing engines and skilled attendants. There were three hotels, the Clifton of 1840, the Railway and the Market hotels of 1847 and 1850. An act of parliament, the Lytham Improvement Act had been passed in 1847; this enabled the building of the Market House in 1848, gasworks in 1847 and the provision of sanitation. All of these aided the development of Lytham as a resort; the hotels were supplemented by thirty-four lodging houses, and eight inns and taverns. The only industry mentioned was a tile manufactory, a shipbuilder, sail maker, two blacksmiths and a block maker.

According to the *Mannex Directory* of 1880, Lytham's development accelerated with the arrival of the Preston & Wyre branch railway in 1846, the line from Lytham to Blackpool was laid in 1863. There was urban development in the east of Lytham in the 1840s, with homes suitable for fishermen and artisans in the Wharton Street area (9 on the map). This will have attracted new members of a fishing community to Lytham. The town formed a board of commissioners after the Lytham Improvement Act was passed in 1847. The same source records the erection of the pier, at a cost of £5,890 (£384,246), in 1864-5

Lytham set up a lifeboat station in 1844, organized by the Shipwrecked Fishermen's and Mariners' Royal Benevolent Society, to be adopted by the RNLI in 1854. The lifeboat house had been provided with a barometer, which probably saved the lives of many Lytham men by allowing them to forecast bad weather. It certainly discouraged them from setting out on the evening before the October storm of 1895. Unfortunately Thomas 'Noms' Rimmer was already out in PN 69 *Jane and Alice*, as he had been trawling from Blackpool. 'Noms', his son Hugh, a Blackpool fisher lad Ezekiel Salthouse and two young holidaymakers, were shanking from South Shore, on towards Starr Ends and towards the Nelson Buoy. The reports of this incident include the first reference we have of hatch boards, as when the storm blew up they fitted their hatch boards, and sent the young Ezekiel and the passengers into the foc's'le. Fortunately after the wind veered to the WNW they were set down onto the Nelson Buoy, which gave them their position and allowed them to run for shelter down the Gut Channel and make their mooring in safety. Thomas Rimmer sold *Jane and Alice* to a Tranmere owner the following year.

The moorings for the twelve to twenty smacks were laid just to the east of the pier, in Lytham Pool, extending round to the mouth of the Liggard Brook. There were seaplanes stationed at Lytham during the First World War; after the station closed the station's wide concrete slipway was put to use by the fishermen to slip their boats for maintenance.

There were some boat builders working at Lytham, and the shipwrights at the shipyard would also undertake work for the local community. Peter Rawstrone prepared a batch of twelve boat timbers for a Mr Henry Davies in 1873. The yard also worked on the following shankers:

Date Entered	Boat Name	Customer	Cost
29 August 1877	Mary Ellen	J. Jackson	
February 1878		Mr Hankison	£3/15/6 (£238.05)
March 1880	Mary Alice		
16 May 1885	Nightingale	Dawson	A contract for £61/% (£4,438)
16 August 1887		Wilson	£0/19/0 (£74.18)
7 November 1887	Lamb	R.L. Ashcroft	£2/6/- (£179.60)
1 August 1886	Golden Arrow	T.R. Ascroft	£22/19 (£1,737)
1887	May	T.R. Ascroft	£3/8/10 (£268.75)
September 1889		R.L. Ashcroft	£5/3/8 (£396.30)
1890	Annie	John Melling	£/17/0 (£65.00)

Robert Lamb Ashcroft came to Lytham from Preston, living 'off his own means' at 11 Park Street, he may have invested in the Lytham smacks, employing skippers to work them. Mr Ashcroft also served on the Lancashire Sea Fisheries Committee, being nominated in 1893 and serving for ten years. The Lytham Town Guide of 1895 demonstrates that Lytham had continued to grow its holiday trade, with 130 lodging houses now advertising. The following fishermen had subscribed to have their names listed:

Anderson Wm, fisherman, 5 St John's Street
Bonney John, fisherman, South Clifton Street
Candlish Rd, fisherman, 16 West Cliffe
Clarkson Matthew, fisherman, 3 Freckleton Street
Clarkson Thos, fisherman, 26 Clifton Street
Hardman Thos, fisherman, 6 Freckleton Street
Parkinson Alf, fisherman, 1 Freckleton Street
Parkinson Jas, fisherman, 29 Westby Street
Parkinson John, fisherman, 22 East Cliffe
Parkinson Wm, fisherman, 13 Clifton Street
Parkinson Wm, fisherman, 42 Clifton Street
Whiteside Geo., fisherman, 3 Victoria Street
Whiteside J.J., fisherman, 19 East Cliffe
Whiteside John, fisherman, 20 West Cliffe
Wignall R, fisherman, 7 Freckleton Street
Wignall Win., fisherman, 30 Clifton Street

Most of the smacks at Lytham were second hand, but it is remembered that earlier ones were built new at Mayor's of Tarleton. John Crossfield has three boats on his list, on 23 October 1893; *Fox* was completed for Mr John Pailey who registered her PN 53 on 7 December 1893 and transferred her to Liverpool on 7 June 1900; *Gentle Annie* PN 77 for Mr M. Parkinson on 25 May 1896 and *Ziska* for Mr J. W Aspoen on 28 January 1903.

The Lytham men, who favoured smaller single-handed smacks, fished the channels and up river to Douglas. They thought a 33ft smack to be big. One of the last at Lytham was the *Coral* at 23ft. Very little detail survives about these small nobbies; the *Ptarmigan*

BWiii survives at Barrow, and the author has seen *Ladybird* at Skippool Creek. Both boats are very shallow drafted in proportion, with little hollow to their floors. *Ptarmigan* had outside ballast, without a moulding, whilst *Ladybird* was ballasted with loose kentledge, and had the typical shrimping nobby moulding under the shear strake around the counter. *Coral* was bought from Morecambe, where it is suggested that nobbies of this size were built as 'old men's' boats. The work included shanking for shrimp, trawling for flats, and they also used the smacks to drift for salmon. Some men kept an 18ft punt, similar to a salmon punt, for musseling.

The Lancashire and Western Sea Fisheries Committee minute books (1891 et seq.) also mention details of the Lytham fishing industry and name some members of the fishing community. They record that in the winter of 1897 at Lytham five to six boats had given up shrimping for fish trawling. In 1898 the Lytham fishermen were complaining of the import of Dutch shrimp. The superintendent noted that a second-class boat was under construction for Lytham in the last quarter of 1901. The class at Roa Island was attended by Thomas Rimmer, 15 Nelson Street, and Isaac Dobson, of 31 Nelson Street, St Anne's; and Peter Whiteside, 12 East Cliff, Lytham, in 1902. The quarterly report for the last quarter of 1902 records that one new-built second-class boat for Lytham, two second-hand boats went to Lytham, one was scrapped and one sold to Whitehaven, one went to St Anne's and one was sold on, and that shrimps were plentiful at the start of the quarter with 100-160qt per day from the Ribble to the Dee.

The quarterly report of March 1903 recorded that all boats were hampered by bad weather, but second-class trawlers made landings of three- to five-score pounds (60-100lb) of plaice and codling per tide in the Ribble. The fishermen who attended the school at Roa Island in March were J.P. Peet, 33 Henry St, and Thomas Newsham, 9 Market St, Lytham (10 & 11 on the map); and Hugh Rimmer, of St Anne's, and from March into April 1903, John Harrison, Clifton Street, and Harry Melling, of Church Road, St Anne's. In 1905 R. Birch and C. Whiteside of Lytham, and N. Johnson and T.B. Harrison of St Anne's attended the school. During the autumn the Lytham men were obliged to go musseling. The superintendent does not state whether this was due to duress of weather of to a lack of fish. In 1906 R. Gillett and W.G. Parkinson of Lytham attended Roa Island (Lancashire and Western Sea Fisheries Committee 1891 et seq.). The town guide of 1907 listed the following members of the fishing community:

Anderson Jas, 5 St John's Street
Bamber Robert Henry, 10 South Clifton Street
Bonney John, 81 Clifton Street
Cartmell Chris, 67 Westby Street
Clarkson Matt., 6 Freckleton Street
Clarkson Robert, 22 West Cliffe
Gillett Robert, 12 Clifton Street
Hardman John, 5 Freckleton Street
Hardman Joseph, 10 South Clifton Street
Hardman Thos, S, South Clifton Street
Parkinson Alfred, 4 Freckleton Street
Parkinson Edward, 35 East Cliffe
Parkinson Edward, 34 East Cliffe
Parkinson George, 10 South Clifton Street
Parkinson Jas, 45 South Clifton Street
Parkinson John, 22 East Cliffe
Parkinson John, 14 Henry Street
Parkinson John Wm, 41 East Cliffe
Parkinson Wm G., 28 Warton Street
Whiteside John, junr, 20 West Cliffe
Whiteside John J., 19 East Cliffe

Whiteside Peter, 12 East Cliffe
Wignall Robert, 10 Freckleton Street
Wilkin Henry, 30 Trent Street

The methods of working the gear differed whether working beam trawls or shanks. Trawling was carried out as at Morecambe, using water sails when broadsiding (called 'sideing'), and dragging a single beam trawl. Shanking fished two shanks, both when siding and trawling, although they sometimes only dragged one. When dragging two 'shanks' they were set from each side of the smack, and spread apart by booming them out. When *Wild Cherry* was sharking under power in 1957-65; she rigged a boomer across the front of the wheelhouse, and towed a third shank from the counter. The trawl ropes went round the stem to be turned up on the forward timberheads (the Lytham men did not use the term nog). The forward shanks were controlled by springers belayed to the aft timberheads. As the 10ft 6in shank covered less ground than an 18ft main trawl and a 7-11ft bow trawl, and were probably lighter and easier to tow, the shanks would influence the smack less, so it is probable that the boomer was positioned so that the smack could be steered by her helm, rather than using a springer to control the pull of the trawl. The boomer had a hole for the trawl rope in each end, so the method of shooting would have gone something like this. The shank ropes was passed through the holes in the ends of the boomer. The smack may have been hove to, or kept reaching slowly ahead. The boomer was laid across the forward end of the cockpit against the shrouds, overhanging to leeward, so that the windward end was within reach. The windward shank was shot away, and the desired amount of rope paid out. This rope was secured to the for'd timberhead, and the springer passed, but left slack. The boomer would then have been slid across to windward, until the leeward end was within reach. The leeward shank was then shot away, and the rope secured. The second springer was then passed, but also left slack, to allow the boomer to be positioned so that both shank ropes ran clear of the hull. The springers were then adjusted so that the smack tracked comfortably on the desired course and the shanks stayed apart to avoid becoming foul of each other (see Fig. 33).

The beam trawls were cut and fished just as at Morecambe, with bobbins on the footrope, and cut backless. One difference is that they used net, not leather rubbers, to protect the tails. The beams were about 15-16ft long, made up out of one, two or three pieces of greenheart. The fishermen braided all of their own nets using twine bought from Preston. There were other nets used by the Lytham and St Anne's men but they were worked without the use of a boat. The power net was, like the shank, rectangular with 1ft stanchions supporting the top beam above a 7ft beam. The staff went into an iron socket on the beam, and came out through a hole made in the back of the net, at a low angle so that the net was pushed from the belly. Davies recorded that a later form had an iron top hoop that rose in a shallow arch (Davis 1958); however, the rectangular frame remained popular, a photograph of Edward 'Teddy' Rimmer (Mayes 2000) has his power net leaning against the house wall behind him, fitted with a wooden chock bored to take the staff, in stead of the older iron socket. The Lytham men also set hose nets, a form of fixed fish weir. The nets were set from rows of stakes set across the tide, spaced 8ft apart. These supported head ropes and foot ropes 2ft apart. Two nets, with a 4ftt by 2ft mouth were rigged between each pair of posts, with between eight and thirty-two nets in a series. The net tapered off over 7ft to a cod end that was secured to a smaller post, set down stream. The nets were braided with ¾-1in mesh using the flat knot and were dressed with gas tar. The nets fished on the ebb, usually at night (Davis 1958).

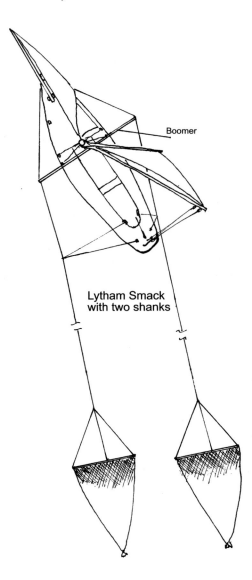

Boomer

Lytham Smack with two shanks

Fig. 33. Lytham nobby with boomer and two shanks.

Chapter 6

Fleetwood and the Fylde

Fleetwood is a Victorian new town, laid out by the local squire Peter Hesketh Fleetwood in 1832. Hesketh inherited the Rossall Manor from his uncle in 1819, and later added his grandmother's surname to his own. His project won him a knighthood but lost him his fortune. In order to finance Fleetwood he sold his lands at Southport to his brother, the Rev. Charles Hesketh, and to Charles Scarisbrick of Scarisbrick Hall. These families profited from their purchase, whilst Sir Peter's fortune sank into the new town (Horsley & Hirst 1991). The first two buildings were completed in 1836, and the rail link inland was opened in 1840; the screw-pile Wyre Light was erected in the same year. The records of a management company of 1844 and of 1874 are referred to by Ashton (1920). The Fleetwood Estate Company also records the growth of the town. In 1841 the population had reached 2,833, climbing to nearly 6,000 in 1861. Census rolls of 1891 list 9,274, and in 1901 list 12,093. The sketch map Fig. 34 sets out the street plan after the docks were dug.

The villagers of the Hesketh estates had always used small boats for subsistence fishing, mooring their small smacks on Rossall beach. A succession of storms leading up to 1814 caused Sir Peter's uncle, Bold Hesketh Esq., the lord of Rossall Manor to move the smacks round to the Wyre and to build huts for their crews' accommodation during the fishing season. There had long been commercial trade to Skippool and Wardleys requiring pilotage. As was often the case the pilots supplemented their irregular income with fishing, and a more formal industry was set up when the Fleetwood Fishing Company bought the port's pilot

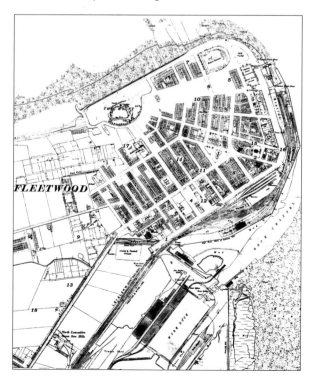

Fig. 34. Fleetwood map. (Ordnance Survey of 1850)

cutter, the *Pursuit*, and in 1841 hired four smacks and crews from Banks near Southport. Next year they bought five smacks from Marshside at Southport. The company survived for several years, after which the Southport men returned home, soon to be replaced in 1850 by four smacks owned by the Leadbetters of Southport. Siltation of the Southport creeks caused the Baxters, Bonds, Rimmers, Wilsons and Wrights to follow them to Fleetwood during the 1850s to 60's. The ex-Ribble smacks must have been of the nobby ancestry, although the name nobby was not recorded by the writers of the time. The community also included the families Abram, Bettes, Boardman, Bond, Colley, Cowell, Hughes, Leadbetter, Perry, Roskell, Salthouse and Wright by 1895. Sam Colley came to Fleetwood as a child with his stepfather John Wright. They were the first to catch prawns, fishing the *Blue Ribbon* at Fleetwood; they sold the prawns in Blackpool, as there was no market for them in Fleetwood.

R.W.H. Holdsworth (1874) reported twenty-seven second-class boats. By 1893 there were forty-six prawn boats. Aflalo (1904) talks of herring taken in stake nets on Pilling sands, and reports there were then about forty shrimp trawlers, whose owners came from Blackpool, fishing out of Fleetwood. The yearbook of 1913 lists thirty-four prawning boats from 4-14 registered tons. This yearbook will have been compiled in 1911, the boats and their owners that it lists were:

Port No.	Boat	Registered Tonnage	Owner
3 FD	*Venture*	8	W. & J. Croft
	Hope	8	M.L. Wilson
	Shamrock	6	E.C. Leadbetter
10 FD	*Thelma*	14	J. Moss
14 FD	*Sea King*	7	J. Wilson Jun.
18 FD	*Jullanar*	11	N. Houston
22 FD	*Dart*	6	J. Wilson
23 FD	*Quickstep*	4	T. Bilsborough
27 FD	*Fox*	9	R. Atkinson
28 FD	*Orphan Girl*	4	Fred H. Pegler
31 FD	*Lottie*	5	N. Houston
35 FD	*Lizzie*	5	T. Sumner
36 FD	*Nelly*	6	T. Knowles
42 FD	*Adam and Eve*	8	Jos McIntosh
46 FD	*Nora*	8	Wm Preston & J. Roskell
74 FD	*Result*	6	M. Wright
83 FD	*Emily*	7	R. Ball
86 FD	*Wild Rose*	8	N. Leadbetter
91 FD	*Prima Donna*	9	W. Wade
96 FD	*Agnes*	4	Wm Wright
105 FD	*Smiling Morn*	3	P. Ball
109 FD	*Black Prince*	3	M. Wilson
101 FD	*Merry Maid*	6	J. Colley
104 FD	*Arrow*	9	T. Lewis
112 FD	*Charlotte*	10	J. Abrams
202 FD	*Celeste*	8	J. Leadbetter Jun
206 FD	*Orient*	7	A. Rawcliffe
209 FD	*Mabel*	9	J. Wright
212 FD	*Nellie*	7	J.T. Bagot
213 FD	*Ailsa*	11	D. Leadbetter
214 FD	*Cistus*	13	J. & D. Moss
216 FD	*Elsie*	13	R. Wright
224 FD	*Albion*	13	F. Parr
225 FD	*Hannah*	11	R. Wright

Plate 12. *Celeste* FD 202. (Courtesy Raymond Sankey)

This documents a fairly steady population of prawners at a port whose fame was as one of the most important far water ports in Britain. *Celeste* appears as Plate 12.

There were four sorts of nobby, mainly called half-deckers, at Fleetwood. They were kebbing boats, prawning boats, cod boats, and yachts. In addition to cod and shrimps or sprawn, they also trawled for flats, went stowboating and longlining. The typical arrangement of those purpose-built for Fleetwood owners was as follows. The kebbing boats were up to 25ft, with loose ballast, and were employed for angling parties. The prawners of 3ft 6in maximum draft had iron keelsons (*Cistus* was ballasted this way), whilst the cod boats drew 4ft 6in and had outside ballast, with loose trimming kentledge. The yachts of 36ft drew 6ft, and had both iron keel and keelson, usually had no rubbing streak, and had a centre bowsprit and two mooring rollers. The Fleetwood men were keen yachtsmen in their own right, and chartered their boats to Midlands businessmen. The existence of Fleetwood's fishermen's yachts, and the similarity between the nobbies and the yachts of the period, makes it difficult to categorize accurately trawling nobbies or yachts. *Laura* is a case in point. The earliest photograph that we have seen is in the book *I bought a Prawning Boat*. The book tells the story of her purchase and refit during the early 1950s, padded out with a misleading version of her early history enlivened with tales of drowning and a ghost story.

The photographs are the important part of the book, and include a view of her aft quarter that shows that her shear streak was thicker than the topsides, and that she had no moulding. This is the same arrangement that William Crossfield & Sons used in the Rivers Class yachts and indicates that *Laura* was built as a yacht. Her proportions are also not typical of fishing nobbies: her 5ft draft is excessive for a 36ft sprawner. *Laura*'s records show that William Crossfield built her in 1908 as a yacht for Mr John Atherford of Morecambe. William Sellers of Fleetwood owned her in 1913 and she was registered for fishing on 21/11/1918 as FD 319, transferring to Douglas, Isle of Man, on 9/12/1922. She was registered D85 on 27/2/1923 until 4/5/1927 when she was sold as a yacht. At the time of writing she has been rebuilt, with a false moulding planted on over her shroud irons, and again sports the fishing number FD 319. The gentleman who rebuilt her, Mr Gayle Heard of Tollesbury, informed the author that *Laura* had a cast iron keelson, and boiler punchings in concrete for her internal ballast, in addition to the external cast-iron ballast keel.

Fleetwood owners commissioned half-deckers from the Crossfield's, as well as Gibson's (later owned by Liver and Wildy), and Armour's. Boats were also bought in second hand. Rawstrone at Freckleton built big smacks for Fleetwood, and may also have built nobbies for Fleetwood owners. James Armour opened his yard in 1880; he was the second son of James who came over from Londonderry. James senior passed away in January 1875. James traded under his own name and then as his three sons (including a third James) joined the business, the yard was then trading as James Armour & Son. In 1887 Kelly's gave an Adelaide Street address (no. 2 on Fig. 34), Plate 13 may represent this early workshop. In 1905 James Armour was at 204 to 210 Dock Street, Plate 14, (no. 1 on the map). The firm traded as Armour Brothers until 1911 when they were called J.&L. Armour. The brothers were James, the third of that name, and Joseph. *Slater's Directory* of 1860 lists Hugh Singleton, shipwright and block maker. As yet only one nobby can be ascribed to Hugh Singleton's firm. They built smacks, including the *Harriet*, now the last surviving Fleetwood smack. *Mannex* of 1880 lists John Gibson, Perry & Roome, and Hugh Singleton, all on Dock Street. A receipt survives from 5 December 1896 for the payment of £112 5s 6d (£9,440) by Mr R. Wright of Rock Ferry to 'W. Singleton and Bros, Yacht Steam launch and Boat builders' of Adelaide Street, Fleetwood, for the prawn boat *Five Brothers*. *Five Brothers* was registered LL 333 on 8/12/1896 until 11/6/1915, to appear as DO 22 on 14/6/1915 until 13/4/1926 when her register closed 'not for fishing'.

Gibson & Butler set up at Dock Street, and were listed in *Mannex* of 1851; however, the 62-ton smack *Margaret and Agnes* was credited to a new company, John Gibson, Shipbuilder, on 21 December 1860. *Slater's Directory* of 1869 lists him trading on the wharf. John Gibson passed away aged 62 on 29 January 1877. His executors continued to run the company until 1881. John Gibson & Sons launched a sailing boat and a steamer for the newly formed Fleetwood Steam Ferry & Pleasure Launch Company in February and August; A.T. Gibson was the ferry company's designer. The yard now built fewer large vessels, producing yachts, pleasure boats, steam ferries, shrimpers, prawn boats, and in 1893 a pilot boat of 70ft length for the pilots Ball, Iddon, Edwards, and McCall. John Gibson & Sons were listed in Kelly's of 1887 with a Dock Street address. Although their offices were in Dock Street their vessels were assembled at the top of the beach opposite Queens Terrace. They sold the yard to Liver & Wilding in 1903 but continued to trade as Chandlers from Lower Dock Street and London Street (3 & 4 on the map Fig. 34), whilst in 1905 Kelly's has them at 206 Dock Street.

In 1868 Gibson's accepted the fourteen-year-old William Stoba as apprentice. William was born in Fleetwood on 8 February 1854. By 1903 Stoba was so comfortable with the cut away nobby hull form that he designed the smack *Reliance* to this model. His reputation had spread so widely that he was commissioned to build a Bristol Channel pilot skiff in 1904 by Peter J. Stuckley. *Alpha*, at 51ft, was so successful that he was then commissioned to build one to beat her. *Kindly Light* at 53ft, built in 1911 when Stoba was at Armour's, was so good that she nearly put the other pilots out of business. Stoba moved to J. Armour's on 5 September 1905. Stoba stayed with them until his retirement in 1927, surviving until 1931. William was living at 31 Livingstone Terrace, Fleetwood (14 on the map Fig. 34) with his wife and three daughters when the 1901 census enumerator called. The census enumerator's entries indicate that he called at six homes on Kemp Street, then recorded twenty-one homes in Livingstone Terrace, before enumerating some homes in Blakiston Street East and turning into Adelaide Street. This suggests that Livingstone Terrace was on Kemp Street, between Lord and Blakiston streets.

John Crossfield's list of boats includes nobbies that he built for customers from Fleetwood, they are:

Johnny	J. Butler	5 March 1893
Ellen Ann	Leadbetter	3 April 1893
Lalla Rookh	Leadbetter Bros	10 July 1899
Armistice	J. Opurr of Blackpool	1 April 1901
Lillie	J. Mybrough	22 May 1901
Lalla Rookh	Leadbetter Bros	29 November 1901
Wild Rose	N. Leatherhead	10 March 1902
Capella	J. Wright	1940

There were also two yachts and a motor launch for Fleetwood customers.

Rigby, who was a noted north-western sail maker famed for his yacht work as well as the working boat sails made in his loft, will have made the sails of many Fleetwood craft. The Rigby loft came to Fleetwood from Freckleton in 1873. The *Mannex* of 1880 also listed Belyeu & Co. of Dock Street, and William Coulburn and James Mason both of Adelaide Street.

Three of the four Fleetwood built boats seen by the author have steamed frames, *Provider* LL 282 having two steamed frames to each sawn, whilst the *Tern* PN 64, now the *Arthur Alexander*, has all steamed frames. The timbers in both boats were cut very much wider than their thickness (3in by 1in in *Provider*, and 1⅞in by 1in in *Tern*). William Stoba designed both craft, which have similar midsections, with an iron keel moulded to a different form from all of the others we have seen. Stoba had a reputation for top quality work and materials, so the use of keels moulded specifically for each craft helps confirm that these were Stoba boats. The iron keels that were cast at Barrow-in-Furness to be used by other builders, were cast in three standard sizes. It is said that all were moulded with a kick up aft, after the foundry man ran aground in a deep-heeled boat.

Both *Provider* and *Tern* were proving difficult to date, received wisdom is that *Provider* was built in 1904, and won a trophy for the best catch of the year in 1905. However, we now know that *Provider* was registered LL 282 on 19 February 1896. Maurice Evans determined that she was built by John Gibson & Sons for Peter Davidson of 53 Upper Dean Street, Park Road, Liverpool, in 1896 which Maurice has confirmed with a cross reference found in the Liverpool Courier of 17 August 1896, with a report of the Hoylake regatta. *Provider* was out sailed by *Eureka*, registered as LL 303 from 1896 to 1900, and also built by John Gibson & Sons in the same year for Mr Ashbrook of Tranmere. *Tern* dates from 1893, and was registered at Preston as PN 64 by Mr J.H. Bullock of Lytham in 1894. *Lloyd's List of Yachts* has her in Mr Bullock's ownership until 1903. She remained on the Preston register until 5/4/1913 when she transferred to Fleetwood as FD 182.

The lines of *Provider*, reproduced here as Fig. 35, record both the as-built keel and the later arrangement, fitted when the centreboard was removed. The centreboard slot was blocked and lateral area added to the hull by dropping the ballast keel, fitting a tapering deadwood, and then refitting the ballast. The original form is the shallower profile, with the form of the hull running from the planking over the wood structural keel and the iron ballast keel in an easy curve with vee'd sections and little hollow in the bottom. Most other iron keels are 'U'-shaped in section with hollow in the garboards.

Tern has some unusual features. It is most probable that she was built as a yacht, with Mr Bullock racing her during the yachting season and employing a crew for fishing when she was not racing. She may well have had wrought-iron floors, since there were no floors in

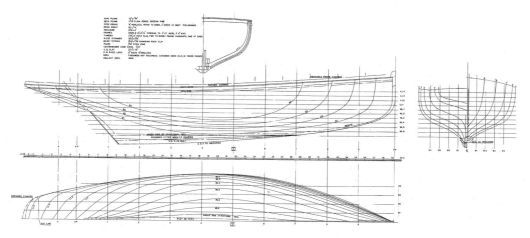

Fig. 35. *Provider's* lines.

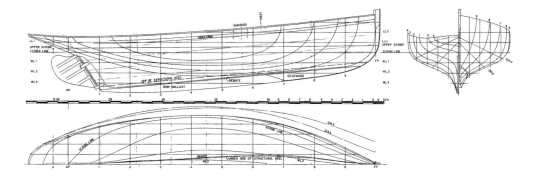

Fig. 36. *Tern's* lines.

her when she was rebuilt in the 1980s. Iron floors would have corroded away in the sixty to eighty years from her building to when she was abandoned on the Tigers Tail at Fleetwood. Her moulding is also of unusual width, as though it replaces a topside plank. Yachts were not fitted with a moulding, unless built as a speculation and then sold for a yacht, and often had wrought-iron floors to maximize useful internal volume. Her lines appear as Fig. 36.

The third Gibson's-built nobby that we have seen is the *Penguin* of 1892. *Penguin* was registered at Preston as PN 33, fishing from both Lytham and St Anne's. Whilst she has no external ballast and is all sawn framed with an open counter without a main stern bulkhead, she does have similarities to *Tern*. She has a long straight keel with lots of drag, and a well-rounded forefoot with hollow water lines in the bow. Although we have had no opportunity to lift her lines, we were loaned a set of photographs from which a half model was prepared. The lines of this model are reproduced here (Fig. 37) as an indication of her form. *Penguin's* counter preserved a distinctive detail. Her builders had left a raised cartouche on the solid of the counter to receive the painting of her name and port. The fourth boat is the 27ft *Ruby* built as a ferry in 1894. Ruby has the same characteristics shown in the lines of the three Stoba nobbies that the profiles all have a deeper round in the forefoot under a straight vertical stem above the waterline. Her keel profile is almost straight, and like all of the Stoba nobbies, her sections all have less hollow in the garboards than nobbies from the other yards. She is framed out with all steamed frames in her topsides, with iron floors made out of 2½in by ¾in cope iron. These are extended up to the turn of the bilge by sawn futtocks. As her beam shelf and shear strake are sandwiching steamed timbers, the assembly is not wide enough to allow a covering board to be fitted, so the deck plank runs over and is nailed down to the shear strake.

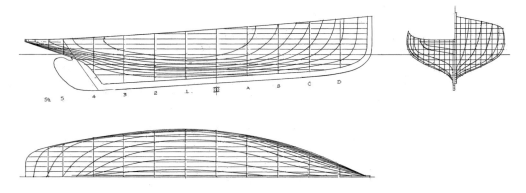

Fig. 37. *Penguin's* lines.

Plate 13. Armour's workshop. (Courtesy F.&B. Lupton)

Plate 14. Armour's Dock Street premises. (Courtesy F.&B. Lupton)

There are reports of steamed framed boats as being a feature typical of Fleetwood, which may be due to the protection afforded by the Wyre channel and docks, allowing a lighter build. Another feature of Fleetwood-built boats was the lack of a main stern (although *Tern* does have one), and the boring of the rudder case out of the solid. Both *Tern* and *Provider* had a king plank, a feature not employed by the Crossfields. Some of the cod boats had grooved stanchions under the coamings to support pound boards, and could carry ice and stay out for several days. Of the Fleetwood-registered boats photographed by Sankey, *Ailsa* FD 213 and *Prima Donna* LR 13 were both built at Arnside in 1908 (Plates 15 and 16). *Prima Donna* was built for James Baxter of Morecambe to be registered on 6/3/1908 until 12/2/1909 when she joined the Fleetwood register as FD 91 on 13/2/1909, where she remained until she transferred to Beaumaris on 10 April 1918. *Foam* (Plate 17) came to Fleetwood from Maryport to be skippered by J. Welsh. She was in the ownership of E. Leadbetter who registered her on 23 April 1913. She was a small nobby at 28ft length and 8ft 9½in beam. She was transferred to J.&R. Ball in 1916, and then to R. Ball of Southport in 1920. She was sold away not for fishing in 1924. The Sankey collection includes three other Fleetwood boats (Plates 18 to 20). The first of these, *Hannah* FD225 shows a characteristic of the nobby at speed. As the stern wave wells up under the counter it spills onto the deck through the scuppers, to run forward and drain back overboard abreast the helmsman.

Yachting Monthly of 1921 published an article on the Fleetwood boats. The *Yachting Monthly* correspondent reports that the boats were nearly all 35-37ft long by 10ft 6in beam, and 5ft 6in to 6ft draught. The boats he described had 'plenty of hollow at the garboard and then springing in a slightly hollow curve to a rather sharp turn at the bilge'. The beam was carried well forward, and the quarters were fine with a narrow, short counter that extended 18in to 2ft aft of the rudder head. They had a booby hatch over the for'd end of the well, giving about 5ft headroom. The motors were installed under the side deck, on the same side as the prop. The foc's'le was painted white with the timbers and frames varnished. There were some details of the rig reported, the *Yachting Monthly* felt the gaff to be long by yachting standards, being the same length as the boom. The jib halyard was rigged through two blocks, one each side of the masthead, the fall to port, and the standing part to the starboard pin rail. None of the boats in the Sankey photos has this feature, although it is admitted that none were Fleetwood built.

Study of these Sankey pictures reveals rigging details. The peak halyard on the larger boats starts at the becket of the lower block on the mast head, being reeved though a block stropped to the middle of the gaff, back up to the lower block on the mast, then to the outer block on the gaff, up to the upper block at the mast head, and then down to the deck to belay. The smaller boats did not need the block at the middle of the gaff, having the halyard made off to the gaff at its mid-span and then reeving through the lower block on the masthead as on the larger boats. The jib halyard is visible on all of the boats except *Ailsa*, and can be seen to run through a double block at the mast head, with a single at the head of the sail, as was usual at Morecambe and on the Annan model. Although *Ailsa* carries a Fishing Registry number in the photo, she is obviously racing, and was often taken out of registry, she can be seen to have patent gaff jaws, a centreline bowsprit, and bobstay and bowsprit shrouds. The pin-rails can be seen to be at the shrouds, which was a popular fashion at Fleetwood, and she has what may be a small booby hatch over the square for'd end of the cockpit.

Ailsa was reputedly built just to catch specimens for the Blackpool Tower aquarium, which may explain her yacht-like details. Several other photographs of Fleetwood half-deckers survive, which also have square ends to the forward end of the cockpit, and round aft ends. One of these craft had battens fitted inboard about 1½in below the top of the inside coamings, running from forward to about level with the forward end of the steering step. These battens were notched on their top edge at about 2ft spacing. Their most likely use was to support hatch boards. It is also possible that the booby hatch in the photograph of *Ailsa* is the forward most hatch board left in place.

Plate 15. *Ailsa*. (Courtesy
Raymond Sankey)

Plate 16. *Prima Donna*.
(Courtesy Raymond Sankey)

Plate 17. *Foam*. (Courtesy
Raymond Sankey)

Plate 18. *Hanna.* (Courtesy Raymond Sankey)

Plate 19. *Cistus.* (Courtesy Raymond Sankey)

Plate 20. *Orient.* (Courtesy Raymond Sankey)

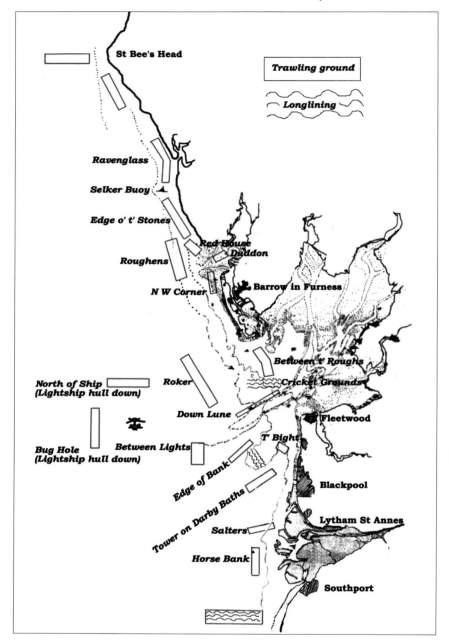

Fig. 38. Fleetwood's fishing grounds.

Some of Fleetwood's social history is revealed by a conversation between Dr P. Wright and Bob 'Sleepy' Swarbrick, recorded as part of research for a thesis. Sleepy was a smacksman, 88 when interviewed, who started fishing at 16 in 1876. He states that there were prawn boats and pleasure boats at Fleetwood 'since I can remember'. On Saturdays the fishermen used to gather in Church Street dressed in their best, 'silk velvet weskit, or blue Devon jacket and weskit, and a velvet collar on your jacket'. Sleepy listed some grounds as: t'Hole, t'Shald, in Mackle, 'Ead 'Ole, and t' Slaughter. He talks of yellow gurnard and plaice as prime fish, and grey gurnard as offal, and of oysters fetching 7s 6d a hundred (£0.37½ per 104). Mackle referred to grounds off Maughold Head, on the Isle of Man.

Plate 21. Appeal poster, 'Effects of the Storm of October 2nd 1895'. (Courtesy of Lancaster City Museums)

The scrap chart, Fig. 38, illustrates the fishing grounds used by the half-deckers from Fleetwood. Most of the names of the grounds are self evident, although Roughens, Bug Hole and Cricket Pitch are enigmatic exceptions. There was unusual co-operation between the line fishermen and trawlers on Shell Wharf. The lines were set far enough apart to allow the small, lightly powered half-deckers to trawl between them. The lines then took cod, whilst the trawlers netted plaice. The lines were normally baited with herring, nine baits to a herring, and mostly set for roker (thorn back ray) on the other longline marks. These grounds were identified by motor-trawler men, but many of them provide echoes of those mentioned in the older records.

There was frequent loss of life due to severe storms. One of 1895 was credited with driving the evolution of the hull form of the boats. Some say that storm losses caused the change from the long keel shape to the cut-away form, although there is evidence that this was caused by a cross-fertilisation from yachting. *Jullanar* was built in 1875, and was later owned by Sir George Pilkington of Southport, and Dixon Kemp (1878) reports the developments taking place on Windermere from 1872. Both *Jullanar* and the Windermere yachts have a cut-away forefoot, so there were plenty of new ideas about to drive change. These developments may have occurred too early for the evolution, which was still underway when *Lottie* was built at Fleetwood, to be registered FD 31 on 22/9/1888, although John Leather reports that racing yachts were still evolving radically in 1893. An alternative form of change driven by storm losses is the reversal of the trend towards shoal draught. This trend developed to allow longer working hours in one tide from the tidal port, but included the penalty of a loss of weatherliness. The Southport nobbies included the cut-away forefoot model with extreme hollow in the garboards in the late 1880s, which suggests that the 1895 storm was not influential in driving change in hull form.

A poster (Plate 21) publicised an appeal on behalf of the dependants of the crews of five Fleetwood boats wrecked during the storm of Wednesday, 2 October 1895, brings home the hazards of the life, recording eight widows and twenty-seven dependent children. Because the holiday season lasted into October, the appeal was successful, raising enough to grant the children 2s (10p, worth £8.32 in 2005 values) a week until they left school at fourteen years of age, and the widow's 2s a week for life. When the payments to the last dependent ceased sufficient funds remained to allow the town's council, who were the trustees, to finance the building of the fishermen's flats on Broomfield Road. It is remembered that this was not a popular decision.

The poster names John Houghton and John Ball, crew of *Daisy Queen* FD 12; Will Scott skipper of *Mariner* FD 100 and Thos. Wright her crew; Robert Weight of *Sarah* FD 116 and James Wright of *Two Sisters* FD 310; 37-year-old Robert Fleming, who was sub Cox'n of the lifeboat *Maud Pickup*, skipper of *Schoolgirl* FD 84; and Cornelius Handgrove.

Of the Fleetwood craft lost during this disaster the *Daisy* was lost under the eyes of the crew of *Mary Ann* (Skippered by Jackson) off Central Pier. The Lancaster newspaper carried a report of a smack, which foundered off of Blackpool Central Pier, with the loss of all three crew and a visitor's son, taken aboard for a trip out; she was *Two Sisters*. The other two crewmembers were J. Roskell and Frederick Bagshaw (21). The *Volunteer* FD 79 was wrecked at the Trafalgar Hydro, South Shore, whilst *Genesta* FD 120 survived, coming ashore opposite Crystal Terrace; both crew survived. Also lucky to survive were the crew of *Blue Bell* FD 33 when she drove on to North Wharf, Fleetwood, as they were able to walk ashore along with the crews of four Morecambe boats. *Mariner* FD loo foundered on Salthouse Bank, to come ashore at St Anne's and be re-floated on Sunday, 6 October. G. Ball was lost from *Schoolgirl* when she foundered on Crusader Bank.

We can learn more details of the trawler men's dress from Plate 21. Two are depicted in buttoned oilskin jackets with cheese-cutter caps; the same caps were worn by some of the men in their shore-going rig. Several were wearing the velvet collars remembered by Sleepy, on jackets buttoned low on the chest in today's fashion, whilst those whose collars were of the same stuff as the jacket were buttoned higher at the throat. One has a bow tie and wing collar, whilst the others are wearing neckties. It is also remembered that the Fleetwood men favoured clogs when working. In fact one of the crew of a sailing half-decker pictured in Horsley & Hirst (1991) is wearing clogs. Their boat also has a square end to the front of her cockpit with a hand-powered capstan fitted between the coaming and the mast, on the centreline. The vertical axis drum was top driven by a horizontal shaft with a portable handle facing aft.

The proceedings of the Lancashire and Western Sea Fisheries Committee (1891 et seq.) refer to Fleetwood directly, and also to prawners, which were originally only worked from Fleetwood. In 1893 they record that the prawn boats were laid up during the cold weather. Two of the fishermen serving on the committee during 1893 were Richard Leadbetter, North Albert Street; and Robert Wright, of North Church Street, Fleetwood (5 and 6 on the map Fig. 34). During the fourth quarter of 1897 longlining had commenced; all except Fleetwood were doing well. Fleetwood prawn boats were less active as most had gone over to fish trawling. The superintendent reported that shrimping was variable in the area whilst the prawn boats were taking 4-5qt a tide up until March 1898, and Fleetwood men were mostly prawning in the quarter ending 30 June. In spring of 1899 the prawn boats fished through, they were normally laid up in winter; they were taking three to 25-dozen quarts (300qt) per day. This continued into summer when most Fleetwood boats were prawning, taking twenty- to forty-dozen quarts (240-480qt) per tide, by the autumn quarter the Fleetwood prawners started quite well but tailed off to average catches.

The quarterly reports of the summer and autumn of 1901 state that Fleetwood prawners were taking twenty- to thirty-dozen (240-360qt) up to fifty-dozen quarts (600qt) per tide, this tailed off to seven- to ten-dozen quarts (84-120qt) per tide, sometimes thirty- to forty-dozen quarts (360-480qt) during the last quarter. The prawn boats did well early in the winter, taking twenty- to thirty-dozen quarts (240-360qt) per day, but were kept

Plate 22. The
Prawn House.
(Bill Curtis,
*Images of
Fleetwood*)

in harbour for much of the time. Richard Wright attended the Roa Island School; he was followed by W. Croft, and J. Croft, of 1 Windsor Place; S.P. Colley, 37 Flag Street; and Robert Blundell, 18 Elm Street, Fleetwood (nos 7, 8 & 9 on Fig. 34). During 1902 two new second-class boats joined the fleet and an order for another was placed; unfortunately the prawners were blown off during the spring. The same season in 1903 saw the following landings made in spite of the weather hampering the second-class boats, which landed three- to five-score pounds (60-100lb) of plaice and codling per tide. Boats that were less affected by the weather included the prawners taking four- to five-dozen quarts (48-60qt) per tide. The fishermen who attended the school at Roa Island in March and April were: John Leadbetter, of 24 North Street; Earnest C. Leadbetter, 51 Warren Street; David Moss, 28 Kemp Street; John Colley, 38 Ratcliffe Street (nos 10 to 13 on Fig. 34); J P Ball Junr of 17 Victoria Street (15 on Fig. 34); John C. Pegler, 25 Flag Street; William Wilson, 97 Upper Walmsley Street (14 on Fig. 34); and Thomas Wilson, 38 Ratcliffe Street, Fleetwood. We can add the names of J. Moss, N. Leadbetter, D. Leadbetter, J. Leadbetter, H. Macmillan, and J. Meadows in 1905 and T. Rawlinson, W. Ball, Wm Wright, R. Abram, R. Ball, J. Leadbetter, and W. Sharpe of Fleetwood and J.T. Bagot of Knott End in 1906.

The Wyre Fisherman's Co-operative Society was formed in 1910, nicknamed 'The Prawn House'. It was set up due to dissatisfaction with the system of independent buyers and distributors called 'Badgers', as also happened at Morecambe and Lytham. The co-operative leased land on Victoria Street on which they built the processing facility and shop (Plate 22). It was on the corner of the lane that ran back to Adelaide Street along the side of the market. It was tacked on to the end of the police station and court building that used to run along Victoria Street from the Queen's Terrace corner (16 on the map Fig. 34). Members bought £1 (£70.80) shares to join the co-operative, and could buy additional shares if they wished. There was a chairman and board, and the members had a say in the running of the organisation. The co-operative employed a manager and about fifty to sixty pickers, with about another thirty home workers. Bill Wright managed the co-op from the end of the Second World War until the co-operative closed down.

The prawn boats unloaded on the shingle beach to the west of the Knott End ferry pier, carrying their catch on a handcart to the Prawn House for processing. The sprawn was packed for the London markets, whilst the browns were mostly sold rough through the Co-operative shop and to local outlets. The picked shrimp were packed in muslin bags for transport after being scalded and dried; these bagged shrimp were placed in greaseproof paper-lined barrels. The co-operative managed the market, as did the Morecambe Co-operative, by placing orders for specific quantities of shrimp with the boats working, these were called 'orders' rather than 'stints' as at Morecambe. The shrimp were measured by the basket of three-dozen quarts (36qt), equivalent to the Morecambe measure of 4st (25kg) to the basket.

At about 1910 the families Moss, Wade, Sumner, Croft, Wilson, Houston, Ball, Bagott, Parr, Bilsborough, Pegler, Atkinson, Knowles, Preston, McIntosh, Colley, and Lewis were recorded as owning or managing prawning boats. In recent memory Ainsworth, Atkinson, Croft, and Hargreaves were part of the Fleetwood community living at Knott End. The records of the Lancashire and Western Sea Fisheries Committee (1891 et seq.) from after 1910 list entire classes of Fleetwood scholars; however, as the syllabus included navigation and other skills of relevance to deep-sea fishing, it is unlikely that they were nobby crew. In 1915 Jeffrey Ball, of 2 Warwick Place (17 on Fig. 34); J.R. Wright, 106 Kemp Street; Stephen Ainsworth, 109 Addison Road (18 on the map); and Jeffrey Wright, of 117 Kemp Street, attended a class with nobby crew from the Lancashire coast. The quarterly reports of 1932 show that there were both the smaller and larger class of boat working at Fleetwood, those of 24-5ft having marinised car engines of 10-15hp, and the 33-5ft boats had paraffin marine engines of 13-15hp.

Although Blackpool is remembered as a resort, it did have a fishing community that will have predated the fashion for sea bathing and holidaymaking. They worked off of the beach in the Church Street area. Ernest Whiteside was living in a two-bedroomed house at Fumblers Hill (bottom of the present Cocker Street) when he added two more bedrooms and became the first Company House Keeper in 1735, and bathing machines were also provided about then. By 1769 a source quoted in Potter (1994) describes a thatched barn, built for use as a theatre in summer, with about twenty or thirty cottages, but no shop. A Sears Brothers engraving, Fig. 39, dated but actually published after 1784, shows six taverns or hotels standing amongst fields atop the cliffs (Ashton 1920). The newer of these hotels are all four-storied buildings, standing amongst the single-storey fishermen's and farm labourer's cottages. The cottages were ill lit, thatched cobble buildings described by 'The Father of Blackpool', Henry Banks, in 1769 as unsanitary dwellings with a stack of turfs to one side of the door, and a putrefying dung heap of fish offal to the other.

The first big hotel was Hudson's, formerly called Lane Ends Hotel, developed from a farmhouse in 1750, rebuilt, and extended until the 1780s. William Hutton and his daughter Catherine, both of Birmingham, visited in 1788, leaving a record of their stay at the seventy-bed Lane Ends Hotel. This was situated on the corner of Church Street on the Promenade. Their fellow guests were manufacturers from Bolton. Forshaw's came next, erected on the comer of Talbot Square and the Promenade in 1769; this was rebuilt in phases to become the Clifton Arms. Next came Bailey's of 1785 on the corner of Springfield Road and the Prom, where the Metropole now stands. Bailey's advertised for visitors in the *Manchester Mercury* as soon as it opened. Bonney's-i-th'-fields was completed in 1787 on the north side of the eastern end of Chapel Street where the King Edward VII Hotel now stands. The 1847 survey (OS) identifies this as Bonny's farm. Finally Hull's was rebuilt as a three-storey hotel in 1788 on the corner of Adelaide Street and the Promenad. All of these

Fig. 39. Blackpool of 1784. (Sears Brothers' engraving)

Plate 23. Uncle
Tom's Cabin.

appear in Fig. 39. By 1788 there were sixty houses strung out over about a mile, with an ale house, bowling greens and archery butts. The barn still served as a theatre, there were a few bathing machines in use, with times set a side for females to bathe, free from the sight of male eyes. Any man caught on the beach at the wrong time was fined a bottle of wine

Blackpool grew up in part of Bispham parish. There are records of fishermen at Blackpool in 1795 assisting in a rescue from drowning, and in about 1815 finding a hoard of porter in barrels, lost from a wreck (Rothwell 1983). Terry Potter (1994) records that Uncle Tom's Cabin, Plate 23, a tearoom and dance hall that was to become a landmark for the Blackpool Closed Ground, dated back to 1850. Uncle Tom was Thomas, brother of the farmer Henry Parkinson who worked the surrounding land and spotted the opportunity to provide refreshment to the visitors walking on the cliffs. This failed in 1861 when the cotton famine interrupted the holiday trade, but the business was bought by two lodging housekeepers who developed it into the form seen here. The parish population grew from 727 in 1801 to 4,334 in 1861 due largely to the growth of Blackpool. The peat-stained stream that gave the new town its name may have still been in existence in 1870, near Fox Hall. This stream is marked on the 1865 OS map named Spen Dyke. It was one of the watercourses draining the Marton Mere area. Comparison with the 1865 map with the modern street plan puts the stream between Princess Street and Rigby Road. The waterways named on the original Ordnance Survey maps indicates that the Lancashire dialect gave the term 'pool' as a name for a stream. The peat stain in the water gave the name Black Pool to the Spen Dyke. Fox Hall, built as a hunting lodge by Edward Tyldsley in 1650 and originally named Vaux Hall (and by 1870 a pub), is marked on the map Fig. 40.

Coaches ran a service to Blackpool in 1780; two or three coaches were running a service three times a week. The *Manchester Mercury* advertised that a service began in June 1783, to run from the Upper Royal Oak, Market Street Lane, every morning (Sunday excepted) at 6 o'clock. By 1816 there was also a daily service from Preston (Potter 1994), with two coaches a day in 1824, when the steamers and coaches brought 1,000 visitors. Blackpool's growth was accelerated by that universal catalyst the railway, which arrived at Talbot road in 1846. The railway caused the first significant change to affect the fishermen. They required ballast for the rail bed, buying it from carters who bought it from the beach at the end of Talbot Road, thereby removing the stable shingle bank onto which the fishermen drew up their boats. 1863 saw the opening of the first, the North Pier, to be followed in 1868 by the Central Pier.

The visitors were a mix of mill workers and mechanics, with middle-class businessmen's families. As there was no main landowner at Bispham the development was piecemeal and unplanned. The Talbot Cliftons did own land and developed Talbot Road before selling up to retrench at Lytham. As a result of this, different entrepreneurs developed their land

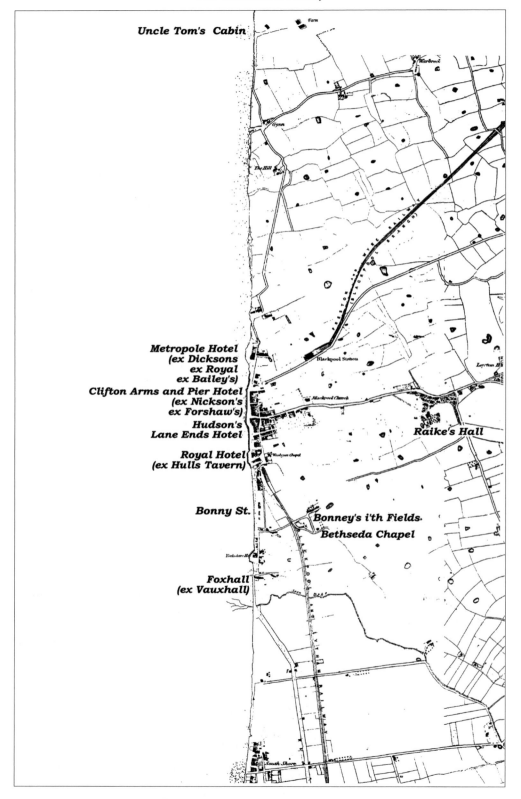

Fig. 40. Blackpool map. (Ordnance Survey of 1847)

as they saw fit, those at North End and the South End estates tending to build well to attract the middle classes, whilst others built cheaper premises that were within the reach of the mill workers (Walton 1978). One example of this was that Bonny, who rebuilt his farmhouse into a hotel, gave his name to the Bonny Street estate, a jumble of narrow back streets on the triangle of land between Bonny Street, Chapel Street and the Central Railway Station. This came to house Blackpool's fishing community as they were displaced from their cottages when the land was developed. These terraced cottages were cleared for redevelopment in the 1960s (Potter 1994). The same source discusses the building of the Bethesda Church. It tracks the congregation from the kitchen of a private house in the 1810s to a chapel built on Bonney's Lane in 1825, then to the chapel on Bethesda Square until it was demolished in the 1970s when the congregation joined the Grassmere Road Methodists. Potter (1994) does not comment on the link between Methodism and the fishing community, which is suggested by the site of the chapel in the Bonney Street area. According to Walton (1978), Methodism was also strong within the boarding house community, both landladies and guests, which tended to make the visitors self-policing. This in its turn helped to maintain Blackpool's popularity as a pleasant holiday town.

The town received its Charter of Incorporation in 1876. Growth continued apace, with the South Pier being opened in 1894. The census returns illustrate the continuing rate of growth of the town, from 14,229 souls in 1881 to 47,346 in 1901. On 1 April of that year John Crossfield delivered *Armistice* to Mr J. Opurr.

The Tower, Blackpool's greatest landmark both in reputation and visibility, was built in 1894, and its lifts were installed in 1901 (Potter 1994). The same year saw the decision taken to widen the Promenade, initially to 60ft, extended to 100ft wide when debated by the full council. The various promenades landscaped and tamed the cliffs that rose and fell from Norbreck to Fox Hall. As the sea reached right up to the foot of these cliffs and to the promenade stonework, there would have been few safe havens for the shrimpers and pleasure boats worked by the fishing community. Old photographs show the boats pulled right up the shore to the foot of, and occasionally partly up onto, the stone pitching that stabilised the cliffs. This would have encouraged many to keep their half-deckers at Fleetwood as reported by Aflalo. However, a sound knowledge of the tides allowed both the Blackpool men and Lytham and St Anne's men to work off the beach at Blackpool, letting the smacks take the ground on the ebb. The photograph of the Metropole, Plate 24, includes

Plate 24. Pleasure boats at the Metropole.

Plate 25. Wellington Hotel.

pleasure boats and hire skiffs. The pleasure boats were full-bodied clinker open boats with a short counter, rigged as sloops. These were peculiar to Blackpool, which differed from other towns, where as often as not nobbies served as pleasure boats.

One photograph of the Wellington Hotel (Plate 25) situated on the top of the shore near Chapel Street opposite the Central pier, has two two-masted open pleasure boats drawn up on the pitching. The photograph dates from *c.*1866. A member of Blackpool's fishing families, Old Bob Bickerstaffe, built the Wellington Hotel in 1851, passing it on to his son John. Old Bob and his nephew Young Bob were both members of the lifeboat crew; Young Bob was its cox'n. Old Bob was son of Edward Bickerstaffe who was nicknamed Neddy Snow. Snow was an alias used by the Bickerstaffes in parish registers to hide their adherence to the Catholic faith. The birth of Molly was registered by John Snow (alias) of Marton Common at Lytham Church in 1788. Walton (1978) does not mention fishing as the occupation of any of the boarding house landladies' husbands so the Bickerstaffes may have been exceptional. At Blackpool, as it developed from green field sites, many of the proprietors came in from the Lancashire and West Yorkshire mill towns that housed their guests. A large proportion of them were single, either spinster, widows, or separated, extending the income derived from savings or annuities by taking guests in season, although some had come to Blackpool as semi-retired couples, using the holiday season takings to supplement their income and to pay for a more comfortable home than their pension would afford (Walton 1978). Walton's oversight of the fishing community may simply have been because there were so few compared to the large number of boarding houses.

The Blackpool community did come to the notice of the Sea Fisheries superintendent, although mainly due to the Blackpool Closed Ground. This conservation measure was imposed in the Byelaws of 1893 covering the area from Uncle Tom's Cabin to Star Inn. Star Inn stood at the head of the beach in the middle of the original Pleasure Beach, roughly where Watson Road meets the promenade. Robert Bickerstaff, of 45 Market Street; and James Parr, of 22 South King Street, served on the committee in 1883. It was reported that the last haul on the Blackpool closed ground took 1,226 young sole 3-7in inch long with the shrimp in a 1¼ hour trawl, and that at this time there were seventy to ninety shrimpers in addition to the push netters working. There were reports of poaching on the Blackpool closed ground by hand shrimpers in the winter of 1898, causing friction with the trawlers. In the summer of 1899 Blackpool fishermen (including the lifeboat cox'n) offered to police the Closed Ground for a retainer of £10 (£797) per annum. After the reorganisation caused by the amalgamation with the Western District, four assistant bailiffs were posted at Blackpool (Lancashire and Western Sea Fisheries Committee 1891 et seq.).

Bad weather interrupted the fishing in the winter of 1901, although shrimping went well, weather permitting, but the boats were only able to work for about half of the time. The Blackpool men also tried line fishing but could not launch due to duress of weather. In the spring of 1902 the Blackpool men tried line fishing at Seascale, Cumbria, helped by the steamer *John Fell* when she took their line boat north. They stayed for a fortnight but had only middling success due to the weather. This implies that the Blackpool community maintained a boat specifically for longlining. 1906 saw E. Salthouse, J. Barrow, and F. Parr attending the Roa Island School. From 1913 to 1915 the school was attended by John Owen, of 112 Handsworth Road, North Shore; Tom Craven, 17 Henry Street; and John Smith, 18 Ashton Road; Thomas Rimmer; Albert Fenton; William Parr; J.T. Fish, 54 Erdington Road, Central Drive; and F. Cartmell, 28 St Helier's Road, South Shore (Lancashire and Western Sea Fisheries Committee 1891 et seq.). These streets are all less than one mile from the old nucleus of Blackpool, and these men may have been the husbands of landladies.

There were some characteristics that identify the Fleetwood, and probably the Blackpool methods of trawling. It was usual for the Fleetwood boats to be crewed by two men. They used greenheart trawl beams; this may have been favoured as it was readily available from the timber importers based in the Wyre Dock, or from the shipyards, having the advantages of durability, and straight, resilient grain. The beam was in three pieces, as they only expected the ends to break. The trawl irons were 2ft 6in to 3ft high and weighed about 56lb (25kg).

The *Yachting Monthly* report of 1929 specified sheet rubber or leather chafing pieces on the shanks, 2in tarred hemp bridles, a 2½in greased yacht manila warp and a 1½in springer belayed to the nog. The fishermen used nets that they braided by hand, as well as those bought from the local net loft.

In the 1950s the prawning fleet was shrimping in the summer and longlining in winter, using herring for bait. The beam trawl was used for shrimp and sprawn until about 1965 when it was replaced by otter trawls nearly overnight. The shrimp- or sprawn-beam trawls were called shanks even though they were of fish-trawl pattern. They did use the broadsiding technique, but called it drifting, using two nets. The trawls had a chain footrope with bobbins, used net rubbers, and had a flapper but did not have pockets. Some sprawn shanks used a veil. Bobbins have now been given up, possibly when the supply dried up due to changes in the far-water trawlers' needs, or through the local timber yards giving up.

There were only a handful of half-deckers surviving at Fleetwood in the 1990s, although those remembered from the late 1960s include Ben Bee's *Annie*, which had a canoe stern fitted after the war, and his brother Gerald (Jid's) *Loella* FD 2. *Loella* was built as *Helen II* in 1910 for G.E. Stonall of New Brighton to be registered as LL 43; she was registered as *Loella* on 11/1/1944. She is a big, full-bodied boat with an outside ballast keel. John Crossfield installed her engine when she was motorised. She dropped her keel in Fleetwood Harbour, where it was replaced by deadwoods, leaving her to sit on the water like a duck.

Half-deckers remembered by fishermen of the 1990s include *Annie Bell*, built for Ben Woodhouse at Arnside, which was brought to Fleetwood by Jud Wright, *Judy*, *Mischief II*

(Crossfield Brothers built in 1903 as *My Lady* LL 417 for John Mealor of Rock Ferry), and Snowy Houden's *Lassie,* which was built at Conwy for Mr A. Kitchen on the Dee, Arty Swayles' Gibson built *Elanora,* and *Short Blue* (built at Conwy as the *Capella* in 1940 for J. Wright). *Capella* (a 36ft boat) sank on her delivery trip when a sack of beach stone stowed as temporary ballast was caught by the starting handle on the engine flywheel and beat her bottom out. Her intended kentledge and scrap iron ballast was awaiting her at Fleetwood; both crew were lost. She was reckoned to be the fastest nobby at Fleetwood in the 1960s.

Ian Greenwood's *Irene* at 39ft was thought to be Millom-built. The Manx line boat *Gien Mie* was fished until recently by Mike Brown and his son. Also remembered were *Advance,* an early straight stem type, built by William Crossfield in 1898 and registered as FD 155 in that year before transferring to Hoylake in 1906, with *May Baxter, Carly Marie, Sea Wolf* (another old type) *Teal, Zora, Speedwell, Queen Alexandra,* and the old Morecambe type *Volunteer.*

Chapter 7
Morecambe

The resort of Morecambe was originally a farming and fishing village called Poulton-le-Sands, named after Poulton Hall. The surrounding ill-drained land produced grain and two crops of potatoes each year. Early commentators recorded the un-hygienic conditions with middens composting garbage at the cottage doors, prior to being used to manure the fields (Kennerley 1982).

Fishing would have been pursued as a subsistence activity supplemented by a smallholding, chickens and a cottager's pig, and probably continued as such up to and into the early nineteenth century. Records survive from Furness Abbey that establish the existence of baulks predating 1330, and from about 1500 include receipts from the mussel fishery owned by the manor of Heysham. During the reign of Henry VIII the manor of Heysham received £11 5s as rent of the mussel beds from fourteen men, out of a total income of £50. Cod and whiting were taken in 1630 (Bingham 1990). A painting (Plate 26) records Shaw's Yard off Poulton Square where Bat Hall was built in 1643. This hostelry became the favoured meeting place for the fishermen of the time.

There are references to catching herring in set nets and baulks in about 1800 and 1813, whilst it was noted that a Poulton fishwife was selling cockles on Lancaster market at the age of ninety-three in 1826. In addition to gathering molluscs and taking fish in baulks (which were activities that farm workers could undertake) boatmen were recorded as

Plate 26. Old Poulton-le-Sands. (Courtesy of Lancaster City Museums)

collecting salvaged coal from a wreck at Piel in 1830 (Bingham 1990). For herring fishing to be worth pursuing with set nets on Middleton Sands implies large dense shoals close inshore. It may be possible that herring were also taken in a beach seine net. At about this time it is recorded that a communal draw net of 150yd length was kept at Barrow-in-Furness for the use of the villagers (Leach 1991) so this technique was known in the vicinity of Poulton. The description of a Morecambe draw net is given as 80yd long, set in by a third which would have used about 120yd of net. It was one hundred meshes at the bunt, and eighty meshes at the tips, braided of 30/32 cotton and dressed with gas tar. The description 30/32 signifies thirty-two threads of thickness 30 laid up into a twine. The thickness measure indicates the length of thread per unit weight, so the bigger the number the thinner the thread (Davis 1958). The importance in which fishing was seen as an occupation is unclear at this time. The census of 1841 did not list fisherman as an occupation; however, a contribution to the Sanitary Inquiry, England, published in 1842 and prepared by Dr Edward de Vitre in 1840 states 'The male inhabitants of these villages are almost exclusively engaged in fishing for herrings, flat-fish, shrimps, cockles and mussels [...], and whilst they are so engaged their families at home are picking and sorting the produce of each previous catch' (Kennerley 1982). Furthermore the *Lancaster Gazette* reported that on 4 February 1845, a Tuesday, 'The Fishermen's Friend Lodge of Odd-Fellows' celebrated an anniversary, so it is strange that fishing was not considered an occupation worthy of note in the census. In both the 1851, 1861 and 1871 census fisherman does appear as an occupation.

Although the sources do not include their calling, research by Eija Kennerley (1982) established the presence of the families who were to become Morecambe fishermen. Listing them in the date order that corresponds to their appearance in official records we find:

Wilson	1746	Willacy	1809	Mayor	1825
Edmondson	1747	Titterington	1813	Burton	1826
Armistead	1750	Raby	1813	Bond	1826
Gardner	1752	Crossfield	1813	Carter	1827
Baxter	1753	Whittle	1317	Airey	1829
Woodhouse	1761	Lupton	1821	Hadwen	1830
Bell	1771	Cockin	1822		
Johnson	1775	Threlfall	1825		

The name Swain, Hodgson, Houghton, Brown, Townley, Jackson, and Mount appear in the following decade. The Titterington family of 1813 were not mentioned in the later narrations. The census record shows that William, who appeared in 1813 when about thirty-seven years of age, had a son William who also followed the fishing. The household of the younger William, aged seventy-two in 1891, included his son-in-law, James Woodhouse. The census suggests that these two were the only Titteringtons to fish for a living.

In addition to its farming background Poulton was also a sea bathing resort from at least 1800. The following advertisements appeared in the *Lancaster Gazette*:

2nd March 1811
TO BE SOLD BY AUCTION, At Miss Noon's, the Royal-Oak Inn, Lancaster, on Wednesday the 10th April next, at six o'clock in the evening.
Lot 1. Two new-erected COTTAGES, adjoining each other, called POOL-HOUSES, with the Court before the same, pleasantly situated on the Sea-shore, near Poulton-by-the-Sands, two mile from Lancaster, commanding an extensive view of the Bay, and Cumberland and Westmoreland Hills which premises are capable of being converted into a neat dwelling-house, at a small expense, fit for a respectable family, during the bathing season, and now in the possession of Christopher Watson and John Woodhouse.
Lot 2. Two other DWELLING-HOUSES, with the Barn, Shippon, and Garden adjoining thereto, situate in the village of Poulton aforesaid, in the possession of Philip Clifton and

Fig. 41. Old Poulton from seaward.

Richard Raby. The tenants will show the premises and for other particulars apply, to Mr E. Atkinson, solicitor, Lancaster.

February 25, 1811.
SEA-BATHING TO BE LET
That convenient Cottage, MORECAMBE-COTTAGE, at Poulton-by-the-Sands, which commands, without exception, one of the sublimest and most picturesque prospects in the country, is chiefly FURNISHED, and, being within three miles of Lancaster, affords every facility for a small genteel family. For particulars apply to Richard Fisher, Friarage, Lancaster, April 27, 1821.

Pool Houses appear on the 1848 OS map, between the Town Hall gardens and the corner of Lord Street.

In 1813 Richard Ayton wrote that both of Poulton's public houses were full of manufacturers from inland towns come for the 'benefit of the physic in the sea' at spring tides (Ayton R. & Daniell W. 1814). Ayton also commented on carts standing outside the inns, with their shafts in the air. These were the tradesmen's carts that the mill hands hired to bring them on their weekend's trip. In 1839 the Tithe map indicated that Betty Edmondson ran a public house on the site of the New Inn. The one other was the Morecambe Hotel on Lord Street, occupied by Thomas Mason and John Gardner. There was also a bathing house, and fish house and yards on the foreshore. During this period the resort's population increased from 177 in 1821 to 540 in 1831 (Bingham 1990). Poulton's appearance at around this time was captured in an image reproduced as Fig. 41.

Whilst it is not recorded that fishing smacks took part, regattas followed by dinners were organised in the early nineteenth century, the first being in 1829, sailed by gentlemen's yachts. Eija Kennerly found records of races sailed on 22 July 1830, again in 1834 and 1836, and by the 1850s the regattas were annual events. There were also regattas held at the other villages around the shores of the Bay. The *Lancaster Gazette* reported regattas at Sunderland Point, in the Lune, and at Poulton. Their report of 20 1829 advised that:

THE REGATTA ON THE LUNE WILL TAKE PLACE AT SUNDERLAND, on Tuesday, the twenty-first of July and Wednesday the twenty-second of July next, when The Following Prizes will be contended for on Tuesday
1st. A Silver Cup, value FIFTEEN GUINEAS, for DECKED Boats not exceeding 30 tons measurements three guineas to be given to the second boat.

2d. A Silver Cup, value FIFTEEN GUINEAS, for Open Boats, not exceeding 7 tons measurement, three guineas for the second boat.

3d. A Prize of THREE GUINEAS to the winner of a Rowing Match, boats not exceeding four oars, and ONE GUINEA to the second boat.

Name of vessels entered	Description	Owners	Coxswains
Princess Charlotte	yacht	H. Hargreaves Esq.	Robt. Gerrard
Lancaster Rose	ditto	P. Hesketh Esq.	Robt. Gerrard
Red Rover	yawl	J. Hunter Esq.	
Swallow	ditto	P. Hesketh Esq.	
William	ditto	John Ellwood	
Ellen (late Harlequin)	schooner	W. Garth	John Baxter
Delight	ditto	J. Redshaw	
Harriet	ditto	C. Gibson Esq.	John Dickenson
John	ditto	J. Simpson	
Unity	ditto	J. Rawlinson	
Good Intent	smack	J. Whitham	J. Whittenham
Amity	ditto	G. Jackson	Capt. Towers
Waterloo	ditto	J. Moore	
Zephyr	ditto	R Atkinson Esq.	Wm Mecold

Thirty-ton craft measured about 48ft by 13ft beam, whilst 7-ton open boats would have been 25ft by 8ft. The *Gazette* of 25 August 1834 wrote:

> The annual regatta on Morecambe Bay took place, and the attendance was numerous and respectable, but owing to the interest of the great will cause, many of the fashionables did not attend.

The regatta of 22 August 1840 at Poulton was written up by the *Gazette*, as were those of 1843 and 1844. The *Gazette* reported an incident on 3 August 1844 after the Silverdale regatta, and went on to report:

> Arnside First Annual Regatta – On Monday last, as beautiful a day for the occasion as ever the sun shone upon these sports came off. The moment the tide began to rise, a flotilla of neat boats appeared mustering from various quarters, and from ten to eleven o'clock crowds of well-dressed persons from the country far and near, assembled near the starting post, in front of the Ship hotel, to witness the gay scene. About 12 o'clock, five handsome sailboats, with a stiff breeze from southwest, started for the prize. Mr Frank Crossfield, whose boat has generally won upon those occasions, took rather too wide a stretch at starting in order to avoid the necessity of a succession of tacks, and was soon seen in the distance – which he could not, with all his clever efforts, manage to recover – and a boat from Poulton, principally managed by a Lancaster gentleman, who, throughout the day, contributed much to the amusement of the company by his drolleries, carried the main prize. Mr Just, of Grange, with his far-famed boat, following closely, and coming in for the second prize. Two rowing boats, only manned by amateurs, started, the one of six and the other of four oars, much skill was evinced as coxswain, by the owner of the latter, but the tide being about one third ebb, she frequently scraped the ground, and finally gave in. Wrestling then became the order of the day, when a man named Hewitson was declared conqueror. There was a great assemblage of tents for the sale of confectionery, cakes, etc., as well as of more useful articles. A company of ingenious and amusing mountebanks graced the ground, and the usual compliment of "Civil Wills", "Bull-ringers", etc., at which games some of the young gentlemen present proved themselves very expert adapts. Mrs. Reid, the worthy hostess, furnished a good homely repast, and the evening was spent with much hilarity and good humour. Following is the account: – A sailing match

for £1. John Baxter's boat, Poulton 1 William Taylor's boat, Carnforth 2 Francis Crossfield's boat, Arnside 3 Jonathan Just's, boat, Grange 4 James Honton's, boat, Grange 5"

The £1 purse was worth £70 in 2005. There followed a detailed list of all of the results, including the heats of the wrestling contests, the report concluded: 'The company then repaired to the assembly-room, where the merry dance was begun. As the owners of the five sailing craft are not 'Gentlemen' with the honorific 'Esq.' this report establishes the participation of fishermen under sail in the regattas.

The handbill for a regatta at Arnside read:

ARNSIDE REGATTA AND SPORTS. This REGATTA and SPORTS will take place on Monday, the 10th of August, 1846, at the house of Mr. J. Titterington, FIGHTING COCKS, ARNSIDE, when the following Prizes will be contended for, viz. First Class, Sail Boats of all sizes, £2. Four Oared Boats, all lengths, £1. Wrestling for £2, with various other Amusements. All disputes to be decided by the Stewards.

Geo. Lee. Printer. Fickle Street Kendal

The £2 purse was worth £150 in 2005. The same newspaper reported a fatal accident thus:

7th September 1839

Melancholy Accident – On Thursday morning a melancholy accident occurred in Morecambe Bay. About two o'clock, the fishing boat *Juno*, which had been trolling for shrimps in the bay, was returning home, with two young men in her, and had got just opposite Bare when a sudden gust of wind caught her, and she capsized. One of the persons on board was seen to rise in the water once, but though every effort was made to render assistance no boat could get to the spot quick enough to give any aid. It is to be feared that the sheets were belayed and there was no time to let go. A more dangerous practice cannot be, and if the fact were so in this case, we trust the melancholy event will prove a useful warning. The names of the two young persons lost were William Edmondson, aged 23 and Edward Edmondson aged 17, brothers. In the evening on the tide going down the bodies of the ill-fated youths were found on the sands. The inquest will be held this day"

The *Guardian* included reports discussing the social conditions and the development of the village.

6th March 1841

Peter Raby, fisherman, of Poulton was brought up by Mr Richard Houghton, the assistant overseer, for the arrears of an order made upon him, amounting to £16 16s (£1,100). Defendant strongly pleaded his inability to pay the money. The overseer stated that he earned in the fishing season a considerable sum – that he had a boat of his own nets etc. but in order to evade payment, he had got his brother's name lately painted upon it, pretending that it did not belong to him. Defendant contended that the boat was his brother's, and that no name was ever on it, until his brother had his own put upon it. Mr Bolder advised him to pay down £5 (£325), and to make arrangements to settle the rest by instalments. Defendant said he was unable to do so, as he had but been recently married. The case was then ordered to be formerly gone into, but as the overseer had forgot to bring the magistrates order – the case was adjourned to this day.

It was reported in 1842 that a fisherman was instrumental in saving life at a drowning tragedy at Arnside, 'Providently a boat belonging to Mr Thomas Houghton, of Poulton Ring, was passing at the time, the crew of which with difficulty, succeeded in saving Mrs C. and the nurse-maid.'

8th July 1843

Charge of Assault Robert Johnson of Poulton, fisherman was charged before the borough magistrates with having assaulted Ann Wise, and stolen from her a black gauze frill on Sunday night last. Johnson was discharged, two young men with whom he was in company, having proved that he never left them, and did not commit the offence. The magistrates were of opinion that the complainant had made a mistake as to the person.

11th November 1843

NOTICE IS HEREBY GIVEN,

That on the 1st January next. Application will be made to her Majesty's Justices of the Peace assembled at Quarter Sessions, in and for the County of Lancaster, at Lancaster, for an Order for turning, diverting, and stopping up a certain part of a certain Highway leading from the village of Poulton, within the hamlet of Poulton, in the township of Poulton, Bare, and Torrisholme, in the County of Lancaster, along the sea shore to the village of Bare, in the said township, and which said part of the said Highway commences at or near to the westwardly end of a certain Dwelling-house or Building formerly used for the purpose of curing of herrings, situate within the hamlet of Poulton aforesaid, and now in the occupation of James Giles, of Lancaster, in the County of Lancaster, Esquire, and extending from thence in an eastwardly direction to the eastwardly end of a certain other Building now used as a Joiner and Wheelwright's Shop, and also formerly used for the curing of herrings, also situate within the hamlet of Poulton aforesaid, and now in the occupation of Marmaduke Hewertson, as tenant to the said James Giles, and that the Certificate of two Justices, having viewed the same etc. with the Plan of the old and proposed new Highway, will be lodged with the Clerk of the Peace for the said County on Saturday, the 2nd December next.

Dated 6th November, 1843,
John Bond,
Surveyor of the Hamlet of Poulton aforesaid.

8th February 1845

Poulton Oddfellows' Lodge – On Tuesday last, the Fisherman's Friend Lodge, of the Independent Order of Oddfellows, held their anniversary meeting, and a most happy meeting it was. At about ten o'clock the Lodge assembled at Mrs. Edmondson's, and having formed in due order of procession, with band, colours, etc., marched to Torrisholme, thence to Bare, and back to Poulton, proceeding to the parsonage house, where they were joined by the respected minister, the Rev. E. Manby, who accompanied them thence to the church, where the rev. gentleman read prayers and preached a most beautiful discourse from Ezekiel chap. 38, verse II: "Turn ye, turn ye, from your evil ways, for why will ye die, of house of Israel." The sermon was listened to with devoted attention, and cannot fail to make a lasting impression. Service concluded, the Lodge returned in procession to Mrs. Edmondson's, where a dinner, of which it is impossible to speak too highly, was served up. The Rev. Mr. Manby occupied the chair, and Mr. R. Speight of Lancaster, acted as vice. The rev. chairman gave the health of the Queen, which was followed by the national anthem. Mr. Speight singing the solo parts. The usual routine toasts were drunk, and the rev. chairman, after giving success to the society, retired, leaving every one delighted with his kindness and affability. Mr. Speight then took the chair, and the evening was spent most convivially, the whole concluding with a dance.

The North Western Railway was completed in Poulton in 1847, bringing in more holidaymakers and providing opportunities for speedier and more efficient marketing of fish that could not otherwise be consumed locally. This is recorded on the 1848 Ordnance Survey map, which includes the location of the Bull Inn, Fisherman's Arms, and Morecambe Hotel. The North Western Hotel was newly erected, opening on Whitsun Monday 1848 (see Fig. 42). The hotel was built on Poulton Rings Point, next to the North Western Railway harbour jetty. The harbour itself was completed in 1850 (Bingham 1990).

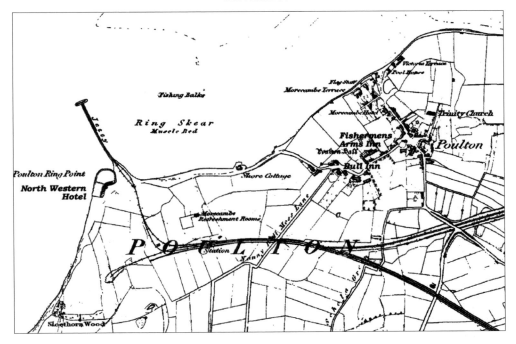

Fig. 42. Old Poulton map. (Ordnance Survey of 1847)

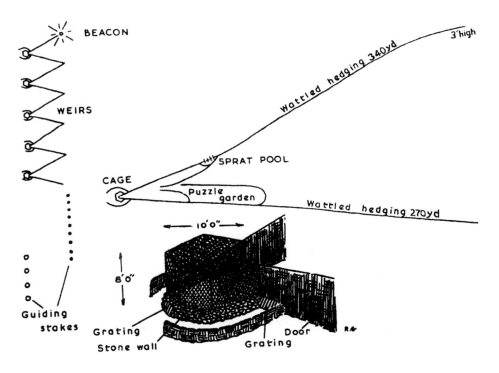

Fig. 43. Fishing baulk. (after F.M. Davis, *An Account of the Fishing Gear of England and Wales*)

The methods of fishing employed during this period were carried out using set nets and the ancient baulks, which caught flatfish and herring, drift netting for herring, and taking cod and flatfish from boats, possibly by both longline or trawl. The baulks continued in use until the 1990s, and so were part of the landscape in which the nobbies worked. They were 'V'-shaped fixed traps, built of wattle fencing with a net chamber at the 'V'. The mouth of the baulk faced up into the bay, so that it fished on the ebb. There were said to be seventy-five baulks between Cockersands and Silverdale in 1900 (Bingham 1990). Old Dick Bond's, Fell's, and Great and Little Gunnel's baulks were off Heysham, Aldren's and Burrow's baulks were opposite the Battery, and the map of Morecambe shows several. Two notable catches have come down on record. Dolly Bill Baxter caught so many salmon in 1845 that he glutted Lancaster market and could only get 2*d* a pound (less than 2 New Pence a kg). Robert Wilson caught 20,000 herring in one tide in a baulk opposite the stone jetty in 1900. The use of baulks gradually died out. Jack Aldren fished his family's baulks until 1976, but by 1990 there were only two or three baulks in occasional use (Bingham 1990). The sketch Fig. 43 is derived from Davis (1958).

The *Lancaster Guardian* quoted the following prices for fish landed by the *Otter* (a large smack built to supply Lancaster with fish), as well as for Poulton herring. In March 1803 soles fetched 6*d* per lb (£3.57 a kg), in November 1804 herring fetched twenty for 1*s* (£3.14). The *Lancaster Gazette* of 25 June 1803 reported:

> On Wednesday last, a fine new fishing boat of 42 tons burthen, called *"Beaver"*, was launched at Mrs Smith's yard, near this town. She is intended to supply our market with fish; and having already experienced the benefit of a supply of turbot, soals, haddock, gurnot, brits &C. by the exertions of the proprietors of the *"Otter"*, lately launched, we sincerely hope, that the subscribers to both boats will meet the reward so justly due to their public spirited exertions.

A later report of 20 February 1808:

> The *"Otter"*, fishing boat (of this port) struck upon a rock, near Ravenglass, during the late gales; the men saved their lives.

The *Gazette* reported a happier event on 22 January 1820:

> A new fishing-boat was launched on Monday last, from the yard of T. Worthington & Co. of this town. She is called the "GEORGE AND AGNES", and about 25 tons burthen.

The *Guardian* then reported:

> 10 December 1831
> William Parkinson, a Fisherman of Bare, last week caught twenty thousand Herrings, which he took to Preston and sold them at one shilling per hundred, clearing £10 (£653) by his journey.

The *Guardian's* report of 26 May 1838 states:

> Supply of Fish – On Wednesday last, the *Greyhound* trawl-boat sent her first haul to our fish market. We should explain that she was driven in by the boisterous weather, and that in consequence the supply which she afforded was not considerable. She has since returned to her ground, and we doubt not her next trawling will be more satisfactory. We hold the town much indebted to the public spirit of Mr Penny Nicholson, the gentleman to whom the *Greyhound* belongs, in thus endeavouring to procure for it a supply of which we were so much in need, and we heartily wish him success. We understand that our coast abounds with fish of the choicest kinds, and if so, there can be no question that with perseverance, the Lancaster fish market will be as well supplied as any in the country.

The reports of 28 July 1838 and after were equally glowing:

> Fish – Our market is now admirably supplied with fish. The catches of Lune salmon, so highly prised, have lately been very abundant, etc. and in addition the boats to which we have before alluded, come in constantly laden either with salmon from Scotland, or fish from our own Coast.
>
> 8th September 1838
>
> Immense Catch of Herrings – One day this week the boats of Poulton-by-the-Sands caught the immense number of 140,000 herrings, all of which were immediately sold and sent off.

By the 1840s the paper was reporting the failure of the herring fishery. In 1840 it was reported that only a few hauls were made in the ten days preceding 22 February, the fish fetching 3s 6d (£11.19) a hundred. The lack of west winds to drive the shoals across the channel was blamed for the failure. The report anticipated the opening of the Lancaster & Preston Railway, which would replace the use of one-horse carts transporting the herring packed in barrels (Kennerley 1982). By 14 November 1840 the herring had returned and were reported as:

> The Herring Season – We rejoice to announce that so far the herring fishing on this coast has been highly successful this season. During the past fortnight, immense catches of fish have been made at Poulton-le-Sands and the neighbourhood. It is said the abundance of fish has exceeded all former seasons, the catches averaging the enormous quantity of twenty tons per day. We are happy to hear further that our Poulton neighbours find a ready market, vast loads of fish being carried off daily by the railroad to Birmingham, Wolverhampton, and other inland places.

On 29 October 1842 a report in the *Lancaster Gazette* stated that:

> Poulton Herring Fishery – Yesterday morning the fishermen of Poulton went out a herring fishing, and were so fortunate as to fall in with a shoal, that on their return with the flood tide, the average catch was between 2500 and 3000 for each boat. Although they have been out three or four times previously, this is the first take of any consequence, and it is supposed that the late strong weather is driving them nearer the land. Brogden's boat took what was computed to be about 9000 in number.

The herring fishery was expected to be a complete failure in a report of 17 December 1842, with many of the boats going over to the mussel fishery (Kennerley 1982). In order to suit the mussel fishery these craft were probably 20-25ft long, flat floored, and undecked.

A lot of developments occurred in the period beginning with 1840. In 1841 the rebuilt Trinity Chapel of 1745 was re-consecrated as Trinity Church. The improved markets opened up by the railway prompted the mussel fishermen to initiate a court case against the lords of Heysham manor to test the control of the mussel fishery. The case was heard at Lancaster Castle with a successful outcome for the fishermen. The trial of 1847 established that the skears between the middle of the Kent to the middle of the Lune were a free fishery (Bingham 1990).

1852 saw the creation of Poulton, Bare, & Torrisholme Board of Health, which indicates the extent of the growth and stature of the young town. Plate 27 illustrates the appearance of the green at this time. The first board was served by the Reverend Edward Francis Manby, of Poulton Hall; James Giles of the Elms, Bare; John Lodge of Bare Hall; John Marr of Poulton; and Robert Bond and James Cole of Torrisholme. Mr W. Tilley, solicitor, served as clerk, and Mr John Bond was the nuisance inspector. An international crisis raised a threat of invasion in 1852 that was to have an impact on the fishermen (sometimes literally) in several ways. A naval force was stationed at the old Heysham mill to protect the harbour. During the Crimean War the Lancashire Volunteers took over the naval campsite. By this time the mill had been reduced in height and roofed in slate as a cottage,

Plate 27. Old Poulton *c.*1850. (R.K. Bingham, *Lost Resort*)

Plate 28. Old Poulton *c.*1860.

named the Round House. The Volunteers used it as their magazine. The troops set up a tented encampment in the fields between the Round House and the railway. These fields were maintained as cattle fields for the temporary penning of livestock from cattle-boats calling at the harbour jetty (Bingham 1990).

The Volunteers welcomed local men in their ranks, promising that calls to duty would not clash with good fishing tides. The fishermen took advantage of a lucrative sideline when they were paid a bounty for returning any cannon balls found on the sand. The disadvantage lay in the artillery battery's bad habit of hitting the occasional boat or ship. In 1863 the Battery Hotel was newly opened next to the Round House. By 1884 erosion had reduced the parade ground in size, so in 1886 a new camp was established at Scalestones Point north of Bare Village (Bingham 1990). The detail from the OS of 1890, copied here as Fig. 44, locates the Mill and the Battery Inn.

Another event that was to prove important to the fishing community was the advent of Methodism in 1853, followed by the building of the Pedder Street Methodist Church in 1855. Farming was still important to the community, which suffered from potato blight during 1847-8, 1855-6 and again in 1869 and 1875. The town's expansion accelerated when Mr Roger Taylor's estate was sold in 1850. This land, between the railway and old Poulton village, allowed sufficient houses to be erected by 1853 that it was reported that

'Morecambe is now so great that there is accommodation for a few thousand visitors and it is not necessary for any to be sent back to Lancaster to seek a bed'. The desire for the benefits of sea bathing was served by eighteen bathing machines in 1853 whilst Mr James Bell offered bathing boats with rope ladders for hire (Bingham 1990).

In 1853 the herring had returned to the Cumberland coast. A report on Wednesday, 5 January 1853, in the *Lancaster Gazette* records that 'The herring boats which went out Monday last, returned with a fair catch of herrings, having taken from one thousand to 600 per boat.' According to Eija Kennerly this report states that the boats sailed up to Maryport and fished as they returned to Poulton. It must have been on one of these trips that four Poulton boats were forced to shelter in Annan in 1854, with the result that a fishing community was set up there.

A record survives that reports cockler's earning £4 (£250) per week in 1860, a very good wage for that time. The census of 1861 as analysed by Eija Kennerley (1982) gives 223 men, their wives and youths listed as fisher folk. This included seven under fifteen years, and twenty-seven between fifteen and twenty. 9 March 1861 saw the *Lancaster Guardian* report that the shrimping industry had expanded so that 'the most distant markets are now supplied – Birmingham, Bristol, London.' They will have been catching a respectable quantity to satisfy the dealers in these cities. The regattas were no longer popular with gentlemen's yachts; by 1860 they were mainly rowing races for fishermen. The fishing fleet peaked at about this time to 150, this will have included mussel doggers as well as trawl boats (Bingham 1990).

The harbour brought a lot of shipping movements to Poulton, so that in October 1855 a lighthouse was erected on Clarke's Wharf. This was supplemented by a flagpole erected on the green in 1861, donated by the Lancaster MP. The town continued to improve itself for holidaymakers; the promenade at the Midland Hotel was extended in 1862 to cover the green. Before these civic works could be undertaken a widow of twenty years had to be bribed to leave her cottage, built on the high tide line on the green. Her family built the cottage in one night in order to claim squatter's rights. The bribe avoided an expensive and long drawn-out inquiry needed to determine who was responsible for the land on which the cottage was built. During the 1850s the green, although at the top of the strand, was literally a village green, unpaved and apt to be messy. The first solution was to lay down boardwalks. These came to be called causeways, a name still applied to pavements by Morecambrians (Bingham 1990). Plate 28 reproduces a photograph of this period, taken from close to the vantage point of Plate 27.

The flagstaff was felled by a gale in 1865. A sense of opportunistic economy caused a mast from the wreck of the *Put Yona* (sic, actually the *Pudyona*) to be erected in its place. This unlucky vessel is still remembered as she gave her name to the skear on which she finally came to rest. She was a barque of 134ft, built in Nova Scotia in 1851, owned by John Stamp Burrell of Lancaster (Rothwell 1983). She hit about one mile east of Danger Patch before being driven over the sands. Her crew was rescued by the tug *Wyre*.

A new map of Poulton was published in 1864 which records the expansion of the town to the west of the railway. The *Mannex Directory* of 1866 catalogues the continuing growth in the number of inns, hotels, and lodging houses. Many of these lodging houses were run by the fishermen's families, who were also employed processing the catch for market. There were also four fishmonger's shops, all in old Poulton. The Pleasure Boat Company had been set up prior to 1867, when they built a wooden landing stage from the green opposite Queens Hotel. The boats took holidaymakers 'kebbing', the local name for hand lining. The Pleasure Boat Company suffered a set back in the following year when the stage was demolished to make way for the new Central Pier, built in 1868-9 and extended in 1871 (Bingham 1990).

The original railway station was replaced in about 1870. The new one was built at Taylor Street, which was renamed Euston Road. In this way a memento of the landowner whose land sale allowed Morecambe to grow was replaced by a reference to the London terminus of the railway company (Bingham 1990).

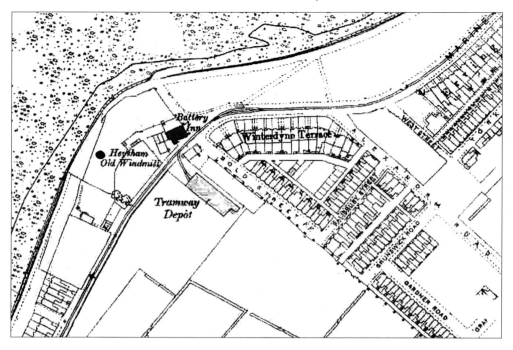

Fig. 44. The Battery. (Ordnance Survey of 1910)

In March of 1871 the Morecambe Deep Sea Fishery Co. Ltd. was wound up, it was reported in 1870 that the directors had purchased the *Beaver* for £710 (£43,690). The 1871 census, again analysed by Kennerly (1982), gives 156 men and boys with fishing as their occupation. As the chapter on the boat's origins sets out, the same year gives us an insight into the form of boats at Poulton by the square tuck-sterned clench-built model cutter now in the Lancaster Maritime Museum collection. This form of craft is confirmed as a trawl boat by the Holdsworth engraving of a single-handed nobby with a square tuck stern and sloop rig, going to or from the trawling grounds in Morecambe Bay, with its trawl on deck, reproduced as Fig. 6. Holdsworth (1874) reported that some boats shipped a boy as crew. Holdsworth lists 122 second-class boats and 101 third-class boats registered at Lancaster in 1872. The fishery that he describes includes trawling for flats and shrimp and longlining in the later part of the year. The longlines take dogfish in addition to the more valued demersal fish. There was a ready market for dogs in Lancashire where they sold as 'Darwen salmon'. Holdsworth describes the shrimp trawl as a conventional beam trawl with a short ground rope and a ½in mesh net. The shrimp was riddled at sea, but if there was insufficient time to do this, the undersized shrimp were used for potting. They were taking 25-30qt a day.

1874 saw a split in the Methodist movement in Poulton, when the United Methodists formed a congregation, buying land for a church that opened in 1876. This building was in Morecambe Street, but the congregation later moved to Clarence Street. The fishing community adopted this Clarence Street Church as their own, with the famous Morecambe Fishermen's Choir being based there (Bingham 1990). 1876 saw the loss of John Edmondson and Adam Raby in the *Leader*. John Edmondson left a wife and eight children, his family had suffered three of six untimely deaths to drowning (Rothwell 1983).

A directory for Lancashire of 1881 gives a useful snapshot of Morecambe. Two railway companies served the town, the Midland with its station on Northumberland Street, and the London & North Western Railway Company with a station on Poulton Lane. Emma Armistead & Sons traded as ironmongers, rope, twine, paint and varnish dealers, blacksmith and whitesmith, at 11 Queen Street. Armistead are still remembered as suppliers of trawl irons and anchors. Roger Bannister of 2 Pedder Street, Thomas Hodgson of 17 Morecambe Street and George Standen of 14 Pedder Street also traded as blacksmiths. There were twelve fishmongers: John S. Edmondson; William Beesley; Thomas, William and James Hadwen; James and Ann Jackson; Richard and Jane Threlfall; and James and William Woodhouse. Four of these traded from the fish market. The secretary of the Palace Sailing Company was William Hadwen of 12 The Crescent; John Brown of Nelson Street was secretary to the Steam & Pleasure Boat Company. There were also seven bathing van and pleasure boat proprietors: Henry Baxter, Robert Birkett, John Bond, William Brown, James Gardner, Wm Hadwen of 12 Back Pedder Street, and Thomas Woodhouse. The directory also listed 271 lodging-house keepers.

The quarterly reports of the Lancashire and Western Sea Fisheries Superintendent, Mr Dawson, made several references to Morecambe. The first reference was that Morecambe shrimpers went drifting for herring in the Mersey in January 1892; the beach fishermen were also taking herring in stake nets on Pilling Sands. In 1893 Morecambe herring boats went to the Mersey without success. Morecambe men took £1,650 (£128,845) worth of shrimp and sprawn in March 1893. The representatives on the committee from the Morecambe area were John Taylor Jnr, fisherman, Townend, Bolton-le-Sands, who would have been a stake net fisherman; John Bell, 39, Lord Sreet, Morecambe; and John Borrow, Cumberland View, Heysham (Lancashire and Western Sea Fisheries Committee 1891 et seq.).

The *Lancaster Observer* reported a meeting of the Morecambe fishermen on 1 April 1892, to agree policy for a meeting to discuss regulating the fishery. The public meeting at the Clarence Street schoolroom took place on Saturday, 26 March, at the request of the Southport fishing community. About seventy fishermen gathered under the chairmanship of Mr A.W. Gorton to elect representatives to attend an inquiry at Southport. The topics under discussion were the new byelaws on mesh sizes administered by Lancashire County Council's water bailiff Mr Dawson, and the restrictions on taking shrimp and mussels. The fishermen were most aggrieved over the mesh sizes due to the combined problems of the natural fibre twine shrinking in use, and inconsistency in the mesh gauges used by the bailiff. Both circumstances caused losses when the nets were condemned and had to be replaced. Messrs Joseph Edmondson, John Gardiner, T.G. Hodgson, P. Bolton, Walter and James Baxter, and Daniel Bell and William Woodhouse spoke on this topic. The meeting also debated the Blackpool closed ground. They resolved 'That this meeting of fishermen hereby condemns the present system of measuring the mesh of the nets, and considers that it imposes hardships of no practical benefit, and this meeting hereby requests the County Council to withdraw the restrictions, and this meeting also requests the County Council to remove the restrictions relating to the fishing area preserved at Blackpool, and thereby restore the rights of free fishing.' The subject of the closed season on mussels was next debated. Messrs George Bond, Edward Woodward, and D. Bell were reported as speaking. The resolution was passed 'That this meeting of fishermen also considers the close time for mussels not needed.' This closed time ran from 1 May to 16 August. Mr Walter Baxter and Mr George Bond were elected to attend the inquiry at Southport.

The fishing community came together to set up the Morecambe Fishermen's Protection Society in 1893. It was later simply known as the Fishermen's Association. This may have been prompted by the creation of the Sea Fisheries District Committee, necessitating a unified and coordinated voice. The society set up the Morecambe Fishing Boat Mutual Insurance Company in 1894. All of the officers, with the exception of the auditor were fishermen. The first fifty boats were insured on thirty-seven policies on 28 February 1894. The values of the craft were given as £2 10s (£200) up to £60 (£4,780) with many boats in the £20 to £30 range (£1,594-£2,390). The company charged a premium of 3d in the pound to cover 'hull, mast, rudder, anchor, chain, sails, ropes and ordinary equipment' against 'accidents of the seas, strandings, fire, thieves, jettisons, arrests and restraints of all the Queen's enemies, barratry of the master or crew and all perils and losses and misfortunes – – – whilst at sea or ashore' (Kennerley 1982). All within a day sail of Morecambe.

The names and addresses of the founding members were listed in the ledger as follows:

Thos. Parr	Main Street	Simon. Gerrard	Euston Road
John Woodhouse	Victoria Street	Chas. Threlfall	Back Pedder Street
James Swam	Poulton Square	William Brown	Cheapside
George Bond	Euston Road	James Dobson	Church street
Robert Threlfall	Euston Road	Geo. Alexander	Queen Street
James Holmes	Back Pedder Street	John Woodhouse	Euston Road
Robert Wilson	Morecambe Street	Thomas Mayor	Main Street
William Brown	Lord Street	Thos. Woodhouse	Euston Road
Thos. Mayor	Lord Street	James Carter	Clarence Street
John Mount	Garnett Street	Cornelius Hodgson	Stanley Street
James Gardner	Lucy Street	Edward Gardner	Clark Street
Thos. Woodhouse	Sun Street	Alf. Threlfall	Green Street
Jas. Woodhouse	Cheapside	Richard Gardner	Sun Street
Joseph Hadwin	Thornton Road	John Hadwen	Queen Street
Rich. Threlfall	Euston Road	John Willacy	Green Street
John Cocking	Oxford Street	Thomas Mayor	Beecham Street
Joseph Bell	Clarence Street	John Wilson	Morecambe Street
Walter Baxter	Clarence street	Jas G. Gardner	Edward Street
Richard Brown	Clarence street		

Even this incomplete sample of the fishing families illustrates the tight community, mostly near neighbours, with shared family names. These streets are shaded grey on the copy of the OS map of Morecambe of 1919, Fig. 45. The Insurance Company ran on until 1956, when lack of custom caused its closure.

The Local Board of Health increased in size from ten to fifteen members in 1893 and in August of the following year, with the development of the West End (nicknamed Little Bradford) the authority was converted into the Urban District Council. As we have seen that most of the fishing community lived in Old Poulton, and as Dick Woodhouse (1979) commented their wives ran lodging houses, there was a difference between Old Poulton and the West End in that the West End landladies were not dependant on the fishing community for their off-season income. In this they were like the Blackpool landladies.

The increase in the number of visitors generated an increase in the pleasure boat industry. These pleasure boat companies catered for the holidaymakers in several ways. In addition to taking parties fishing, and for trips around the bay, they carried parties to Grange or Fleetwood, returning later in the day to return them to Morecambe. The dangers of sailing on the bay, with its treacherous fluky wind, was tragically demonstrated when *Matchless* capsized in 1894. A newspaper report of the accident claimed that about 300 boats plied the bay; these would have included open mussel boats with standing lugs, as well as the decked Bay boats. The accident occurred on Monday, 3 September, at about a quarter to twelve. Samuel Houghton, of the Princess Sailing Company, owned *Matchless*, a boat measuring 33ft on deck. The *Matchless* had thirty-four souls on board, having departed at about 10am in the company of seven other Bay boats. She capsized in the channel to Grange after the fleet had passed Silverdale. The first two boats reached Grange without their passengers being aware of the accident, but the boats of Edward and Richard Gardner returned and were able to take up nine survivors, including Samuel Houghton. They and a third boat also recovered four bodies. The *Lancaster Guardian's* report commented on the Gardiners' 'admiral presence of mind' in first quelling the panic amongst their own passengers, and then in managing the rescue by instructing their passengers to support the survivors at the gunwales of the boats until as many as could be were saved.

Of the eight passengers who survived, six were from Burnley, one from Skipton, and one was from Ramsbottom. Those lost included nineteen from Burnley, with one each from Bolton, Bradford, Cleckheaton, Gorton, two from Ramsbottom (one the husband of a survivor), and one from Skipton. The preponderance of folk from Burnley in the list of passengers was due to the system of Wakes Weeks, groups of manufacturing towns closing for a different holiday week through the summer, with most of the holidaymakers visiting the same resorts. Four of these towns are in Lancashire, whilst Bradford, Cleckheaton, and Skipton were in the West Riding of Yorkshire. As Walton (1978) reports, the mill workers in these towns accumulated enough savings from the family income to be able to afford a holiday, which allowed the Wakes Week system to develop, which in its turn lead to the growth of Blackpool and Morecambe. Even as late as 1957 Bolton Burnley and Ramsbottom Wakes Weeks overlapped, suggesting that towns adhered to their traditional weeks for their holiday. The *Guardian* reported the testimonies at the coroner's inquest verbatim. Edward Gardner testified that the Bay boats had main, topsail, and jibs set, with the foresails stowed. He reported that the gust, called a bluff, first hit the boats ahead and caught their sail aback. It then hit his boat abeam, behaving more like a whirlwind. The gust was strong enough to blow the billycock hat from the head of one of the *Matchless* passengers. Plate 29 is a photograph of a Bay Boat dried out at Grange, awaiting the return of the tide. It illustrates the shallow draft and large cockpit of this form of nobby.

The fishing community of Morecambe felt the disaster so strongly that the Morecambe Fishermen's Protection Society commissioned and crewed their own lifeboat. The first was a tank whammel boat called *Gyakhan*, built by Crossfield's, fitted out as a rowing lifeboat. She served from 1895 to 1907. Next was a 25ft sailing vessel called *Rescue*, followed in 1934 by the auxiliary sail motor nobby *Sir William Priestley*. Both of these were also built by Crossfield's, the *Sir William Priestley* can now be seen at the Lancaster Maritime Museum.

The Lancashire and Western Sea Fisheries Committee (1981 et seq.) received a letter read at their meeting of February 1895 from the Morecambe Fishermen's Association seeking a ban on stake netting, citing conservation, as agreed at a meeting of 26 January. This prompted letters from all of the net fishermen's village groups blaming shrimp trawlers for destroying immature fish. The committee's decision was to limit stake nets to 300yd long, and poke nets to 150yd. The superintendent reported that thirty-four small boats were set adrift by ice in Morecambe Bay; most boats had been laid up. The Northern Division of the District had seventy shrimpers, forty-three Fleetwood prawners, and seventeen fish trawlers from the Lune and Barrow. Most men were pleasure boating on the bay or on Windermere as paid yacht hands in the summer.

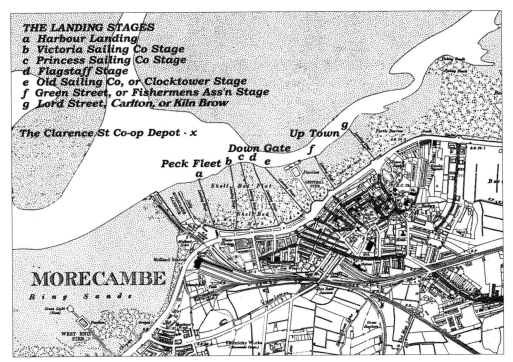

Fig. 45. Morecambe map. (Ordnance Survey of 1910)

Plate 29. A Bay boat awaiting the tide at Grange. (Collection of R. White)

The *Lancaster Observer* of 5 July 1895 reported on the import of foreign shrimp. The paper produced 26½ column inches (at 70 words to the inch, some 1,880 words) describing the import of shrimp from Germany and the Dutch, the quality of the shrimps, how preparing them for sale further damages their flavour, and how they are marketed as 'fresh boiled' or 'fresh picked'. The need for the deception was recorded as the poor supply of Morecambe-caught shrimp due to climatic conditions, and because the fishing community could earn better wages following other callings. The same edition set out the orders for the week of the Royal Artillery at the battery. All of the drills were in the afternoon, and included riding drills, trumpeters' practice, signallers', recruits' and gun drills.

The fishing grounds used by Poulton (and those of Fleetwood, Blackpool, Lytham, and Southport) were exposed lee shores for some of our worst weather. One of the storms was so bad that it is now part of folk memory. It occurred on the night of Tuesday, 2 October 1895. At least nine Morecambe boats had been trawling the 5fm line for flatfish and haddock. Due to the light air, most boats were riding to anchor between midnight and 4am, on the last of the ebb, when the storm struck. The *Lancaster Guardian*'s report names one Morecambe nobby, the *Genesta* (in error as *Genesta* was registered FD 120 at the time). She was noteworthy as her crew saved themselves by leaping onto the passenger steamer *Greyhound*. The *Greyhound* had been at anchor off Blackpool's north pier when the storm struck. As she ran for Fleetwood, passing Cleveleys, James 'Marro' Wilson ran *Genesta* alongside the steamer to save himself and his crew, Colley. *Genesta* was driven ashore, without much damage, under the cliffs at Bispham. The report also records that the first-class pilot ketch from the Ribble was driven from her anchorage near the Wyre Light to be wrecked on Bernard Wharf. The paper also reported:

Those (boats) belonging to Robert Gardner, Oxford-street, William Brown, Lord-street, and James Woodhouse, Cheapside, drifted onto Heysham Rocks, but the occupants fortunately managed to get ashore, while S. Houghton and A. Woodhouse, who were in charge of boats, got away from the shore, and returned safely to Morecambe. Harry Woodhouse and Richard Woodhouse, Joseph and George Parkinson, and Adam Woodhouse, Graham-street drifted near to Fleetwood, where the boats belonging to the first three sank, and that of the latter is reported to be safe. The escapes from drowning have been marvellous, considering the grave peril in which some of the fishermen have been placed. The boat belonging to John Wilson, Morecambe-street, was driven into Fleetwood with sails torn, and that of Henry Mount, Green-street, who was accompanied by his son, drifted towards the same place and is reported to be lost on Pilling sands, that of James Woodhouse senior, Main-street, went ashore off

Blackpool and it is uncertain as to whether it is lost or not, that of Wm. Baxter and his son drifted up the Lune and landed at Snatchams. James Swain, Poulton-square, who was musseling, lost his boat, but was fortunately saved from being drowned by Edward Woodhouse, who was also Musseling.

William Woodhouse Sr., Euston-road and Mr Willacy, Green-street returned to Morecambe on Wednesday.

The body of Richard Baxter, aged 30, of Clarke-street, Morecambe, who was skipper of the smack *Resolution*, was washed ashore at Fleetwood ... He ... had with him as assistant James Woodhouse, aged about 22, of Euston-road, Morecambe. Their boat- – - is now stranded at Larkham (Larkholm), about three miles from Fleetwood.

The *Resolution* was registered LR 43 from 1892-1895. The Morecambe boat *Tit Bits* LR 80 was successfully refloated from the Wyre Bank nearly opposite Lune Bank, by shifting her ballast and fastening on her hatches. The other 'Morecambe prawners' ashore at Fleetwood were the *Sarah Ann* LR 93, *Kittiwake* LR 34, and *Blue Ribbon* LR 82. Snatchems is on the north bank of the Lune, just below Salt Ayre, over three miles up stream, the public house Golden Ball stands on the bank there.

Reports from Lytham (Mayes 2000) record that James Woodhouse Sr was working Thomas Woodhouse's *Ada*; Cornelius Hodgson's *Edith* LR 58, crew Ralph Gerrard, was badly damaged. Both came ashore on Salthouse Bank but were salvaged and refitted. James Woodhouse Sr survived the stranding. *Blue Ribbon* was crewed by James Woodhouse and Josiah Ball, *Kittiwake* was crewed by Harry and Richard Woodhouse, and *Sara Anne* was crewed by Joseph and George Parkinson and Adam Woodhouse. The differences between the reports of the Lancaster and Lytham newspapers indicates the difficulty experienced by journalists in the days before the telephone. Some of the nobby owners and their craft appear in the ledger of the Mutual Insurance Co. Those insured in 1894 were:

James Swain of Poulton Square with *Annie* at £8 (£637.80).
John Willacy of Green Street with *Bran* and *Sally* at £30 (£2,392), *Dolphin* at £20 (£1,594) and *Clara* at £5 (£398).

Those insured in 1895 were:

William Brown of Lord Street with *Martha Brown* LR 81 at £40 (£3,328), replaced by *Lizzie* at £30 (£2,496).
Robert Gardner of Oxford Street with *Swan* LR 8 at £40.
Cornelius Hodgson of 65 Stanley Street had *Edith* LR 58 insured for £40
John Wilson of 27 Morecambe Street with *Custom House* LR 41 at £40.
James Woodhouse of Main Street with *Reindeer* LR 52 at £40.
Adam Woodhouse of Back Pedder Street with *Nora* at £40.
Edward Woodhouse of Carlton Terrace with *Alice* for £10 (£832).
James Woodhouse of Cheapside with *Anny* at £40 (£3,363) moved house to Euston Road in '96.
Thomas Woodhouse's *Ada*, which was insured for £25 (£1,930).
Those insuring boats in 1896 after the disaster were:
William Brown, who had moved to Clarence Street, with *Rose* at £30 (£2,522).
Robert Gardner of Oxford Street with *Swan* at £40, she was sold to Heswall in 1908.
John Wilson of 27 Morecambe Street with *Custom House* at £32 (£2,690), re-valued from £40.
Adam Woodhouse of Back Pedder Street with *Nora* at £40.
Edward Woodhouse of Carlton Terrace with *Alice* for £10 (£840).
James Woodhouse of 1 Main Street with *Reindeer* at £40.
William Woodhouse of Euston Road who insured two nobbies, *Eve* LR 63 at £30, *Midnight* LR 16 at £32 and the *Me-Me* at £8 (£672.60).

Plate 30. *Tit Bits*. (Courtesy of Lancaster City Museums)

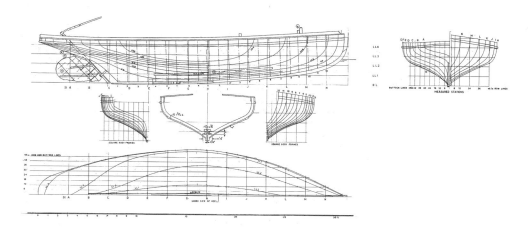

Fig. 46. Lines plan of *Edith Nora*.

Sara Anne was insured in 1895 for £48 (£3,994) by Joseph Parkinson of Townley Street, to be replaced by *Mayflower* at £40 in the same year. *Sarah Ann* was new built by Crossfield Brothers on 14 April 1895.

Henry Mount's son Jack, living at 45 Green Street in 1952, remembered the gale in a report in *The Visitor* of 1952. He was thirteen years old and crewing for his father in *Tit Bits* LR 80, Plate 30, on that night. They abandoned their boat when it hit Pilling Sands, and Jack was carried ashore on his father's back. The nobby was washed further on to Pilling Marsh and survived undamaged. Local farmers dragged her down to Knott End with their horses. *Tit Bits* was delivered from the Top shop of Crossfield Brothers on 17 May 1893.

Jack Mount started fishing full-time in 1891 at ten years of age; he had been out 'once or twice' when about eight. His first trip was on a Saturday at 1.30am, fishing for sprawns off Fleetwood. They landed three apple barrels full. Jack then received 6d (2½p) for a twelve-hour day, six-day week. Jack got his own boat, *King Fisher* at age sixteen. She cost £62 (£4,990). She was built by Crossfield Brothers and registered LR 114 on 8 July 1898, until transferring to Parkgate on 24 January 1910 to be registered by Mr Higgins as CH 28. Because they worked hard in those days, Jack remembered being a big eater. Breakfast was ½lb bacon with an egg, a pint of tea and three or four slices of bread. Cold bacon or beef sustained them afloat, and a big dinner was consumed after the day's work.

During the spring of 1898 the superintendent reported that Morecambe men were doing well at fish trawling, many shrimpers were now trawling for fish. This may imply a change of custom, where the Morecambe men previously specialised exclusively in shrimp, prawn or fish. In the summer of 1899 the Morecambe shrimp and prawn were the best for some years. During 1900 Morecambe trawlers were taking ten- to twelve-score (200-240) of plaice in one haul. Morecambe then had a large fleet of second-class boats (Lancashire and Western Sea Fisheries Committee 1891 et seq.). After the amalgamation of the fisheries districts an assistant bailiff was posted at Morecambe. During the summer of 1901 the Morecambe men were taking starfish and selling them for manure. Morecambe prawners were taking twenty- to thirty-dozen (240-360qt) up to fifty-dozen quarts (600qt) per tide, whilst longlining was not pursued in the summer quarter. During the autumn there was little trawling, most were shrimping, taking 40-100qt per tide. When the weather was good trawlers were taking 20-30lb of sole a day and four-score pounds (80lb) of fluke (plaice and dab). The prawners were taking seven- to ten-dozen quarts (84-120qt) per tide, sometimes thirty- to forty-dozen quarts (360-480qt). There were four new boats at Morecambe with four more on order during the twelve-month. The report for the year's end stated that there were six new boats at Morecambe in the year, and Crossfields were full of work for the district. One of these boats was the *Edith Nora*, registered as LR 129 on Jan 1902. Her lines appear as Fig. 46. She was built with a centre plate, and was said to have been intended for use as a Bay boat in summer and for shrimping in winter. This may have been the reason for her centre plate, as she will have required shoal draft as a Bay boat, and a plate to grip the water when fishing. Bad weather interrupted the fishing; shrimping went well weather permitting with one 100qt taken per tide. 20-40qt per tide was frequent but the boats were only able to work for about half of the time (Lancashire and Western Sea Fisheries Committee 1981 et seq.).

Four Morecambe men attended the Roa Island School in 1902: William Beesley, William Woodhouse, John Johnson, and Edward Gardner. John Bell, 39 Lord Street and James Allan, of 17 Queen's Terrace, served on the Sea Fisheries Committee. Later in the year the second-class trawlers were fishing well: the Lancashire coast yielding six or seven boxes of plaice and dab per tide. Thirty Morecambe shrimpers were trawling for fish. Shrimps were plentiful at the start of the quarter when Morecambe shrimpers took fair catches. During 1903 all boats were hampered by bad weather. Second-class trawlers made the landings of plaice and flounder at Morecambe; boats that were less affected by the weather included those line fishing from Morecambe who took three- to four-score pounds (60-80lb) of one- to four-pound cod per tide.

The Roa Island scholars (Lancashire and Western Sea Fisheries Committee 1891 et seq.) for the years 1903-15 included

James Carter	Clarence Street	James Johnson	Pedder Street
Wilfred Woodhouse	Euston Road	J.G. Gardner	Edward Street
		(Secretary Fisherman's	Association Morecambe)
James Bond	Rose Street	George Bond	Euston Road
William Brown	Lord Street	John Birkett	Green Street
J. Threlfall	J Bell	A. Woodhouse	D Bell
J. Johnson Jnr.	A Wilson	T. Woodhouse	W Wilson
P. Baxter	G Parkinson	R. Gardner	T Gerrard
R. Ellwood	Walter Hadwen	T. Woodhouse	Thos Cocking sen.
Johnson Raby			
John Bell	7 Edward Street	James Parkinson	54 Kensington Rd
George Mount	10 Rose St	Thomas Cocking Jnr.	Green St
Thomas Gerrard	Lancaster Rd	Thomas Bond	Pedder St
Richard Bond	Lord St Morecambe	Richard Curwen	Snatchems
Edward Woodhouse	Cheapside	John Woodhouse C/O A. Woodhouse	West End
Peter Wilson	Beecham Street	Eardley Hadwen	Lamplough Street
J.W. Woodhouse	Samuel Bond		
R Johnson	Bolton-le-Sands	J. Wilson	Bolton-le-Sands
William Taylor	Bolton-le-Sands		
William Stackhouse	Gordon Cottages		Bolton-le-Sands
Frederick Davies	Packet Bridge		Bolton-le-sands
Thomas Ghorst	Nicholas Lane		Bolton-le-Sands
Arthur Townley	Sunderland Point	R. Laytham	Heysham
Walter Mayor	Primrose Street	Wilfred Woodhouse	41 Edward Street
W. Butler Jnr. C/O Robert Butler	6 Thurnham Terrace Glasson Dock	T. Smith	Overton
Richard Braid	Overton	Harry Cowperthwaite	Main Street Flookburgh
John Burrow	Market Street Flookburgh	James Hill	Main Street Flookburgh
James Hill	Flookburgh	John Butler	Flookburgh
William Hodgson	Flookburgh	Thomas Shaw	Flookburgh

The development of the town as a resort continued apace. After some argument about ownership of the land the promenade was extended to Bare in 1897. The work took eighteen months to complete. The district council organised a public meeting on 15 May 1900, where a resolution was passed that resulted in a petition to HM The Queen to apply for a Charter of Incorporation. When this was granted in June 1902, the town celebrated with decorations of bunting and flags, a two-mile procession and an ox roast, concluding with a water carnival. In 1904 Ward's ship breakers took the now redundant harbour on a long lease. This had circumvented plans by Morecambe's council to buy the harbour from the Midland Railway. Shipping movements had ceased when the non-tidal Heysham Harbour was completed. The ship breaking activity was an eyesore that Morecambe attempted to mask by the building of civic amenities. The holidaymakers apparently were not too worried, and enjoyed the opportunity to see over the ships awaiting demolition. Of more relevance to the fishing community were the twin benefits of regular employment as 'jetty fellows' away from fishing, and as a source of materials for boat maintenance and landing-stage construction. The demolition process would have been very labour intensive: their peers also called the workers hammer men, as without oxy-acetylene burning the vessels were dismantled with hammer and cold chisel. Ward's continued at Morecambe until 1931 when a bill from Parliament enabled the sale of the harbour frontage to Morecambe and Heysham council. The agreement with the London, Midland & Scottish Railway included the rebuilding of the Midland Hotel in its present form. The new hotel was erected to seaward of the original building, which was then demolished (Bingham 1990).

Mr James Cooper founded the Morecambe Fishermen's Choir during 1905. In Dick Woodhouse's time there were fifty or more members, who performed all over the north of England and down into Cheshire, their fame spreading so that in 1934 the choir performed a radio broadcast. A sporting event began in 1907, which was to continue until after 1952. After a group of amateurs made the attempt to swim the ten miles from Grange to Morecambe, The Victoria Club of Grange asked Professor Stearne of Manchester to accept challengers for a cross-bay swim. His first swim took place on 13 June 1907, but was a solo event, as he had no competition. A collection was taken on the Promenade from which a quarter was used to finance the Morecambe Bay Swimming Association. Lord Ashton (the Lancaster linoleum magnate) gave £25 (£1,838) to provide a shield to be competed for annually. The second challenge took place on 26 August of the same year (Bingham 1990). Morecambe fishermen supplied the support boats and acted as swim pilots, usually six were required. The article in *The Visitor* of 1952 celebrating Jack Mount's life, records that he was at that time the Inshore Swim President, a member on the Cross Bay Swim committee, and Chief Pilot, and had held the post of Swim Chairman.

The fishing establishment came up against officialdom in 1907 when the older fishing families had their rents increased for the four best stages from £1 p. a. to £5 p. a. (£367.50) and to £3 (£220) for Green Street and £2 (£147) for the Lord Street stage. The old families were criticised for protectionism in that they refused to allow other fishermen access. They were also criticised for treating the promenade and its shelters as their property, using the shelters when they sorted their catch (Bingham 1990). The stageless fishermen rented access to the foreshore from the Midland Railway to resolve the issue of beach access. This allowed them to erect a new stage, named the Harbour Landing.

The Morecambe fishermen seem to have stopped placing orders with John Crossfield by 1908, as the list taken from his workbook shows:

29 Jan 1892	*Princess Annie*	John Woodhouse
17 May 1893	*Tit Bits*	H. Mount
14 April 1895	*Sarah Ann*	J. Parkinson, insured for £48 (£3994
4 Sept 1895	*Red Rose*	R. Wilson, insured for £50 (£4,160)
5 Nov 1895	*Cedar*	John Willacy, insured for £30 (£2,414) in 1899
13 Jan 1896	*Ellen*	Harry Woodhouse, insured for £80 (£6,656) in 1895
1 July 1896	*Eleanor*	Sam Baxter, insured for £50 (£4.025) in 1899
3 Feb 1897	*Lizzy*	Harry Woodhouse
17 March 1897	*May Flower*	Jas Parkinson, insured for £40 (£3,363) in 1896
30 July 1897	*White Rose*	William Brown, insured for £30 (£2415) in 1897
14 Sept 1897	*May*	John Woodhouse
7 Feb 1898	*Snowdrop*	John Woodhouse
12 March 1898	*Albert*	Jas Hadwen
25 April 1898	*May Baxter*	James Baxter, insured for £70 (£4,955) in 1910
25 May 1898	*Kingfisher*	H. Mount
11 Aug 1898	*Olive*	W.M. Brown, insured for £42 (£3,348) in 1898
4 Oct 1898	*Agnes*	Thomas Wilson, insured for £32 (£2,551) in 1898
11 May 1899	*Jane*	Joe Wilson
5 Oct 1899	*Orient*	Richard Woodhouse, insured for £50 (£3,900) in 1900
28 Mar 1900	*Baden Powell*	W.M. Woodhouse, insured for £30 (£2,342) in 1900
13 Sept 1901	*Cormorant*	J. Parkinson, insured for £40 (£3,088) in 1901
30 July 1904	*Three Brothers*	David Willacy, insured for £40 (£2,997) in 1904
22 Oct 1904	*Mabel*	Bert Green
5 Aug 1905	*Red Rose*	R. Wilson, insured for £60 (£4,541) in 1906
1905	*Ann*	Mr Woodhouse
4 Aug 1908	*Clara Mount*	H. Mount

Plate 31. *Red Rose.* (collection of M.P. Evans)

A photo of Robert Wilson's *Red Rose* LR 96 (Plate 31) survives from her time registered as RN 28, from 1908 to 1923. She has the long gaff on her mainsail that caused many of the boats' gaff jaws to wring and strain. Plate 32 records her launch on the beach at Arnside; she sits on the bogy on which she was brought down from the top shop. David Willacy's *Three Brothers* was named for his sons Gilbert, Rueben (second), and Amos (third). She worked her way south with new owners, to be photographed at West Kirby (Plate 57), and finishing up on the Beaumaris register.

A souvenir pamphlet published to commemorate the National Union of Teachers Conference of Easter 1909 held at Morecambe included a study of the fishing industry by Mr Andrew Scott (Hatch 1909). This study records that in 1906 72,676 long tons of mussels were exported from Morecambe, with a value of approximately £6,000 (£454,150). Over 100 men, working a season from September to April, worked in this industry.

The fishermen were encouraged to protect their livelihood by trials that resulted in success in 1903 with the experiment of relaying mussels from overstocked skears to prevent their being smothered by younger mussels from later spat falls. The study also records the classes run by the Lancashire and Western Sea Fisheries Committee at their laboratory at Piel (actually at the old summer residence of the Victorian iron master, Mr Schneider, on Roa Island). The classes took fifteen fishermen, selected by the local associations, and lasted for a fortnight, giving twenty lessons of two hours each. The subjects taught included the life history of economically important fish, chemistry, physics, and oceanography. The fishermen were supported with a grant during their stay at the laboratory.

1909 also saw the widening of the Marine Parade by 20-30ft. All but one of the rails crossing the road to the harbour was lifted and the area received general improvements. The material used in the construction of these promenades was dug out of the high ground of the harbour cattle fields, leaving the levelled ground recently occupied by the amusement park called Frontierland (Bingham 1990). This widening will have caused the rebuilding of the beach accesses used by the fishermen and pleasure boat companies.

A list of pleasure boat company stages, made in Bulmer's directory of 1912, includes:

Calton Landing stage,
Promenade East End,
Fishermen's Association,
Harbour Sailing Co.,
Harbour Landing Stage,

Plate 32. *Red Rose* on her launching trolley. (Courtesy of Lancaster City Museums)

Old Sailing Company,
Clock Tower Landing,
Flagstaff Landing,
Princess Sailing Company,
Victoria Sailing Company,
Morecambe Steamboat Company.

This lists two more stages than appears on the OS map of the time. The Morecambe Steam Boat Co. may have worked from one of the piers, whilst, as Dick Woodhouse states, there were wheeled stages working on the beach at Poulton Ring, just to the west of the Harbour Jetty. Alternatively the Bulmers agent may have listed both the name of the stage and of the company, as the Old Sailing Company used the Clocktower stage, and kept a road roller's living van on the promenade at the clock tower as a company office (photographed by Francis Frith in 1906). The Harbour Sailing Co. probably and the Harbour Landing stage are probably also the same.

Dick Woodhouse (memoirs 1979) listed:

Green Street Landing,
The Clock Tower Stage
The Flagstaff Stage
The Princess Landing
The Victoria Landing
The Harbour Landing
Back o't' Dock, (mussellers with wheeled stages)
The Palace Landing,
Kiln Brow.

Keith Willacy remembers the Lord Street stage as mainly a pleasure boat stage, and Green Street as mainly a fishing stage, these are identified on the copy of the OS map of Morecambe of 1919, Fig. 45. These may have corresponded to the Carlton and Fishermen's Association stages in the 1912 list. Kiln Brow is in front of the town hall, which would refer to the Carlton/Lord Street Stage. The town hall site was originally occupied by Carlton

Villas. The OS of 1890 recorded two further stages, one at Regent Street, which was later replaced by the West End Pier, and one between Regent Street and the battery. Keith Willacy also identified the moorings used by the fleet. The Peck Fleet were shrimpers. Down Gate was mostly used by sprawners, and Up Town were mostly shrimpers with some sprawners. The stages were busy from Easter until mid October during Dick Woodhouse's time (he was describing the period at the start of the First World War) (Woodhouse 1979). He remembers each stage having at least thirty men to sail big Bay boats, mussellers to take out fishing parties, and men with big rowing boats. Top men and Stage men assisted with the customers. Some valued the pleasure boat work, as it was difficult to keep the shellfish fresh in the hot weather, causing wasted labour and loss of income. The seasons work commenced with repair or rebuilding of the stages in the spring. Dick Woodhouse wrote thus:

In those days large amounts of railway sleepers were bought and brought by the mussel ponies and earls on to the promenade. Then long lengths of eight seven or six inch deep two or three inch thick pieces of wood were bought. Depth and thickness was not as important as the price because you could make all do. And when you had a ship breaking you might be lucky. These were the side bits. Next you wanted pieces for head lumps and foot holders. These could be four or six inches deep and one inch thick. Then middle bits, these were three by three because they carried the middle of the top planks that the passengers walked on. Last, top planks, they were ordered the exact width of the stage. Just to come nearly to the edge but not quite so that boats coming alongside did not knock them off.

First in the building of a stage was the digging of the hole for a pair of posts. These were at least six feet long and three feet wide. These holes were set across the hole (sic) and three feet the width. Although the posts were only at the most, eight by six, the most used being railway sleepers, eight inches by three to four, the hole was made to allow for shuddering (caving in).

How-over, all the men came together and work started, the old hands organised all the tools, shovels, hammers, crosscut saws, nail bars, levers, nails and nail-drawers and Uncle Tom Cobleigh and all. Next the wood gang who made the posts ready and wheeled them down to where the shovel gang had been getting their holes ready. Then the gang with shovels, who are worth mentioning, they were mussellers who lived with a shovel in their hand and my word could they use them. They soon went down be it clay, sand or shingle. When they were deep enough the posts were put in, the foot holders nailed across the bottom a head lump nailed across the top. Then they were sighted and the holes filled in. I never saw any modern theodolites or anything like that. All was done by the wrack o't eye and twist oft mouth. That meant just squinting at it. Although the men did not graduate at school with A levels or B levels they knew what a b-y level post was like.

Now […], these men started at the Promenade and built down towards the sea so that all stuff could be wheeled down on a cart as you completed the stage. First the posts, then the side bits, next all the head lumps, ready to nail the middle bits on followed by the planks. Our stage was four hundred yards long, so it took time, labour, money and an awful lot of goodwill at a flat rate of one shilling per hour per man. My Uncle, Walter Bell, who was always in charge told me that it cost ten shillings a foot to put a landing down.

Top boards were set one and a half inches apart. Firstly to allow water to get through. When it could not get through it washed it up. So the boats that were using the stage had to have somewhere to put the grapnel when they came alongside. It was hooked between the planks and over the middle bit. So they had to be strong.

When the museling was finished the mussel doggers were hauled out, scrubbed and painted, and submitted for survey by the local Corporation. Everything was made ready for the official start of the season on the last Sunday in June, which was Bolton Holidays. The working day on the stages commenced at six a.m. The Old Sailing Company enforced this by sending home anyone who was not on the seaward side of the tramlines by six. First away were the fishing parties, in mussel doggers, small bay boats, and the larger rowing punts if required. In all they could have two hundred hand lines fishing by six-fifteen.

They gave two hours fishing, then back for breakfast. They dare not be late because nearly all their wives ran boarding houses. Whilst they were out fishing, the men left were digging bait ready for the next sessions, ten and half past one when they went out again.

At eight or sooner if any one came, hourly sails started and punts were all ready for any one who fancied a row on the bay. At the same time Grange over Sands was being shouted out by the top man and at a given time away to Grange went the fast sailing boats. They had to get back for half past twelve dinner at the boarding house so the length of time ashore was governed by the wind conditions. Morning trips were run but afternoon trips were more popular because trade winds that blew in the bay in those days were so reliable. On other days, Fleetwood was advertised and boats left on the ebb. It was flood tide when they got back as it was always an afternoon trip it was towards seven or eight-o-clock when they got back.

Nearly always, the boats came home all right but, if they were not in sight at a certain time because of being becalmed, the best young rowers, four to a big punt, went to meet them. When they got to them, a towrope was put aboard and the men started to tow the big boat home. As these men would be ready for home there was no need to tell them to wire in and if it was a long tow, as soon as the other men were free they came with more boats. It was always the select boats that ran on this sail. Swift good boats, the pick of the fleet and good reliable men in them. The *Coronation Rose* and the *Princess Royal* were the greatest of rivals on the Grange and Fleetwood runs. My father sailed the *Rose* for the Old Pleasure Boat Company and Uncle Walter Bell skippered the Royal for the Princess Landing Stage.

Dick mentions two memories of relevance to the connection between the boating companies and the boarding houses. Dick reminds us that many fishermen's wives kept boarding houses. This will have been of benefit to Morecambe as a whole, as it helped avoid the hardship of the seasonal nature of the holiday trade. At Blackpool many boarding house ventures failed because of the need to make the year's income during the season, whilst the fishing allowed an income to be generated all through the year at Morecambe. The second memory relates to the rigid adherence to meal times. This was less the tyranny of the 'battle-axe' landlady of the variety theatre comic, than to the holiday makers' desire to adhere to the habits of the rest of the year when meal times were set by the factory hooters.

Walter 'Mad Ike' Bell was a jack of all trades, and according to his nephew Dick Woodhouse (1979) a master of most. He was a single-handed shrimper and a musseler in season as well as Bay boat skipper. Walter also worked as a boat builder. Dick Cockling ran a boat yard near Clarence Street Church, building punts and mussel doggers with a few nobbies including *Seagull*, *Marguerite*, and *Western Queen*. Walter started with him as a young man, and when Dick Cockling died took over the yard. The photograph Plate 32 is of the author's *Nora* being refitted in 1952 by the 85-year-old Walter.

The Bay boats included *Coronation Rose*, *White Heather*, *Shamrock*, *Daffodil*, *Iris*, *Marguerite*, *Princess Royal*. *Coronation Rose* went to Liverpool to fish as LL 168 from 16/9/1918 until 22/11/1943. Her hull is now in the collection of the Lancaster Maritime Museum. She is extremely shoal drafted for a sailing vessel, and still has the remains of her sailing thwart kneed in with both standing and lodging knees. This was used instead of a deck sailing beam due to the wide cockpit arrangement of the Bay boats, that extended forward of the mast.

The following Bay boats were also registered for fishing: Princess *May*, *Victoria*, *Queen Mary*, *Telegram*, *Mauritania*, *Topsy*, *Fram*, *Queen Alexandria*, and *Edith Nora* (later renamed *Day Star*).

Some of the smaller lug-rigged boats had sails sponsored by the chemist John Birkett, who advertised his perfumes 'Am o Dell' and 'Sea Breeze' on them.

Plate 33. Walter
Bell and *Nora*.
(Collection of
Frank Brooks)

A report survives of the 1910 regatta. The nobbies sailed for a Challenge Cup donated that year by Mr Saul Bercott. The course was of three 7-mile laps from the Central Pier to the Reap Skear Buoy, across to a mark boat at Humphrey Head, and back to the start finish line between an anchored passenger steamer and the pier, then round a mark boat off Bare Ayre and back. The smaller nobbies were allowed a time allowance of a minute per foot. The mussel doggers open handicap for boats under 23ft sailed a shortened course. The winning nobby was *Clara Mount*, by 16 minutes, she had returned from fishing at Southport the evening before. *Clara Mount* was built at Conwy in 1908, at 35ft over all, with a mast rising 30ft above the deck. Her bowsprit extended 20ft outboard, which gave a 35ft hoist, and a foot of 23ft to the big jib. Her topsail had a 27½ft yard (called the gaff at Morecambe and Freckleton) with a 15ft leech; 5t of ballast helped her to stand up to her canvas. Mr Harry Mount helmed her, with his son Jack on the foresail and jib sheets. They shipped two others as racing crew. *Clara Mount* was registered as MT 61 on 7/10/1908 until 7/2/1911 when she transferred to LR 29 on 9/2/1911. She then transferred to Liverpool on 12/1/1914.

The report also described other events, the 'Pick a pint of shrimps' contest and a 'Handy Man Race'. This was an event for fishermen to prove who could get under weigh single handed in the smartest manner. Each man started by his punt on its anchor. At the starting gun he had to recover its anchor, scull with one oar over the punt's stern to his nobby, loose and set sail single handed, and cast off, leaving the punt on the mooring to sail round the course. The 1909 regatta programme, one of the surviving programmes in the collection of Lancaster Maritime Museum from the period 1909 to 1922 lists two classes of nobby.

Half-Deck Fishing boat Handicap

Boat	Owner	Location	Handicap	Position
Clara Mount	H. Mount	Morecambe	4m 44s	
Cistus	J. Moss	Fleetwood	Scratch	
Peggy	Jas Baxter	Morecambe	3min	(1st)
Crusader	W. Baxter	Morecambe	6min	(3rd)
Hannah	R. Wright	Fleetwood	3min 22½s	(2nd)

Half-Deck Fishing boat Handicap under 32ft

Ploughboy	J. Jackson	Barrow	2min 50½s	
Maggie	J. Rome	Barrow	1min 3½s	
Rotha	R. Woodhouse	Morecambe	1min 26½s	(3rd)
Ada	J. Gardner	Morecambe	Scratch	(1st)
Three Sisters	T. Cocking	Morecambe	38½s	(2nd)
Syren	John Birkett	Scratched		

J. Jackson was a farmer from North Scale, and a keen yachtsman who commissioned three yachts, including *Ploughboy*, from the Crossfields.

The Handy Man Race was contested by:

Three Brothers	T. Willacy	Morecambe
Tit Bits	H. Gardner	ditto
Young John (2nd)	J.W. Woodhouse	ditto
Teutonic	Thomas Threlfall	ditto
Jennie (1st)	C. Willacy	ditto
Meteor (3rd)	J. Baxter	ditto
Iris	Alf H. Thompson	Barrow

The rules included 'Sealed Ballast. No Jackyard Topsails, Balloon Jibs, or Balloon Foresails allowed, and no booming out. Sounding by lead.' These prohibited shifting 'packing weight' to weather, and shoving the boat along with an oar when sounding the depth of water. In 1910 the contestants were:

Half-Deck Fishing boat Handicap

May Baxter	Jas Baxter	Morecambe	1min 52½s	(1st)
Peggy	C. Schofield	Fleetwood	Scratch	
Clara Mount	H. Mount	Morecambe	2min	(2nd)

Half-Deck Fishing boat Handicap under 32ft

Cricket	John Mount	Morecambe	2min 52½s	(1s)
Three Sisters	T. Cocking	Morecambe	39min ½s	(3rd)
Beatrice	Wm Baxter	Morecambe	1min 22½s	
Ada	J. Gardner	Morecambe	Scratch	(2nd)
Primrose	J.H. McKinnell	Barrow	11min 15s	

The Handy Man Race was contested by:

Maud	John Baxter	Morecambe
May (2nd)	J.T. Woodhouse	ditto
Young John	J.W. Woodhouse	ditto
Jane (1st)	John Mount	ditto

Quick (1964) records that there were 150 nobbies at Morecambe before the First World War, with 500 supporting the industry. Quick also explained the origin of the Upgate and Downgate names of the fleets mentioned on the Morecambe map, Fig. 45. Upgate fishermen lived around Poulton Square and Downgate men lived around Queen Street. The author's 31ft shrimp nobby Nora LR 59 was built for Robert (Rodding) Wilson by William Crossfield in 1912; she was named after his daughter. Next year The Morecambe *Visitor* of 4/6/1913 summarised Dr Travis Jenkins' report as Superintendent of the Lancashire and Western Sea Fisheries District for the quarter ending 31 March. He reported that the Morecambe was profitable with keen demand from the London markets, the Morecambe and Lune mussel fishery had both done very well. The value of wet fish landed at Morecambe during the quarter was 812cwt (41.289 tonne) valued at £322 (£21,778), against 551cwt, £309, (£30,898) in the same quarter of 1912, whilst 22,767cwt (1,157 tonne) of shell fish valued at £2,865 (£193,770) was landed in 1913, an increase over 14,772cwt at £1,654 (£111,865).

The Sea Fisheries committee minutes of 1913 record that bigger and better Morecambe sprawners are being built. They record that shrimps are packed 4st to a margarine box, or 1cwt to a grape barrel. In 1914 a demand for whitebait was developing, being the by-catch riddled out of the sprats taken in shrimp trawls. Due to the perishable nature of whitebait they were marketed in small quantities, but the sprat became a commercial fishery. This prompted the start of stowboating in 1915 in order to meet the demand for fish due to the reduction in deep-water fishing during the war. Morecambe did better in summer than winter at this fishery, taking 20-30st of boxes of sprat in a few hours. The grounds were to the west of Heysham skears, whilst a ground off the Gynn at Blackpool was fished for a brief period (The Lancashire and Western Sea Fisheries Committee 1981 et seq.).

There was a view that in 1915 shrimpers and sprawners begin to evolve to common size. This will have been a slow process as Dick Woodhouse (1979), who started fishing full time at age fourteen in this year, remembered *Blanche* being ordered by his father in 1916. *Blanche* was a 35ft sprawner, at the larger end of the 32-6ft range for Morecambe sprawners, whilst shrimpers were then 28-31ft long. This evolution took until the 1920s to complete its process, and may have been an effect of the loss of the men folk during the Great War reducing the number of third hands. *Blanche* was registered on 19/11/1918 as LR 193 until she ceased fishing on 10/5/1930. When Dick started he remembered that there were 'well over two hundred' men fishing. Another sprawner for which records survive is the 35ft *Nance*, built for Percy Baxter by Crossfields in 1917 and registered LR 181 on 11/4/1918. She was 10ft 4in beam and drew 5ft 4in. Her mast was of black spruce. She cost £125 (£4,832) for hull and spars, and her sails would have cost £20 (£773) from a sail loft. The Lancashire and Western Sea Fisheries Committee (1891 et seq.) reports continue to record the value of the fish caught. In 1915 mackerel were earning £12 (£663) a week for those hand lining for the fish and hawking them, whilst a quarter to two-thirds of its value went to middlemen if the catcher's family could not hawk his own fish. Plaice were fetching three shillings (£8.28) a score during the third quarter of 1915. Plaice continued to fish well into 1916 with fifty-score pounds (1,000lb) weight taken per day off Walney. The mackerel fishers usually worked during the early morning so that they could hawk their catch on the Top (the prom) at about lunchtime (Woodhouse 1979). Although fishing continued apace, the pleasure boats work ceased for the War's duration.

Morecambe played its part in the Great War. In addition to her men volunteering to join up, Morecambe became a barracks town, and also both housed and provided workers for the National Projectile Filling Factory at White Lund. This factory still lives in Morecambe's folk memory because it caught fire and exploded on the night of 1 October 1917. The fire started at 10.00 at night, causing panic in the area, as people sought shelter from the force of the explosions and the debris and shells raining down. Ten people lost their lives, and one section of the site was destroyed. Fortunately the main magazine survived, and even though fires and explosions continued for days, the factory was operating again by Christmas (Bingham 1990). Shrimp prices were quoted in the Lancashire and Western Sea Fisheries Committee (1891 et seq.) reports at six to seven pence per quart rough and one and six to one and seven picked, retailing at four pence a gill rough and two and six to two and seven a quart picked in 1917, spratting was the most productive fishing at Morecambe.

The summer of 1918 saw a hundred quarts of shrimp taken on one tide, fetching 2s 6d a quart, going to 80 to 100qt a tide at 10d rough and 3s picked. A report in the *Visitor* of November 1919 on the resolution of a problem with stake nets gives a snapshot of the trawling industry. The Lancashire and Western Sea Fisheries Committee at Lancaster held an enquiry into the issue. Messrs S. Compton of Preston and J. Formby of Southport conducted this enquiry. The superintendent, Dr J. Travis-Jenkins; the Sea Fisheries Officer, Mr E. Gardner; and the Fishermen's Representative Mr J.G. Gardner were also in attendance.

The issue arose over the interpretation of a new byelaw regulating stake netting. The trawler men were lead by Walter Baxter, who was supported by Harry Mount, James Baxter, Martin Allan, and Mr Cocking, to argue that the stake net men (from Hest Bank, Silverdale, and Bolton-le-Sands) were completely obstructing the channels by setting their nets at low springs, right across the channels. By setting them where they would be completely covered and by leaving them in place they were denying the trawlers access to the fish and putting the pleasure boats at risk. When the stake nets were set and left in place in this way they could not be fished for nineteen days out of the twenty eight, but deprived the trawlers of access to £1,000 (£31,700) worth of fish a month. As nobbies were now costing £300 (£9,510), the trawler men argued that their greater investment and expenses, with their earning capacity justified their demands that the stake nets men did not block the freedom of navigation. Mr J.G. Gardner reported that the channel was blocked all of the way to Grange, with the consequence that 'five or six stake netters were taking the living from about seventy men'. The committee, after considering the issue in camera, ruled that the byelaw must be enforced, and any owner of a stake net remaining in the water was 'liable to be proceeded against for obstruction' (The Lancashire and Western Sea Fisheries Committee 1981 et seq.).

After the Great War problems with marketing fish, especially the higher value shrimp and prawn caused unrest. This was not a new problem as Southport experienced a minor riot in 1913 over the passing off of Dutch imports as 'Southport Shrimps'. The system for marketing the catch at Morecambe was operated by members of the fishing community, called badgers, who purchased the catch and forwarded it to the big city markets. James 'Titeram' Baxter and 'John Tomas' Woodhouse were remembered as dealers. The badgers could wield considerable power, and one was reputed to exercise this power by refusing to purchase the catch from one of his regular fishermen in order to enforce a form of discipline. Other suspected abuses included the issuing of a condemned note, which left the fisherman with no income and a rail freight bill to be paid. The shrimp was inspected for its fitness for sale after transport in non-refrigerated rail vans, but it was suspected that the City dealers would arrange for a condemned note if they had agreed to take more fish than the market could absorb. Titeram Baxter was both a fisherman and badger. His son Harry took over the fish and shrimp shop that he established, but did not follow the fishing (Woodhouse 1979). The return of the deep-sea trawlers to fishing after the war caused the demand for whitebait and sprat to fall right away, so the stowboat gear was given up in 1919. The nets were cut up and used to make fish and shrimp trawls, whilst one arm was cut off of the stowboat anchors to allow their use as mooring anchors.

The Morecambe Trawlers' Co-operative Society Ltd was set up by forty-five members to open for business in October 1920. The directors were Walter Baxter (chairman), David Willacy, Will Baxter Jnr., Martin Allan, Richard Woodhouse, John Mount, Percy Baxter, Richard Mayor, and John and Robert Gardner. The co-operative was set up with £3,000 (£82,000) capital raised by the members from their savings.

The society built premises on Clarence Street, marked on the OS map of Morecambe. This were a single-storey building, with space to receive, weigh and process the catch at one end and a fishmonger's shop at the other. The founders of the society had come together in 1919 but suffered delays due to difficulties with building the Clarence Street shop. The co-operative was able to manage the fishery by placing orders with the members' boats, so that they could better meet the needs of the city buyers. Each crew would catch the shrimp needed for picking, and boil it, and then they would add more salt to the copper so that the subsequent catch could be boiled to be sold rough. The extra salt helped to preserve the shrimp, but made it harder for the pickers to shell. The fish was delivered to Clarence Street and weighed. The secretary, Herbert 'Nibbler' Willacy, recorded the amount caught in a receipt book, and a copy of the receipt was handed to the fisherman. The society employed about thirty wives and girls to pick the shrimp, which was then packed in muslin bags and paper-lined apple barrels ready for the train. Shrimp was also sold locally through the front shop of the depot and shrimp shops in Morecambe. This improved the family life of the members considerably, since before the co-operative the shrimps had to be picked, scalded and packed or potted at home, mostly by the wife, on top of her household duties.

The society also managed the fishery by sharing out the work when demand was slight. The boats working were assigned part orders called 'stints'. Single-handed shrimpers were assigned two stints, and the bigger skipper-and-third-hand sprawners were appointed three stints. The manager of the trawler co-operative had to anticipate the number of boats likely to work when calculating the size of the stint; if he misjudged the numbers too much or too little was caught. It is remembered that on one occasion three days' orders were met on one tide. The society paid out periodically, using the receipt book to calculate each member's credit.

During the first eleven weeks of trading the forty-five founding members of the society achieved sales worth £3,359 (£91,820), generating £95 (£2,597) surplus after the expenses were covered. By the end of the first year the membership had grown to fifty-nine, and by June 1921, when the report in the *Visitor* from which this is culled was written, there were sixty-six members with thirty-one members' boats fishing out of a total of forty nobbies at Morecambe. The industrial unrest of the time caused the fledgling society difficulties, both with the supply of coal for the tallegorams, and in disruption to the railway timetable. The buying power and organisational abilities of the society and its officers enabled them to overcome these problems. The co-op continued to grow, and to support its members by stocking chandlery, which included specialist items like cast-iron boiler pans, and shrimp riddles, and by setting up a net loft to cut and make up trawl nets from bought-in cotton netting. The cotton nets would last about six months, so there was a constant steady demand for new nets.

The social life and attractions for the holiday trippers gradually restarted after the war. *Annie*, Plate 34, won her class at the 1919 Regatta. *Annie* was built in 1914 for Joseph Parkinson of 19 Townley Street, at 33ft 7½in long by 9ft 9½in beam. As with most nobbies she moved from port to port. She was registered as LR 7 from 12/10/1914 until 28/7/1932. She had an auxiliary motor reported to the registrar in 1926. She was registered at Liverpool as LL94 on 30/9/1932 until 17/5/1933. She must have changed hands as she was reregistered by Herbert Jones of 15 Chapel Road, Hoylake (who had bought her on 17 July 1933) as LL94 from 17/5/1933 until 8/11/1949 when she went to Fleetwood. She sold on 26 October 1949 to Harry Ainsworth of Springbank, Wyreside, Knott End, who renamed her *Carl Rosa*, and registered her FD51 from 10/11/1949 until 19/6/1964 when she transferred to Lancaster as LR133 on 17/10/1964 until 30/4/1971 when she transferred to Maryport as *Christine* MT33 on 30/4/1971. Her tonnage dimensions were 32ft by 9ft 8in by 3ft 2in deep registered as 8.77t, later re-registered as 6.49t, Official Number 182476.

1920 saw the cross-bay swims re-start, with up to six a year. The organisers again used the skills of the fishing community to provide the pilot whilst Councillor Walter Townsley loaned his motor yacht as pilot boat. There had been discussion in 1919 about removing the bathing vans, with sea bathing being allowed providing the swimmers changed in a bathing tent or at home. The bathing vans lingered on until 1932 when eight were ceremonially burned, six went to the Lancaster Road School as dressing rooms, and eight were given to unemployed men to use as allotment sheds (Bingham 1990).

There had been a sprat and whitebait industry in the bay documented by the Sea Fisheries' quarterly reports. These record catching rates, methods and how the fish was marketed. In the autumn of 1913 sprats were packed at a rate of 4st (25.4kg) in a margarine box, and 1cwt (50.8kg) in a grape barrel. These fish were sometimes salted. In the spring of 1914 twenty to thirty 4st boxes of sprat were taken in shrimp trawls in a few hours. The following year the price of whitebait had fallen in London in the second quarter so the boats were sprawning. They were spratting in the spring of 1918 and 1919, but the both the catch and the prices were bad in 1919. Enquiries and a public meeting in 1919 established that fishermen (thirty-six men) on the North Wales coast and at

Plate 34. *Annie* LR 7 at
the Morecambe regatta
of 1919. (Courtesy of
Lancaster City Museums)

Morecambe were not in favour of motor trawling, Morecambe had then twenty-five trawl
boats. The sprat fishing failed. In 1921 forty boats were shrimping from Morecambe. In
1920 the fishermen were pleasure-sailing during July, August and September, with trawling
taken up in earnest in October. Shrimp were fetching 4s to 4s 6d a stone, retailing for 5d
a quart. *Florence Baxter* was built for £95 (£2,597) in 1920, and registered as LR 29 on
6/7/1920, to transfer to Fleetwood on 6/1/1937 and be registered as FD 76 on the 15th; she
was known as *Florrie Baxter*. 1924 was also a poor year for sprat and whitebait, with the
stownet failing, whilst some sprat were caught by trawling (The Lancashire and Western
Sea Fisheries Committee 1981 et seq.). Stowboating was mentioned in the quarterly
reports as a sideline in 1935. Dick Woodhouse claims that his father first altered Essex
stownet gear in 1915 to fish from Morecambe, but his description of the resulting net is
from the 1960s (Woodhouse 1979).

A Morecambe institution started as a peace celebration after the war. The victory
celebrations lasted for four days from 20 July, commencing with a 2-mile parade of civic
dignitaries, school children, scouts clubs and societies, and war orphans (Bingham 1990).
This was to develop into the Carnival Parade, with its associated celebrations of ox roasts,
baby shows, Venetian water fetes, country fairs and Highland gatherings. The parade
was supported by the fishermen when the co-operative entered a float in the parade. In
1920 they put a Bay boat on a lorry, and a photograph of 1925 records a mussel dogger
or boarding punt dressed as a steam trawler on a horse drawn lorry. The pleasure boat
companies started up again as peace allowed the holidaymakers to return. With the
availability of reliable marine engines the pleasure boat companies had started using
motorboats by 1922. These proved so popular that the sailing Bay boats were given up,
many being sold away and the remainder being laid up at anchor behind Bare Dub. Plate
35 is from a post card showing both Bay boats and motor launches at the jetty at Grange.
It provides a good view of the outfit of the Bay boats cockpit with its side benches for the
passengers.

The regatta programmes from 1920, 1921 and 1922 included events raced by:

In 1920:

Plate 35. Bay boats at Grange Jetty. (Collection of R. White)

Yachts of 15t and over

Boat	Owner	Location	Handicap	Position
Sue	A. Mansergh	Morecambe	Scratch	(2nd)
Capela	S. Brown	Fleetwood	6min	(1st)
Wallaroo	J. Spur	Blackpool	2min	
Mimosa	N. Worsley	Fleetwood	12min	

The Hallam Challenge Cup, presented by the late R.T.R.W. Hallam Esq.

Deva	H. Baxter	Morecambe	Scratch
Jossett	P. Smith	Morecambe	6min 31¾ sec

Half-Deck Fishing boat Handicap, 33ft and over L.O.A.

Speedwell	R. Croft	Fleetwood	Scratch	
Nance	P. Baxter	Morecambe	8min 15sec	(1st)
Blanche	R. Woodhouse	Morecambe	8min 20½sec	(3rd)
Linda	D. Willacy	Morecambe	46¾sec	(4th)
Fanny	R. Willacy	Morecambe	26¼sec	(2nd)
Annie Bell	M. Worsley	Fleetwood		

Half-Deck Fishing boat Handicap, 27ft to under 33ft L.O.A

Elsada	Jno Woodhouse	Morecambe	Scratch	(1st)
Jane	H. Wilson	Morecambe	18¾sec	(4th)
Seven Sisters	J.T. Woodhouse	Morecambe	33¾sec	(3rd)
Hannah	H. Hodgson	Morecambe	46¾sec	(2nd)
Peggy	Jas Baxter	Morecambe	48¾sec	(5th)

The handyman race, 29ft to 32ft L.O.A.

| *Two Sisters* | Jas Woodhouse | Morecambe | (1st) |
| *Young John* | J.W. Woodhouse | Morecambe | (2nd) |

In 1921 races included:

Half-Deck Fishing boat Handicap, 33ft and over L.O.A.

Nellie Crane	A. Baxter	Barrow	Scratch	
Annie	J. Wilson	Fleetwood	1min	
Thelma	D. Moss	Fleetwood	1min 49sec	(3rd)
Celeste	J.T. Woodhouse	Morecambe	2min 18¾sec	(2nd)
Blanche	R. Woodhouse	Morecambe	6min 11¼sec	(1st)
Connie Baxter	S. Baxter	Morecambe	7min 5½sec	
Alice Allan	M. Allan	Morecambe	7min 7½sec	
Speedwell (LR 31	P. Baxter	Morecambe	8min 39sec	

Half-Deck Fishing boat Handicap, 27ft to under 33ft L.O.A

Spray	J. Baxter	Morecambe	Scratch	
Jane	H. Wilson	Morecambe	1min 15sec	(2nd)
Seven Sisters	J.T. Woodhouse	Morecambe	1min 22½sec	(3rd)
Peggy	Jas Baxter	Morecambe	2min 43sec	(1st)

There was also a race for yachts of 15t or over

Sue	A. Mansergh	Morecambe
Capela	S. Brown	Manchester
Moya	W. Townsley	Morecambe
Mimosa	N. Worsley	Fleetwood

These same yachts competed in 1922, the fishing boats competing were:

Half-Deck Fishing boat Handicap, 33ft and over L.O.A.

Nellie Crane	Jno Hall	Barrow	Scratch
Celeste	J.T. Woodhouse	Morecambe	2min 16¾sec
Alice Allan	M. Allan	Morecambe	7min 5½sec
Peggy	J.W. Gardner	Morecambe	7min 46¾sec

Half-Deck Fishing boat Handicap, 27ft to under 33ft L.O.A

Elsada	Jno Woodhouse	Morecambe	Scratch
Jane	H. Wilson	Morecambe	24¼sec
Seven Sisters	J.T. Woodhouse	Morecambe	31¼sec
Peggy	Jas Baxter	Morecambe	1min 52½sec
Ploughboy	T. Thompson	Barrow	2min 31½sec

There was also a race for the motor launches now used by the pleasure boat companies, boats not to exceed 30ft length. The competitors were *Red Rose*, *White Rose*, and *Moss Rose*. Plate 36 was taken at the 1921 regatta; *Annie* is the lead boat in the photograph. She was built by Anderson's at Millom in 1915. The following nobby is the *Alice Allan*.

Plate 36. *Annie*, FD 108, at a Morecambe regatta. (Courtesy of Lancaster City Museums)

There had been some debate within the Lancashire and Western Sea Fisheries Committee (1891 et seq.) about trawling under power. The Welsh fishermen had requested this in 1914. It was discussed again in 1917, and been allowed in the Western Region since 1919, but their Morecambe colleagues resisted the change until 1925 when trawling under power was allowed throughout the region. The first motors fitted at Morecambe were a Widdop, fitted to *Anne*, as she was finishing off at Crossfields, a Lune Valley Engineering Co. steam engine installed in *Blanche*, and a 4hp Evinrude outboard engine for the Willacy's *Linda* LR 24. Walter Bell fitted an engine in *Volunteer*; Dick Woodhouse claims this to be the first (Woodhouse 1979). *Blanche*'s Lune Valley boiler was fired by a pressurised paraffin burner that had a bad habit of blowing back when being lighted. It is remembered that you could always recognise *Blanche*'s crew by their lack of eyebrows.

The Baxter's had *Star of Hope* LR 39, built in 1925; she was the first to be modelled by Crossfields' at Arnside for a motor. They filled out the hollow in the floors, which increased her carrying capacity as well as making room for the engine. With the reliable power provided by engines, trawling methods evolved at Morecambe, and broadsiding and topsails could be given up. It is remembered that the topsail yards were set up at the end of the fishermen's back yards to support wireless aerials. 1925 saw 62st of plaice taken in one tide off Walney in the summer.

The *Morecambe Visitor* of 24 February 1926 summarised the report of the superintendent to the Lancashire and Western Sea Fisheries Committee. The report was a good one for all aspects of the industry. The Morecambe boats had found good-quality plaice off the Walney grounds in October, the plaice being sold in three sizes, the largest for filleting, and the smallest for hawking locally. The superintendent reported that the Morecambe Trawlers' co-op had refused to accept plaice under 7in length, and were considering raising the limit to 8in. There had been a prolonged frost in November that drove the plaice out into deeper water, but caused fluke (flounder) to move down out of the upper estuaries, so that good catches continued to be made. Shrimping had gone well during the quarter, in spite of the cold November and December, although fewer boats had pursued the shrimp, some boats going to the Solway for herring, others sprawning, and others fishing for plaice longer than usual. The superintendent attributed much of the success to the fitting of motors, reporting that, during the calm weather in the November frosts, sailing nobbies could not work, whilst motor nobbies were returning with 100 to 150qt of shrimp a day. The prawn fishing also received good reports, some of the Morecambe boats returning with 40st (254kg) from the Lune outer grounds. The mussel fishery was increasing, most of the fish going to the east coast to supply the long line fishery, so that little mussel was now sold for human consumption.

The returns for fish were reported to be:

Year	Weight, Shrimp	Value	2005 Value	Wet fish	Shell Fish
1924	16,976cwt (863.2 tome)	£25,447	£986,600	2,739cwt	25,405cwt
1925	15,714cwt (799 tonne)	£20,019	£774,000	3,442cwt	26,777cwt

The same edition of the paper quoted from the report of the sixth annual meeting of the Morecambe Trawlers Co-operative Society:

> The feature of the year has been the increase in motor trawling. During this period fifteen more of the members installed motors in their boats, making a total of nineteen in all. The landings of fish were much heavier than in previous years, this fact being due to the installation of motors.
>
> To instance the increase in weight of fish landed in January, 1925, the Society's boats landed a total of 853 stones of plaice and flounders, while during the week ending January 23rd, 1926 841 stones were landed. The total for the month of January 1926 was 2,500 stones. This increase was also partly accounted for by the failure of the winter prawn fishing.
>
> During the year the Society landed 3,075 cwts. of prawns, a large proportion of which were picked, necessitating the payment of £1,204 (£47,730) for this class of work, an increase of £54 (£2,140) on the year 1924, £468 (£18,553) was paid for railway carriage. Altogether the total sales realised £12,422 (£492,450), an increase of £1,500 (£59,460) on the previous year.

The superintendent, in his report, stated that all of the Morecambe men now landed all of their catches at the co-operative society. The fleet were fishing the grounds off Black Coombe in 1927, motoring three to four hours, and taking 100st of plaice in the three or four hauls that they could make on the grounds before returning home.

The superintendent's report of 1928 referred to another innovation in trawling. The inshore trawlers adopted bobbins from the Fleetwood smacks gear for their sprawn gear. This will have been of great benefit since sprawn is found on rough ground. According to Dick Woodhouse (1979) when he started fishing, shrimp trawls had a plain, thin, chain footrope, and fish trawls used rope, lapped round with junk rope and fastened with staples. As they had abandoned broadsiding when using engines they would have put the shorter bow trawl ashore, then as the trawlers evolved towards common gear, they would have used the same beams and footrope with bobbins, but would have rigged the appropriate net. The method of rigging the trawl with bobbins is set out in the chapter on fishing gear and techniques. The initial supply of bobbins came from the deep-sea trawlers of Fleetwood. The timber yards serving Morecambe soon turned up a supply of bobbins, which were stored in water in iron vats. The fishermen always pushed aside the floating bobbins, and reached down for those that had sunken to the bottom of the vat. The bobbins had to be kept in a waterlogged condition or they would lift from the ground and pass over the fish. Dropping the trawl into shallow water and stirring the bobbins with a booted foot tested their weight. If they lifted, after drying out too much when boarded on the trawl deck, they would have to be taken off of the footrope, and replaced by heavier bobbins from a supply stored under the landing stages below the tide line.

The Maryport herring season failed in 1929, but the Blackpool closed ground yielded 300qt in three hours in early 1930. The Lancashire and Western Sea Fisheries Committee reports thirty-nine nobbies fishing full time in 1930, and mentioned capstans. These will have been fitted as the boats were re-engined, with their motors fitted in the fore bay of the cockpit, or to new boats. *Nora* LR 59's first engine was a two-cylinder 6/7HP Kelvin fitted in the mid-bay, under the thoft. As the motors were moved forward a power take-off from

Plate 37. Powered capstan on *Little Wonder*.
(Courtesy of National Museums Liverpool
[Merseyside Maritime Museum])

the front of the engine could be used to power the capstan. This drove through a gearbox
with a crown and pinion drive controlled by a friction clutch. Plate 37 depicts the capstan
with its foot pedal controlled clutch fitted to the nobby *Little Wonder*.

The annual meeting of the Morecambe Trawlers Co-operative Society Ltd held on 29
Jan 1931, found that 1930 had been the best year of trading. Their total sales valued
£12,000 (£554,000), and £1,380 (£63,725) had been paid in pickers' wages. Of the thirty-
nine boats mentioned by the superintendent's report, thirty belonged to the co-operative,
the remaining nine were independent full-time shrimpers, and there were four part-time
independents. 1931 saw 2,238st of shrimp delivered to the trawler co-operative in July and
1,869st delivered in August.

The Lancashire and Western Sea Fisheries Committee were considering the problem
of poaching by the mid-water boats during 1932. To prepare for byelaws to control this
problem the committee requested the superintendent to report on engine types used by the
inshore fleet. The Morecambe boats were found to be fitted with marine engines of 8-12hp
in 32-4ft nobbies. The reports of the fishing had 40st of fluke landed on occasion during
January and February, with 700qt of shrimp and or prawn landed in one day at the year's
end (The Lancashire and Western Sea Fisheries Committee 1981 et seq.).

Two nobbies were caught up in the drama when the Central Pier took fire on the
afternoon of 31 July 1933 (Bingham 1990). A stiff onshore breeze fanned the flames so
that the pavilion was completely consumed in barely an hour from 5.40pm. The breeze
and its resulting firestorm carried embers to start secondary fires within the town. The
spectators who were attracted to the disaster also witnessed the fishermen's lifeboat put
out fires on two nobbies moored near the pier. 1934 started badly for the trawlers, but
improved as the sprawn returned in the third quarter of the year. About half of the fleet
belonged to the co-operative, and many owners were selling up. In 1935 the nobbies were
trawling off Blackpool, twenty-dozen quarts (240qt) per day were taken off Norbreck in
August. September saw them off the Shell Wharf Buoy, and from October to November
they were taking fourteen- to eighteen-dozen quarts (168-216qt) a tide from Shell Wharf
to Norbreck (The Lancashire and Western Sea Fisheries Committee 1981 et seq.).

The Lancashire and Western Sea Fisheries Committee (1891 et seq.), whose remit was
to foster the inshore fishing industry, maintained several patrol boats. In addition to the
task of enforcing byelaws, these craft were used to find new trawling grounds and remove

the snags. Both were tasks that the working fishermen could not afford to undertake due to the risk to costly gear entailed in such work. The quarterly reports of 1936 record an instance of the Lune grounds being cleared of snags by the committee's boat.

By 1937 the motors were becoming sufficiently powerful and reliable so that the rig was cut down further. Bowsprits were given up and masts were often shortened, as the mainsails were cut shorter in the hoist as though a reef was tied in. The greater engine power allowed the otter trawl to be used for flatfish. This was a great convenience, since the trawl with its boards stowed neatly in a fish box, and could be kept aboard when the shrimp trawl was also shipped. The quarterly reports comment that the Bay boats still have sail, and in a separate report that the pleasure boats were catching on Bernard's Wharf. The Lancashire and Western Sea Fisheries Committee quarterly reports for 1939 record that there were only twenty-nine second-class sailing boats in the entire region, with 303 second-class motor boats. This is effectively the end of the sailing nobby era.

Mention has been made of the different size of the sprawners and the shrimpers. During the closing years of the sailing era a smaller class of nobby was built, at about 23-5ft long and shoal drafted. They were built to a size that the older men could handle alone. The Morecambe nobby's arrangement is described in the chapter on construction, which is based on the Morecambe shrimping nobby *Nora* LR 59. She has been described as a standard 'sawn off by the foot' shrimping nobby. Most Morecambe shrimpers were arranged with a gammon iron to one side of the stem, and with the mooring roller to the other. They had a pair of bowsprit bitts and a mooring post with a hook for the mooring buoy chain. When the bowsprits were taken out stowboating, nobbies often replaced the gammon iron with a second mooring roller. There were always nogs on the foc's'le, and three pairs of fairleads for the jib sheets. The nobbies that went after herring at Maryport fitted a hatch in the foc's'le deck. Most shrimpers had a pin rail in front of the mast, whilst most of the bigger sprawners had pin-rails at the shrouds. Many shrimpers had nogs fitted by the shrouds. The cockpit ballast boards were in one level, at a height to suit the stature of the skipper so that he could use the cleaning deck as a worktable. The ballast boards were laid athwart ship and were divided into three panels. There was a steering step aft, with a hatch for access to a stowage. The cockpit was divided in two by the thwart, which had pins for the headsail sheets. The pump used to be on the centre line, with a trough on the thwart discharging the bilge water through the shear strake. Later boats had the pump to port in the trawl deck. The cleaning or crab deck was to starboard, and was kept clear to facilitate lifting the shrimp with a shovel. The counter had a pair of nogs, a large cleat, and the sheet horse. The nobby's bottoms were originally tarred and black-leaded, and then as antifouling paint became available red or copper appeared. The topsides showed a great variety of colour schemes as colours became available, whilst the decks were either red-leaded or painted tan or pale green.

The Morecambe fleet was busy during the Second World War. The problem of the correct marking of stake nets recurred, and there was debate about mesh sizes for fish trawls, centred around the issue of whether a 6in plaice was marketable. The shrimpers were taking 20qt a tide in the spring of 1946; however, this dropped to only 200qt in total for the entire summer. These were worth 8s (£10.45) a quart picked. 1947 started badly, with only 3cwt (152.5kg) of shrimp worth £9 (£219.56) delivered to the Morecambe Trawlers' Co-operative Society Ltd during the first quarter, and no sprawn at all. This improved through the year, shrimp becoming so prolific that it was reported in the third quarter that one drag of the shrimp trawl 'filled the net to the beam'. The sprawn had returned at the end of the year with 30-50qt being taken in one three quarter hour drag (The Lancashire and Western Sea Fisheries Committee 1981 et seq.). Wartime rationing made potting the shrimps impossible because of the consumption of margarine, ½lb a quart of shrimps. The ban was communicated to the MP Sir Ian Fraser by the Minister of Food Dr Edith Summerskill (Bingham 1990) and was not lifted until 1951.

The author's own *Nora* LR 59 was in the ownership of John 'Shiney' Mount from 1935 until 1951. John worked her, mostly single-handed, until ill health forced her sale on his retirement. *Nora* appears in the Mutual Insurance Co. ledgers, and was remembered by Harry Allan and William 'Young Knocker' Baxter. *Nora* was built for Robert 'Rodding' Wilson by William Crossfield & Sons in 1912 and named after his daughter. Robert insured the 31ft shrimper for £65 (£2,577) in 1926. He also insured his punt for £10 (£396) paying a premium of 19s 7d (£38.80). John Mount insured her for £60 (£2,855) in 1935, keeping her with the Mutual until 1943, when she was insured for £265 (£8,400) for a premium of £13 os 5d (£413).

William Baxter remembered crewing for Shiney on and off for about seven years on Saturdays. The Morecambe trawler co-operative placed fewer orders for shrimp on Saturday because the pickers wanted to finish their work early. Saturday was also 'make and mend' day and no one worked from Morecambe on Sunday. This reduced demand for shrimp freed Young Knocker to crew for Shiney. They made between £1 and £1 10s each for their day's labour (dependant on which period in Shiney's ownership this could have been from £30 to £70). Young Knocker was courting his wife at that time, and remembered that in the half-hour that it took him to wash, dress in his best, and meet the train, the pickers had shelled and packed their catch to put it on the same train. Young Knocker also remembered going on one of the last trips to the Maryport herring. They went in *Star of Hope*, first of all making the boat habitable, by rebuilding the foc's'le bulkhead. Many Morecambe men had friends or relatives at Maryport with whom they could lodge, but they sometimes had to live aboard. They always took a crewman on these trips, even in the smaller shrimpers. The boats that pursued this fishing were also fitted with a skottle (hatch) into the foc's'le so that a look out could be taken with out going through into the cockpit. The only thing of note about the gear was the homemade weights for the foot of the net. They were made from clay gathered from the Red Bank at Carnforth, moulded and carved to shape and baked in the range.

Harry Allan also remembered a trip crewing for Shiney Mount trawling for flukes in Longlight Hole in 1941. Harry had a more vivid memory of *Nora*. They were heading out to go sprawning off Blackpool at 1-2am on a foggy night in 1937 when the Allan's in *Alice Allan* LR 170 and Shiney in *Nora* got in amongst the Fleetwood mid-water fleet just past the NW Buoy off Fleetwood. It is apparent that Shiney decided against motoring through the press of bigger boats and put *Nora*'s helm up to go back. Unfortunately Shiney continued to watch the lights of the Fleetwood boats, rather than *Nora*'s heading and rammed *Alice Allan* in the broadside, cutting her down to the water and smashing the pump. Shiney was known to be a bit deaf, and Nora's engine drowned out the Allan's warning shouts. They kept *Alice Allan* afloat by shifting the trawl and all loose gear over to starboard, and by using rags to plug leaks until they could put her on Bernard's Wharf. The photograph of *Alice Allan* being repaired by Fred Crossfield appears as Plate 38.

The production of courlene netting caused the Morecambe Trawlers Co-operative Society Ltd to close its net loft in 1953. Courlene was so much more durable than cotton net that the need for a net loft ended, and the goodwill was sold to one of the loft's last apprentices, Mr E. Nicholson. Mr Nicholson still had the records of the loft's final year trading; this included a net made for *Nora* LR 59 in 1952, a 17ft shrimp trawl costing £17 10s (£328). The record has the mesh counts for forty-five nets, a complete range of shrimp, sprawn, fluke, and otter trawl, made both full-backed and backless. The loft oiled some nets, only one was roped, and their weight was usually listed. The prices varied from £23 (£430) for a 23ft oiled backless shrimp net, and a 19ft roped backless shrimp net weighing 18lb, to £2 15s (£51.50) for a 6ft backless oiled net weighing 1lb 9oz. The nets were made for customers in Annan, Dalton, Fleetwood, Glasson Dock, Lancaster, Llanerch-y-mor, Sunderland Point for Harold Gardiner, and Widnes, whilst the customers included Mr Aldren, Blowney and Sam Baxter, F. Hudson, Jas Leadbetter, Mr Morley, G. and J. Mount, R. Preston, J. Swain, Mr White, Amos, G.J. and Reuben Willacy, and Ben, Fred, and Dick Woodhouse.

A slow decline in Morecambe's fishing industry was marked in 1956 when the Mutual Insurance Co. folded with only twelve policies. It was about this time that the co-operative changed its name to the Trawler Co. to avoid confusion with the Co-operative Wholesale

Plate 38. *Alice Allan* under repair. (Courtesy of National Museums Liverpool [Merseyside Maritime Museum])

Society. Keith Willacy has made his notes available that record the reintroduction of stowboat gear in Morecambe in 1958, due to links with Young's fish merchants through Judd Willacy. Because of the pollution in the Thames, the manager of Young's Seafood's Ltd at Annan, George 'Judd' Willacy, had a stownet tried in the Solway, using one of Young's boats, but there were too many blebs to make it worthwhile. Judd then asked the manager of the Trawler Co., George Gregory, if anyone at Morecambe would try the gear. The only fisherman who had used the stownet in the First World War who was still fishing was Amos Willacy, who undertook to try the gear in *Linda* LR 24. Young's sent up a set of gear on trial, fishing began in November 1957, though to February 1958, fishing eighty-six tides and averaging 3-4st a day, earning £1 1s a stone (£2.65 a kg). Young's collected all of the whitebait each day from their Flukeborough depot. During the same period the rest of the Morecambe fleet was shrimping off Blackpool, landing approximately 4st a day, if fishing, at 18s a stone (£2.27 a kg). In addition to the higher value of the catch *Linda* out earned the other nobbies, as she only had to steam at most two miles to the mark, and used ten gallons of diesel for the eighty-six tides, whilst the others had to steam for six hours each way, and trawling for six hours, consumed fifteen gallons in one day.

Keith records that the winter of 1958 was wiped out by a hard frost, which drove the fish and shrimp out of the bay; only ten days' fishing produced any earnings. The boats started shrimping in March 1959, and the winter saw Keith and Amos Willacy taking *Linda* to Maryport after sprawn. They were accompanied by Sam and Jack Baxter in *Connie Baxter* LR 22, Ted and Frank Gerrard in *Nance* LR 181, *Edith* LR 32 crewed by Ben and Harry Woodhouse, Harry Allan and Johnston Raby in *Alice Allan* LR 170, and Jack Willacy in *Day Star*. The crews of *Linda, Nance*, and *Alice Allan* lived aboard. When the sprawn season finished in February 1960 the fleet went shrimping off Blackpool. *Linda* took the stowboat gear back aboard, fishing seventy tides between the end of February and mid-April. They averaged 10st a day at £1 1s (£15.83) a stone. They were joined by *Speedwell* LR 27 crewed by Bob Woodhouse and Frank Lee, with gear made by the Trawler Co. for £200 (£3,015), with anchor and chain costing £75 (£1,130), and in January 1961 by *Connie Baxter* and *Nance* using second-hand gear bought from Tollesbury for £200 each, fishing until the season closed in March. The four boats averaged 40st of bait a day.

In order to process the whitebait Young's placed a Jackson plate freezer at the Trawler Co. Young's expressed their thanks to the Willacys for opening up the fishery by giving them the stowboat gear.

The Essex gear proved to be far too heavy for a nobby to work (see a description in Benham 1977). The gear was very soon cut down, substituting 18ft scaffold poles for the 22ft baulks, rope for the winding chain, and by shortening the net from 75-80yd, down to 50-60yd. Although it provided another source of income and came to be used by all of the boats working at Morecambe, the gear was held in such affection that it was called a bogey net. In addition to the stowboaters the whitebait fishery included about fifty to sixty set nets between the Stone Jetty and Scalestones Point, some in the Lune, and a very active fishery in the channels on the north side of the bay. During the 1962/63 whitebait season the Lancashire and Western Sea Fisheries Committee patrol boat, the 65ft John Beardsworth, carried out a trial with mid-water trawl gear, with some success. The gear was offered on loan to any one within the Lancashire & Western Sea Fisheries District. Boats from Morecambe (Dick Woodhouse's *Mascot* LR 1, *Connie Baxter*, and Bob Hodgson's *Ann* LR 63), from Fleetwood, the Ribble, and Liverpool tried it; however, the cost of fuel prevented this gear from being able to compete with the bogey net. Keith Willacy also records that Amos and he tried the fly net for about a fortnight. It proved to be easier to use than the modern middle water trawl, was as efficient a catching engine and used less fuel to tow.

Several members of the Baxter family were involved with the Trawler Co.: Parson Bob and Sam Baxter managed the co-operative, Pop worked in the net loft. Sam worked at the Trawler Co. for almost twenty years after giving up his *Girl Helen*, to retire in 1989 (Bingham 1990). The Trawler Co. also stocked chandlery, rope, and bought sailcloth from the Lancaster cotton mills.

The chandlery included a stock of boiler pans for the Dutch pots or tallegorams. These were cast at a Manchester foundry called Baxter's. As the pans were all of slightly differing diameters the cases were made to fit, and the fisherman had to search the stock for a replacement of the same diameter. This lead to one of the practical jokes remembered by the Morecambe community. The pans had to be replaced when they became thin and at risk of burning through. One of the big boat skippers had an idea for a joke on his crew when he was in the chandlery whilst another skipper was sorting through the pans. He took the old pan and swapped it for his own in the boiler. His crew always complained of cold feet, and had his own way of warming them. The joke came off, with the boats of everyone in the know trawling as close as they dared, when the crewman decided to warm his feet as he was used to doing, by stepping in his Wellingtons into the pan of boiling water. The bottom of the old pan went through leaving him standing on the hot coals in a cloud of sooty steam.

Although the Trawler Co. purchased sailcloth, the fishermen made their own sails, or asked one of the more expert fishermen to do this. Harry Allan remembered James Gardner, Robert Gardner and Walter Bell making sails. Harry used to help his mother after school by treadling the sewing machine as she seamed the cloth for his father (Kennerley 1982). Dick Woodhouse describes his father sail making. First of all the cloth was false seamed, some fishermen relied on their wives for this or they might employ a man called Hodgson. This was necessary to strengthen the cloth, by putting a seam up the middle of what would otherwise be too wide a panel. A professional sail maker would have cut the cloths first as he would have worked shape into the sail by increasing the width of the seams towards the edges of the sail, a process called broad seaming.

The cloth was then cut, Dick's father used the Green Street schoolroom as a sail loft. Dick and his brother were roped in to help, the first task being to set out the shape of the sail with a chalk line on the floor. The cloths were then laid out and cut with a sharp knife. Dick called the cloths breeds. In laying the breeds out allowance was made for shrinkage and for 'seeing'. The breeds were handed over to Dick's mother for seaming, and then his father roped the sail and worked the cringles (Woodhouse 1979). The working sails (main, forestay sail and topsail) were dressed for preservation. Dick remembers using tar, black lead, and boiled oil. Keith Willacy remembers a different recipe. The sail was first dampened with seawater so that it would not take too much tar. It was then brushed over with tar, followed by a coat of boiled oil coloured with some red lead and red ochre. It has been suggested that some men started to use red lead because they obtained the oil by draining it from off the top of red lead paint that had settled out.

Mention has been made of some of the nicknames used at Morecambe. Young Knocker was the youngest of a line of three William Baxters. His grandfather became Old William, and his father Old Knocker. Dick Woodhouse (1979), Eija Kennerley (1982) and R. Bingham (1990) all list nicknames. The three sources, combined into one tabulation as an appendix, list 136 nicknames. Some were simple, like Lile, Gurt, Young or Old linked to a contraction of the Christian name, and others were obscure. A sample of those that can be explained are tabulated here:

Nickname	Family Name	Given Name	Comments
Lile Neb	Allan	Harry	Both lile and neb mean small
Graham Street Dick	Baxter	Richard	From Graham Street. Third hand.
Polly's Dick	Baxter	Richard	Polly's son. Third hand.
Noisy	Baxter	Robert	Bass soloist in the Choir. Third hand.
Parson Bob	Baxter	Robert	A Methodist preacher.
Gentleman Joe	Bell	Joseph	A member of the Liberal Club.
Duckanoo	Brown	William	Always said duckanoo instead of 'W'.
Billy and Tommy	Brown	William	
Tommy and Billy	Brown	Thomas	
Old Rafty	Gardner	Richard	The nickname 'Rafty' was given to a lot of Richards.
See Me	Mount	John	Always prefaced statements with 'See me'.
Ned Russian	Willacy	Edward	'Russian' usually denotes a foul temper.
Seaweed	Willacy	James	Recited a weather rhyme about seaweed.
Jerkem	Wilson	Herbert	Cried 'Jerkem in' when mackerel fishing.
Gurt Hamper	Woodhouse	Arthur	Talked of a 'gurt hamper full' of shrimp.
Christie Jimmy	Woodhouse	James	Worked for Christie.

Third hand referred to the crew of a two-man nobby, called 'Third hand' because he received a third share: one was for the boat, one for the skipper, and one for the crew. In addition to the nicknames to come down to us, there were dialect words used by the fishing community. We have already seen the contraction 'lile' for little and 'gurt' for great, and the word 'breed' for a panel of sailcloth. The word 'tagel', the correct pronunciation for two pulley blocks rove with rope, became an adjective to describe the size of a cod end as a 'good tageling bag'. 'Slape' referred to that state of a sandy bottom, when it was smooth and fluid, so that the ripples usually formed could not be felt through the trawl rope. Scour pits that form around rocks and pilings in sand are called 'bell graves'. Standing waves that build as a fast stream runs over a steep sided submerged bank are called 'gillimers'. When the waves form, move up stream in series before collapsing, so that the waves are always moving but the series of waves is always over the obstruction, they are called 'running gillimers'. The beach was called 't' slutch', which is evocative of the silty mud and sand at Morecambe. In addition to the 'tallegoram', the nobby's gear included a 'whisket', a sixpence ha'penny clothesbasket holding about 18qt, and an enamelled quart pot called a 'mollinger'.

The Morecambe men fished, as we have seen, both within and outside of the bay. Whitebait was taken within the channels of the bay, and shrimp both in the channels and on the sandy bottom off Blackpool. Fish were taken both in the channels and on the mussel beds off Walney and to the north of the bay. The sprawning grounds were more limited as the sprawn was found on rough ground in about 6fm (12m) on the edges of Lune Deeps and off Rossall Point. These marks are illustrated on the scrap chart Fig. 47, using the names for the grounds related by Young Knocker Baxter and Harry Allan.

Dick describes trips after shrimp, sprawn, and flatfish in his memoirs. He remembers the shrimpers being of 25-30ft in length. His favoured ground was The Hollow, whilst Pickles, Heysham Bank and Black Hollow fished with variable results, and Ring Hole was fished if the weather was wild. The selected ground was located by landmarks, and confirmed by sounding with lead line or oar. It will have been chosen on the basis of how well it had been fishing, and whether there was wind enough to allow it to be worked and to get the catch home again. Getting home again was important, as the shrimp had to be prepared in time to meet a train. If they were delayed by a mishap or by failing wind they could work the channels by tide edging. This is the practice of using slack water at the side of a channel to make headway against a contrary tide. With the strong currents running in these channels it was the only way to make headway, if the wind failed entirely the crew were forced to row.

When on the chosen ground the nets were set, and the trawl rope checked to feel for the bottom. If there were no tremors felt the bottom was slape and no shrimp would be found. If all was well the nobby towed away. The shrimper would check the nets regularly, feeling for the tremors that denoted the bottom, feeling the weight on the net to be sure that it was not sanded, and occasionally hauling the bow trawl to see what fish were there. Sanding

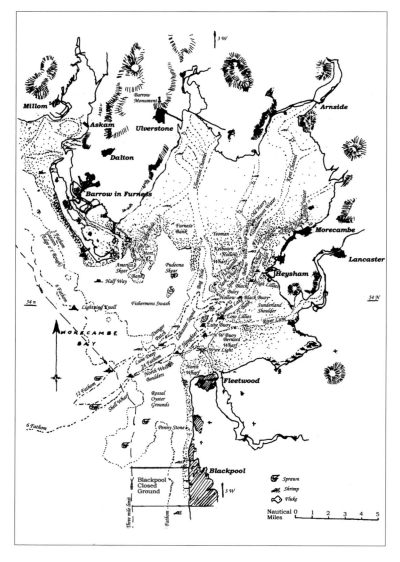

Fig. 47. Morecambe Bay fishing marks.

was caused by weed blocking the meshes and trapping sand, so that the net became so heavy that it could rip out of the beam. If all was well the nets were hauled and the cod ends emptied into a hamper to be sorted and riddled. The number of old pennies, farthings, and ha'pennys that they would pass sized the riddles. The undersize shrimp went back to grow some more. If the catch included large shrimp, called cobs, these could be separated out with a cob riddle for marketing separately, usually as rough shrimp, whilst the smaller ones went for potting. The catch could be taken ashore live in the cool of winter, but had to be boiled aboard in the summer (Woodhouse 1979).

The Dutch pot was prepared by cleaning the pan thoroughly inside and out, and filled with three buckets full of seawater. Then the fire was lit with small coals, and made to draw with a draughter. This was a piece of board hung on the top of the chimney with a bent nail. When the water was boiling the shrimp were poured in, about a dozen quarts (12qt) at a time, and stirred with the lader. As soon as the water came back to the boil the fish were cooked, and were lifted out into a washer in a half butter tub. The lader was made from ¼in iron rod bent into a hoop with a 1ft-long handle, filled with a loose circle of shrimp net. The washer was a sack made from shrimp net. After the shrimp had cooled it was transferred to sacks that could hold between 5 and 6st. Shrimping started in January off Blackpool, but the fishing was a bit hit or miss until the spring rise (woodhouse 1979). Dick Woodhouse told Ms Kennerly that a lot of shrimping was done at night, as the shrimp were more active in the dark, and it also allowed the pickers to be finished in good time for the trains.

Prawning generally started in May and went on through to September (Woodhouse 1979). The day started half an hour before high water, and as with shrimping you needed to choose your ground by taking account of sailing time, train times and the state of the weather. Sprawning gear was heavy, so only one net was fished, broadsiding down the tide with the head sails lowered. The crew had to be constantly on the alert for fasteners, which were common on sprawning grounds. If the net was caught, the nobby had to be swung round head to net. The nobby was then pulled up to the net in the hope of lifting it over the fastener. This was achieved by sheering the boat in the tide by putting the helm over. If the net could not be got free the nobby would be stuck until the tide turned, when the net would come off the way it went on. Another hazard was picking a boulder up in the net, if the footrope went under a rock instead of jumping it. The rock could either wear out the belly of the net, or go down into the tail where it could go through freeing the catch, or mash and break up the catch of sprawn. If the net came free the trawl was paid out again and the drag continued until it was time to haul. Some of the sailing nobbies had hand winches, but as these were slow most used Armstrong's Patent.

When the bridles appeared both crew hauled on the same bridle until it became too heavy. They belayed their gain and went to the other bridle, bringing the net in end after end until the beam was along side. The bow end trawl head was boarded with a fish tackle, when the nobby was still fully rigged the jib halyard was used, but latterly a fish tackle was rigged from the hounds. With the bow end set up a few feet above the deck the two crew could lift the aft end onto the counter. With the bow end lowered on to the deck and the first few bobbins boarded, the fish tackle was hooked into a length of chain shackled to the footrope that was fitted to allow the footrope to be lifted aboard. Then came the net, one man to each side until the tail end came up. If you had a nice haul the fish tackle strop was passed around and it was lifted aboard (Woodhouse 1979).

The sprawning mark in Heysham Lake was from High Lillies in about 8fm (16m), trawling down to Low Lillies in slightly more water (Woodhouse 1979). This was a bad weather mark, which was fished as a last resort or by the smaller boats as it produced mixed bags of sprawn and shrimp, which had to be sorted by hand for the market. It could be fished as it received some shelter from Clarke's Wharf. If you missed your marks you could get in amongst a submerged forest, which filled your net with rotten peaty wood. This was called Moss Wood Hole, and lay inside the hard ground and below the Dummy Buoy, and outside the Lake Skears. The two Lillies buoys were named for a vessel wrecked on Bernard's Wharf in November 1863. In addition to Lillies and Pudiona Skear, Kelburn

Hollow on Yeoman Wharf was named after an iron barque driven ashore there on 27 August 1910.

The Lune Ground shot away in about 9fm, and broadsided down until the Wyre Light was on the Grain Elevator. Next to Lune Ground was The New Ground. This was discovered by Jack Mount and Dan Woodhouse in the *Invincible*. Dick remembers that their first haul contained ten apple barrels of sprawn, with soles, plaice, skate, and lobsters. Unfortunately it was an anchorage for Fleetwood and was foul with wrecks and lost anchors. Dick remembers lifting about one anchor a week when he started out in 1915. The nobbies could manage anchors up to 6cwt, but a steamer from the harbour helped them with the bigger ones.

The Back Side ran from Rossall Oyster Grounds down almost to the North Pier. Dick Woodhouse remembered it as several marks, called Green Hill, Church in t' Street, Big Wheel outside the Tower, Mill in t' Gap, and Below t' Gap. All of this ground was within the 3fm line, and could be as shallow as 2fm. It could be very productive ground, but with a high risk of fasteners, all of the marks were beam breakers. This ground fished well with easterly winds, as you could trawl down southerly and up northerly, and you always had sea room to make long tacks as you sailed home on the flood. It could get very rough on these grounds as the bottom shallowed in any winds from the south round to the north (Woodhouse 1979).

Danger patch and North Side were sprawning grounds along the north edge of the Lune Deeps. The sprawning ground was along the twelve to twenty fathom lines. As the breast of the Lune Deep was steep sided the track was quite narrow, but the length was 'terrific' (Woodhouse 1979). If you missed the fasteners a drag could last three hours on the ebb. Because the mark was so long a fleet of nobbies could be strung out one behind the other, so one fastener could snag two boats' sets of gear, then both had to wait for slack water to recover the trawls, and lose a tide's fishing. If you did free your net from a fastener in deep water, you had to recover all 300ft of rope until you could see the beam to ensure that when the beam went back to the bottom it was the correct way up. The bobbins would destroy the net if the trawl dragged on its back. Because the track was so narrow you could easily move off into too shallow water, and catch nothing, or fall off of the breast into 40fm. Then came the labour of lifting 5cwt (250kg) of gear by hand (Woodhouse 1979).

Dick described a trip down the North Side, sailing down to the ground on a west wind and 'going like lilty'. Shooting away past the big Lune Buoy, and broadsiding with the bow pointing inshore as the west wind would then help you to keep your track. The third hand was sounding with the lead, looking for 15-20fm (pronounced 'faddom' by Dick). After about two hours you would have reached a shallower bank in about 12fm, and it was time to haul. If the wind was right the skipper could sail the nobby to the trawl, so the third hand had only to coil down the slack as it came aboard. With good fortune one drag would suffice, with a girt tageling bag of prawns with a few soles and maybe five or six lobster. Then 'set thi foresail, that'll do us' and away home whilst the third hand boiled the prawn and cleaned the fish. The prawns were boiled at about 12qt a time in brine made with rock salt. The prawns were boiled in washers, and then cooled in seawater. It was important to get this done quickly: the prawns should be boiled before they died, and they then needed to be cooled quickly and got out of the sun to keep them cool (Woodhouse 1979).

As the sprawner approached the moorings, the catch was bought up on deck. The prawns were washed with cold seawater and covered with oilskins to keep the sun off. Then you stowed the headsails, the fore sail was lashed to the bowsprit heel, and the jib rolled up and stowed below. The topsail was rolled, and if fine left on deck for the next day, or if doubtful put below, the heel went into the foc's'le as far as it would go, and the peak put under the side deck (Woodhouse 1979). With the mooring picked up and the mainsail stowed, the catch was put in the bow of the punt, taken ashore, salted, barrelled up and away for the train. The punts that were used to tend the nobbies at Morecambe were outwardly a standard rowing stern punt, with one difference. The main thwart was heavily built, fitted with a clamp on the riser, so that it would be strong enough to withstand the thump of a fisherman jumping from the nobby in a seaway. The punts were also ceiled up to the thwart riser to help to keep them clean, and used thole pins instead of oarlocks.

Dick also described trawling for fish at the Piel Fishing. This was a summer job; from July through August, many turned to this because they lost too much shrimp or sprawn to spoiling in the hot weather. The boiler and sprawning gear was put ashore and the fluke trawls shipped. The fleet set off at the first of the ebb, sailing round to the mussel beds of Mort Bank and America skear. These grounds fished well because the mussel spat attracted the fish. You could get several drags on ordinary tides, but the feed ebbed out on springs, so you had to hurry a drag, and then anchor until the flood covered the ground again. An armed lead was kept handy to help ensure that you were on the grounds. With luck a sprawner's gear could take twenty-score (400) of prime plaice in one drag, they were only ½-1lb weight but very rich from feeding on the small mussel. If the weather turned bad they sometimes anchored at Barrow-in-Furness, some staying with friends at that port, and selling to a Barrow-in-Furness dealer at the Deep Water Berth. Dick referred to the Top, Middle Low and Vectra feed. Another mark called Tom Tutch is near Walney Lighthouse. Dick took Shiney Mount to Long Light Hole (Back o' t' Lights) trawling for 2-3lb flounders. Flats were also taken in the river channels in the Bay. Dick's uncle Old Wilt and his son in *Spray* took 120st of prime plaice (760kg) from the top of the bay (Woodhouse 1979).

Some of the Morecambe men went hand netting for shrimp, walking down to Half Moon Bay under Heysham with a push net. This is very hard work, as the shrimp had to be carried back on foot, before being boiled, picked, and packed for sale. The design of the Morecambe power net used a withy bow of about 18in to 2ft high, which stood upright when the net was fished, so that the staff came out through the back of the net. The net was pushed from the belly.

Unfortunately the decline in Morecambe's fishing industry continued, no new nobbies had been built since the late 1930s. Storms destroyed the boats as they parted their moorings and drove onto the stones of the landings and promenade. There were still good years, 30,000cwt of shrimp was exported in 1968, valued at £100,000 (Bingham 1990) (£1,167,500). When Dick Woodhouse was setting down his memories in the 1970s there were only two boats working full time, and by the end of the 1990s the Trawler Co. had closed. Only one nobby, *Maud Raby*, and a glass reinforced plastic copy of the *Sir William Priestley*, remained at Morecambe.

Chapter 8

Annan

This history of Annan is recorded from the memories of Annan fishermen who remember the end of the sailing era, from 1918 through the 1920s. The earlier history is compiled from written sources.

In 1814 Richard Ayton visited Annan in preparation for *A Voyage Round Great Britain*. Ayton gives a detailed description of the town of Annan, then of 1,800 inhabitants, its buildings, amenities, and trade. Ayton also reported on the fishing industries, that of salmon being worth £2,500 (£125,000), for a rent of £900 (£45,110) per annum, the fish selling for an average of 1*d* a lb (£0.46 a kg). This was prosecuted using traps, similar to hedge baulks, made entirely out of net, and laid out to fish on both the flood and ebb, and by a three-pronged fish spear on a 20-24ft shaft. A few miles west of Annan on the river Lochar, Ayton found a hamlet of twelve cottages called Powhellin, whose inhabitants made a living from both sea and land, boiling sea salt and shrimping, as well as farm work in season, and again at Caresthorn below the mouth of the Nith, Ayton observed shrimpers on the sands (Ayton R. & Daniell W. 1814). There is a farm called Powhillon on the north shore of the mouth of Lochar Water.

The context of boat building at Annan is established in a note in *Mariners Mirror* (1951). This recorded fast Annan-built schooners and their builders. After the yard closed in 1865 two of the yard's employees went on to build boats for the longshore community. Mr Rabbie McCubbin, who was stated to be the yard's boat builder, continued to build

Plate 39. The silver presentation model. (Dumfries Museums, Nithsdale District Council)

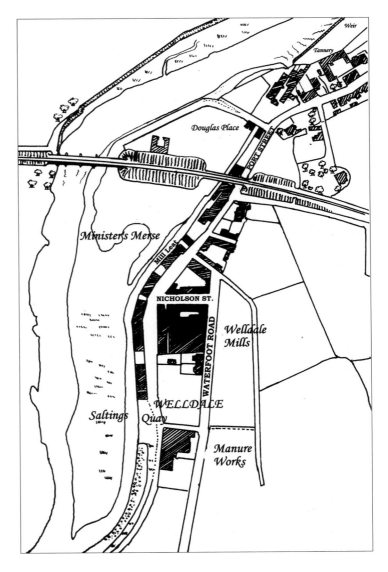

Plate 40. Annan-built
motor nobby.

Fig. 48. Welldale,
Annan, map. (Ordnance
Survey of 1896)

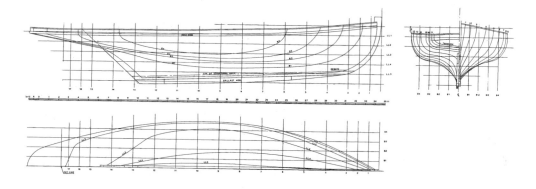

Fig. 49. *Samantha's* lines.

small craft. Mr William Wilson set up the business that became Wilson & Son, building
fishing and utility boats and at least one yacht. The *Dumfries & Galloway Saturday
Standard* described Mr James McCubbin as 'late boat builder' of Waterfoot in a report of
24 April 1897, which stated that he had produced the accurate model of a trawl boat as a
prototype for a silver model, presented to MP Sir Robert Reid. The model is of a '31 feet
Solway trawl boat in full sail, to a half-inch scale. It measures from the stern to the end of
bowsprits 22½ inches, and from the keel to the higher point of top-sail yard 25 inches." It
was 'Clyde-built' to the order of Mr John H. Wilkinson, silversmith, Annan. Two views of
the model appear as the Frontispiece and as Plate 39.

Shaw and Nielson were both reported as 'boat builders, since deceased', in
correspondence of 1932 preserved in the Science Museum, with the intelligence that Mr
Wilson's son was building at Waterfoot at that time. Mr Thomas Willacy remembers
that his grandfather Mr William Wilson was building from about 1885 until about
1920, records show that he built the centreboard yawl *Sentinel* to a Mylne design in
1900. His yard moved from a site south of the manure works behind Welldale Quay
to the old shipyard site between the manure works and Welldale Mills just before he
ceased trading. The quay had been extended southwards over the end of the shipyards
slipway. Mr Thomas Willacy also remembers Mr Ben McCubbin operating a yard near
Douglas Place off Port Street below the weir. William Wilson's son Willy built *Gypsy
Queen* there in 1939. The boats launched at Welldale Quay were brought to the south
end of the quay on rollers, bilged over and without a cradle. They were taken past the
end of the quay and allowed to roll down the steep grass bank into the top of the tide
as a fast endwise-dynamic launch. All of these sites are illustrated on the scrap plan of
Annan, Fig. 48. Thomas Willacy can remember five Annan built boats up until 1920.
Many boats were also ordered from Arnside, and if of suitable form, bought second
hand during this time. John Crossfield recorded three boats in 1892, *Lily* for J.T.
Willacy, *Barbara* for John Baxter, and *Agnes Helen* for Richard Lupton, then *Agnes* for
J. Rae in 1898.

As discussed above and in the first chapter, correspondence has been preserved in the
Science Museum's collection. This describes the first Annan boats as half-decked cutters,
clinker built with a square stern. Unfortunately we know of neither drawing nor model
of these Annan boats, although we can assume that the Morecambe boats drawn by
Holdsworth in the 1870s were still representative of the type.

The Science Museum model of 1880 is either of a large boat, at 39ft, or a 26-footer.
These lengths are derived from a length 19½in of the model and an assumed scale of ½in
or ¾in to 1ft. She has the straight floors, long straight keel, and straight stem of the early
form, drawing either 4ft 6in or 3ft. She has a short, squarish elliptical counter running up
to the deck. Her draft, fullness and freeboard imply the smaller shrimping form.

The later model of Annan boat, called trawl boats, were built with a straight or only slightly rockered, raked keel. They did not carry rocker right aft so that there would be no kick under the sternpost. The use of rocker under the stern would mean that they would screw about on the beach as the tide rose, which was known to be unsafe. The drag meant that they lay on the beach bow down, and would lift about the heel of the stern, and give them about 4ft 6in draft. The deep round in the forefoot of *Samantha's* lines, Fig. 49, was fairly common in Annan boats, and may have been a result of the straight keel, but was not universal, as Mr George Willacy's *Anita* BA 442 had the high cut away forefoot, typical of the southern nobbies. She was an Arnside-built boat of 1904, registered LR 1 in 1904, and sold to Girvan in 1908.

Annan-built boats cost £50 (£1,367) to build when sailing, and about £80 (£2,187) fully equipped. Engines were fitted as conversions in 1920, with the shaft put through the port quarter. *Anita* was the first with a Brit petrol/paraffin motor. After engines came in no sailing nobbies were built at Annan, although the older fishermen retained the sailing rig in the converted boats. *Gypsy Queen* was built for Bob Wilson by his brother Willy in 1939, of full if conventional nobby form but with a centre line shaft, whilst Tom Willacy built *Ivy Willacy* in 1950 with the same shallow nobby model and low freeboard but with a broad shallow MFV canoe stern and a foc's'le raised by one streak. There is an Annan-built motor nobby lying derelict at Harrington, Plate 40. She has a conventional nobby stern with the shear strake running round the counter above the moulding, above a centre line propeller aperture. She is of full form and very strongly built forward. The breast hook is notched around the first cant and buts the second. Her ledge covers the second cant and extends aft to the thirteenth frame; she has a thwart at the eighteenth frame, whilst her main stern forms the twenty-seventh frame. Her forward nog is let into the inside face of the ledge at the fourth frame.

Study of the silver presentation model establishes the form and outfit of the boats at the close of the nineteenth century, whilst Mr T. Willacy described the boats of the 1920s. Sailing trawl boats were almost identical to Morecambe boats in construction and outfit. They had the doubled sawn frame construction of the southern boats, with close-butted futtocks, unlike the more common Scottish method of single futtocks with clamps. The Annan boats were not fitted with cast iron keelsons, but did fit ½t ballast keels cast by Pratchetts of Carlisle. The model, whose photographs are published as the frontispiece and as Plate 39, reveals that the 1897 form has a nicely curved forefoot and a slightly square-ended round counter. The deck fittings hark back to the North Lonsdale square tuck-sterned boats discussed in Chapter 1. There is no mooring post, and the bowsprit heel is housed in a transverse chock. The outside coaming is interrupted by and butts against the forward nogs, whilst it moves nearer to the deck edge further aft. The stern nogs are fitted abreast the aft end of the cockpit, called the hold at Annan, which places them further forward than on *Nora*. They have horizontal pins fitted for belaying ropes.

The deck fittings on the later boats had more in common with the boats from the rest of the range. They had a thwart across the hold about 9in below the deck. The silver model has a deck beam crossing the hold, with the discharge from the centre line pump built against its foreside, discharging through the shear strake. Hold ends were rounded on de-luxe boats and square on the economy models, with carlings supported on pillars from the thwart. The presentation model, and some later boats used the sailing beam as a pin rail for the halyards, as was also the case elsewhere (see *Eva* FD 184, Glasson built in 1895). The topsail and oars were stowed under the side deck as at Morecambe, but the anchor was kept handy in the hold, and the half bulkhead that formed the after half of the topsail stowage rack was sometimes fitted on both sides. There were parting boards running for'd and aft to separate the stowage's from the hold floor area. The foc's'le had pipe cots, and a stove bought from the Carlisle iron founders, and as the model shows a sliding hatch on the foredeck.

The most unexpected feature of the model is the bowsprit rigging, with a bobstay and shrouds spread by whiskers from the stem head. The whiskers are modelled with eyes on their inboard ends, passed through horizontal eyes formed in the end of the mooring roller axle and on the gammon iron. These may have been the modellers attempt to represent portable fittings. The bowsprit shrouds passed through holes in the coaming to deadeyes whose lanyards went through eyebolts about 18in for'd of the mast beam. If the whiskers were portable they may represent the fishermen's love of a regatta. The bowsprit shrouds and bobstay could then be rigged for racing, but as they would be in the way when broadsiding they could then be unshipped.

The masthead and gaff rigging is also worthy of note. The shrouds have soft eyes seized in, bearing on the hounds mast band. The upper mast band is fitted below the topsail sheave and accepts the jib and upper peak halyard blocks. There is a single eye mast band for the lower peak halyard block, and the double mast band that forms the hounds carries the forestay and throat halyard block. The standing end of the peak halyard is spliced into an eyebolt on the gaff, whilst the span is a strop, clove hitched round the gaff at both ends, led up through a bull's-eye on the halyard block. There is no room for pins in the beam that replaces the thwart, so the head sail sheets were belayed to cleats outside the coaming, whilst a cleat is visible inside aft, possibly for the springer. In 1932 all but two of the boats had all rope rigging.

The details not visible in the photos include the layout of the hold, and the halyards. There was no slide in the foc's'le bulkhead, so the only access to the foc's'le was through the hatch on the foredeck. The ballast boards were in three levels. The fore bay, from the mast to the pump, was at about the same level as at Morecambe, but laid for and aft. They had a lifting ring by the pump and two ceiling planks forming a margin on the face of the frames. Between the pump and the steering step the ballast boards were laid athwartships, about 6-9in below those in the fore bay. The steering step sloped up about 3in as it ran aft, its planks running for'd and aft. Sketch Fig. 50 illustrates this.

The running rigging belayed to the pins in the sailing beam are as follows. To port is an eyebolt for the topsail halyard whip, next inboard is the peak halyard. The jib whip goes to an eyebolt in front of the coaming. Next inboard is the throat and then the fore staysail halyards. To starboard of the mast gate is the jib standing part, and the topsail downhaul whip. The model maker did not include a topping lift. A rope through the boom end, to be belayed to the reef tackle cleat, secured the mainsail clew. This rope (laid up from two fine silver wires) has parted allowing the boom to drop. Other details include a deck light in the foredeck alongside the bowsprit, eyebolt fairleads for the headsail sheets, and the mainsheet horse right aft on the end of the counter, just inside the coaming. There is no turning block on the counter, so the sheet goes directly from the block on the boom to belay to a stern nog. Plate 41, published as

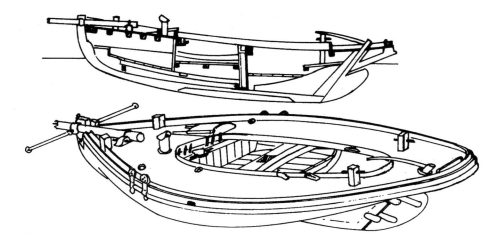

Fig. 50. Sketch of Annan model.

Plate 41. A nobby at Annan.

a post card, was taken where the Mill Leat rejoins the Annan and has a nobby moored in the foreground. She has her trawl stowed on the starboard deck, and her topsail rolled around its yard lying in the port deck. The foc's'le hatch is visible to starboard; this and the topsail stowed on the side deck confirms the full bulkhead between the foc's'le and hold. There is a sculling notch in a chock on the counter's outer coaming. The foc's'le stovepipe is visible to port; the jib halyard is stowed by being hooked into a strop, and the rather high transverse chock for the bowsprit heel can be seen on the foredeck. A brig is moored in the middle ground, waiting for the tide to lift her, and the masts of a second brig can be seen further up river.

The trawl boats were nearly all 30-2ft, or 35ft on deck, and were used for shrimping, trawling for flats and cod, and for herring drifting. They also trawled for skate off Maryport, and occasionally dredged for mussels with oyster dredges. Warrington Smythe, in *Mast and Sail in Europe and Asia*, wrote of winter fish trawling, with two crew, and spring and summer shrimp and prawn fishing alone or with a boy crew. When the boats had a crew of two, they worked a three-share system. There is some evidence of fish dealers. The 13th Decennial Census of Scotland of 1921 reported twenty fish and poultry retailers at Annan. The same census recorded seventy-five fishermen working. An Annan historian, Mr J. Thomson, reported memories of William Anderson who operated from about 1890 until 1939, buying from the trawlers and haff net men, packing the fish into ice boxes and carrying the fish to the station for dispatch to the markets with a horse drawn lorry, often making two trips a day. Another dealer named McGlasson also ran a fishmonger's shop in Annan High Street. There was not a large organisation of buyers until Young's bought into a business set up by George 'Judd' Willacy, who came from Morecambe, and there was no co-operative, hence there was no stint system in times of glut.

Holdsworth (1874), gives a brief mention of 'shrimping and trawling for flounder, with a little inshore line fishing for codling' in the Solway. Both the Cumberland and the Lancashire Sea Fisheries records mention Annan fishermen. In January of 1892 seventeen boats from both Morecambe and Annan went to the Mersey after herring (Lancashire and Western Sea Fisheries Committee 1891 et seq.). In 1898 the Annan men were in trouble with the Cumberland bailiffs, with the result that they submitted petition requesting a change to the byelaws or their enforcement to allow the bunching of the tail of the shrimp trawl as was allowed in Morecambe Bay (Cumberland Sea Fisheries Committee 1889 et seq.). The petition was drawn up by a lawyer's office and had the following names appended, all fishermen of Annan:

George Bryson	Richard Woodhouse Sr.	John James Rae	Joseph Bryson
James Hunter	Christopher Baxter	John Rae	Martin Ewan
John Woodhouse	William Rule	Robert Beattie	William Ewan
Andrew Nicholson	George Hadden	John Baxter	James Ewan
Thomas Willacy	J.J. Woodman	William Woodhouse	Edward Rae
Richard Houghton	John Irving	James Irving	John Robinson
James Woodhouse	Hugh Woodman	George Nicholson	William Edgar
Richard Woodhouse	James Irving	William Woodhouse	Thomas Wilson
Joseph Woodman	William Nicholson	Thomas Woodman	Thomas Rae
Jacob Robinson	Andrew Rae	William Beattie	Richard Lupton
Daniel Baxter	James Baxter	George Willacy	John Mirnor
Matthew Irving	James Rae	Thomas Woodman	George Gordon
William Baxter	John Rae	William Woodman	Joseph Lupton
William Baxter	John Woodhouse	James Woodhouse	William Raby
John Woodman	Thomas Houghton	George Irving	Thomas L. Willacy
James Johnson	John Irving	Matthew Irving (Sen)	John Wilson
Dick Woodhouse	Crichton Woodhouse	James Anderson	
Joseph Woodman	William Woodhouse	Edward Rae	
Joseph Woodman Jnr.	Thos Woodhouse	James Irving	

In 1899 the Cumberland bailiff prosecuted James Irving and his son James of Annan for using an illegal trawl. The inspector bought prosecutions against James Johnson, James Anderson, John Robinson and Thomas Rae of Annan, amongst others, for taking berried lobsters in 1900. The railway at Annan exported 162t 19cwt of flounder at £1,955 (£152,660) and 200t 11cwt of shrimp at £4055 11s 4d (£316,693) in the same year. In 1902 eighty boats were shrimping and prawning from Maryport to the Solway Viaduct, some twenty miles. They were broadsiding with two trawls of 18-19ft with a chain footrope. Aflalo (1904) when interviewing the Maryport fishermen in 1904, recorded that brown shrimp was trawled from the Solway lightship to the Viaduct. By the 1920s the shrimping grounds were in the Southerness, Dumfries, Blackshaw, and Powfoot Channels on the north side, and occasional drags in the Silloth Channel on the south side, see Fig. 51. There are older newspaper references to Annan men trawling as far west as Luce Bay.

The trawling methods remembered by Mr Tom Willacy differed from Morecambe practice. Both trawl ropes were belayed to the bowsprit heel and passed round and to forward of the forward nogs when broadsiding. The forward trawl springer was belayed to a pin in the thwart, and the aft went to the stern nog. The aft trawl beam was about 18ft long, to stow from the shrouds to the counter, made from two or three pieces of ash. Both sails and nets were made at home, the nets being braided during the winter.

The nets were made both full backed and backless, with pockets and a flapper as appropriate, being dressed with boiled oil and red lead. As they were shrimpers, and not sprawners, they used chain footropes with out bobbins. Their sails were dressed black, including the jibs, and the hulls followed the same sorts of colour schemes as at Morecambe. Local blacksmiths made all the ironwork for the boat and fishing gear.

There were about thirty to forty boats at Annan, at about 1920, and about a dozen at Silloth where some Annan families had settled. Silloth Dock was built in 1861 as an out port for Carlisle and a sea bathing resort. The Annan men would have moved there to take advantage of the shrimp grounds near Allonby Bay, and the prawning grounds further south. Holdsworth who, in 1874, lists eighteen second-class boats registered at Carlisle and ninety-three at Dumfries provides an earlier record. Some of the Carlisle boats would have fished from Silloth, and the Dumfries boats would also have worked from Kirkcudbright, leaving perhaps fifty boats belonging to Annan. Most Annan boats at the end of the sailing era were registered at Ballantrae.

The moorings were in the mouth of the river on the west side, an area called the Harbour. As the moorings were sheltered the crews could use conventional punts, and did

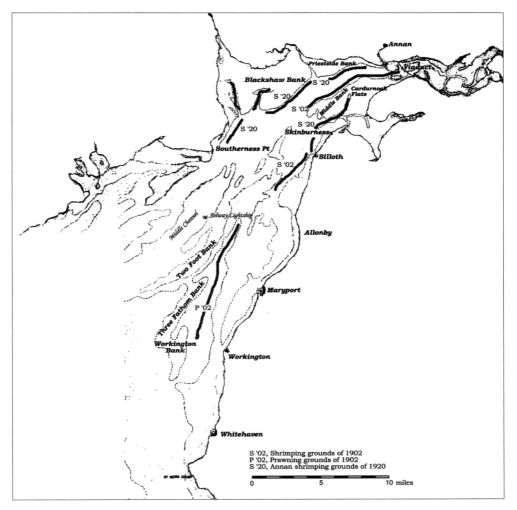

Fig. 51. Scrap chart of the Solway.

not ever need to jump onto a thwart as at the exposed Morecambe moorings. A few of the fishermen had huts near the moorings, on top of the old eastern sea wall, to store their gear. There were racks erected on the bank between the sea wall and the river channel on the east bank for drying the drift and whammel nets. The tidal stream running into the river mouth was so strong that the trawl boats would anchor off, until the run slackened. This is why the anchor was always stowed handy in the hold.

About half of the Annan community lived 'Back o' t' Hill' (Kenizels on the map Fig. 52) in the 1920s, and half in Annan itself. The community of about forty-five families included the Houghtons and the Ewanses, the Baxters, Holmeses, Willacys, Woodhouses, Woodmans, the Nicholsons, Irvings, the Raes and the Mariners. There seems to have been less need for nicknames, perhaps because there were eleven family names amongst forty-five families, although some are remembered. Their use has largely died out today, although 'Professor' or 'Pro.' Ewans is remembered, as was 'Wonk' and 'Lecky' (Jimmy) Nicholson, and 'Judd' Willacy. The Professor's by-name was recalled in a conversation about work wear. Pro. always wore clogs, and never managed to launch his punt dry shod, so he always started his working day drying his socks on the nobby's cabin stove. The community, although compact, found about half of their marriage partners amongst themselves. The formation of the Annan Waterfoot Fisherman's Association, who commissioned the presentation

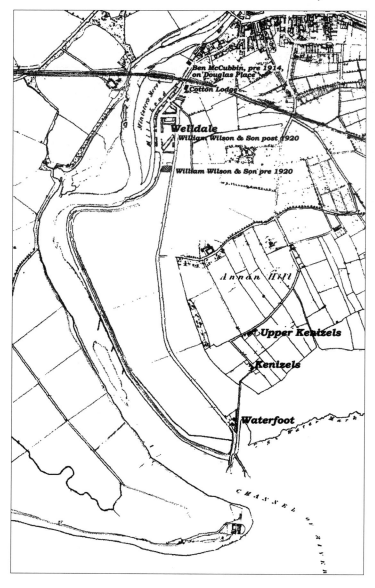

Fig. 52. Map of Annan and Keniziels. (Ordnance Survey 1896)

model for their MP, indicates that this was a cohesive community. The association ran a benevolent fund, paying out if a member could not work in case of accident or illness, in addition to lobbying in the interest of the industry.

There was a ready sense of fun: practical jokes were played, and the fishermen enjoyed testing their boats in regattas, the last of which was held in 1921. When regattas were in their heyday the boats were all of about 32ft, so that they could race on equal footing. The fishermen often played a game of quoits, using iron rings, on the ground behind the boat stores at the Harbour after the day's work. Bowls was popular in their leisure time. Because the pattern of work followed the tides round, most fishermen were moderate drinkers, enjoying a bottle of stout or a pint at the weeks end. The community worked the same week as their Morecambe forebears: Saturday was make and mend day, and Sunday the day of rest and social discourse. The men would don their Sunday clothes and meet at the Harbour for a gossip, and would then walk back into town. Unlike Morecambe, there was not a fishermen's choir, nor a teetotal movement as at Southport. Annan was never a seaside resort, so the fishing community will not have supplemented their income by running lodging houses as at Morecambe.

The Annan fishermen felt under threat due to the attentions of several Royal Commissions that enquired into the Scottish fishing industry. This apprehension was felt both for the conflict of interest between the salmon fishermen at sea and inland, and due to the confusion caused by the use of the term 'trawling' for pair seining for herring, which the Loch Fyne community wanted banned. The Annan fishermen were ably represented by their MP Sir Robert Reid, in recognition of which the silver model was presented.

In making the presentation to Sir Robert at a public meeting reported by the *Dumfries and Galloway Saturday Standard*, which took place on Wednesday, 21 April 1897, several leading members of the fishing industry spoke. Amongst the speakers, John Holmes (one of the first to come from Morecambe) recounted the ups and downs of the fishing community. The first six years of their existence were peaceful, but from then there were conflicts about their right to fish, possibly exacerbated by misunderstandings about the fishing techniques employed. There was an enquiry set up in 1862 into fishing on the Solway shores, followed by a royal commission in about 1871, both of which went badly for the Annan men. This was followed by an abortive Scottish Salmon Bill, which was resisted all over Scotland. Sir Robert attended the Annan demonstration against this bill, held in the Port Street Hall, having travelled from London for the meeting. Then came two attempts to enact a herring bill, the first of which would have prevented trawling within the three-mile limit, this would have prevented all but the whammel boats from fishing at Annan. This then was the act desired by the drift net fishermen of the Lock Fyne area to prevent seine pair 'trawling'. At the second attempt to enact this bill Sir Robert was again able to advise the Annan community, with a successful outcome. Mr George Bryson, also an active fisherman, referred to Sir Robert's efforts and his successes in inserting a clause exempting the Solway from the provisions of the bill. Then came the royal commission of 1896 that caused the Annan fishermen to wish to show their appreciation of the dedication and interest in their cause shown by Sir Robert, reflected in their commissioning of the model.

Chapter 9

Ulverston, Barrow-in-Furness and the Duddon

Ulverston has always had a fishing community; however, as Ulverston is so far up the sand, it has mainly pursued a stake net fishery and carried out cart shanking for shrimp. Several of the families have kept nobbies, which are called prawners at Ulverston. Dick Woodhouse remembers about five, there would have been nine at most, which would have had moorings at the edge of the channel at Canal Foot (Plate 42). There has long been a need for an oversands guide, as the sands provided the only link from Low Furness to Lancaster before the turnpike roads, and indeed by using the routes over the Duddon sands northward linking Lancaster to the Cumberland coastal routes. As at Grange-over-Sands the guide at Ulverston has always been appointed from the fishing community. The Ulverston families following the fishing were Benson, Burrow, Butler, Gardiner, and Tallon. Bill Bird fished the *Topsy* (registered LR 179 between 1917 and 1937) from there. Peter Butler had *Hearts of Oak* built by Dan McLester to be launched in June 1912. She has a fairly full bow, external cast iron ballast and was built with a centre plate. The gear fished from Ulverston was fairly standard, as they were shrimp and fluke trawlers they did not use bobbins, but used chain footropes.

Ulverston is mentioned in the Doomsday Book, the 'ton' ending placing it as a settlement created by the Anglian tribe that came to Furness in the early seventh century. It was of secondary importance to Dalton until the plague started a movement of trade in the seventeenth century. Ulverston developed into a market and industrial town with water-powered corn and textile mills, a brewery, and a tannery. There was coastal shipping from Greenodd at the head of the bay, carrying raw material for iron and copper smelting. Greenodd became the busiest port in Low Furness from 1781 until Ulverston canal was dug in the period 1793-6. Greenodd's shipyards continued until after 1868 when the railway crossed the estuary. Ulverston had four shipyards, the canal, coal, and ore wharves, and it exported local products including gunpowder, iron products, and copper.

This trade was taken by Barrow-in-Furness, the transfer being speeded by silting in the channel from Ulverston to the open sea, and by the railway, which threw a bridge over

Plate 42. Nobbies at Canal Foot. (Collection of D. Hughes)

the canal denying sailing vessels access to the canal head, and taking the iron ore trade to transport by rail rather than round the coast to the Welsh valleys.

William Fisher, who farmed in Barrow-in-Furness, kept a diary in part as a logbook of the farm's production and the climate, but also to record his family's activities and local curiosities culled from gossip and the local news journals. This diary, published with a commentary (Rollinson & Harrison 1986) provides much of the story of early Barrow. In 1780 Barrow-in-Furness was a hamlet of five farmhouses. Four years later an iron ore-loading quay was built, followed in 1790 by a wooden jetty. By 1801 it had grown to eleven dwellings with sixty-five inhabitants (Rollinson & Harrison 1986). After a further four years two inns were open, and the village was both a resort for medicinal sea bathing and a port exporting iron ore, oats, malt, and barley (from West's *Antiquities of Furness* quoted by Rollinson & Harrison [1986]). By 1822 there were twenty houses, with blacksmith, butcher, and shoemaker in residence. 1833, 1839, and 1842 each saw a new ore-loading pier built (Rollinson & Harrison 1986).

In 1846 the Furness Railway linked Kirby slate and Dalton ore to Barrow-in-Furness. The railway signalled the start of the development of this small farming hamlet into a port and industrial town. The status of the channel and its sheltered anchorage was originally as a 'creek under the Port of Lancaster', it would have been a haven of refuge as well as serving the south-western end of Furness for centuries. The castle, the Piel of Fowdrey, was used as a warehouse for sea-borne trade more than as a defensive fortification by its builder, the Abbot of Furness Abbey. Samuel Pepys had started to set up a dockyard to build a Third Rate of 937t in 1668, but relations with Holland were improved, removing the need for the warship. In the eighteenth-century Rampside was a bigger community than Barrow-in-Furness, with two inns and a ropewalk, several pilots and customs officers with a King's Boat. In 1814 Ayton visited Rampside and Barrow-in-Furness in preparation of *A Voyage Round Great Britain* (Ayton & Daniell 1814). They were able to hire a boat at Rampside, 'a humble bathing place', to carry them over to Piel and Walney. They next stopped at an inn at Barrow, and commented on the ore boats which were trading to Hull, Chepstow, Neath, and Cardiff.

Greenodd and Ulverston overshadowed Barrow, until a combination of silt and the railways moved maritime trade into Barrow. Ashburner launched the *Jane Roper* into Barrow Channel in 1852, and the first iron furnace was lit in 1859 (Rollinson & Harrison 1986). From this point on Barrow's development as a heavy industrial town took off at an incredible pace.

William Fisher's diary (Rollinson & Harrison 1986) does include some cryptic references to fishing. In 1838, William recorded 'Man belonging to a fishing boat drowned at Piel of Fouldry' unfortunately without recording to which port the boat belonged. In July 1843 a fisherman rescued Captain Rimmer of *Fanny* (carrying slate) landed at Piel, this could have been a Rampside man with a rowing punt. In October 1850 Fisher noted that 'Samuel Todd, a fisherman from Dalton, on Duddon sands shot a ships carpenter in an affray'. One cannot imagine what a Dalton fisherman was doing with a gun on Duddon sands unless he was wildfowling, but for our purposes this establishes that there were fishermen of some sort in Low Furness.

There is little tradition for fishing for a living from Barrow, one commentator, W.E. Roberts, Esq., stating that the Barrow villagers had access to a communal draw net of 150yd for an autumn fishery during the period from 1830 to 1850 (Potter 1994). There exists an engraving of a view of Piel with fishermen in the foreground, Plate 43. They have been shrimping with power nets, and are using leaps to carry their catch. There are rowing punts drawn up on the beach, and small sailing craft are in view. There are some references to fishing along the shore of Lonsdale North of the Sands in the minutes and reports of the Lancashire and Western Sea Fisheries District. The representatives on the committee of 1893 included John Edmondson, of Roosbeck Aldingham, and Thomas Tweedale, Over Sands Guide, of Ulverston. The minutes of May 1894 examined the Rooscote fishery. There were four fishermen who also farmed, using set nets on the skears. These were set on sites known as stalls identified by permanent stakes. There were many more stalls than

Plate 43. Power netters at Foulney, off Rampside, Piel in the background.

set nets in use at any one time, there was concern that the stalls were so close together that fish might not be able to pass between the nets. The set nets were of two arms, one long at about 100yd, and one short with a pocket at the 'V' (The Lancashire and Western Sea Fisheries Committee 1981 et seq.). Davies (1958) refers to these as Poke Nets.

The superintendent reported in 1902 that a fisherman at Barrow had a new boat built. Fishermen from Baicliff (sic), W. Wilson, and S. Mott of Bardsea, attended the Roa Island school in 1905 and 1906, they will have been set netters and cart shankers studying the biology of the fish and shrimp. William Wilson of Baycliff followed his namesake in 1911.

As the town grew, and the island of Walney became one of the town's dormitories, there was a need for ferrymen, the docks required pilots and boatmen, and many of the workers kept a boat for part time or pastime fishing. There have always been nobbies moored in Walney Channel, either used as a cheap yacht or for a bit of part-time trawling. Older Barrovians remember nobbies being purchased from Morecambe, to be refitted using materials available in the shipyard and iron works, only to be sold on again after a few years. At the time of writing there are no longer any nobbies fishing from Barrow-in-Furness. The Nobby named *De Wet* LR 131 from 1902 to 1936, rebuilt as the yacht *Quest*, was here until 2001, and three smaller nobbies, one a ferry by Stoba, one a ferry or small Bay boat, and all outfitted as yachts many years ago, are on moorings in Walney Channel.

On the north coast of the Furness peninsular is the Duddon estuary, which is the only English sea loch or fjord, and is home to two small fishing havens. Askam is on the Furness side, a little too far up the sand to be a convenient trawling station, but with a small fishing community. Askam is a Victorian new town, laid out in the shadow of the iron works that opened in 1865. The slag from the blast furnace was tipped towards the shore, so that part of the slag bank formed a loading pier. A small drying harbour formed in the lee of this pier, used by the small fishing community. Askam was primarily an iron town, and as it was located next to, and practically joined with, the farming community of Ireleth, most of its townsfolk looked inland for their employment. Our contact, Jim Allonby, spent five years in farm service before buying his first boat, and was also employed setting charges and blasting in the local quarries.

Those that did look to the sea for income pursued a very mixed fishery, and as Askam is on the shore of a relatively shallow estuary, with only one main channel, they favoured smaller craft. Only one nobby was kept at Askam at any one time. *Hannah Hambleton* was fished by the Proctors; *Ptarmigan* BW III, a very narrow and shallow nobby, fished from Askam; and Aleck Mellon of Haverigg sold *Hearts of Oak* to an Askam man. The more usual trawl boat at Askam was a converted mussel dogger, a 20ft clinker punt, transom sterned, decked over and cutter rigged. They were used for the winter shrimp fishery with

Plate 44. Nobbies in Haverigg Pool.

a 16ft beam trawl, working the sand from Askam round to Roanhead, and then onto a ground called Hardacker, and grounds just outside of the Duddon Bar.

In addition to the Proctors, the fishing families included Alexander, who fished the *Lunesdale*, a mussel boat from Overton, and worked a salmon drawnet; and the Constables, who were mainly stake netting, supplemented by draw netting with a little boating. J.G. Constable of Askam attended the Roa Island School in 1906. Most people set trotlines, called longlines locally, on the beaches and in the pier hole.

On the north side of the Duddon the village of Haverigg had a community of nobby fishermen. Haverigg and Holborn Hill were originally farming communities that are now thought of as being parts of Millom. Their development is a parallel to Askam and Ireleth, the town of Millom being created when iron ore was found at Hodbarrow and an iron works set up to smelt it. Haverigg, at about 1850 between the arrival of the railway and the opening of the Hodbarrow mines, was a hamlet of about half-a-dozen homes on a lane running down to the mouth of a creek called Haverigg Pool. Plate 44 illustrates two nobbies in Haverigg Pool at the top of a big tide, one is registered at Barrow as BW 63. As Millom and the iron industry developed, piers were built to export the ore and the finished iron at Berwick Rails and Crab Marsh Point. These attracted chandlers and a shipbuilder, which lead to the establishment of Anderson's boat building yard behind Hodbarrow Pier on Crab Marsh. This family, who are discussed in the later chapter on builders, produced nineteen nobbies, mostly of the 35 or 36ft size preferred by Fleetwood men, some of whom who settled at Haverigg and bought nobbies from Anderson's. It is said that some of the Fleetwood families moved many of their goods and chattels in their nobbies from Fleetwood when they settled at Haverigg.

This founding community is said to have favoured the bigger boats because they followed the offshore cod fishery, and did not trawl for shrimp in the Duddon. More recently they have pursued a mixed fishery, shrimp trawling, cockling and draw netting for salmon. Davis (1958) recorded a fluke trawl on a 12ft beam, braided from cotton. The families at Haverigg that are associated with fishing now include Mellon, Taylor, and Davies, Bonny John Davies came from Morecambe, his sons were Sam and George. Allan and Billy Davies followed their father Sam into the fishing. Jonty Proctor of Askam married Sam's widow. George 'Brab' Davies fished the *Mispha* that was the only nobby at Millom when he was fishing. The Iron Works transferred *Hearts of Oak* to Millom from Ulverston, acting as a rescue boat for the airfield at Haverigg during the Second World War. She was then powered by a single-cylinder, hot bulb engine.

Chapter 10

The Isle of Man and the Cumberland Coast

The Isle of Man was not a major trawling centre, being most famous for their herring industry. This was first pursued in cutter-rigged, double-ended craft with the round stern that was also to be seen on the flats and coasting schooners of the Lancashire coast. These cutters evolved into the 'dandy', to be replaced by the 'nicky' and the Manx nobby.

The next most important fishery was a longline fishery. This started out in baulk yawls, double-ended, open, clench-built boats with a clear Viking ancestry, which after 1850 were built with transom sterns. Then came the half-decked boats of 1880-90, these 'line boats' were counter-sterned, cutter-rigged half-deckers. The shape of those built at the turn of the century being of a similar form to the Lancashire nobby, worked out in nearly 50ft on deck and a good 5ft draught. Later boats had a cabin over the front half of the cockpit. The local paper referred to these craft as 'yachts' and 'half-deckers' when reporting their launching ceremonies.

Two of this fleet serve to illustrate the type: *Master Frank* of 1895, and *Gien Mie* of 1913.

Gien Mie, which means 'Goodwill', 'Good Humour', or 'Good Mood', was built at Piel by Neakle and Waterson for J.&C. Cowell, James being skipper with 22 shares. Charles and William Henry had 21 shares each. Her register number was 67864, coming in at 13 82/100t gross, 5 90/100t nett. This was calculated from the register dimensions measured as length from fore side of stem to aft side of rudder – 41ft 5/10, beam to out side of plank – 12ft 7½/10, depth from deck to ceiling – 5ft 4½/10. The report of her launch, on 9 January 1913 gives her length at 47ft overall and a 13ft beam. She was first registered as PL 83 on 1 February 1913.

She had a moderately raked sternpost, and had deep draught at about 7ft. Her keel was well raked, running up to a shallow curved forefoot and straight stem. Her deep draught allowed well-hollowed garboards. She was built with an elm keel, oak stems, frames, main beam, and knees, and pitch pine for everything else including the aft deadwoods. She had an iron ballast keel. The frames from the mast to the fashion timbers were all double, those forward were single and double, whilst there were two pairs of cants, and knightheads supporting the apron. The counter was framed out with cants and a pitch-pine horn timber. Her hull planking seems to have been conventional, with a sand streak, and a thick shear streak to form a rubbing bend. There was a stealer in her tuck in the run.

The deck beams were supported on a clamp and were tied in with lodging knees. The deck was laid with a king plank and a nibbed covering board. The rail on *Gien Mie* was a plank on edge, and she had the line-boat wide rectangular cockpit. This finished further forward on line boats than on the trawl boats, ending nearer the handle of the tiller than its mid-length as on trawl boats. She was fitted with timberheads forward and just aft of the cockpit, and had a scuttle just behind the Samson post.

It is apparent that she was built with provision for a centre line propeller, and was re-registered on 8 June 1914 after a 13hp two-cylinder Kelvin engine was fitted in October of 1913. It is said that she was at the Kinsale fishing when the *Lusitania* was sunk, and helped in the rescue of survivors. She was sold to John Wright Dixon of Whitehaven who registered ownership on 11 January 1929. He worked her until her registry was closed on 8 December 1937. Her new owner intended to take her to Montreal, Canada, but only got as far as Peel, were she began her life. After a couple of years Dave Helm of Fleetwood bought her. He sold her on to C. Scott, who was unlucky enough to have her go onto King Scar after engine failure on 16 December 1957. Up until 1937 she was registered as PL 83, and from 1954 as FD 5.

During the 1960s she was owned by Arthur 'Arty' Swales. Charles Swales bought her on 1 March 1967 for £300 (£3,590), her bill of sale described her as an auxiliary motor boat with a 50 BHP installation. 'Ginger' John McDonough also owned her in the 1970s. Next came R. Bradshaw of Birkenhead who bought her as a bare hull and fished her on the Mersey. She was then bought back to Fleetwood by W. Dix. The last owners to fish her with success were K.P. Brown and his son Simon who worked her from June 1983 until the end of the 1980s. As the registered length was unchanged until after 1967, it is probable that she had not then replaced her original rudder with its propeller aperture with her last installation that had an upright stocked rudder hung on a skeg. *Gien Mie* was broken up on 11 July 1996 at Fleetwood after being damaged following a knock from a larger vessel on 29 or 30 June. As she was dismantled it was discovered that her deadwoods were doweled together to enable the bearding to be carved in one go before the bolts were bored and driven.

Master Frank of 1895 was the third of about nine line boats built by Clucas & Duggan who worked alongside the Ramsey boat yard, in a field next to Marsden Terrace. The first of the series was the 28ft *Maggie* of 1893 and the second the 32ft *Britannia*. *Master Frank* is 38ft long, 10ft 6in beam, and 5ft 6in draft, and is heavily built for her size. *Master Frank's* counter was framed out big boat-style with the cants radiating from the sternpost and filled in with timber chocks. She was planked with pitch pine on the bottom and larch topsides, over horse chestnut frames. The rudder case was stave built. She had 1in thick bulwarks on separate stanchions, and unusually for a cutter a skottle to allow the mast to lower. This may have been to allow her to pursue drifting for herring. Her form is very hollow in the bottom and bow, with a raking sternpost, slightly rockered 18cwt ballast keel beneath a straight elm keel and rebate, and rounded forefoot. Her counter is squarish, similar to but longer than the Annan trawl boat of 1880.

Master Frank was named after the son of Frank Shankley of Whitehaven who had her built, he only kept for about a year when she returned to the Isle of Man to be worked by Joe Kinnin. She had a crew of four until she was fitted with a Kelvin 7/9 in 1914. The Kinnin family worked her through to 1976 longlining for cod and skate, with occasional trawling for flatfish. She was registered as WA 63 from 15/2/1895 until 24/8/1899 when her registry transferred to become RY 95.

Although both boats were built for line fishing and have different deck layouts and broader counters than Lancashire nobbies, their profile and beam-to-length ratio is very similar. This may have been an example of parallel evolution, with the builders drawing from yacht hull-form developments, since the other fishing boat traditions and the method of fishing pursued on Man were both so different. However, the Lancashire nobby 'bloodline' and the Manx fishery will have met at the Maryport herring fishing and mainland nobbies were purchased by Manx fishermen, so there may have been cross-fertilisation as well.

Of the nobbies that did fish from Man, we know that *Wild Cherry*, a 33ft 10in nobby was registered at Ramsey from 1910 to 1918. *Five Brothers* was registered DO 22 from 1915 to 1926, and *Laura* was at Douglas from 1923 to 1927. Others included *Campainia*, *Comrades*, The Rivers Class *Esk*, *Lady Elanora*, *Naiad* (built as a yacht at Armour's) PL 57, *Two Brothers*, and *Useful*.

Davies (1958) records backless fluke trawls at both Whitehaven and Workington. He records that the Whitehaven net was rigged to a 50ft beam, which can only have been fished from a deep-water ketch, and states that the Workington net was small without giving a length to the beam. The taste for big smacks that could work a 50ft beam may explain why *Gien Mie* was sold to Whitehaven, and Frank Shankley commissioned *Master Frank*, both being large Manx line boats. These Cumbrian ports exist due to the presence of the Cumbrian coalfield. Coal was mined in the sixteenth century along the valley of the Pow Beck at Whitehaven, and carried by packhorse to Whitehaven cove from which it was trans-shipped.

The land-owning families of the early seventeenth century industrialised the mining industry, and laid out the ports of Whitehaven, Workington, and Maryport. Scott-Hindson's history of Whitehaven harbour (see Bibliography) records that the new town was laid out alongside a fishing village that belonged to the priory of St Bees. The harbour began with a quay at the head of the cove in 1634, and was extended through the 1870s and beyond. The need for strong ships to carry coal, initially to Ireland, allowed Whitehaven ship owners to trade with the American colonies. They could do this, as their ships were strong enough to sail to America, lay afloat as warehouses in the river estuaries until they had traded their cargoes for tobacco and sugar, and then return without spoiling their vulnerable cargoes. There is a reference from the 1790s that establishes the continuing presence of fishing craft at Whitehaven, when compensation of 10s 6d (£28.45) was awarded to John Dixon for the loss of his boat, which was crushed by a ballast hopper. A photograph in Scott-Hindson's history established that the fishing fleet used the corner between the north side of the Old or Sugar Tongue and the West Strand. The photograph includes two nobbies, ketch-rigged smacks, two steamers and two topsail schooners.

On 5 June 1813 the *Lancaster Gazette* reported that:

> Saturday last, a fine new smack, intended for the coast fishery (about 30 tons burthen) was launched at Whitehaven, called the "Caesar", and built by Mr. Cowan. – A very awful occurrence took place on this occasion: – Mr. Richard Power, of the Rams – Head public house, Chapel Street, who named her, had no sooner thrown the bottle at her, than he dropped down and expired!

Richard Ayton visited several ports and havens on the Cumberland coast in 1814 in preparation of *A Voyage Round Great Britain*. Ravenglass was found to be 'a dirty, ragged, forlorn looking town" whose inhabitants eked out a living from fishing and farm work. Ayton made no mention of fishing craft, actually bewailing the lack of a ferryboat, rather than recording the existence of boats. Further north Ayton came to St Bees and Whitehaven; his account claims an ancient record that names St Bees Head 'Preston Isle', and the discovery of a large anchor in the floor of the valley that runs between Whitehaven bay and the town of St Bees. It is of note that the chart of the northeast coasts of the Irish Sea, prepared by Collins in 1689 indicates a large estuary of the River Ehen reaching into Egremont. Ayton recorded that 204 vessels belonged to Whitehaven in 1814, with sixty-two trading to the West Indies, America, the Baltic and other British ports in general trade, whilst the rest were colliers, of a total of 15,122t burthen. Progressing north Ayton came to Parton, where he observed a fleet of herring boats at anchor, waiting out a calm. Next came Harrington, a coal port home to sixty-four vessels of 7,388t, six of which were in the foreign trade. Ayton recorded that Workington had 200 vessels of 27,899t, and that Maryport had 143, of which twenty-one bearing 4,125t traded to foreign ports, but did not work out of Maryport (Ayton & Daniell 1814).

Ayton was interested in the antiquities to be seen on his voyage, and also wrote at length on the new technologies. He was not concerned with fishing unless it was an important or novel aspect of the social history. Ayton's sponsor and co-traveller, William Daniell, illustrated the *Voyage* with excellent aquatints; all of his sea views are populated with accurately observed cargo vessels of which most were cutters.

Blake (1955), refers to a grant made to Holm Cultram by Thomas de Multon of the fisheries of the Solway, in addition to 'both sea and sand fishing' at the mouth of the Wampool, these included the right 'to have and to hold a fishing boat with pertinents at the mouth of the Alne', the name Alne evolved to become the Ellen. The new town of Maryport was laid out by the Stenhouse family alongside the fishing village of Ellenfoot, beginning in 1749. The port was created on the authority of a Parliamentry bill, and built between 1854 and 1857, to allow the export of coal and iron products. The docks were under-utilised, the later Stenhouse Dock of 1888 being little used from the outset, as Workington's development took its trade. This allowed the fishing industry to continue and grow at Maryport. Workington's development paralleled that of Whitehaven, but Whitehaven was always the larger.

The fishing fleets reflected this in the returns of 1872. The three ports fleets were as follows (Holdsworth 1874).

Port	1st Class	2nd Class	3rd Class
Maryport	4	48	2
Workington	-	14	
Whitehaven	17	15	34

Holdsworth (1874) reports that the first-class smacks trawled grounds between the English coast and the Isle of Man, whilst shrimping is an important fishery in 'many districts' alongside inshore trawling for flatfish.

The minutes of the Cumberland Sea Fisheries Committee (1889 et seq.) record statistics and descriptions of the inshore fishery. The minutes of 12 October 1898 record that the herring season ended poorly in July, but the mackerel fished well with some excellent hauls. The Solway Firth was 'literally alive with shrimp'. On 19 January 1899 they heard that the second-class boats that fish from Maryport north were taking plaice skate and cod, the shore fishermen were taking sparling (smelts). The shrimping had been poor due to the cold. The AGM of 20 April 1899 received a report that second-class boats were landing shrimp at Maryport, Allonby, Silloth and Skinburness, a total of 10t 19cwt at 5d per qt valued at £77 15s 6d (£6,260). During the quarter ending 30 June 1899 the shrimp trawling had progressed well, prawns were found off Maryport, with some twenty to thirty Morecambe Bay boats trawling for them. 5t 2cwt of prawn valued £63 9s 9d (£5,110) was landed at Maryport and Silloth. By the quarter ending 30 September 1899, 71t 1cwt of prawn valued £833 (£67,040) was landed at Maryport, and 1t 10cwt 1½qt of shrimp valued £47 5s (£3,803) were landed at Allonby, Silloth, and Skinburness.

During the quarter ended December 1899 the boats working to the north of Maryport were taking plaice, the prawning grounds still abounded with prawns. The statistics of fish landed by the second-class boats included:

Weight	Catch	Price	2005 Value
8t 13cwt 0qt	Prawn	£106/%	£8,531
1t 13cwt 0qt	Shrimp	£51/6/8	£4,131
31t 12cwt 3½qt	Plaice in Solway	£569/11/9	£45,843

In the summer of 1900 prawns still abounded off Maryport and Workington; however, the prawners were still taking sole and plaice. The landings included 49t 13cwt of prawns valued at £771 10s (£60,245) and 2t 10cwt of shrimp at £77 15s 6½d (£6,073). The summer of 1901 saw a similar pattern, whilst shrimps were also plentiful. The landings included 4t 2½cwt of shrimp at £127 19s 2d (£9,880) and 78t 19cwt of prawns at £950 (£73,356) (Cumberland Sea Fisheries Committee 1889 et seq.).

During the quarter ending 30 September 1901, second-class boats near Silloth were taking 20-30st of plaice per boat per tide in 7in mesh trawls. In 1897 when the byelaws were adopted there were two two-man boats at Maryport, there are now (1901) up to forty boats, twenty-four of which belong to Maryport. Some of these boats earned £16 (£1,235) per week. 55t 18cwt of prawn at £594 (£45,867) and 4t 15¾cwt of shrimp at £149 (£11,505) was landed in this quarter, and in the final quarter the landings of fish included 3t 7cwt of shrimp valued at £83 7s 8d (£6,439), and 54t 13cwt of prawn at £876 (£67,642) at the Cumbrian ports; second-class boats from Maryport were catching plaice, skate and ray, but shrimp and prawn were scarce. The herring fishery was a failure in both 1901 and 1902 (Cumberland Sea Fisheries Committee 1889 et seq.). The Lancashire and Western Sea Fisheries School was attended by John Nichol Armstrong, 30 Esk Street, Silloth, and John Ferguson, 56 High Street, Maryport, in 1910, evidence of continued inter-district co-operation (The Lancashire and Western Sea Fisheries Committee 1981 et seq.).

In his enquiries Aflalo bypassed Whitehaven and Workington and went directly to Maryport. Here his informant stated that the shrimpers did not fish from Maryport until two arrived in 1897, but that there were about two-dozen resident and about a dozen visiting the port regularly. He must have been misinformed in this, as we know that the nobby's Morecambe progenitor fished off Maryport in the 1850s, and that there were forty-eight second-class boats in 1872. Aflalo recorded that the shrimp were fished from the Solway lightship to the viaduct, and that prawn were trawled from Maryport to the lightship, whilst they were known to spawn on well-defined ground off Workington. Two hands worked the shrimpers, the catch paying four shares, one each to boat, nets, and each of the crew. The working owner might cut his and the boat's share to one-and-a-half in lean times, but even then might make a Sovereign a day in the season. Aflalo also recorded that longline fishermen sold skate to a Workington dealer at 6*d* a fish (Aflalo 1904).

Chapter 11

Runcorn and the Mersey

The Mersey was clean enough to attract visitors who wished to enjoy sea bathing in the eighteenth century. The shore at Liverpool was provided with bathing huts in 1721. The clean waters supported a fishing industry, both from boats and from fixed engines. Mr H.F. Starkey writing in *Schooner Port* quotes C. Poole, *A History of Widnes and its Neighbourhood* stating that on 4 August 1728, 30,000 herring were taken at Hale. March records that at the end of the eighteenth century trawlers were supplying Liverpool with soles and shrimps, the fish fetching 3-4*d* a lb (£1.75 a kg) and the shrimp few pennies a quart. Herring were also sold at Liverpool for about 1*s* (£3.27) a hundred (Holdsworth 1874). Much of this fish would have been taken on grounds to the north and west of the mouth of the Mersey, in addition to the estuary fish and shrimp catch taken before pollution forced all of the boats out into Liverpool Bay. The hamlet of Oglet of the 1860s housed shrimp fishermen who were catching in abundance. The presence of fish within the estuary is borne out by the number of fishing vessels registered at Runcorn, a port twenty miles' sail from the open sea. Holdsworth (1874) in his 1872 tabulation lists three first-class, thirty-five second-class, and seventeen third-class boats registered at Runcorn. We have to thank Mr H.F. Starkey and Mr Percy Dunbavand for the information and photographs on fishing in the upper Mersey that they have provided.

Runcorn developed from a small 'sea side' village into a transhipment port, although twenty miles up the estuary the Mersey is still tidal and wide. Sea bathing was so popular that a terrace of boarding houses named Belvedere Terrace was built next to All Saints' Church. The cleanliness of the Mersey, linked to the improvement in communications provided by the newly opened Bridgewater Canal of 1876 prompted this holiday trade, but the canals and the nearby salt deposits of Cheshire allowed soap and chemical industries to be set up, which destroyed the popularity of sea bathing at Runcorn by 1830. Cargoes from the deep-sea fleet were transhipped into Mersey flats, to be transhipped again, with coasting cargoes from places like Cornwall, into narrow boats serving the Potteries and inland industrial centres. The opportunities created by this commerce attracted shipbuilders, chandlers, brokers, coal and salt merchants, two rope walks and six sail lofts, and some of the wealth created was ploughed back in through ship ownership, both of coasting schooners and flats, and middle-water trawling smacks. Against this background inshore fishing at Runcorn and the nearby centres of Warrington and Widnes became part-time and fall-back employment, to provide an income when dock work was hard to come by as trade fluctuated. By 1883 there were only thirteen boats of all classes, with only four out of the thirty fishermen working full time. As the numbers rose and fell the fleet peaked at forty boats.

Both the census returns and registration records yield the family names of fishermen and their home addresses. *Schooner Port* records that the White family had been fishing from the early years of the eighteenth century from Ince and Elton, before moving to Runcorn in the 1840s. Woods and Edwards also fished from Ince in the eighteenth century. The Register document, from 1862 to 1893, shows that most of the Runcorn smacks of that era were second-class, and all were two men or a man and a boy crew. The Runcorn smacks, their later registration numbers, and their owners are listed below. The number in brackets refer to the map Fig. 53.

Smack	Tons	Register Length	Owner
Elizabeth Ann (Sloop) LL 87 from 1889-1901 RN 23 1903-1920	6.00	24ft	J. Hambleton, 13 Heath Road (11) E. Dunbavand, 30 Mason Street (2) Walter Moore, 13 Lowe's Court (3) William Hushin, 2 Water Street (1903) (4)
Pursuit, RN 24 1903-1920	9.00	33ft	Ernest Gleane of Crowton
Edie, RN 22 1901-1910	3.07	22ft	Robert Smitham, 82 Church Street (5)
Katie, RN 6 1912-1917	7.37		Charles Woods, Pool Lane (6)
Merry Maid, RN 8 1903- 1915	6.61	29 x 9 x 4ft	William Shaw, 3 Norfolk Street (7)
Maggie, RN 9 1913-1929	7.69		Joseph Green, 2 Brook Street (8)
Fanny, RN 10 1913-1931	5.33		Arthur Lomax, 29 Princess Street (9)
Lady Lathom (shrimp & trawl) RN 1 1901-1922	8.45		Thomas Jones, 22 Norfolk Street (7)
Shamrock (shrimp & trawl) RN 2 1914-1924	6.44		William Shaw, 3 Norfolk Street (7)
Moonlight (shrimp & trawl) RN 3 1913-	8.87		Samuel Dutton, 28 Wyvern Place (10)
Roses, RN 4 1915-1919	7.97		Joseph Alberton, 10 Rock Mount (1)
Banshee, RN 16 1916-1926			Henry Illidge, 64 Loch Street (12)

A sample of the 1891 census returns gives a valuable insight into the home economics of the Runcorn fishing family. The household at 3 Rock Mount, pictured here as Plate 45, was run as a boarding house. The daughter of the head of the family was married to a Hambleton, of Hambleton Toffee fame. This boiled sweet business developed from a common practice at Runcorn where the wives made sweets for sale to add to their husbands' erratic opportunities for gainful employment. As at Morecambe, the catch included shrimp, which were preserved by potting. Although Hambleton's Toffees developed into a large business the family continued with fishing, so that Mrs Hambleton, owner of the toffee business, had *Hannah Hambleton* built for her grandson. Plate 46 depicts her at Arnside before delivery to Runcorn. *Hannah Hambleton* later came north to the Duddon. The census returns include the following fishermen, again the numbers in brackets refer to Fig. 53.

Plate 45. Rock Terrace.

Plate 46. *Hanna Hambleton.* (Courtesy of National Museums Liverpool [Merseyside Maritime Museum])

Name and Address	Relationship	Age	Occupation	Place of Birth
3 Rock Mount (1)				
Sarah Furnival	Head of Household	45	Charwoman	Runcorn
Annie Hambleton	Daughter	23	Fish Dealer	Runcorn
Peter Furnival	Son	11		ditto
John Hambleton	Son-in-Law	26	Fisherman	ditto
James Hambleton	Grandson	5		ditto
Elizabeth Hambleton	Granddaughter	7 mth.		ditto
Henry Hambleton	Boarder	50	Fisherman	London
James Hambleton	Boarder	15	Cripple from child	Runcorn
Thomas O'Gara	Boarder	31	Carpenter	Runcorn
60 Cooper Street (13)				
Moses White	Head of Household	44	Fisherman	Runcorn
Ann White	Wife	45		ditto
Charles Henry White	Son	6		ditto
Clare Alice White	Daughter	4		ditto
29 Foresters Court (14)				
Joseph Woods	Head of Household		Fisherman	Widnes
Aim Woods	Wife			Runcorn
Mary Woods	Daughter		Charwoman	ditto
Margaret Woods	ditto			Widnes
Joseph Woods	Son			ditto
1 Wilsons Row (15)				
John Antrobus	Head of Household		Fisherman	Farnworth, Lancs
William Antrobus	Son			Runcorn

Farnworth is a suburb of Widnes. These streets appear on the map Fig. 53, whilst a photograph of the top end of Water Street appears as Plate 47. A postcard survives depicting one of the courts off Cooper Street; it depicts an entry just wide and high enough

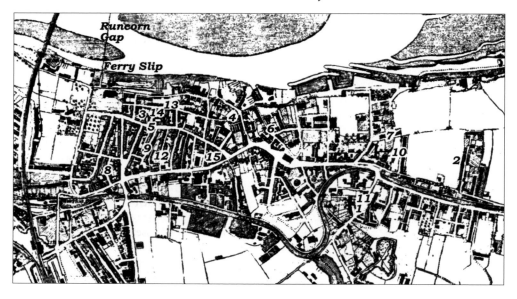

Above: Fig. 53. Runcorn map. (Ordnance Survey of 1882)

Left Plate 47. Water Street by W.A. Mack. (Courtesy P. Dunbavand)

to pass a horse and cart over rough and broken flags. The court is surrounded by two-storey terraces and the blank rear wall of a neighbouring building, all built out of rough un-coursed ashlar stone.

The Runcorn smacks were photographed on the pitching at the Old Ferry at Runcorn in 1885 (Plate 48) by Chas A. Timmins and again in 1886 (Plate 49). The smacks were all sloop rigged, with the stay to the stem head, there were two hull-form variants pictured. The Runcorn registered smacks, 1 RN and 4 RN, and two of their unregistered sisters had full hulls, 5ft depth of side, with straight slightly raked stems, no round to the forefoot, and a square-ended counter. The midship section had straight floors with a moderate rise, a quick turn at the bilge, and flared sides. Maurice Evans has identified 4 RN as *Old Ben*, registered from 1890 to 1908. The other form was of a Liverpool registered smack 325 LL, of finer form. Her stem was straight and not raked above the waterline, she had a round forefoot below. She carried her bilge high, made apparent by the prominent bilge rubbers fitted amidships. Unfortunately her counter ending is not visible. The shipyards on the Runcorn bank, whose mainstay was building coasting vessels, also built smacks in the 9-17t range in the period from about 1840 to 1860. It is possible that the smacks 1 RN and 4 RN on the Old Ferry pitching were the products of these yards. The Runcorn register also lists four other smacks. *Water Lilly* RN 15, *Polly*, and *Red Rose* RN 28 from Widnes, and the *May Flower* RN 26 from Warrington.

Runcorn changed significantly when the Manchester Ship Canal was built along its river frontage during the period 1887 to 1894. Its quays, shipyards and docks were demolished or altered, and the smacks were obliged to lay moorings on the riverside of the new canal wall. Their crews had to cross the canal by the high-level bridge, and descend to the canal wall to gain access to their boarding punts. The older boats were gradually replaced with both nobbies and other forms. A photograph of 1902 (Plate 50) includes one of the older sloops, a modern nobby picking up its mooring, with a sloop-rigged flat sailing in the middle distance. Both smacks have one beam trawl on deck, of a length to fit from aft of the shrouds to the counter. The nobby is fitted with a bobstay. A later photo, Plate 51, taken at some time before 1950, depicts two nobbies and a third small trawl boat on drying moorings by the tidal openings at the Old Quay. All three boats have one beam trawl on board. The small trawl boat is a clinker-built sloop, the aft end of the trawl obscures the stern, but she may be one of the Lytham smacks, or a converted ship's lifeboat. These were certainly fished from the upper Mersey as photographs show.

Photographs provide evidence of fishing from the Widnes shore, on the West Bank. They date from the 1930s, at a time when the upper Mersey was clean enough to allow a day at the seaside. The first two photographs indicate that fishermen were using converted ship's lifeboats, which were a cheap way to get afloat if you were able to build a deck and rig. The Transporter Bridge, prominent in one of the pictures alongside St Mary's Church Runcorn, was completed in 1905. The third Widnes photo of RN 13, Plate 52, is of Mr Bob Garner's nobby *Primrose*, with her beam trawl on deck. She is cracking on under all lowers, and if her skipper wanted to set the topsail he would have been frustrated by the loss of the topsail outhaul, one end of which is streaming away from the gaff, after it has got free of its belay. She has pin-rails at her shrouds, and details of her rig differ from Morecambe practice in several ways. Her forestay has a soft eye at the mast into which the standing end of the peak halyard is hooked; the peak halyard itself is more complicated with two spans on the gaff, and four blocks instead of Morecambe practice's two. The jib halyard is simpler, with a whip at the sail's head and only one fall. Mr Garner lived on Mersey Road, Widnes, and *Primrose* was registered RN 13 from 1897 to 1939.

A Warrington fisherman, Mr S. Wilkinson, ordered a 23ft shrimp trawl from the Trawler Co. net loft in 1953, costing £23 (£493). After about 1950 there were no full-time fishermen, and the last smack left Runcorn in the early 1970s. Without a regular, substantial supply of fish the market remained local. The fishermen hawked their catch around the pubs and supplied their families and friends. They were obliged to go out to Rock Channel, occasionally going to Hilbre and Point of Ayre, where the shrimping was better and cleaner.

Plate 48.
Runcorn smacks
at the ferry pier,
1885. (Courtesy
H.F. Starkey)

Plate 49.
Runcorn smacks
at the ferry pier,
1886. (Courtesy
H.F. Starkey)

Plate 50. Smacks
at Runcorn,
1902. (Courtesy
H.F. Starkey)

The Runcorn fleet included the following smacks from time to time: *Anna Mable, Ploughboy, Pastime, Etna, Excel, Emily* (fitted with a motor in 1932), *Minnie, Tempest, Lena, Doris, Lily, Welcome, Robert, Harlequin, Tern, Thora, Wild Duck* (at St Anne's from 1891 to 1921 when she went to Fleetwood; came to Runcorn in 1938), *Bat, May Baxter, Fram, Gipsy* (from Warrington), *Joan, Uno, Amy,* and *True Love.* We know that *May Baxter* and *Fram* were Morecambe nobbies (being told that both were built for members of the Baxter family).

William Ashton (1920) states that when King John awarded a charter to Liverpool it was then a fishing village. There were substantial smacks belonging to Liverpool at the beginning of the nineteenth century as the *Lancaster Gazette* of 4 March 1809 reported that 'A sloop has been found at sea by a Liverpool fishing boat, laden with rum and staves, with out any person on board, and full of water, about four miles to the westward of Pile of Foudry, and taken in there. The name "MARY", of Plymouth painted on her stern.'

The port's commercial interests eclipsed Liverpool as a fishing station, so that Aflalo's reports (1904) ignore its fishing industry, whilst giving credit to the work on shrimp and juvenile fish, shellfish and pollution carried out by Professor Herdman of the University of Liverpool. Holdsworth's statistics of 1872 list thirty-five first-class boats, 137 second-class boats, and ten third-class boats. These would have included boats from Hoylake to Southport, so we will have to rely on more subjective information to discuss the size of the industry. Holdsworth goes on to state 'Liverpool is the oldest of the deep-sea trawling stations on this part of the coast, but this fishery appears never to have been prosecuted with much energy, and the number of smacks there has been subject to great fluctuation.' Holdsworth also states that the bigger smacks "work a good deal in Caernarfon and Cardigan Bays' (Holdsworth 1874). Incidentally Davis (1958) describes a Liverpool stake net for mackerel, of 300ft long by 3ft 6in high, set in a crescent parallel to the shore.

The Lancashire and Western Sea Fisheries Committee (1891 et seq.) records refer to the Mersey from their inception. They listed the following shrimping fleets in 1891:

Hoylake shrimpers	15	Dingle shrimpers	4	Garston shrimpers	5
Tranmere shrimpers	17	Cockle Hole shrimpers	10	Speke shrimpers	4
New Ferry & Rock Ferry	17	Widnes shrimpers	7	Ince shrimpers	2
New Brighton & Egremont	10	Runcorn shrimpers	6	Formby shrimpers	1

These, with the Welsh towns along to Rhos Point in Colwyn Bay, formed the southern division of the early district (1891 to 1900). There was shrimping in both upper and lower Mersey in 1891. The Sea Fisheries Committee debate continued during 1892 on the size of trawl mesh. The committee wanted 7in, whilst the Mersey men wanted 4-5in: the theme through out the committee's minutes indicate that the Mersey inshore men were the most profligate of all of the district in their disregard for conservation of immature fish. Some Mersey men laid up their inshore boats in winter to go trawling in the first-class boats. The committee boat was used to try southern division grounds include Jordan Flats and Queens Bar, Rock and Horse Channels, and the Crosby Channel (see Fig. 54). Some Morecambe men followed the herring to the Mersey. In January 1892 seventeen Annan and Morecambe shrimpers went to the Mersey after herring, the Mersey men were reported not to drift or use longlines (The Lancashire and Western Sea Fisheries Committee 1981 et seq.).

Fish merchants of Liverpool, Manchester, and Blackburn each wrote to the Sea Fisheries Committee suggesting minimum fish sizes in 1883. The Liverpool letter was signed by thirty-seven merchants, twenty-two of which were single names, the rest were & Co., & Son, or partnerships. The meeting of August 1893 recorded that John Formby Esq., of Formby Hall, wrote regarding carts coming from areas outside of the Formby Estates working the estate's foreshore and damaging the grounds, contrary to the practice of the local cockle fishermen. Shrimp hose nets were fished at Ince and Garston. The fishermen of Ince applied to use hose nets with pockets for shrimp, designed to fish both flood and ebb,

Plate 51. Moorings
by the tidal openings,
Old Quay *c.*1950.
(Courtesy P.
Dunbavand)

the pockets were to retain the fish as the tide turned. Pockets were not normally allowed in shrimp nets in order to prevent the destruction of immature fish that they would trap (The Lancashire and Western Sea Fisheries Committee 1981 et seq.).

The committee discussed a letter during February 1894, from the fishermen of the Mersey Fishermen's Society, Seamen's Bethel, Mann Island, Liverpool, signed by Daniel Robinson, forwarded by the Board of Trade. They demanded:

> Representation on the Board from Liverpool, South Toxteth, Birkenhead, New Ferry and New Brighton.
> Mesh sizes of 7" measured dry, and dressed.
> No closed season for shrimp, and permission to keep the bye-catch if of six to seven to the pound.
> A commitment to buy out the fishermen if these demands were not met.

These demands were rejected. A letter was received from the Mersey Fishermen's Association repudiating Daniel Robinson's letter. There was friction because the Mersey men were used to keeping the by-catch from the shrimp trawls, and were aggrieved at giving up this practice, attempting to throw a bailiff overboard in the Mersey when challenged (The Lancashire and Western Sea Fisheries Committee 1981 et seq.).

Formby herring stake nets were catching during spring of 1894. Mersey fishermen were shrimping from the Dingle to above Garston, but were suspected of trawling illegally for fish. During first weeks of 1895 a meeting was arranged at Liverpool to discuss shrimping. The Mersey fishermen gave much contradictory evidence, claiming that mechanisms preventing taking fish in shrimp trawls and a closure of the Burbo Bank ground would drive them out of business. The shrimp trawl, being about the same length as its beam, allowed fish to swim out forward, 150 nets in northern division then complied with this design. The Mersey men wished to continue using a net with the same ratio of length to beam as the fluke trawl. There was discussion on a close season in the Mersey, to close the ground from the Hoylake lower light to seaward, the Hoylake lower light to the Bar lightship, to the Formby lightship, to the Crosby Light to Bidston Light house. This was later withdrawn, as it received no support from the Board of Trade. It was proposed that the shrimp trawl be limited to no more that 2ft longer that the beam length. The Crosby Channel was shrimping well. Thirty Mersey shrimpers went over to trawling in March 1896 (The Lancashire and Western Sea Fisheries Committee 1981 et seq.). *Jane and Alice* was bought from St Anne's by T. Thompson of Tranmere, to be registered LL 310 in 1896; she stayed on the Liverpool Registry (changing to LL 1 in 1914) to transfer to Beaumaris in 1925.

Plate 52. RN 13 *Primrose.*
(Courtesy P. Dunbavand)

The autumn of 1898 saw concern expressed about killing fry when shrimping on the Burbo Bank. Arguments arose between the Mersey and the Hoylake men over shrimp trawling. The ground behind the Burbo Bank is mud, and reported to be unsuited to the Southport shank which can only fish a sand bottom. Trials were conducted with a Mersey pattern shrimp trawl, fishing in company with up to fifty shrimp trawlers. They usually took up to 36qt of shrimp, with one bag of 64qt and one of 80qt, hauling after 1-1¼ hours. Each time thousands of immature fish were killed. During the summer of 1899 thirty-seven shrimpers per day were working the Burbo Bank; two were prosecuted for taking young soles in the shrimp trawls. Second-class trawlers were taking big hauls of haddock and soles around the southern division. The shrimpers had done well over the entire region. The minutes of February 1899 included a report of negotiations with the Mersey shrimp trawlers about closing the Burbo Bank sole nursery (The Lancashire and Western Sea Fisheries Committee 1981 et seq.).

After the amalgamation with the west region, the committee minutes became less specific; however, there were further mention of the Mersey. The amalgamation required the re-assignment of the bailiffs: No.2 District from the South bank of the Ribble to Rhos Point was assigned three bailiffs and a cutter at New Brighton. In the summer of 1901 there were seventy shrimpers working the Burbo Bank; fewer fry are caught in cold weather. Later in the year one second-class boat was purchased for Rock Ferry. In the spring of 1902 dab was found in abundance especially at the Mersey Light vessel, being taken at the rate of 600-800lb a day, weather permitting, but prices were low. By the year's end the Mersey's cutter was moved to New Quay, one secondhand second-class boat came to Rock Ferry, and one was ordered from Fleetwood. The second-class trawlers were fishing well: off the Mersey they were taking sixteen boxes per tide. Shrimps were plentiful at the start of the quarter with 100-160qt a day from the Ribble to the Dee. In 1901 three new boats were purchased for Rock Ferry with one building, mostly to replace old boats (The Lancashire and Western Sea Fisheries Committee 1981 et seq.).

The quarterly report of The Lancashire and Western Sea Fisheries Committee of March 1903 reported that one new boat was added at Rock Ferry. All boats were hampered by bad weather. Second-class trawlers managed a little fish trawling in the Mersey with three- to five-score pounds (60-100lb) of codling per day; the shrimpers from Southport were doing well in the Mersey. During 1909 Liverpool shrimpers were working in the Crosby Channel. In that year Liverpool sent Frederick Houghton of 18 Grampian Road, Edge Lane, Liverpool, and Joseph Beck of 4 Winifred Street, Wavertree Road, Liverpool, to the Roa Island School with

Left: Fig. 54. Liverpool fishing marks.

Below: Fig. 55. Wallasey and Egremont.
(Ordnance Survey 1882)

Jas Murray of Egremont, and Wm Cross of New Brighton. Later, in 1910, Ralph Brooks, Raven Meols Lane, Formby, attended the Roa Island School. Liverpool and Birkenhead boats trawled Horse Channel, off Jumbo and Nelson Buoys. Hose nets for shrimp were set at Ince, Garston, Crosby and Formby. Those at Ince still had pockets fitted to retain the shrimp taken on the flood as the net fished the ebb. In 1911 Mersey shrimpers were on grounds at North Bank, Burbo Bank, Crosby Channel, Jordan Flats, and Mad Wharf.

Of the families that worked from towns near the mouth of the Mersey, the Murrays are remembered. They lived at 44 Withens Lane, Wallasey, and in addition to fishing they ran a fishmonger's shop at 9 Stringhey Road (see map Fig. 55). Richard Murray started the fishmonger's, and was later joined by his son John. James Murray, one of the Roa Island students, was a member of this family. They were racing *Camellia* with racing number 3, Plate 53, in the regattas of 1911, 1912, and 1913. *Camellia* was known as 'the fastest plank on the river'. The Murrays also fished *Playmate*, *Greyhound*, and purchased *Cedar* from Thomas Mealor of Parkgate in 1934. Their moorings were off the Mariners' Homes. *Camellia* beat *Helen II*, Plate 54, in the 1911 Royal Mersey Yacht Club race, to lose on handicap to *Five Brothers*. *Helen II* was built in 1910 for G.E. Stonall of New Brighton to be registered as LL 43. The following week *Helen II* won the Magazines Yacht Club Regatta; *Camellia* was disqualified after the race for crossing the start line early. The run of rigging on *Helen II* is of interest, including the pin-rail visible at her shrouds.

The next mention from the Lancashire and Western Sea Fisheries Committee is of 1914 when Liverpool boats were in the Sloyne and off Egremont. The Sloyne Roads were on the Wirral side from Tranmere to past New Ferry. During the First World War many of the Mersey grounds were closed to all boats in support of the war effort. During 1919 there was a longlining revival at New Brighton and Egremont, whilst the second-class boats began to fit motors. By 1920 six boats had motors on the Mersey; two more were on order. Mersey boats were shrimping the Formby and Crosby Channels and the Burbo Bank. 1921 saw the Mersey men shrimping, and five boats trawling. The following year's minutes state that Mersey half-deckers experience best fishing in summer and autumn, so some lay up over the winter, whilst their crews take up casual labour. 1923 saw permits issued to trawl by motor in the Mersey, in the following year the Mersey men were shrimping, as there was little fish, they were catching five- to eleven-dozen quarts (60-132qt) per tide.

The nobby fishery has continued, with between twenty-five to thirty boats working from the Mersey in the 1930s when our informant, Mr C.H. Mealor of Rock Ferry started fishing. If we assume between four and half-a-dozen at Runcorn, that leaves between twenty and two-dozen nobbies to be shared between Liverpool and Birkenhead. There were eighty-one vessels registered at Liverpool in 1932, of which thirty-eight were nobbies, about two-dozen working from the Mersey and fifteen from Hoylake. The nobbies used the South Ferry Basin (the Cockle Hole) on the Liverpool side, this is a small tidal dock just upstream of the Albert Dock, and Rock Ferry, Tranmere, and New Brighton on the Wirral side. In addition to the Mealors and Murrays, the Slack, Shaw, Hay, Wright, Jones, Stonall, Martin, and Morris families owned nobbies.

John Crossfields list adds one or two other families

26 Aug 1896	*Minnie*	James Whittle	New Brighton
4 May 1897	*Dancing Girl*	J.R. Lee	New Brighton
15 March l899	*Spindrift*	E. Rae Esq.	Birkenhead
9 Jul 1901	*Onward*	Thomas Slack	Tranmere
28 Jul 1903	*My Lady*	J. Mealor	Rockferry
2 Apr 1904	*Darling*	G. Stanley	Birkenhead
17 May 1904	*Primrose*	W. Kay	Birkenhead
1935	*Emma*	Mealor	Rockferry

John Gibson and Sons also built for the Mersey, including:

Plate 53. *Camellia*. (Collection of M.P. Evans)

Plate 54. *Helen II*. (Collection of M.P. Evans)

Plate 55. *Onward* LL 106. (Courtesy P. Dunbavand)

A Shrimper	T. Slack	Birkenhead	30 January 1891
A yacht	Mr Slack	Rock Ferry	9 October 1894
Provider, a centre-board fast sailer (Mersey Trade)	Peter Davidson	Liverpool	25 February 1896
Eureka, a centre-board for fishing and racing	Mr Ashbrook	Tranmere	8 May 1896

The honorific 'Esq.' given to Mr Rae probably denotes a gentleman's yacht. *My Lady* was registered LL 417 by J. Mealor, and *Emma* LL 130 by Mr C.H. Mealor's father. In addition to buying in nobbies from away, there was a succession of builders on the Wirral side, lumped together under the generic term 'Tranmere nobbies'. Their builders worked on and off from 1840 to 1930; they were most likely shipwrights from the shipyards and repair yards of Birkenhead, their output when working being only about one each year. The Slack family worked several of these nobbies, whose characteristic form was a full bow, and a short, wide counter.

In the 1970s and 1980s the trade had fallen off so that only one boat, John Neary's *Comrade*, was fishing full time. William Crossfield & Sons built *Comrade* as a yacht in 1936. She was registered to fish at Runcorn as RN 22 from 1939 1940, and as RN 28 from 1940 to 1942, before transferring to Chester as CH 141 in 1942. John has fished her since 1962.

The fishery used nobbies from 25ft up to 40ft, using the smaller sizes for shrimping, and trawled for cod with the bigger boats. They used backless nets with three-part greenheart beams, the fish trawls being fitted with a flapper as well as pockets with roller bobbin ground gear. The shrimp trawls used rope. Davis (1958) reports a Rock Ferry shrimp trawl on a 19ft beam. With the fishing industry being relatively small at Liverpool the fishermen did not generate enough business to support a net loft, but cut or braided their own. With the proximity of the Liverpool fish market there was much less likelihood of shrimp spoiling, so this and the size of the industry did not prompt the formation of a marketing organisation, but promoted the use of local dealers. There is no tradition of the fishermen making their own sails; there will have always been sail lofts to service the commercial shipping and the yachting of the Mersey.

The photograph of the *Onward* LL 106, Plate 55, has many features of interest. Dick Hynes owned her before the Second World War at Runcorn, but the photograph was taken within one of the Liverpool docks. Her registry as LL 106 ran from 1/3/1912 until after the Second World War. The details of note in the photograph are as follows:

The forestaysail has large 'Ω' hanks.

There are no bowsprit bitts; the Samson post is on the mid-line and has an iron ring to constrain the heel of the bowsprit.

The jib halyard block has sister-hooks hooked into the loose hook on the outhaul traveller.

A fisherman anchor is stowed with its stock up and down outboard of the port bow nog.

Two jib sheet fairleads can be seen just inboard of the outside coaming.

There is a wire sheet horse shackled to the forward shroud deadeye strap. This has a traveller ring into which are spliced a pair of sheets. These run through bull's eyes that are shackled to eyebolts in the forward ends of the pin-rails, which are placed at the shrouds. The sheets disappear into the cockpit.

The shroud irons are properly fitted around the moulding, but do not extend to the height of the outside coaming as at Morecambe. The deadeye straps are long enough to place the deadeyes above the coaming.

There appears to be a large tin can placed over the stove chimney alongside the mast. The top of the topsail tack downhaul eye cleat is visible in front of the mast.

The heel of the bowsprit is resting on the rounded forward end of the cockpit. There is one hole for the heel fid visible.

The bow trawl iron stands upright on the starboard side of the cockpit; the beam is ruler straight, possibly made from three pieces, and overhangs the counter. The trawl iron is similar to the Morecambe pattern, but the bridle staple is made of a bar fitted through

Plate 56. Trawlers in the Hoyle Lake. (Courtesy of National Museums Liverpool [Merseyside Maritime Museum])

the eyes of two eyebolts. The shrimp net with its rope woulded footrope is hauled up to the masthead to dry.

There is no evidence of an engine, so the photograph will probably have been taken before 1920, with only one net on board the *Onward* was probably used for sprawn fishing and fish trawling.

One of the popular Mersey grounds, the Rock Channel, leads us from the Mersey to the Hoyle Lake. The town of Hoylake is just outside the Dee, having easier access to the grounds at the mouth of the Dee and in the Rock Channel. The Rock Channel used to be the only access to the Mersey until the newer channel through the Burbo Bank opened up. The channel from Dove Point between the Hoylake coast and the Hail or Hyle sand, which was only covered at extreme spring tides, once provided an anchorage in the shelter of the Hoyle Bank that caused the villages of Little and Great Meols and Hoose to house a community of mariners. In 1687 the Hoyle sand measured 13 by 3¼ miles. In 1700 the Hoyle Lake was ½ mile wide, and 15ft deep at its shallowest. This protected roadstead once sheltered Britain's fleet (Bailey 1955) and was an embarkation roadstead for the transports that took William III's 10,000 troops to Ireland (Roberts 1992). The Hoyle Lake was used as a lightering roadstead where the bigger craft were lightened to gain access to Liverpool as this port grew. As the commercial trade moved to Liverpool when the channel through the Burbo bank opened up the seafaring community took to deep-water trawling, so that by 1860 a fleet of ketch-rigged smacks was at its peak (Plate 56). The Hoyle Lake was now sanded up, and as its depth became inadequate for the big trawling ketches at about 1880 they moved to the Albert Dock in Liverpool, the fishermen having to commute to work by rail (Roberts 1992). The Hoylake fishermen then began to use nobbies.

The importance of the Hoyle Lake to the merchants of Liverpool prompted the Liverpool Docks Trust to re-site their lifeboat at Hoose, near the lower lighthouse in 1803. The Tide Surveyor Daniel Manlove was charged with her care and the recruitment of a crew from the local fishing community. In 1808 the lighthouse keeper took over this responsibility and was charged with ensuring that the crew exercised in the lifeboat once a month. The crew were to be paid 3s (£8.36) each time they exercised, and were rewarded for each time that they were called out. The Liverpool Committee of Underwriters and the West India Company furnished the funds disbursed to the crew and for the maintenance of the boats. The system occasionally failed when the funds were not forthcoming, so that in 1845 the

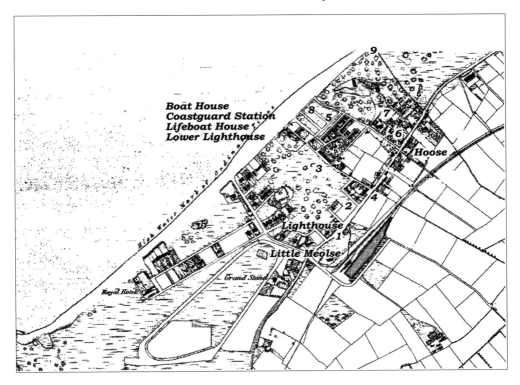

Fig. 56. Hoylake map. (Ordnance Survey of 1881)

rates were fixed at 10s (£38.11) for the master and 7s 6d (£28.59) per day for the crew, with an annual retainer and extra gifts for successful services. The silting of Hoyle Lake reduced its depth so that by 1847 it was impossible for boats to enter before quarter flood, after which it was only used by flats and coasters (Roberts 1992).

Most of the fishermen lived in Hoose, with the rest staying in Great Meols. The boundary between Hoose and Little Meols lay under what is now Lake Place and Alderley Road. The parish registers and census quoted by Roberts (1992) yields the following statistics quantifying fishing families.

Date	Little Meolse	Hoose	Great Meolse	Surnames
1759-1789		Paul Lineker	7 families	
1790-1820	6 families	12 families	6 families	
1841	38 out of 107 households fish			6 Sherlock households
				5 Eccles households
				5 Jones households
				3 Bird households
				Davies, Hughes, Becks and Roberts with 2 households each

In addition to trawling there was a cockling industry in the later nineteenth century, and small craft were used for shrimping. Roberts (1992) uses the tithe maps and the 1841 census to populate the villages of 1844. A cluster of fishermen lived on Grange Road in Little Meols in cottages between the present day Queens and Cable Roads (No. 1 on the map Fig. 56). They were Joseph Armitage, Joey Powell, Robert Beck, and John Pugh. Next was Bobby Parr between Cable and Alderley Road (2). There were thirteen cottages on Lake Place, mostly occupied by fishermen (3). John Barlow lived opposite the Ship Inn on Grange Road where it enters Hoose (4). John Beck was one of the fishing communities

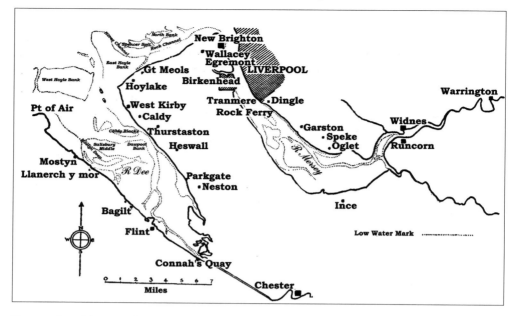

Fig. 57. Dee fishing marks.

that occupied the cottages on Sea View (5) and Back Sea View. Market Street housed another cluster of fishermen between Grange Road and the turning into School Lane (6), the blacksmith John Hazlehurst, and the boat builder Thomas Linacre lived at the foot of this Lane (Roberts 1992) (7). These lanes are indicated by numbers on the map Fig. 56.

The Church of England recognised the growing community by creating the parish of Hoylake in 1833. The pastor of 1840 to 1854 referred to the community as 'Hoyle-Lake', whilst the town's name had settled on the modern spelling with the publication of a town directory in 1897 (Roberts 1992). This completed a process of amalgamation which started with baptismal register entries referring to Hoylake from 1774.

Hoylake was mentioned in the Lancashire and Western Sea Fisheries Committee (1981 et seq.). There were fifteen shrimpers and thirty-seven first-class boats in 1891. The proposed byelaws were so unpopular at Hoylake that the committee boat was vandalised and public disorder occurred after a public meeting, but they were won over so that they withdrew their objection to the byelaws in 1895. Fishing trials were carried out in 1893, which identified the fishing grounds accessible from Hoylake, shrimp grounds were: from the Salisbury Buoy to the H.S. No.5 Red Buoy in the Dee, along the West Hoyle bank, SE side of Hoyle bank, towards the Seldom Seen Buoy, crossing Hilbre Gut and Welshman's Gut, from Mostyn Deep to near the Lightship. Some of these marks are identified on the map Fig. 57. Both fish and shrimp off Prestatyn Gutter, off Rhyl Pier towards Abergele, Colwyn Bay. Fish were taken on Constable Bank, Hilbre Swash, Mostyn, and from Mostyn to Point of Ayre Light. Thomas Banks, Great Meols; Robert Aldred, Market Street, Hoylake; James Eccles Sr. Lake Place, Hoylake; and Robert Holmes, Market Street, Hoylake served on the committee in 1893.

The reports of 1898 mention that Hoylake trawlers (smacks) were trawling the Welsh coast taking plaice and soles. The inshore trawlers were also taking plaice. In 1901 it was reported that two new first-class boats joined the Hoylake fleet. By the year's end a third new smack was added, second-class trawlers were with few exceptions shrimping and doing well, those fish trawling were taking sole, but not doing as well. In 1902 three first-class boats sold from Hoylake, and four were bought in. James Dickinson Esq., 13 Hamilton Street, Hoole ,served on the committee for 1906, alongside Frank Lees, 3 Alexandra Terrace, Bedford Road, Rock Ferry; Thomas Jones, Marmion Road; Thomas Davies, Westward Ho, Prussia

Road, Hoylake; and William Dean, 3 Hilbre Road, West Kirby. The reports of the classes at Roa of 1910 included Herbert Jones, Aston Villa, Groveland Avenue; Douglas Bevan, Laurel Cottage, School Lane; Frederick N. Evans, 19 Marmion Road; and William Eccles, 6 Sea View Hoylake. By 1919 the first-class boat numbers drop from forty-five in 1891 to seventeen. The decline in numbers continued so that in 1920 there were only seven first-class boats at Hoylake. They moved to the Mersey later in the year and started to fit motors. There were only six left in the district by 1925, two of which were motorised (The Lancashire and Western Sea Fisheries Committee 1981 et seq.).

As the big smacks were driven away the fishermen had started to use nobbies (Roberts 1992). March, in *Sailing Trawlers,* quotes a smacksman, Mr Thomas Cooper of 1878, who talks of the 'smaller cutters working inshore spent only a day at sea. They fished with a twenty six foot beam.' A bad storm of 7 October 1889 (a Monday) coincided with a spring tide, the storm surge raised the tide from 18-23ft. Several big smacks were damaged but three nobbies, belonging to Mr Jones, Armitage, and Sherlock each became a total loss (Roberts 1992).

The lifeboat records of 1916 the following fishermen in the crew, posed for a photograph on the occasion of the funeral of their 56-year-old Coxswain Thomas Dodd.

Macki Armitage	Fiddler Evans	Four Eyes Jones
Turk Armitage	Stephen Housley	Daw Jones
Yonk Beck	Little 'un Hughes	George Norrie
Long Ted Beck	Walter Hughes	Danny Rainford
Jeff Beck	Scroggie Hughes	Prophet Rainford
Twigger Beck	Tom Jackson	Conger Sherlock
Joe Cooper	Father Jackson	Soap Smith

There are unpublished records of fifteen nobbies at Hoylake in the 1930s. The 42ft *The Ivy* was bought to Hoylake in 1907 to be registered LL 108 by Cox'n Thomas Dodd. Thomas passed *The Ivy* on to Arthur Dodd, who sold her to W. Harry Jones. Harry Jones was fishing her with two crew, A. Baker and C. Leatherbarrow, in 1948. Ackroyd fished the Crossfields' *Enid*, built at Arnside in 1935. Jones, Hughes, Armitage, Housley, and Bird also fished from Hoylake.

George Crossfield's two sons George and Herbert moved to Hoylake in 1914, building at least four nobbies at the old Latta's Yard before closing their business. Their nobbies were *Nancy*, for the Bushell family of Parkgate; *Annie*, for Samuel Evans of Neston; and *May*. The *Mona* LL 29 of 1919, one of their smaller boats at 26ft 5in by 9ft 5in deep, suffered a capsize and rolled the full 360°, when skippered by Ben Armitage. A formal enquiry into the incident was inconclusive, but the incident and the seriousness in which it was viewed may have helped to close the yard. Herbert died in 1921, possibly as a result of injuries that caused him to be invalided out of the army in the First World War, and George retired to live in Conwy. Maurice Evans researched the history of boat building at Hoylake. Alec Latta, a captain of Everton Football Club, opened a yard at the turn of the century. His business address was 23 Lake Road (8 on the map), but it is unclear where he worked. By 1902 Alec was working as manager of Smith Brothers' boat yard opposite the slip by Hoyle Road (9 on the map Fig. 56). The Smiths' main business interests were building and joinery, and it is apparent that they were not comfortable with diversifying into boat building, as they put the business on the market in February 1905. Even though the Smiths owned the yard, it was widely known as Latta's, and Alec may have bought the business from Smith Brothers to continue building until the Crossfields bought the yard. The yard did not produce nobbies, building cruising yachts and racing craft until the Crossfields came to Hoylake. The site of the yard is now occupied by housing that was built before the 1927 edition Ordnance Survey.

Hoylake hosted a regatta that grew to be the largest in the Dee. It was established in 1887, and continued until 1938. It began with a race for the local smacks and nobbies, patronised from the first race by Thomas Dodd in *Gipsy Dan* LL 160, and Joseph Bird in *Leader* LL 147. The first prize in 1890 was £6 (£460) in cash and a voucher for 3t of coal, these attracted boats from Hoylake, Heswall, Tranmere and New Brighton. An unidentified artist sketched scenes from the regatta some time prior to 1897, possibly as early as 1890. The montage of scenes includes nobbies racing (the caption states 'Race for nobbies [small fishing boats]') and a race for the boats of the New Brighton and Mersey sailing clubs. The newspaper reports of the regattas of the early 1890s listed races for 'Bona fide fishing boats' at the Mersey regattas, whilst Hoylake alone used the name nobby. By 1907 there were races for fishing boats, shrimpers, fishing boats' punts, and a tug of war. The Hoylake Sailing Club organised races on the same day, and a carnival atmosphere was created ashore, which included a torch-lit parade.

Chapter 12

The Dee and the Welsh Coast
to Rhos Point

We have to thank Maurice P. Evans of Heswall for providing much of the information that is not derived from the quoted references in this chapter, and to Mr C.H. Mealor for his reminiscences.

Nobbies came late to the Dee, the fishery having been pursued in Jigger boats. These are 20-30ft double-ended and transom-sterned yawls, with a foresail on a bowsprit, gaff mainsail and topsail, and sprit mizzen. They were originally clench built but later were carvel, the *Capella* of 1923 measured 23ft by 7ft 8in, by 4ft 1in deep. They were used mainly as fish trawlers and occasionally for shrimp, and although some of the Dee fishermen consider them less safe there continued to be new Jigger boats built up to 1939. Some men distrusted the type, as they were less manoeuvrable so unable to be managed by one of the crew if the other suffered an accident. Their experience of the cutter-rigged nobbies, and their concern about safety prompted the Dee men to build cutter-rigged jiggers, on the same hull form. The first nobbies came to the Dee during the 1880s, so arrived in their later, fully developed form.

The Dee, in common with all estuaries widened by glacial action, is silting up. Chester was the premier port on the West Coast until the end of the fourteenth century. Silting of the channels moved its trade to Shotwick, from where Henry II set sail to campaign in Ireland. By 1673 trade had been driven to 'New Key' at Neston, where in 1684 there was 30-40ft of water at the quay at spring tides. There would have been a fishing community at Neston, as an ancient smoke house survives, serving a herring fishery. Commercial shipping then had to move to Parkgate. Whilst the head of the Dee estuary was silting up the channels at its mouth were changing. The Hoyle bank was originally one bank extending some fourteen miles across the mouth of the Dee. The Hoyle Lake Channel that gave Hoylake its name, and allowed Hoylake to support a fleet of deep-sea trawling smacks, separated it from the Wirral. By 1840 the new Dee Channel had divided the Hoyle Bank into its East and West banks, and the Hoyle Lake has continued to sand (Ashton 1920).

Parkgate was named from its nearness to Leighton Park, and developed from a waiting place for weather-bound passengers for Ireland and beyond. By the eighteenth century Parkgate had grown into a fashionable bathing resort with as many as thirteen hotels, and continued to be the port of departure for Ireland, accommodating royalty on occasion. In 1813 there was a packet service between Parkgate and Flint, to connect the coach services from the Mersey ferry through to north Wales (Ashton 1920). Until the encroaching sand drove its fleet away Parkgate was the hub of the Dee's fishing industry. During the heydays of the fishing Parkgate rail station took more revenue in one week than all of the other stations on the Hooton-West Kirby line took in a year. In addition to the shrimp fishery the Parkgate men exported twenty to thirty trucks of cockles and mussels every Saturday. In 1872 cockles or mussels sold at 5s (£14.46) per bag, with freight costs of 1s 6d (£4.34) per bag, generating £450 (£26,024) for the railway. By 1893 this had increased to 25,218 bags of cockles and mussels at 2s 6d, each generating £3,152 (£246,135) profit. These were gathered using large third-class punts to drift down to the flats and banks at Heswall Point, and The Blacks, Caldy, on the ebb, returning on the next flood tide (Pearson 1990). The mussels were gathered with 26ft-long rakes, and craams were used to gather the cockles.

Although the Lancashire Sea Fisheries district ran past the mouth of the Dee estuary, the superintendent did report on the Dee itself, listing the fishing grounds in 1893 as shrimp grounds from the Salisbury Buoy to the H.S. No. 5 Red Buoy in the Dee, along the West Hoyle bank, SE side of Hoyle bank, towards the Seldom Seen Buoy, crossing Hilbre Gut and Welshman's Gut, from Mostyn Deep to near Lightship. Both fish and shrimp off Prestatyn Gutter, off Rhyl Pier towards Abergele, Colwyn Bay. Fish were taken on Constable Bank, Hilbre Swash, Mostyn, and From Mostyn to Point of Ayre Light. There was mention of fishing at Neston and Parkgate in the spring of 1894, although the report does not clarify whether the boats were based there or if the fish was caught off these ports. The Dee Conservancy Byelaws were approved by the Board of Trade in 1895. In the summer of 1898 inshore trawlers from Rhyl and Abergele were taking ten boxes of plaice and ray in one trip; however, the Welsh and Wirral shrimpers were not doing well. The second-class trawlers were taking big hauls of haddock and soles around the southern division during 1899 (The Lancashire and Western Sea Fisheries Committee 1981 et seq.).

After the amalgamation of the Lancashire and Western districts the Dee and North Wales coast to Rhos Point joined with the Lancashire coast to the Ribble to form Division 2. In 1901 the second-class boats of this division were catching sole; the shrimp were plentiful on the outer grounds. The Prestatyn ground yielded 100qt of prawn per tide. In 1909 Cheshire paid the fees to allow T. Matthews Jnr of Neston, and W. Mealor Jun. of Parkgate to attend the Roa Island School. Liverpool merchants complain of undersized fish from trawlers at Neston and Parkgate during 1912. The war effort restricted fishing in the division when areas off Point of Ayre and off the Foryd Point closed for rifle ranges in 1915. As the desire to modernise by the adoption of motors was spreading from the west, trawling under power was allowed under licence with 7in mesh in Menai Straits and off Rhyl (The Lancashire and Western Sea Fisheries Committee 1981 et seq.).

The Parkgate community were self-sufficient, shelling their own catches in the evening. The older sons of the family would help by taking the catch by pony trap to the dealers waiting at Rock Ferry, setting off at 5.30 in the morning and returning for breakfast and school. Some of the fish was sold locally from tables outside the families' homes. The fisherman John Peters of Parkgate developed a dealership, buying the catch at Rock Ferry and Eastham. The families also knitted the nets used in the fishery, both shrimp and fish trawls, and draught and trammel nets for salmon. They called the knot that they used the 'shoute' knot. Like the other main nobby havens, Parkgate held a regatta. The 'Parkgate Fisherman's Regatta' was a big event, as befits a resort as important as Parkgate, and attracted entrants from all of the Dee fishing havens, and spectators from all over the Wirral. The nobbies sailed a fifteen-mile course, to Heswall, Mostyn, and back to Parkgate, whilst the smaller boats sailed and rowed over shorter courses. There were events for the children, and rowing boat tug o' war, all conducted in front of an enthusiastic crowd. The nobbies and jigger boats were presented with winner's pennants, whilst the band played a tune that had some mention of the boat's name. The regatta finished with a high tea for the competitors, and games and dancing on the green for the children (Pearson 1990). The regattas were held in 1898, 1899, 1903, 1913, and 1914. There were attempts to restart them after the war, in 1921, but without any real success.

There were about twenty-five to thirty boats in the Dee in 1932 as remembered by Mr C.H. Mealor. Mr Mealor's great grandfather and grandfather were both at Parkgate. William Mealor entered *Kitty Darling* in the regatta in 1867, and Mr C.H. Mealor's grandfather, who died at Rock Ferry aged ninety-eight in 1946, claimed to have had the first nobby at Parkgate in 1890. The Mealor family were living at Parkgate when the brothers Roy and Henry ordered the 23ft *Two Brothers* CH 36 from John Crossfield. The 7ft 9in beam, 1ft 9in draft Jigger boat was completed in February 1939. *Cedar* had been bought from Morecambe in 1922, and was not re-registered until sold to Liverpool in 1934. There were eighteen nobbies and thirteen jigger boats registered at Chester in 1932; however, as Thomas Mealor was fishing *Cedar* without re-registering her, others may also have avoided the registration fees, and as Liverpool registered boats will also have worked from Dee ports the higher number is feasible. The Wirral fishermen were able to avoid the enforcement of the registration regulations because the Dee Conservancy bailiffs were based on the Flintshire shore, and rarely came over to the Wirral. Thomas's brother William Mealor fished the *Lizzie* CH 17 in 1932. Two of the Peters family boats are recorded as *Onward*, winning the regatta for Dick Peters, whilst Christopher owned *Ethel* CH 31, from 1937, she was John Crossfield built, finished on 23 October, but remained at Conwy until the November.

Christopher Peters and his brothers James and Albert were some of the last Parkgate men fishing. In addition to the Peters, the families fishing from Parkgate were Higgins, Evans, Mealor, Smith, Lewis, Campion, Robinson, Fewtrell, Mellor, and Bushell. Parkgate continued as a fishing station until after 1930 when the encroaching sand drove the boats to moor at Heswall. The Parkgate residents continued to work by motoring to their moorings in vans.

In spite of the accretion of silt, erosion was pushing back some of the coast of the Wirral. Erosion at about two meters a year occurred between 1873 and 1897 at Heswall and Caldy. Ashton also mentions rapid erosion at Thurstaston, and the building of sea walls at Heswall in 1889 and at Parkgate (Ashton 1920). The fishing community began at Heswall in 1886 with the completion of Station Cottages. The Evans, Brierly, Higgins, and Lewis families moved in, followed by the occupation of homes on Banks Road, and in the 1920s Mostyn Avenue. Richard Evans set up a boat building and repair yard at the bottom of Banks Road in about 1910, alongside the new premises of the Dee Sailing Club. Until then the nearest building or repair facilities were at Hoylake and Chester. The moorings also included Parkwest, off The Targets at Heswall, and later at Caldy.

The Higgins worked *Cachalot* CH 10 out of Heswall from 1938 until 1988. Richard Evans purchased the Runcorn smack *Merry Maid*; she transferred from the Runcorn register in 1915. John Crossfield built for Heswall owners, including the 38ft *Lassie* for Alan Kitchen in 1936. She fished out of Hoylake for many years before going to Fleetwood; the *Betty* CH 45 at 36ft by 12ft, by 4ft 6in deep for William Evans; followed by the smaller *Polly* CH 98 for William in August 1938. The size of the industry reduced from the two-dozen or more boats of the 1930s to nine in 1963, four of them being worked by members of the Evans family.

West Kirby is just within the Dee, having easier access to the grounds at the mouth of the Dee and in the Rock Channel that runs parallel to the Wirral shore between Meols and the Mersey. West Kirby is not remembered as a major nobby station, although the *Amanda*, which Arnside Crossfield built for Annan in 1920, fished there for some years along with the *Seafisher* WO 49. There are photos of *Three Brothers* on the slip at West Kirby, Plate 57.

Wirral fishermen also fished for fish and some shrimp from the Flintshire harbours of Connah's Quay, Flint, Bagillt, Llanerch-y-mor, Mostyn, Rhyl, and Bangor, alongside Welsh fishermen. The Welsh were predominantly salmon fishermen; the Bithell family of Flint was well known for large catches in the river. They continue to use the trammel for salmon, from early March until late August, and trawl for shrimp in winter. The Roberts and Dennis families were shrimpers. Lemuel Evans worked the nobby *Novice* CH 8 from Llanerch-y-mor in 1891. She was the only Dee nobby recorded to work longlines. Lemuel's brother George fished the nobby *Mostyn Lily* CH 24 from Bagillt for shrimp, and was the 1914 winner of the Parkgate regatta. John Jones of Connah's Quay ordered *Wild Cherry*, a 33ft 10in nobby with outside ballast from the Crossens, Southport yard, to be completed in January 1904.

Rhyl grew up as a seaside resort; at the opening of the nineteenth century there was nothing but the haven at the mouth of the River Clwyd called the Vorryd (the Foryd), where small vessels loaded corn, timber and farm produce. By 1840 a resort had developed, served by steam packets from Liverpool, and in 1848 the railway arrived, to accelerate the growth of what became a very select resort.

Captain Richard England, writing of his childhood between the wars and his experience after the war in the book *Schoonerman*, remembered as a child befriending a Liverpool

Plate 57. *Three Brothers* at West Kirby. (Courtesy of National Museums Liverpool [Merseyside Maritime Museum])

fishermen living aboard his nobby at the quay by a bend in the Clwyd at the Foryd. The young Richard's friend was John Henry, who fished *Lizzy*, a 38ft Crossfields of Arnside nobby, trawling for flats, and hand lining mackerel. Freddie Harrison was working *Three Brothers* CH 69 from the Foryd at the same time. She raced in the 1914 Parkgate regatta and was registered by the Mealors of Parkgate from 1918 to 1928 when she transferred to Beaumaris as BS 76. Captain England wrote that the Welsh were intolerant of the English fishermen, and caused John Henry to abandon Flintshire and return to the Mersey, selling *Lizzy* for conversion to a yacht. The descendents of the Wirral fishermen recall the difficulty that their relatives also experienced. Job Mealor of Parkgate placed an order with the Morecambe Trawler Co. for a 19ft backless shrimp trawl from an Llanerch-y-mor address in 1953, so the Wirral men obviously persevered.

J. Hughes of Rhyl was a regular customer of John Crossfield, with boats completed in 1929, 1933, 1937, and 1939. The boats all had 'Royal' names, as they were pleasure boats for Rhyl's holiday trade. The boats in the Crossfields list built for the Dee included:

1929	*Duchess of York*	J. Hughes	Rhyl	Pleasure Boat
1933	*Majestic*	J. Hughes	Rhyl	Pleasure Boat
1936	*Lassie*	A. Kitchen	Heswall	
1936	*Betty*	W. Evans	Heswall	
15 May 1937	*Queen Elisabeth*	J. Hughes	Rhyl	Pleasure Boat
23 Oct 1937	*Ethel*	C. Peters	Parkgate	Jigger
30 Apr 1938	*Tamara*	Gardner & Young	Prestatyn	£230 (£9,995), 30ft x 9ft x 3ft 3in
Aug 1938	*Polly*	M. Evans	Heswall	
Feb 1939	*The Brothers*	Mealor	Parkgate	Jigger 23ft x 9ft x 1ft 9in
July 1939	*May Queen*	J. Hughes	Rhyl	Pleasure Boat

The details of the fishing gear and methods come mostly from the era of the motorised nobby. The favoured net was a 21ft backless shrimp trawl. The beam was made from greenheart, sometimes spliced into a bow, the length being governed by the available material. The later generation of fishermen bought sheet shrimp net from Morecambe to cut and sew for themselves. They favoured backless nets, as they believe that fish fry could escape between the beam and back of the net. There used to be a fishery for *Pandalus montagui*, called shanks on the Dee, which ceased in the 1930s. Davis (1958) describes a Hoylake Prawn Trawl, having a 4ft beam on the usual 1ft heads. The belly wings being about 1ft long. The net was said to be for trawling over very rough ground with large rocks.

The main cash-earner used to be fish trawling for plaice, sole, and ray, sold to Liverpool market, but latterly the fishery was concentrating on shrimp, which were hawked around the Liverpool pubs on Friday night, or picked and sold through family outlets and to merchants. A member of the Evans family named Jane, who married a Sissons, was a successful merchant. Jinny Sissons sold the fish caught by the Wirral Evanses, whilst the Welsh Evanses sold fish through Blunds at Manchester Fish Market. There was no Sunday fishery as there was no market on Sundays. One of the favoured grounds was off Point of Ayr, in 30-40ft of water, with 60fm of trawl rope. The shrimp fishery began in spring, catching small shrimp during mid-summer until the first week in September they averaged 30qt a day of big-shelled shrimp. The winter fishery was for flatfish, when it was actively pursued. Most boats were worked double handed. Surviving cine film of the motorised nobbies shows that they retained auxiliary sail, and rather than using the Morecambe-style of tallegoram, boiled the Dutch pot in a brazier placed on top of the engine hatch, this was so that the whole lot could be shoved overboard if the crew needed to get rid of it in a hurry.

Chapter 13

Conwy and the Menai Straits

Conwy was a port, a fishing harbour, and the home of John Crossfield's boat building enterprise. Prior to the coming of the railway Conwy's main fishery was for pearls from mussels; however, the improvement in transport allowed a mixed fishery to develop to supply the industrial cities. The shellfish were collected from rowing punts by long mussel rakes with handles of both 12ft length and of 18-30ft. The fishermen's wives were collecting in the shallows whilst their men folk were working from the punts (Jenkins 1991). The mussel fishery continued with the building of purification tanks, gathering for food instead of pearls. The nobby fleet, which were called nobbies rather than half-deckers or prawners, were used in pursuit of flatfish and cod, trawling with otter boards since the 1930s (previously the boats used 30ft beam trawls). At this time there were about ten to fifteen 35 to 40 foot boats, as well as some 25 to 30 footers.

The trawls did not use roller bobbins, whilst the beams were made Fleetwood-fashion of three pieces with iron banding on the splices. Alfie Crossfield remembers the fishermen hanging their trawl nets over the town wall by the boat shed to coat them with gas tar. The wall still bears dribbles of tar to this day. Possibly because the bigger boats specialised in cod, or came from Fleetwood, they were fitted with pounds under the side decks. The nogs were fitted at the aft end of the cockpit, there were no mid-nogs, and the sheet horses were always fitted on the mid-line. None of the boats were fitted with a forestaysail sheet horse.

The first records from the Sea Fisheries reports appear after the districts merged in 1900, the reorganisation that this required allocated one of the patrol cutters to Caernarfon. This part of the coast was within the new Caernarfonshire district, which extended from Rhos Point to Nevin. The superintendent reported that one second-class boat was new built for Conwy, one was sold to Menai Bridge, and one to Bangor; one second-class boat was also new built for Bangor during 1902. During the following spring the Menai Straits fished well up to February, the shrimpers were taking 16-100qt a day, Jonathan Williams, of 2 Little Lane, Beaumaris, served on the joint committee in 1903. Both shrimps and prawns were taken during the third quarter of 1905 in the Menai Straits. The report of 1909 noted that two secondhand boats came from Southport and Hoylake to both Bangor and Caernarfon and one left Caernarfon for Pwlhelli. There was trawling in Menai Straits, and two boats each caught 4-5cwt in 5 hours in Conway Bay (The Lancashire and Western Sea Fisheries Committee 1981 et seq.).

The superintendent reported the growth of the industry in the Caernarfonshire division.

	July 1903		Totals		March 1910		Totals	
	No. of Boats	No. of Men	Boats	Men	No. of Boats	No. of Men	Boats	Men
1st Class Sail	7	28			9	28		
2nd Class Sail	28	61			26	60		
3rd Class open	241	241			103	108		
Steam	1	4						
Shore Fishermen		68	277	402		225	138	421

It is of interest that most of the second-class boats were crewed by two men, and some by three. It was noted that boats worked Conwy and Redwarf Bays trawling in 1910. In the language of the reports these will have been after flatfish, not shrimp. The patrol cutter was reallocated to Bangor in 1911. There was little else reported in the minutes until the movement to allow motor trawling. In 1920 trawling under power was allowed under licence with 7in mesh in Menai Straits. This was extended as the prohibition was lifted completely in 1923.

Unfortunately neither Holdsworth in 1874 nor Aflalo in 1904 mentioned Conwy. It will be difficult to identify nobbies from amongst the herring and mussel boats used in the local fisheries. The fishing families included the Cravens from Blackpool and the Rimmer-Hughes. A study of the Caernarfon register identifies thirty-five nobbies with certainty, most moving from the Liverpool register and some of those having come from Southport and Morecambe, the Caernarfon fleet rose from ten in 1885 to above sixty in the 1920s, peaking at eighty-five in 1932. The Beaumaris and Conwy registers will have shown a similar story.

There were no ancillary organisations, the fishermen making their own sails and nets and doing their own marketing, although one of the buildings on the quay forming part of the Crossfields saw-mill and chandlery complex, was originally an ice-house for the fishing fleet. Davis (1958) refers to other fisheries. He credits the Conwy men with developing an oyster dredge that although having more complicated smith work, did not dig in and jump. Both Conwy and Bangor men used draw nets, at Conwy having 150yd of sixty meshes stapled in to 100yd. The net was braided from 3/24 cotton. The Bangor net was used for pollack, being 120yd, set in to 75, made from thirty-ply cutched cotton. The Conwy men also set longlines for flatfish, both as trots and as longlines. They were interchangeable: the trots were pinned down with wooden toggles, and the longlines weighted with rocks. The lines, called Tee lines, had thorn or pin hooks on snoods at 8-15in, with twenty hooks to a bow, and six bows to a line, baited with lug.

Conwy was a popular destination for holidaymakers and did cater for their needs. There were pleasure boats and steamers, but no sailing tripper boats as at Morecambe and Southport because the pleasure boats always went up river, under the bridges. John Crossfield's business was manager and part owner of the St George's Steamship Co., running steam paddle and motor pleasure boats on the River Conwy. They had a boat shed at the north end of the quay against the town wall with a floating jetty running down the wall into the tide. There were also three boatsheds up river at Crumrid Point on the Conwy side, for winter storage of yachts and the pleasure fleet from Llandudno, Rhyl, and Colwyn Bay.

Much of John Crossfield's output was yachts and motor pleasure boats, with repair work on boats including herring drifters. John was also commissioned as boat inspector for Aberystwyth, Conwy, Llandudno, and Penmaenmawr councils. John's list included the following boats:

Jan 1904	Cigfran	J.R. Craven	Conwy	
1905	Spika	Major Marshall	Bangor	
1927	Silver Star	Tom Parry	Llandudno	Clinker Motor Launch
1927	Shannock	Ben Clarkson	Llandudno	Clinker Motor Launch
1927	White Heather	J.A. Roberts	Llandudno	Clinker Motor Launch
1927	White Thistle IV	Jones & Williams	Llandudno	Clinker Motor Launch
1929	Sunbeam	G. Rowlands	Colwyn Bay	
Oct 1932	Heatherbell	A. Atherton	Deganwy	
1933	Betty	J. Emery	Conwy	
1933	Winifride	J. Humpherys	Llandudno Junction	
1934		A. Atherton	Deganwy	
Jan 1936	Rannock	Collins	Glan Conwy	

Aug 1936	*Mary*	J. Nicholson	Conwy	
Jan 1936	*Minnikin*	Whittaker	Colwyn Bay	
April 1938		Collins	Glan Conwy	25ft x 8ft x 2ft 6in
May 1938		Collins	Glan Conwy	25ft x 8ft x 2ft 6in
June 1938	*Sally*	R. Oliver	Bangor	Morris Navigator 26ft x 8ft x 2ft 6in

A. Antherton's yacht *Heatherbell* came out at 34ft by 11ft. She was registered to fish as CO 193 from 1941. The chapter on the builders discusses the yard's work in more detail.

Chapter 14

Cardigan Bay

Nobbies were used from the ports and havens on these coasts where the harbour provided sufficient shelter, mainly as herring drifters, and also as trawlers and as yachts. Where fishing had been prosecuted from open beaches the native small open beach boats continued in use. Neither Holdsworth (1874) nor Aflalo (1904) recorded a large fishing industry. Holdsworth found that many of the grounds were fished by big English trawlers, the Welsh confining themselves to longlining and herring drifting in small boats for consumption in the immediate vicinity, whilst smaller nobbies were not noticed at Welsh ports by Holdsworth, although there is a mention of them at welsh ports *c.* 1850. J. Geraint Jenkins (1991) gives an excellent overview of the Welsh fishing industry. The main industry was the autumn-winter herring fishery. This took place after the harvest was gathered and finished as the herring spawned. There was a little trawling and longlining where the boats were suitable, and this often depended on the nature of the harbour.

Aflalo (1904) felt that this part of the Welsh coast may 'be dismissed in a few lines'. He found a little inshore trawling at Aberystwyth, no commercial fishing at Barmouth, and Brixham and Milford trawler working out of Pwlhelli. This pattern continued into the nobby era, with Liverpool and Hoylake smacks working the Welsh trawling grounds. The Cumberland Sea Fisheries Committee minutes (1889 et seq.) recorded that Morecambe crews were living aboard their nobbies somewhere on the Welsh coast in 1897. Having become familiar with nobbies, the availability of secondhand nobbies from Southport and Morecambe Bay allowed the fishermen from the Welsh ports to change over from their native craft. The Southport boats became available due to the silting of the channels at Southport. One branch of the Wright family moved to Aberystwyth when their home port became unworkable. The Morecambe boats became available during the boom time at Morecambe when the fishermen were able to have new boats built every four to six years.

The bailiffs of the Lancashire Sea Fisheries Committee assisted the Western Sea Fisheries Committee policing the grounds off Aberystwyth in 1898. The Hoylake trawlers (smacks) were trawling on the Welsh coast taking place and soles. After the amalgamation of the districts in 1900 the first meeting of the Lancashire and Western Sea Fisheries Committee agreed to purchase a sailing boat for £200 (£15,617) for the northern division of the Welsh district. Shrimping was doing well except in the Aberdovey division. Line fishing and netting mackerel was good, especially south of Holyhead. There were problems with the southern men failing to letter and number their boats, one caught in Cardigan Bay was prosecuted. The patrol cutter *Eric* of 19t was stationed at Anglesey, Lytham's cutter was sent to Pwlhelli. The limit of beam length of 45ft was determined to be applied in the Western Region all year from 1901. South Cardigan Bay was reported to be shrimping well. In the autumn of 1901 in Division 3, the larger trawlers were doing well, the south coast trawlers were fishing in Division 4. The Aberystwyth boats were passenger sailing, working from the pier to the north of the castle. The herring catch was poor except at Pwlhelli, but the prices there were poor. The minutes report movements of boats in 1902, one second-class boat came to New Quay, one was sold from and one bought for Pwlhelli, by the year's end two second-class boats were bought for Pwlhelli, one came from Southport, and one from Falmouth, one second-class boat was bought for New Quay from Pwlhelli. Drift netting was a failure, the north Cardigan Bay was yielding poor fish in abundance (The Lancashire and Western Sea Fisheries Committee 1981 et seq.).

The superintendent's report for the winter of 1905 referred to fifteen trawlers at Pwlhelli, of which twelve laid up for the winter. By 1909 this had increased to twenty-two second-class trawlers. John Crossfields list includes the Norah, built for Jos Shallby of Pwlhelli. The nobbies took trippers out in summer, some were two-man boats, and they then went back to trawling later. A Pwlhelli owner purchased a yacht from Liverpool, a first-class smack was sold from Aberystwyth for a yacht. The minutes of 1910 record that boats were trawling Caernarfon Bay, Tremadoc Bay, and Killin ground. The Pwlhelli fishermen's incomes were raised due to the billeting system, a greater demand for fish, and a demand for pleasure sailing throughout the year from the soldiers billeted there in 1914. The Tremadoc Bay trawlers went over to drifting for herring. In 1921 Nicholas Parkinson, spokesman for the Western district, petitioned for a byelaw to allow motor trawling (The Lancashire and Western Sea Fisheries Committee 1981 et seq.), the issue of motor trawling having been on the minds of the Welsh men since it was proved possible to trawl under power.

Ashton provides evidence of one nobby at Barmouth. When researching for *Evolution of a Coast Line* in 1910, Ashton was taken out to a sarn by the Barmouth lifeboat's coxswain in his yacht. The yacht appears in the background of his photograph of the sarn, and is clearly a nobby. Barmouth received its harbour in 1902, so it will have come late to the nobby scene, especially as the advent of war in 1914 seems to have signalled a rapid decline in longshore fishing.

Three nobbies are recorded in a photograph of the Nefyn regatta, Plate 58. All three have tanned sails so may have been trawl boats; one is registered either CO 50 or CO 60. CO50 was the *Eva* at 36ft 2in x 11ft 1in x 4ft 7in keel 31ft registered as 13.88t. She was registered from 11/8/1915 until 17/2/1925 (ceased fishing). *Eva* was reputedly built in Southport. By 1915 she was owned by Thomas Hooks of Arfolyn, Abersoch, then sold on 13 January 1923 to William Harold Winterbotham, of Craig-y-Mor, Abersoch. CO 60 was carried by *Schoolgirl* (Ex LL275) from 1908 until broken up in 1936. She was a Southport boat that had a new mast fitted by R. Lathom. She fished from Abersoch from 1908 to 1911, then from Porthmadog until 1925, and then from Pwlhelli until 1936. The other vessels two with tanned sails may have been nobbies only recently sold as yachts.

There were two-dozen boats fishing from Pwlhelli in 1914. In 1915 thirteen were laid up and the crews of eight had joined up; this total had declined to eleven by 1930 (Jenkins 1991). The Stansby family is remembered from 1936 fishing Pwlhelli and Conwy. The Criccieth nobby *Benita* CO 78 appears in a photograph of Pwlhelli, Plate 59, lying in the river in front of the Gimlet Rock. She was built by Mr Nell in 1913 at 20ft 6in. There is a CO-registered lifeboat conversion lying astern of her.

Aberystwyth has long been a fishing centre. Records of herring catches date from 1206 (Troughton 1997) although the herring industry was by necessity seasonal. There were two types of boat in use in Aberystwyth in the eighteenth and early nineteenth centuries: second-class double-ended rowing boats, and small, sloop-rigged, open, second-class boats. These were unusual as herring drifters, being gaff-rigged with a bowsprit. This will have suited their other employment as they fished for herring from September until December, and carried coastal cargoes of bark, timber, and lead ore for the rest of the year. There were fifty-nine of these sloops using the harbour in the 1748 season.

The commercial development of Aberystwyth began in 1763 when the Customs Office was moved there from Aberdyfi, followed by an act that allowed harbour improvements to be commissioned from 1780. This attracted considerable coasting trade, blue water shipping, and shipbuilding to the port. This boom lasted until the arrival of the railway, which took away enough trade for the fishing industry to regain its importance. The layout of the town and its port are set out in the map Fig. 58. There is an excellent sketch from around 1820, of three little, transom-sterned, cutter- or sloop-rigged, open boats on the tide line. These may well be the descendants of the herring sloops of the 1740s. Although completely open, the boat in the foreground has a beam trawl stowed along her gunwale. The records from 1872 listed eighty-three boats of which seventy-five were third-class,

Plate 58. Nevin regatta. (Courtesy Gwynedd Archives Service)

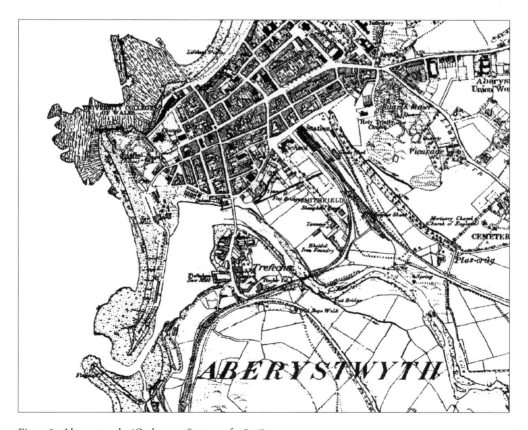

Fig. 58. Aberystwyth. (Ordnance Survey of 1846)

Plate 59. *Benita* CO 78 at Pwlhelli. (Courtesy Gwynedd Archives Service)

Plate 60. *Snowdrop.* (By Permission National Library of Wales)

Plate 61. Unidentified nobby. (By Permission National Library of Wales)

Plate 62. Unidentified nobby. (By Permission National Library of Wales)

and six were second-class (Troughton 1997). The fishing register lists twenty-nine boats in 1885, rising steadily to seventy-seven in 1896, when steady decline in numbers reduced the fleet to thirty in 1930.

The first nobbies arrived during the 1890s, to fish for herring, mackerel, and to trawl. The ex-Southport nobby *Violet* came round from Conwy in 1907. The National Library of Wales has photographs, dating from the 1920s, of the *Edith* AB 26, of about 25ft. She was registered between 10/5/1921 and 25/9/1922 when she was sold for a yacht. The *Snowdrop* was pictured with her trawl on deck and her crew selling their catch on the quay (Plate 60). *Snowdrop* was built for Richard 'Hutch' Wright of Cottage Brow Marshside, at 36ft 6in by 11ft 1in beam and 4fr 6in deep. She was registered as LL 336 from 25/10/1897 until 23/3/1921 when the family moved to Aberystwyth. The silting up of the Southport channels would have caused this migration. *Snowdrop* was registered as AB 52 from 2/4/1921 until 7/8/1930 when the register was closed 'not for fishing'. She may have been sold, as she was re-registered as AB 24 on 9/2/1931. She had been motorised and fitted with a capstan when the photograph was taken. It is likely that she was converted when she was taken to Aberystwyth, due to the timing of permission to trawl under power in 1921 discussed in the chapter on Legislation. Nobbies became very popular at Aberystwyth, adding the role of pleasure boat to their repertoire. The boats working as pleasure boats, which included the local open double-enders, worked off the beach next to the pier to the north of the town. Plate 61, which includes at least three nobbies, and Plate 62 are also the collection of the National Library of Wales (Troughton 1997); however, they do not carry fishing registry numbers, making identification difficult. The two gentlemen selling *Snowdrop*'s catch of mackerel in Plate 60 are the same two pictured on the deck of the nobby in Plate 61. Both photographs were taken around 1925. There were at least fifteen nobbies registered at Aberystwyth of which *Enid* was the only one purpose built for the Cardigan Bay coast.

The herring season varied according to local tradition. At Aberystwyth the second week in November was believed to be the best, at Aberporth the fishing was from September until Christmas, at Moelfre it extended from October until February, at Nefyn from September to January. Where nobbies were used they were from the full range of lengths available, some were built in Welsh ports, although Geraint Jenkins does not identify where, and some were re-rigged as ketches. At Pwlheli and Criccieth the nobbies set fleets of thirty-five nets of 30–40yd in length; each net had five buoys in addition to the head rope corks. The Aberystwyth boats fished from Porthmadog to New Quay. They set fleets of fifteen to twenty nets each of 30yd by 24ft depth with a mesh of one and ¼in. The foot rope was weighted with beach stone, each secured by being wrapped in a rag and tied to the footrope with twine, about a hundred to each net (Jenkins 1991).

The trawling grounds off Aberystwyth lay between New Quay and Aberaeron, and from five miles south of Aberystwyth to New Quay Head where lying inshore a clay bottom known as the Gutter was prolific, and a sandy bottom further off but within twelve miles off was also reliable. The big English and Milford smacks worked these grounds before nobbies made the grounds accessible to the local men.

Chapter 15

The Builders

The most famous builders of Lancashire nobbies in their home range is probably the Crossfield family of Arnside, Westmoreland, although William Stoba, whose reputation earned him commissions from as far a field as the pilots working out of the Bristol Channel, could also claim that honour. There were nobby builders in ports or fishing stations from Annan to Criccieth, although some are only known by the survival of single boats and unfortunately little is now recorded about many of them.

Due to the efforts of Mr H.E. Crossfield, who was kind enough to make his genealogical research available, the family tree of the boat-building Crossfields, simplified by omitting descendants of the children who were not involved in boat-building, can be published.

The family has been traced back to the mid-seventeenth century at Polton-le-Sands (now Morecambe) in Lancashire. The next four generations remained at Polton as husbandmen, and then came Edmund, a cooper who served his time at Lancaster. A husbandman farmed between ten and forty acres of land and had his own house or cottage. Edmund moved to Liverpool were he married before moving back to Lancaster. There they occupied Pot House, situated on the south bank of the Lune at the corner of St Georges Quay and Lune Road. Three of Edmunds sons learned trades associated with shipping, one as a sail maker, one a shipwright; John, born 1782, served his time as a ship's carpenter. John went on to work at shipyards at Greenodd and at Ulverston before trading as a lath river. Whilst in Furness he fathered two sons and four daughters, they then moved to Milnthorp in 1817-8, and then on to Arnside where he traded again as a ship carpenter. In the census of 1841 John was listed living in his son Thomas's household at Woodbine Cottage (Plate 63) as

Plate 63. Woodbine cottage.

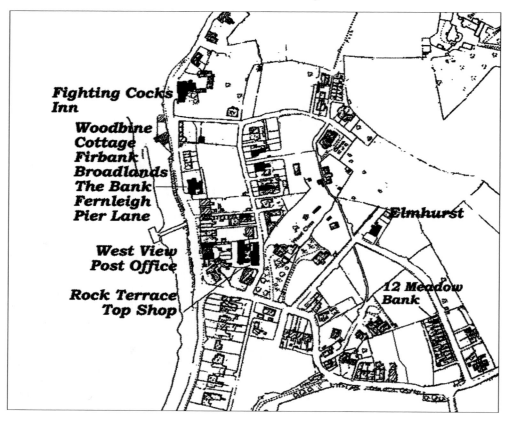

Fig. 59. Arside map (Ordnance Survey of 1846)

was his second son Francis John. Woodbine Cottage is on the lane that leads up from the Promenade by the Crown Hotel to Church Hill (see the map Fig. 59). The addresses given here were recorded in Bretton's *A History of Arnside*, which reports that Francis John built his first boat in 1838. A report in the *Lancaster Gazette* of 7 March 1840 records:

> Rare Shot – On Thursday week, Mr. F. Crossfield, of Arnside, killed at one shot, on these sands, nine wild grey ducks, out of a flock of 16. About six weeks ago the same person killed 40 seapyes at one discharge. He is provided with a small boat and large gun for fowling. One day last week the same person killed a goosander, a beautiful bird. The goosander is a very rare bird in this part.

The same newspaper in 1844 credits Francis as a winning helmsman with a fast boat in its report of the first Arnside regatta.

Francis John married in 1842, and lived until 1849 in a thatched cottage on the site now occupied by the Bank, which is just north of the pier. They then moved to West View on the Promenade. By the time of the census of 1851 they had an apprentice and an indoor servant living in, and employed three men at a carpentry and boat building business. Francis John's first boatshed was near West View, but its site is now lost. It may have been in the complex of buildings behind the Post Office marked on the OS of 1862, which may in its turn have been the cottage that they occupied until 1849. The OS map shows only this one set of buildings between the Fighting Cocks Inn and the Albion Hotel. It is remembered that the boat yard was higher on Church Hill before moving to the Rock Terrace corner, but this may be apocryphal. Francis John's family then moved to Pier Lane, Plate 64, to the house later used as the police station on the corner of Church Hill, and built the Rock Terrace Boat Shop Plate 65.

Right: Plate 64. Pier Lane

Below: Plate 65. Top Shop

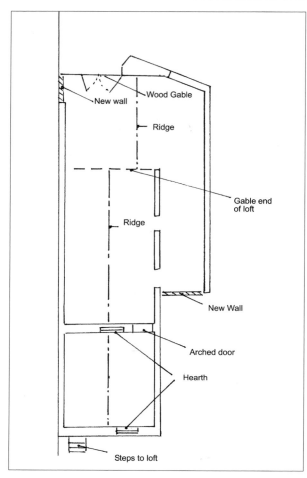

New wall

Wood Gable

Ridge

Gable end
of loft

Ridge

New Wall

Arched door

Hearth

Steps to loft

Left: Fig. 60. Plan of Top Shop.

Below: Plate 66. Francis John, Mary Crossfield and children. (Courtesy of Lancaster City Museums)

The boat shed is little changed; some windows have been blocked, and the timber board gable ends renewed, whilst internally the loft has been divided, a new stair provided and the heavily loaded roof truss under the loft gable has been shored up with a pillar. A sketch plan appears as Fig. 60. At the back of the workshop, through an arched opening, is a room with two hearths. It is possible that one may have been for a steam box boiler, it may be that one was for a smithy hearth as John, when at Conwy, ordered his boats iron work from the family at Arnside. The last steam box was at the back of the building, between it and the Rock Terrace backyards. Francis John was widowed at 41, and married again after a year, fathering a total of nine children. Plate 66 is a picture of Francis and Mary with five of his sons and one daughter. Considering the probable ages of the children, and relating them to the dates on the family tree, we can suggest the identities of the children pictured. Going clockwise from 12 o'clock we have William, Frances James, Thomas kneeling, John (seated), George, and Jane. Margaret would be married in her own household, but Mary Hanna, who we could expect to be in the picture is missing. Francis John's five surviving sons, William, Francis James, Thomas, John, and George, continued in the boat-building business, although Francis James and Thomas eventually moved away from Arnside, both to trade as joiners.

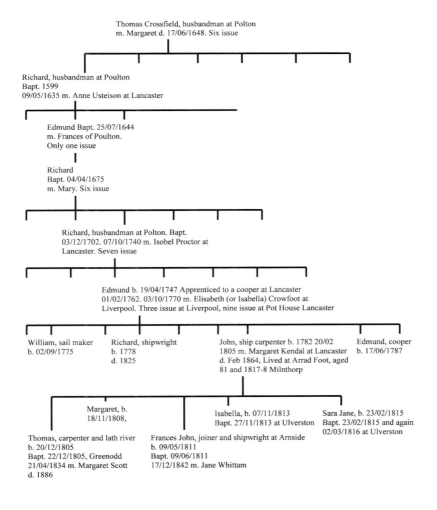

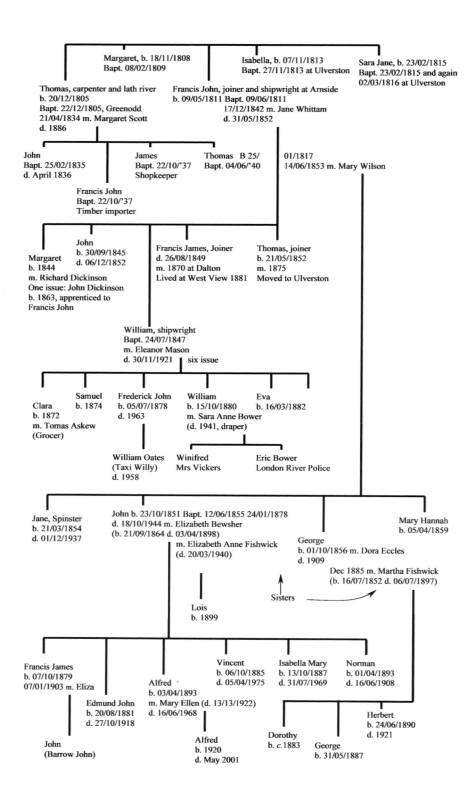

The 1881 census lists Francis John living in the Post Office, employed as postman and joiner with his grandson, John Dickinson, as a live-in joiner's apprentice. The Post Office was probably next-door but one to the Albion Hotel. There were three dwellings called West View between the Post Office and the Pier. The middle one, Plate 67, was occupied by Francis John's son Francis James, his wife Margaret, and children Mary Jane, Charlotte E., Eleanor M., Mabel, and Francis. William was living in Prospect Villas, and John and George had each set up home in a Rock Terrace property (Plate 68). The census enumerator recorded that two more of the Rock Terrace cottages were still building in 1881, leaving the fifth to be started after the census date.

Bulmer's Directory of 1885 lists Crossfields Brothers, implying that Frances John had retired. He was then seventy-four, and passed away aged eighty-eight in 1899. All five brothers were running the business, and it is likely that William will have done much of

Plate 67. West View.

Plate 68. Rock Terrace.

Plate 69. William Crossfield and staff. (Courtesy of Lancaster City Museums)

Above left: Plate 70. Firbank.

Above right: Plate 71. Firnleigh.

the designing, as he is the only brother credited by *Lloyd's List of Yachts* as the designer of their craft at Arnside. Some of the brothers were known to have been employed as crew on the Windermere racing yachts, and the business built for Windermere, giving them useful experience in the developments taking place in hull forms. Bulmer's lists them as pleasure boat proprietors, as well as boat builders and joiners, whilst William was also listed as keeping lodgings at Prospect Villas. Family papers revealed that the joinery work was also undertaken. William left Crossfield Bros., to build a new boat shed, in 1892 or 1893. He was probably managing the partnership up until that time, as the evidence for the 1892 date of the split is derived from the start of John's list of boats built, whilst Bretton quoted 1893.

William's new premises were built in an old quarry on the beach to the south of the village, using the quarry face as the rear gable wall. This later proved too small for one of his commissions, so a recess was cut into the living rock. Plate 69 records Frederick, his father William, brother William, uncle Frances James, and employee John Burrow at the top of the beach in front of the shed.

The first mention of the Rock Terrace boat shop was in 1894, where they were listed in Kelly's Directory, however this site will have been occupied before the 1881 census. The same Kelly's entry lists a Francis Crossfield at West View, this may be Francis John living retired in the house that housed Francis James. Rock Terrace housed Francis James, John, and Thomas. George's wife kept apartments at Fir Bank, Plate 70, and William had moved to Fernleigh, Plate 71, were his wife now kept apartments. Bretton quotes a news paper clipping of 8 of April 1893, stating that Crossfield Bros launched Airside's biggest boat on the previous Tuesday (the 4th). She was 38ft 6in long by 10ft 6in beam and 6ft draught, intended for cod and prawn fishing. John's list has her as the *Ellen Anne* for Mr D. Leadbetter of Fleetwood; she was registered as FD 102 from 7/4/1893 to 21/07 1899. Rock Terrace is part way up a moderately steep hill – the new boats had to be manhandled down Church Hill, turn onto the steeper Silverdale Road, and run down onto the beach. The promenade and its slipways was not there in 1893, as it was built to celebrate Queen Victoria's Jubilee in 1897. We were told that launches were arranged for Fridays, and the school allowed the boys to help manhandle the boats, declaring a holiday so that the children could then watch the boat float off of her cradle. Plate 32 is a photograph of *Red Rose* at one such launching.

Plate 72.
Broadlands.

The 1901 census recorded that four of Francis John's sons were living at Arnside. William with his family and son-in-law Thomas Askew occupied Fernleigh. Frances James was living at Kent Villa with Margaret and their five children, his son-in-law, and a domestic servant. John was living at Rock Terrace, and George was at Broadlands, Plate 72.

Whilst John was keeping his list of boats built at Arnside, Crossfield Brothers averaged over five boats a year, building ten in 1896, a total of seventy boats in thirteen years. The business also employed apprentices who probably stayed on as journeymen; with this throughput of nobbies and yachts the joinery and other woodwork undertaken by the business may have been its mainstay. This is supported by their declared occupations in the census as joiners rather than boat builders. Alfie spoke of his grandfather John's extensive knowledge of wooden farm and builder's equipment including gates and wheelbarrows.

In addition to the nobbies mentioned in the chapters on the fishing ports, John built the following yachts and boats:

6 Aug 1892	*Mag*	James Clarke	Arnside	
19 March 1894	*Seagull*	Mr Higgins	Bolton	Yacht
27 March l894	*Ethal*	James Jackson	Barrow	Yacht
2 July 1898	*Iris*	James Geldert	Barrow	Yacht
2 July 1898	*Naiad*	Isaac Geldert	Barrow	Yacht
17 Sept 1898	*Hubbane*	Dr Shepherd	Arnside	Yacht
13 Feb 1900	*Flying Fish*	John Jackson	Barrow	Yacht
15 Aug 1900	*Ruby*	Crossfield Bros	Arnside	
22 Dec 1900	*Cock-o'-the-North*	J. Jackson	Barrow	Yacht
7 Aug 1901	*Ploughboy*	J. Jackson	Barrow	Yacht
8 May 1902	*Estrel*	Mr Galloway	Fleetwood	Yacht
11 Nov 1902	*Jean*	W. Raby	Piel	
6 Jun l903	*Sirroc*	R. Kirkham	Peel	
11 Jul 1904	*Jean II*	Crossfield Bros	Arnside	
1905	*Britannia*	Robert Kirkham	Peel	
6 Jun 1905	*Norgi*	J. Stevenson	Fleetwood	Motor Launch
28 Oct 1905	*Albert Edward*	A. Friendly	Bradford	
19 May 1906	*Wallaroo*	J. Spurr	Fleetwood	Yacht
1908	*Mauretania*	Miss Williams & Davis	Aberystwyth	
1913	*Ein-na*	From *Lloyd's List of Yachts* 1919		CB cutter
1914	*Olga*	From *Lloyd's List of Yachts* 1919		Auxiliary Yawl
1928	*Thelma*	E.L. Vickers	Betws-y-Coed	Yacht
1929	*Patricia*	Robertson	Manchester	
1930	*Naiad*	H. Stott	Manchester	
1933	*Mayflower*	Thomas	Aberystwyth	
1935	*Calloo*	A.D. Staite	Birmingham	
Jan 1936	*Lotus*	O'Farrell	Morfa Nevin	
1 Aug 1936	*Dolphine*	Tom Lilley	Port Dinorwic	
15 May 1937	*Sea Hawk*	White Bros	Aberystwyth	
10 Aug 1937		Tom Lilley	Port Dinorwic	

William's business continued as W. Crossfield & Sons, closing after the Second World War. William's two sons, Frederick John and William (Plate 73) were building nobbies up until the war, also producing the last of the Morecambe fishermen's lifeboats, the *Sir William Priestley* in 1934. She is now preserved at Lancaster Maritime Museum. Frederick appears in the photo of the launching of a big nobby, possibly for Southport, included as Plate 74. William died in 1941 but Frederick (Plate 75) continued, building his last two boats, a 14ft and a 16ft punt in 1946. Dick Woodhouse, who wrote memoirs of the sailing industry, remembered W. Crossfield building four to five boats a year. He states that the quickest that he remembered

Right: Plate 73. Frederick John and William Crossfield. (Courtesy of National Museums Liverpool [Merseyside Maritime Museum])

Below: Plate 74. Frederick J. Crossfield at the launching of a nobby. (Courtesy of National Museums Liverpool [Merseyside Maritime Museum])

Plate 75. Frederick J. Crossfield. (Courtesy of National Museums Liverpool [Merseyside Maritime Museum])

was three weeks and four days, for £45 delivered to Morecambe. It has been assumed that this involved working fifty-hour weeks; however, Alfie Crossfield reminded the author that without electric light you could only work when the sun was bright. At Conwy, and probably also at Arnside, work stopped at Saturday midday. Saturday afternoon was for the barber, so that you could get spruced up for your Sunday best.

Unfortunately little documentary materiel now survives from William's branch of the business, although the Mersey Nobby Association published an estimate Frederic John & William offered in 1933. The prospective owner was from Warrington, being quoted £152 (£7,383) for a 30ft trawl boat, hull and spars, with boiler punchings in concrete for ballast. They also quoted £182 (£8,840) for the boat rigged with sails. Even though engines were usually fitted from 1925, there is no mention of supplying or fitting one in the estimate. Their bill for the building of the yacht *Nanette* also survives, totalling £169 4s 5d (£8,220) complete and provided with sails and equipment. Some of her outfit included a cabin stove for £4 5s (£206), fixing cost 6s (£14.57), beaching legs, £1 5s (£60.71), gold line 18s (£43.72), and 20lb of yacht manila rope at £1 6s 8d (£64.76). Their letterhead proclaimed (alongside a photograph of a small nobby or yacht under all sail):

W. Crossfield & Sons, (F.J. Crossfield & Wm. Crossfield) YACHT & BOAT BUILDERS, Etc. PROMENADE, ARNSIDE.

The letterhead had the first three digits of the year 1933 pre-printed, some eight years after their father had passed away. Bretton records that Frederick, who lived at 12 Meadow Bank Plate 76, finally retired in 1952.

John had been invited to holiday in Conwy, by the owner of a new boat who was weather bound at Arnside, having come up by train to collect his boat. John's list includes *Cigfran*, built for Mr J.R. Craven of Conwy dated 18 January 1904. The new boat's owner was staying as John's guest until the weather abated. John had mentioned that there was not enough work for all of the family at Arnside during conversation at dinner, which prompted the idea of moving to the Welsh port. *Cigfran*'s registration details have her

Plate 76. 12 Meadow Bank.

Plate 77. Elmshurst.

built by Crossfield Brothers in 1904, Register number 109638, register dimensions 39.5ft x 12.4ft x 6.3ft and 12.18t. Mr H. Kneeshaw of Beaumaris owned her in 1905 to be renamed *Amasis* by Albert Leach of Beaumaris by 1913.

John made the trip south, and having seen the opportunities moved to Deganwy in 1906, purchasing the site for a boat yard at Conwy. Kelly's of 1906 lists his brothers Francis James at Elmhurst, Plate 77, and George at Broadlands. George is known to have traded as George Crossfield with his sons, George and Herbert joining him. After their father's death in 1909, George and Herbert went on to continue the business, re-establishing the name Crossfield Brothers until they moved to Hoylake in 1915. They built *Jean* and *Moya* at Arnside in 1910, both appear in the Lloyd's list of 1919. William continued designing and building yachts and fishing boats including *Laura* and *Maid Marian* in 1908 and *Arabis* and *Sapphire* in 1912 (all from Lloyd's list of 1919), to be followed by his sons at Beach Walk. Both boat sheds are still standing, the Top Shop on Church Hill is a builder's workshop, whilst Beach Walk has continued as a boat shed, although somewhat altered and doing less business with time.

Neither of George's sons stayed long at Hoylake. Their health was broken by their service in the Great War, Herbert did little building and some fishing until his death in 1921. George retired to Conwy in the same year, they had only built a small number of nobbies whilst on the Wirral.

John took all but one of his family to Conwy, his oldest son having moved to Barrow-in-Furness to work at Ashburners shipyard. John's two sons Alfred and Vincent worked at the family business, and his daughter Isabella Mary served as company secretary. The business throve, producing many fine yachts and fishing boats. John took over the Pensarn timber yard, running it from 1910 to 1920. The boat sheds appear at the northern corner of the town walls, with Pensarn opposite the castle to the south on the sketch map. The war years kept them busy making spokes and poles for army wagons and limbers. The family also had shares in the St George's Steamship Co., managing a small fleet of pleasure paddle steamers, running trips up river. The author was fortunate to have been introduced to John's grandson Alfie, who told of the fishing boats and yachts built by the yard, as well as other wooden products including wheel barrows, farm gates etc.

The first boat shed was built over a small dock, purchased from Conwy's mayor, Sir Albert Wood. The dock was formed from a 6ft wide sandstone quay under the spur of the town wall, with a second buttressed sandstone quay 18ft off. The dock was about 6ft deep, with a shingle bottom on which the keel blocks were set. The hull was set up with the turn of the bilge at the level of the cope, which saved on staging. As the business grew two more sheds were built at Conwy, and three sheds were built up river to provide winter storage.

The boat yard used the shed of the St George's Steamship Co. for storage of the plank stock. Much of this was pitch pine in 14in wide boards, long enough to plank the hull in single lengths. This timber was delivered from Liverpool on the steamer that delivered flour to the areas bakers twice a week. The framing timber came from Arnside and Denbigh by rail to be stored by the sawmill. This saw mill and a chandlery was at the castle end of the quay, as indicated on the sketch map. The buildings were originally a brewery and an icehouse. The old customs house by Porth Bach, now the Harbour Master's office, was used as both the boat yard and Steamship Companies office, run by John's daughter Isabella. These appear on the map Fig. 61.

There was also an engineer's and blacksmith's business (J.&A. Higginbottom) in premises on the quay, which carried out the installation of the engines in the Crossfield boats. Alfie remembered the difficulty of moving timber between the saw mill and the building shed, and of sawing out keels set up on trestles and fish boxes on the quay, when it was thronged with summer visitors. When Alfie started his apprenticeship with his grandfather there were five other apprentices, earning 5s a week for the first three years and 7s 6d for the last two (£12.00 and £18.60). The business employed about fifteen in total, with the journeymen earning about £2 10s (£120) a week.

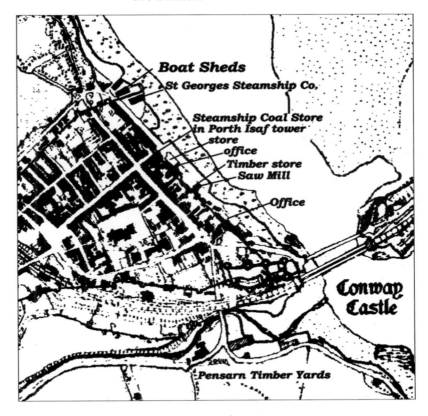

Fig. 61. Conwy map. (Ordnance Survey of 1846)

The yards two largest boat sheds were capable of building two boats each. When John took semi-retirement he purchased a shed at Deganwy Dock for building. Again this arm of the business expanded, to total three sheds. John passed away in 1944, to leave his children to manage the yard until they sold up in 1947. The business and the Crossfield name was bought by Mr McDonald, and continued in other hands until at least 1987, but the boat sheds, Fig. 62, were demolished in 1994. Although there were four other builders working, when Alfie set up after the Second World War Crossfields were the only builder of nobbies at Deganwy and Conwy.

John built trawl boats for owners at Annan, Aberystwyth, Deganwy, Fleetwood, Lytham, Morecambe, Heswall, Parkgate, Rock Ferry, and Southport. Boats were also built for owners in Arnside, Bangor, Barrow, Betws-y-Coed, Birkenhead, Birmingham, Blackpool, Bradford, Colwyn Bay, Llandudno, Manchester, Morfa Nefyn, New Brighton, Port Dinorwic, Prestatyn, and Rhyl; this second part of the list includes pleasure boats and private yachts, and may include trawl boats. John's list records the building of two boats in 1906, one in 1907 and five in 1908. Only one boat is listed for 1909 through to 1920, when John was running Pensarn timber yard and doing war work. *Nama* was built for Sir Richard Williams-Bulkeley in 1913. She was sailed to Tahiti in 1930-31 when renamed *Pacific Moon*. She had a moulding that ran right round her counter in shrimping nobby style. She was modelled for a yacht at 6ft draught on 36ft length. Unlike his brother William, John seems to have used fishing boat details on his yachts, even though their proportions are of deep-drafted yacht forms. The list goes on to include thirty-seven boats from 1920 to 1940, of all sizes up to the *Thelma*, a 75ft yacht for a merchant at Betws-y-Coed. Alfie remembered the casting of her keel with the mould set in the beach below the boat shed. She was so big that they had to take her over to Deganwy Dock to step her mast.

Fig. 62. John Crossfield's boat yard.

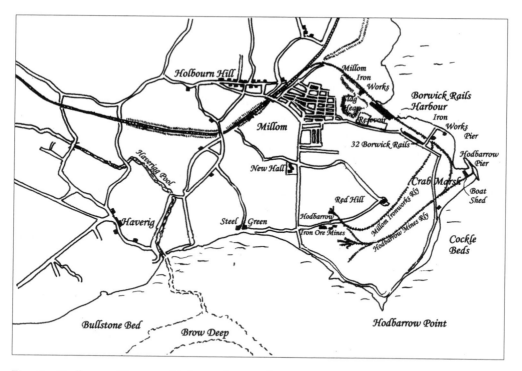

Fig. 63. Hodbarrow Pier map. (Ordnance Survey of 1846)

Trawl boats were also built at Annan, Millom, Barrow-in-Furness, Ulverston, Morecambe, Overton, Glasson, Fleetwood, Freckleton, Hesketh Bank, Crossens, and Marshside near Southport, Tranmere, and at Criccieth. Those builders working in the major fishing ports are discussed in the chapters on the fishing stations. The author has not been able to uncover as much about these builders as has survived to commemorate the Crossfields; in two cases only a picture of one boat bears testament to the existence of a builder. This implies that there may have been builders that are still unknown to us.

William Anderson worked at Millom, in Cumberland (now Cumbria), alongside the shipyard on Hodbarrow Pier (see map Fig. 63). William had come from Whitehaven to 32 Borwick Rails, the end of a terrace of large houses by the iron works. He probably moved down the coast in 1866 or 1867, bringing his son Wells. His second son Vincent Edmundson was born in 1868 at Millom. William was then 35 and Wells was 18. The census of 1871 listed William as a shipwright. It also listed a shipbuilder at Crab Marsh, and a pier master. William's wife Jane died some time between the census of 1871 and 1881. The listing of 1881 has him maintaining a household on the pier, with a live-in domestic servant, trading as chandler and ship's carpenter. In Bulmer's directory of 1883 he was listed as a boat builder and chandler. By the 1891 census William had remarried to another Whitehaven lass. Vincent was still living at home on Hodbarrow Pier, but Wells had married and moved in with his widowed mother-in-law. William was still trading as chandler, and Wells as a shipbuilder.

William's sons may have been in the boat-building and chandlery business since 1883, but the brevity of both the directory and the census entries gives us no clues about the structure of the business. A dip into *Lloyd's List of Yachts* of 1919 lists five yachts built between 1897 and 1913 all built by W. Anderson. The author was invited aboard *Ellidi*, built in 1912 as a yacht to a design by Vincent, although she carried the Barrow fishing registry number BW 111 from 1/5/1918 to 17/9/1919. She is rather full in the bow, with a very long counter, implying a long run. The counter has been shortened; unfortunately there is nothing to show how the counter was originally finished off. Her bow profile is cut away, with a chin to the front of the ballast keel, a yacht profile with the beginnings of a fin keel. *Ellidi* has iron floors, double sawn frames, and a bilge stringer. The deck is laid on widely spaced beams; there has been some reworking of the beam shelf, so her deck may have been more or less altered in her 86-year life. The Andersons also built the 30ft *Heloise* in 1900. She fished for four years before being sold for a yacht. Mr A.W. Ardagh entered her in the under 25ft water line event of the 1906 Roa Island regatta. *Heloise* survived until at least the mid-1990s at Salcombe, having spent some time at Hamble, and then in the Orwell.

William was listed in the directories as a shipbuilder from 1894 to 1906, working on Duddon Wharf. William will have been seventy-three in 1906. Wells was listed as a shipwright in 1901; folk memory has him in the family business, but he may have been working for the schooner yard. By 1906 Wells, then aged fifty-six, was listed as a Private Resident, implying that he had retired with independent means. Vincent was not listed in any of the directories, so he must have worked in his fathers business, and probably lived with father until moving in with Wells. W. Anderson was credited in Lloyd's with the design of a yacht built in 1897, and two in 1909, and the builder and designer listed for a yacht of 1913 was Wm. Anderson & Sons. We did not find a record of the burial of William or of his wife at Millom. This may have been because the record was not available to us, or possibly because they both returned back to Whitehaven to enjoy William's retirement.

The yard was listed in Kelly's as yacht builders from 1910 to 1929. The last boat was started for Vincent's own use, a 35ft boat to be called *Tarn*. Vincent was one of the only two designers, William Stoba being the other, who were remembered as working entirely from paper. The Andersons produced about twelve to fifteen trawl boats for Millom owners. Four of these were in the 40ft range, as some of the Millom men looked offshore for cod and deeper water fish. We are advised that many of the Millom fishing

Plate 78.
Cachalot
bow quarter.
(Courtesy
of National
Museums
Liverpool
[Merseyside
Maritime
Museum])

Plate 79.
Cachalot
stern quarter.
(Courtesy
of National
Museums
Liverpool
[Merseyside
Maritime
Museum])

Plate 80.
Ingram's boat
shed.

community settled there from Fleetwood, coming from the cod fishers of that port. The *Irene* of 39ft was fished out of Fleetwood, and claimed to be Millom built. Vincent died in March of 1926, to be buried from Wells' house. Vincent's own yacht lay in the boat shed planked up to the bilge until the Anderson's estate was settled after Wells died in January 1933.

The 1904 *Kelly's Directory* lists two boat builders at Barrow-in-Furness: Hugh Bannister of 4 Hindpool Road and David McGruer of Ferry Road. Unfortunately no one remembers a builder working before Ingram & Parr, so we have not been able to confirm either of these as nobby builders. Ingram and Parr, trading as the Limit Motorboat Co., built the only known Barrow nobby, *Cachalot* (Plates 78 & 79), for Mr George Mount of Morecambe. Richard Ingram was the boat builder, whilst his partner's main employment was as engineer on the dredger that kept Walney Channel clear. Ingram's boat shed survives on Ferry Beach (Plate 80) as part of Barrow Sailing Club. The shed was one of several built as emergency accommodation for the rapidly increasing population of workers attracted to Barrow. Ingram's shed was the Mission hall, whilst two of the dormitory huts still survive. Unfortunately Parr's boat shed and the sawmill that linked them were demolished in July 1996.

We were fortunate to meet Mr A. George who had persuaded Mr Ingram to allow him to work as tea boy in the summer of 1930 when *Cachalot* was building. He has clear memories of Mr Ingram walking around the boat when it was in frame, with a plane in his hand sighting to check for fairness, and later he remembers the steaming of the cockpit coaming. Her planking of 1⅛in larch and her framing was heavy at 2in by 4in doubled. Close study of Plate 79 reveals the unusual run of the garboard and next strake, which run down from stern rebate to the keel so that the garboard is triangular.

Cachalot was registered LR 13 on 14/7/1930 until she transferred to Parkgate on 1/11/1934, she was still working, to come up for sale in 1994. She was the only nobby built by Richard Ingram, who built several motor launches for the Morecambe pleasure boat companies, and usually supplied a double diagonal-built punt with his commissions. Plate 80 shows that the shed had to be extended to make room for a 40ft motorboat for Morecambe, whilst Plate 81 is of one of his punts. She is double skinned, diagonal inner and fore and aft outer, over closely spaced, steamed frames, and is a lovely piece of work. It is said that Mr Ingram died relatively young, due to lead poisoning developed from exposure to the pastes used for luting in the double skin planking of the punts.

Plate 81.
Double-skin
punt.

Plate 82. *Nora* FD 46. (Courtesy Raymond Sankey)

Plate 83. *Eva.* (Courtesy Raymond Sankey)

Of the several trawl boats built at Ulverston, one produced in 1912 still survives. Dan McLester built her for the Guide over the Sands from Flukeborough to Canal Foot, Ulverston. She is called *Hearts of Oak*, as a testament to the quality of timber selected for her frame. Her builder served his time as a shipwright at one of the Ulverston shipyards, but was running the pub at Canal Foot when he put her together. *Hearts of Oak* BW 40 worked her way up to Maryport through a varied career, where she was purchased by a member of the Mersey Nobby Association, and taken down to Liverpool to start a new life as a yacht. As the sands guide was also the pilot retained by the Iron works at Ulverston, it is likely that the iron works contributed to her build. She was fitted with an iron ballast keel, which looks as though it had warped as it cooled, so *Hearts of Oak* was built with a hog to her wood keel. She has a distinctive curved stem creating a snib bow appearance above the water. She is also one of the few to have been built with a centre plate and has slightly more freeboard than is usual, possibly because Peter Butler intended her for use as a tripper boat as well as for shrimping.

Moving south again, and bypassing Arnside and Morecambe, we reach Woodhouse's of Overton. This yard produced salmon whammel boats, mussel doggers, yachts, and trawl boats. Several of their whammel boats have survived, the youngest being built in 1923, still drift-netting salmon in the Lune. Dick Woodhouse also remembered the *Sue* being built at Overton. She was a Woodhouse boat. Records survive of *Maud Wilson* being built by Woodhouse's in 1893. She was registered LR 83 at 29ft by 8ft 9in by 4ft deep, and of *Peggy*, LR 6 (later LR 100) built for William Brookes of 2 Walton Avenue, Morecambe, in 1929. She was a 24-footer. Kelly's of 1904 refers to Mr J. Gardner building at Overton. *Nora* FD 46, Plate 82, was built at Overton to be registered on 8/4/1892, but her registration documents do not record by whom. One of a pair of irons bolted to her side two or three frames aft of her shrouds can be seen in her photo; these were fitted to take the beaching legs, and were often supplied even when the more modern deck eyebolts were fitted. *Nora* was re-registered on the Fleetwood registry to become FD 116 on 13/11/1900.

Upstream on the opposite bank of the Lune to Overton is the port of Glasson. The Firm of Nicholson & Marsh had their yard and ran the graving dock in the outer basin, building trading schooners (and the Barrow pilot schooner *Argus*). The yard's buildings were along side the entrance gates, with the slipway launching into the river outside the dock gates. The Fleetwood registry records that *Eva* FD 184, Plate 83, was Glasson built in 1895, but give no record of by whom. *Eva* is of interest as hers is the only photo we have illustrating a southern-built boat with the halyards belayed to pins in the sailing beam. *Eva* was built for Samuel Haughton of Morecambe to be registered from 2/1/1895 until 2/5/1913, when she transferred to FD 184 from 28/5/1913 to 26/6/1920. She then went to Liverpool as LL 84.

By-passing Fleetwood we come to the Ribble. This estuary gave access to a creek and a river on which there were three boat yards. Rawstrone had their yard on the cut at Freckleton. An account book, and its supporting day-book kept at the yard survives, listing boats for Fleetwood, Lytham St Anne's, Preston, Hesketh Bank, Banks, Marshside and Southport. Six were Bay boats, there were trawl boats for Fleetwood, and there were fifty-eight shankers built and repaired for Southport, Lytham St Anne's, Banks, and Marshside owners.

Robert Rawstrone and George Rigby set up the yard in 1814 as shipbuilders and wheelwrights. William Rawstrone was working as a wheelwright in 1852 and John Rawstrone later owned the boat yard. Peter Rawstrone's surviving accounts ledger and the rough daybook cover the period from 1870 to 1893. In May 1881 Peter took his employee Henry Allunson into partnership.

The ledgers list the yards employees and their wage rates on the bigger jobs. This also allows the yards employees to be identified year on year. The data reveals the following names and daily rates.

Year listed	1870	1871	1872	1875	1879	1887
Value of 1s in 2005	£3.08	£3.08	£2.89	£3.07	£3.38	£3.90
P. Rawstrone	4s			4s 4d	4s 4d	Wage not given
H. Rawstrone	Wage not given	2s sawyer				
H. Allunson	4s				4s 4d	
J. Butler		4s				
J.T. Battersby	4s			4s 4d		
J. Iddon		3s			4s 4d	
J. Whittle	2s					
J. Parker	Wage not given					
J. Wright		4s				
N. Bannister		4s				
T. Hargreaves		1s		4s	4s 4d	
R. Richardson			4s	4s 4d	4s 4d	
G. Rigby			2s		4s	
W. Sumner			2s	3s sawyer	4s	
E. Nickson				4s sawyer		
J. Halsall				2s 6d	3s 6d	
G. Richardson				2s 4d	3s	
R. Rawstrone					2s 8d	
W. Cook					4s 4d	
I. Sumner					3s 6d	
F. Hacking						Wage not given

Three of the new-built boats provide a record of the man-hours expended; they were:

Shanker for Benjamin Ball of Southport 1881		Moon Light for Lawson of Southport 1884		Nightingale for Dawson of Lytham 1885	
P. Rawstrone	17¾	P. Rawstrone	13¾	P. Rawstrone	13¼
H. Allonson	32¼	H. Allonson	9¼	H. Allonson	9¼
R. Richardson	19¾	T. Battersby	28¼	T. Battersby	50¾
J. Iddon	2¾	J. Iddon	3	J. Iddon	24¾
H. Rawstrone	9	H. Rawstrone	8¼		
G. Rigby	12¼	G. Rigby	28¼	G. Rigby	½
W. Sumner	19¼	W. Sumner	16½	W. Sumner	23¾
J. Halsall	8			J. Halsall	15½
G. Richardson	9¼	G. Richardson	8¼	G. Richardson	13
R. Rawstrone	27	R. Rawstrone	3	R. Rawstrone	16¼
T. Rawstrone	12¾	T. Rawstrone	8¼	T. Rawstrone	26¼
		E. Hacking	2½	E. Hacking	13
W. Cook	2½	T. Iddon	17	T. Iddon	24¾
T. Sumner	16¾				
Total man-hours	189¼	Total man-hours	146 ¼	Total man-hours	231

The daybook included much information about the materials and items of outfit used in the shankers and Bay boats, the most enlightening of which is summarised in the following tabulation:

Mary	Bay boat	J. Rimmer	Copper nails and clench nails, larch, pine, Quebec elm
	Bay boat	Mr Jas Robinson	Including spars, mast 13½ft, boom 4½ft
		Mr Richard (Henry Cotty) Wright	Making iron keel mould, fettling 4 shroud irons, spar for mast 16½ft
Clipper	Bay boat	Mr Richard (Henry Cotty) Wright & John (Bull) Rigby	Spar for mast, Quebec elm and oak, pitch pine
Clipper	Shanking boat	Richard (Henrys) Wright	1gal black varnish, 5 gallon gas tar
	Shanking boat	Peter (Cotty) Wright	New elm logs for keel and timbers, yellow pine plank
Alice Ann	Shanking boat		New boat & hatches, iron work £3 2s (£211), Pump 14s (£47.72)
	Shanking boat	B. Ball	Iron keel, 8cwt 2qtr, @6s 3d £2 21s 1d (£222), 1 barrel cement 9s (£33), sand 1s 10s (£36.38)
Moon Light	Shanking boat	Lawson	Contract for hull iron work spars hoops, and hatches, pump 17s 2½d (£59.79), Iron work £2 5s 11d (£159.53)
Nightingale	Shanking boat	Dawson	4 men 6 days planking up, iron keel 20cwt 3 quarters @ 6s £6 4s 6d (£452.88)
	Shanking boat	B. Ball	Iron keel, 8cwt 2 quarters, @6s 3d £2 13s 1d (£193.10), cast @ Preston
New boat	Shanking boat	W. Watkinson	8½cwt iron keel, launched 8 December 1885
Golden Arrow	Shanking boat	T.R. Ascroft	6lb black lead, varnish inside and out, getting ballast out 6s (£23.42), 14ft oars, J. Harrison 40½hr @ 6s per hr paid for coating sails
Bertha	Shanking boat		2 shank runners 8d (£2.60)
	Shanking boat	Peter Kellett	3qt black varnish, 22¼lb paint

Several boats were fitted with bought-in pumps, unlike the Crossfields' wooden pumps, and there were several entries for new rudder backs, their term for wooden rudderstocks. Black varnish is a compound of varnish and tar that dried to a high opaque black gloss, which was commonly used on the topsides of commercial craft. The quantity quoted for spars will have recorded the measure in cubic feet, whilst the reference to logs and sawyers indicates that the yard converted its timber with the pit saw.

The costs of the shanking boats built at Freckleton (in 2005 values) was fairly steady, as can be seen from this tabulation the contracts varied from £3,420 up to £4,433, with an average cost of £3,463.

Entered	Boat Name	Cost	Man days
April 1872	Bay Boat	£1,732	
1873	*Clipper* (Bay Boat)	£1,405	67 man days
8 Oct 1875	*John*	£1,133	
28 June 1876	*Mary*	£1,231	42¼ man days
23 Jan 1878	*New boat*	£3,932	
Feb 1878		£239	8½ man days
24 Oct 1878		£1,459 wages	
1879	*Mistress of the Banks*	£3,038	10 men employed
22 July 1879	*Wonder*	£3,126	
19 Nov 1879	New boat		£1,906
Jan 1881	*Polly*	£3,093	
1881	*Little Nellie*	£268 labour	11¼ man days
1881	New boat	£3,420	13 men, £1,971 wages
Aug 1882	New boat	£3,964	
14 Feb 1883	*Little Willie*	£716	29¼ man days

April 1883			£1,906 wages
1883	*Alice Ann*	£3,474	£1,928
10 June 1884	*Northern Light*	£316	13½ man days
23 April 1884	*Alexandra Eccles*	£468	15¾ man days
15 Feb 1884	*New boat*	£3,681	
1884	*New boat*	£4,171 contract	
10 June 1884	*Northern Light*	£316	
July 1884	*Moon Light*	£4,095 contract	12 men, 146¼hr £1,928
16 May 1885	*Nightingale*	£4,433 contract	13 men, 231hr, £2,646
1 Aug 1886	*Golden Arrow*	£1,743	557¾ man hours
16 Aug 1887		£74.17	
1888	May	£104	94 man hours
1889		£291	94 man hours
Aug 1889	*Teapot*	£994	301 man hours
1890	*Annie*	£65.20	211¾ man hours

The yard continued as Allunson's for a couple of generations before changing markets and a fire closed the yard. We know from a magazine article by John Leather that Allunsons built a ketch-rigged smack to the fully developed nobby model.

The River Douglas enters the Ribble further up the estuary on the southern side. The villages of Hesketh Bank and Tarleton are both situated on the western bank of the Douglas, and both villages supported boat yards. Both Lathom and Wright set up yards at Hesketh Bank from about 1901. One of them survives as Shepherd's yard. The Mayor family ran the Tarleton yard, and are known to have repaired clench-built Lytham-type smacks.

The most southerly built nobby on published record was found by Commander McKee, when researching his *Working Boats of Gt. Britain*. This clench-built nobby *Benita* CO 78 was built at Criccieth, at 20ft 6in long, in 1913 by Nell. She has the typical nobby deck layout, but with a centreline bowsprit and no mooring post. Her hull form is of very shoal draft, with little drag to her keel, and no hollow to her flat floors (McKee 1983). She is all in all quite a throwback to the old shallow Morecambe boats of the 1880s. The later Conwy motor nobbies were of the same form but retained carvel construction.

Chapter 16

Construction

The construction of nobbies was strong but economical, as befits a working boat. The scantlings of the boats we have measured are generally as specified in *Lloyd's Rules for Yachts* of the period, or in excess of them. The exception to this was the omission of iron hanging knees, the proportions of the steamed timbers, and the use of cut boat nails instead of through fastenings. The steamed frames seem to be wider and thinner than specified in Lloyd's, or in common use today. Lloyd's at the turn of the century specified the minimum cross-section area of longitudinal members. This allowed the builder to make his beam shelf of plank stuff, whereas today's standards would require the siding to be nearer to the moulding in dimension. As a follow-on from this most nobbies were fitted with a ledge, a longitudinal timber with its moulding laid horizontal, bolted under the beams, instead of a clamp-fitted under the shelf. One exception to this is the *Judy* (formerly *Millie*) preserved at Fleetwood Museum. She is a big boat, built for a Welsh port, and is fitted with lodging knees over a plank-type beam shelf. Another exception was *Little Nellie* (Plate 84) a Southport boat of 1881 or earlier, wrecked in the Ribble estuary. The photographs taken to illustrate the newspaper report of the loss of her crew were of the boat put ashore near the Lytham lifeboat station and windmill. Her foredeck was found near the hull, and was placed upside down in the stern when she was salvaged. She was ceiled in the cockpit, her thoft was kneed in with lodging knees and iron standing knees, and she had lodging knees on the main and mooring bit beams.

The design and construction methods described by Alfie Crossfield, and evident in the surviving boats, allow us to set out the method of design and building of a typical nobby. Not all of these methods will have been used by the yards that Stoba worked for, as they occasionally built all steam framed nobbies. There may well have been different methods favoured by the other yards as well, and we know that from the silver model at Annan

Plate 84. *Little Nelly.*

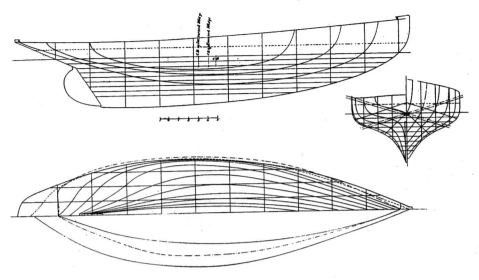

Fig. 64. John Crossfield's half model. (*Yachting Monthly* May 1910)

there were differences in layout through time. The boats used as sources are identified in the text when appropriate.

When contracting to build a boat, the first thing to do was to determine what the customer wanted. Many had new ideas to try out, and providing that they judged them safe the Crossfields would accommodate their customer's wishes. Perhaps the most extreme of these ideas was tried in the *Fram*, whose owner had been to Norway or Denmark, and seen the praam-bowed working boats. He was so taken with this form of bow that he commissioned a nobby with a praam bow. Unfortunately this form of bow is unsuited for the short steep seas of Morecambe Bay, and the nobby slammed and stopped dead every time she pitched into a wave. Her motion was so violent that her owner was obliged to return her to the yard, where by saving as much planking as possible, they were able to rebuild her bow in a conventional form, for the sum of £7 (£540). *Fram* LR 124 was registered by Thomas Mayor on 18/2/1901, and sold to Simon Gerrard to be re-registered on 12/7/1904. She continued a successful career after her surgery, later being fitted with vivier tanks. Not all owners wished to express an opinion, so John Crossfield was able to build several hulls from the same half model. The lines of this 35ft 6in waterline model were published in the correspondence page of the May edition of *Yachting Monthly* of 1910, reproduced as Fig. 64. The correspondent stated that the model was used for several boats, and then fined down in the bow and in the run to be used for several more.

When the size and form of the boat was agreed and a deposit paid, a half model was prepared. Alfie remembered John's customers placing a gold sovereign on the workbench as deposit. Both John and William Crossfield & Sons used lift, and bracket or bird's nest models, but lift models have mostly survived from the Crossfield yards, the Southport yards, and one of our sources tells of stacks of Stoba's half models in storage at his home at the end of his life. The Science Museum also has plaster casts of two Annan lift models. Even though it is remembered that he worked on paper, Stoba's designs will have been modelled to show the owner the form of the boat, and possibly to test the fairness of the design. Most surviving lift models were built of lifts up to the design water line with a solid block above, fixed to a backboard, although the Wright's of Southport model for the *Sir George Pilkington* was built with lifts throughout. The lifts described the form of the hull out to the rebate, whilst the backboard established the profile of the stem, keel, and rudder. These models require interpretation, as the backboards were cut from board of arbitrary, and often not uniform, thickness. The rebate on the boat would not have described a flat

Plate 85. *Lottie*. (Courtesy Raymond Sankey)

plane as the keel would have tapered to the siding of the stem and sternpost, so we can only assume the boat's beam by using the stem siding from *Lloyd's Rules for Yachts* with the half breadth of the model.

Not all models were agreed with their prospective owners, hence the mistake in the bow of *Lottie*. As can be seen from her photograph, Plate 85, she was built with a raking motorboat stem. Folk memory tells that her owners requested a boat with the 'new' form, but her builders were not familiar with the developments, and misinterpreted the form of cut-away bow requested. The report of the opinion of her new owners when they first saw the completed hull makes it obvious that they had neither seen a half model nor visited the builder when she was framed out. Their first comment on seeing her became her nickname 'Th's buggerdit'. She was registered at Fleetwood as Fleetwood built, and dated 1888.

When the model was finished it would be sent off to the new owner. He would return it to John, bringing several more gold sovereigns as a stage payment. With the model agreed, John Crossfield sent off an order for the ironwork from his relatives at Arnside. This also implies a fair amount of standardisation in both form and detail. The hull lofting was carried out, the profile and five frames being scaled up to full size (*Nora* was built from five frames but Alfie Crossfield spoke of lofting seven frames). The frames and profile were drawn out on a screive board or floor, made of inch pine boards. Moulds were made for the frame futtocks and mid line components by transferring the scribed lines onto one quarter inch waste board. These moulds were taken to the sawmill, where the crooks and compass timber was stored. The bends were selected and sawn out on the band saw, to be returned to the building shed at the other end of the quay. The chapter on the builders records the speed at which the nobbies were built, and discusses the structure of the working week. One of the reasons for the speed of construction, and for the economical cost of the boats was that no wood was sawn that did not eventually become part of the boat. Another reason given by Alfie Crossfield was that the men working on the boats knew exactly what they and their colleagues needed to do. The result of this deep knowledge was that after the morning's greetings, and any inquiry after the health of family members, there was no need to speak during the working day. The building yard workers would know from the sound

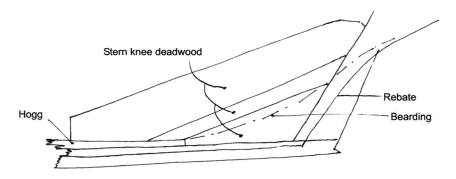

Fig. 65. De Wet deadwoods.

and rhythm of the tools when a colleague needed a hand to move a trestle or staging, and the one best able to lend a hand would make the adjustment un-asked. In this way all of the working day was devoted to work. It also meant that they could wear out a plane iron or rip saw in a month. Alfie described his grandfather hand sawing both sides of a 40ft keel in one day, and four men taking about a month to build a 38-footer.

The building commenced with the backbone and the five or seven frames being assembled on the screive board, along with the arch board frame that defines the shape of the counter. The frames were assembled from a floor, with short arms, first futtocks bolted to the floor, second futtocks butting the arms of the floors and extending above the bilge, and top timbers butting the heads of the first futtocks. The Crossfields used black iron ⅜in coach bolts to assemble the frames. Black iron was used for economy, since the planks were nailed into both futtocks, which held the frame together when the bolts rusted. These units were stacked against the shed side as the screive board was dismantled and set aside for re-use. The form of the keel would have been determined by the decision to fit outside ballast, or a centreboard, and to suit the timber available. Boats with outside ballast had the Lloyd's minimum scantling in the vertical thickness, the top and bottom being flat and parallel. The cast iron keels used by William Crossfield were moulded with 1in square vertical tongues on their square ends; these tongues were fitted into groves made in the deadwoods that formed the forefoot and heel. The ballast keels of the two Stoba boats we have seen are different, having a scarf face cast in forward. Because their structural keel raked more than the Crossfield models, they do not have an after deadwood but their iron keels run out to the heel of the sternpost. The ballast keel on *Hearts of Oak* ran out both for'd and aft with no deadwoods. Where the ballast keel was joined to deadwoods, provision was made for a keel bolt, and a ½in step was cast in to accommodate the keel band, which was countersunk to take the carrot head of the keel bolt. All other keel bolts had square heads let into pockets cast in the keel. The later Southport builders used lead ballast keels, salvaging the keels from old boats on the beach by dropping them just before the boats ebbed out.

Alfie told the author that John's business ordered their iron keels from the Barrow ironworks. Alfie remembered one keel being delivered from Conwy station by the railway's two-wheeled cart, with one horse between the shafts, as the carrier tried to slide the keel off of the back of the cart its end dug into the gravel road surface and tipped up the cart, lifting the poor cart horse in the shafts off the ground.

The nobbies without fixed ballast, like the author's own *Nora*, built in 1912 by William Crossfield, have the minimum scantling in the width of the keel, which tapers to the ends, whilst the depth is curved to suit the profile, and moulded to provide the cross-section area. The scantlings are 4in siding by 9in maximum moulding. The builders of the *De Wet*, now named *Quest*, cut the boarding surface on a hog, bedded down on top of the keel, this hog stopped at the lowest stern knee chock, to be overlaid by the rest of the stern knee.

We were told that this is a feature of newer boats, so this may have been adopted because the Crossfields at Arnside could no longer find a tree of sufficient dimensions. The sketch Fig. 65 illustrates this.

The forefoot was a large crook, fastened down on top of the keel, and moulded so that its top surface ran in a fair curve down the back of the stem and on to the keel. On *Nora* the stem of 3¾in siding was scarfed onto the forefoot, with a plane scarf running from outside upwards and inwards, doweled with two blind treenails. This joint was doubled with a stemson, called apron at Morecambe, of 3in by 3in scantlings, nailed on with large cut boat nails. The stern knee was formed from a stack of 3½in siding chocks in *Nora*; the lowest triangular layer was fastened down with cut boat nails. The sternposts were tennoned into the keel and fastened with a dowel. *Nora*'s sternpost was sided 3in by 8in at its heel. There were economies made here as well: any joint in major components are usually fastened with three or four through bolts, but on *Nora* they used only two in each arm of the stem knee. On boats with outside ballast, keel bolts will have been driven through the deadwoods, in addition to the carrot headed bolts securing the keel band and stem bit into the recess in the ballast keel ends. The other fastenings securing the keel band and heel bit were 6in by ½in dumps. *Nora* has three pieces to her keel band, the heel bit, middle bit, and stem bit. Her heel bit was bent around the skeg in the keel and has the bearing cup for the rudder stock forge welded into its angle, the Rivers Class yachts had no skeg, so the heel bit was bent round and welded to an iron chock. When all of the keel bolts and fastenings were driven in the keel, the whole assembly could be rolled upright onto the keel blocks and set plumb.

When the backbone was erected, the square frames set aside after assembly on the scrieve board were then erected on the keel. The frame assembly was fastened down with a single headless ½in iron drift driven blind through the bosom of the floor. The last frame lifted from the model will have been the main stern or last cant frame on the stern knee in an open counter boat. *Nora*'s mainstern is assembled from three 1¾in transverse planks with doweled joints let down into the back of the sternpost, and nailed in with cut boat nails. There is strong folk memory that the boats were built without a bulkhead at the sternpost, until leaky counters prompted the inclusion of this bulkhead. It is called the main stern at Morecambe and a tuck in the south. Alfred Crossfield was told that his grandfather started to build bulkheads into nobbies after having the counter of a pleasure trip boat he was skippering damaged by gunfire from one of the coastal artillery batteries when off Blackpool.

The archboard assembly can now be erected, springing aft from the after most frame, and supported by the horn timber. The author is familiar with archboard assemblies made in two ways. Those with the moulding running out before the end of the counter (*Nance*, *Christine*, and *Lottie*) had the archboard carved from two crooks, joined on the mid-line. Those with the moulding running round the counter under the shear strake (*Nora*, *Maud Raby*, and *Day Star*) have the archboard formed from 2in frame stock in two layers, with the butts staggered. The moulding and the rebate for the bottom planking hood ends was carved from the solid of the lower layer. Planting a third layer of timber on top formed the full depth of the shear strake. Some archboards butted up to the back of the main stern, being supported by the shear strake alone, whilst the upper layer of *Nora*'s archboard passed through the mainstern to be sandwiched between the shear strake and the shelf, and secured by the bolts in the arm of the quarter knees. The horn timbers were of different forms although no reason for these differences is apparent. Nora had a larch piece sandwiched between two oak sides. The sides formed the bearding of the rebate for the counter planking, with caulking seams against the sides of the centrepiece. Other boats had the horn timber formed from the solid, without a rebate, so that there was a caulked seam on the centre line between the ends of the planking.

The lower end of *Nora*'s horn timber was secured by notching it round and nailing it to the lower of two strong backs that clamp the rudder case to the back of the main stern. The rudder case was usually made from two pieces, joined with loose tongues in grooves

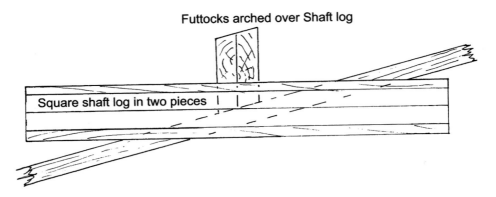

Fig. 66. John Crossfield's shaft log.

worked in the faying surfaces, although Fleetwood built boats had cases bored out of the solid. The case was clamped in place, so if it became damaged by gribble, its clamps could be freed off and the case driven upwards without disturbing the structure of the counter.

With this framework erected and horned in square, battens were nailed around the frames from rebate to rebate. Alfie Crossfield called these laggings. At Conwy and probably at Arnside they were off-cuts from the plank stock. *Nora* was reviewed at this stage, and the forward two moulded frames were firred out about a ½in. The rest of the frames could now be made, the shape of each timber being lifted from the inside of the battens with a chain. The chain was an assembly of wooden links riveted together with copper boat nails and roves to resemble a bicycle chain. The links were about 7cm long, 2cm wide and 5mm thick. This was rendered stiff enough to hold its shape by soaking in water before use. Alfie recounted that in nobbies built for engines the frames supporting the shaft log were moulded to fit over and support a square log, see sketch Fig. 66.

Limbers would have been bored when the frame was ready for erection. On *Nora* they were in the mainstern, and at the bottom of all of the floors; however, on *Nance*, which was concreted by her builder, they were bored at the top level of the concrete in each floor. This meant that they rose from the top of the keel forward to the top of the floors amidships. On boats with a narrow deep keel (like *Nora*) the first futtocks extended down the side of the keel, whilst on *De Whet* and *Day Star* the first futtocks double the floors and cross the keel. When the last frame was erected the spaces between the rebate, the top of the keel or deadwoods and the frames were filled with softwood blocks. On *Nora* there were also oak fillers of frame stock nailed to the side of the keel to extend the floors down to the rebate. Many of the boats concreted by their builders had iron boiler punchings mixed into the concrete. Alfie told of a large pile of punchings and swarf, purchased from Vickers at Barrow. This had rusted into a solid mass, and had to be broken up with a pickaxe and hammers before it could be used.

A keelson was set on top of the floors, secured by the keel bolts, in *Nora* these were 6 off ¾in square headed bolts. They were driven clear of the floors through 2in by 3in pillars cut from the lop and top wood from the trees felled for plank stock. The keelson was normally about 2½in thick and 9in wide tapering to 5in at its ends. A mortise (called the tabernacle at Morecambe) was worked in for the heel of the mast. Those boats with iron fixed-ballast keelsons also had wood keelson ends scarfed on to clamp the floors down in the ends. Boats with centre boards had a keelson worked in forward of the case logs.

The planking was larch or pitch pine finished to just over 1in thick. Alfie explained that pitch pine was used on boats for Fleetwood since their sheltered moorings and soft bottom did not lift the grain on pitch pine in the way that the hard bottoms of the other more exposed ports would. On the yachts that were built without a moulding, the shear streak was made thicker, at about 1⅛in thick, with the bottom edge chamfered off. Planking was hung working down from the shear and up from the garboards. The frames were dubbed fair with the adze at Conwy, leaving flats to fay the plank. There is no evidence that William and his sons at Arnside worked this way. The inner surface of the planking was planed up in the topsides unless ceiling was requested. It was always left rough from the saw below the level of the ballast boards and forecastle benches better to take the tar with which the bilge was finished. The planking was hung at Conwy without recourse to steaming, using sash cramps to edge set the plank to place, pulling against the keel or the shear strake. Alfie remembered the shutter plank being driven into place with a sledgehammer against a piece of scrap.

The planking was fastened with two off 3in galvanised cut boat nails per frame, driven into a pilot hole and counter bore. Any plank butts landed on the frames. There were no attempts to nib the plank ends into joggles, so there were some very fine ends to the planks in the forefoot. The nail heads were set down with a punch at Conwy, Alfie talked with admiration of the Scottish boat builders who could set the heads of their nail with a blow from a pin hammer. The process of driving the nails was eased by the use of green frame timber.

The fishing nobbies were planked with a moulding of oak as a rubbing bend, approximately 3in wide, below the shear strake. The moulding was made of 2in thick stuff, rounded off where it stands proud of the plank. On *Nora*, *Wild Cherry*, and *Day Star* the aft end of the moulding would have been let down into the archboard framing that carried its form around the stern. On *Arthur Alexander*, *Christine* and the boats with the knuckled or half-round treatment to the archboard, the moulding is faired off as it runs out aft. On *Lottie* it was nibbed into the shear strake, and the cove line ran onto the flattened moulding plank, off its butt and on to the shear strake again. On the other boats the moulding ran into the rebate worked into the archboard to be faired off as it ran out.

A 1½in-thick oak sand streak (called a bilge clog by John Crossfield and bilge plank at Morecambe) went in to the midship bilge, to take the wear on the beach.

Alfie recounted a clever piece of craft used when planeing the edges of a plank in poor light. When the plank was lined off on the plank stock, nail holes were made with 1in or 1½in oval nail hammered in all along the marked line. After the plank was sawn out, the edge could be planed with confidence down to remove half of the width of the nail holes, which could be felt through the plane as well as seen.

Alfie remembered that before the shutter plank (the last plank hung between the bottom and topsides) was fitted the timber used for the screive boards were passed in to make the ballast boards and foc's'le sealing. They were passed in through the gap left by the shutter plank, marked to length, pushed out on one side and cut, then back out of the other to be cut at that end. With the planking finished, and the nail heads punched down, the hull was planed fair, round-soled backing out planes being used under the tuck aft. A local boat builder, who served his time at Allunsons of Freckleton called this process 'flogging off'.

The beam shelf was cut from plank stock. *Nora*'s measured four and a half inches deep, and was fitted up to fay the deck plank. *Nora*'s breasthook was replaced along with the beam shelves forward of the nogs, and Samson post deck beam, when her stem top and Samson post were replaced. *Nance* and *Dart* were not fitted with a breasthook, the space between the stem, plank, first frames, and shelf was filled with a chock, with its grain vertical in *Nance*. It is most likely that the Crossfields used this form of chock, with the grain either fore and aft or vertical, through-bolted to the stem, the shelf would have been nailed to both the arms of this chock and to the first futtock. The shear strake will have been nailed to rebate and with four to six nails into the chock. *Nora*'s shelf was in two pieces butted on a frame three rooms and spaces forward of the mast step. A three-quarter by one-quarter chamfer was planed along the lower edge. In *Nora*, and other boats with main sterns, quarter knees, sawn from 1⅞in frame stock were fitted, skew-nailed to the main stern and bolted through the shelf, arch board frame and shear strake. A ledge of 2in depth by 5½in width was bolted to the shelf supporting the two sailing beams and the next two beams forward. The ledge was bolted through the shelf and frames, using four

Plate 86. Under deck pillars.

½in bolts a side. Alfie Crossfield remembered their yard using the same galvanised bolts as those that the General Post Office used for assembling their telegraph poles. At the time of writing an unnamed Annan motor nobby is hauled being out at Harrington, on the Cumbria coast. She has an aperture for a centre screw and is of full form, which makes it most likely that she is an Annan fishing nobby and not a yacht, which was the only other type of craft of this form built with a centre screw. Her foredeck is missing, which reveals a local variation in build technique. She is fitted with ledges that extend from the mast partners right into the eyes. *Helen III* is different again, she has a second pair of ledges spanning the frames before and aft of the bow nogs.

Provision would have been made for the thwart before work started on the deck beams, and it was probably installed before the shelf. *Nora*'s thwart is supported on a rising of 2¾in by 1in, with a ¼in ovolo moulding at its top and a ¼in by ½in chamfer at its bottom, whilst the Willacy's *Linda* had a heavy clamp notched round four frames and faying the plank. The dimensions of *Nora*'s thwart are reconstructed from fay marks, at 9in by 3in. It was kneed in with a standing knee at each end, fastened by one bolt through knee, shelf, frame, and shear strake.

Nora's beams are larch, sided 2¾in, moulded 3in on the ledges, whilst the other beams were reduced at their ends, and in the ends of the boat, they round up one ½in to the foot. The half beams at the thwart were supported by turned pillars, just visible in the original of Plate 86, an unknown nobby at Barrow. These pillars are ornate, especially so for a trawler, being reminiscent of Victorian piano legs, the photo also records the pins in the thwart for the headsail sheets, which gave all of the appearance of coach bolts driven down into the thwart. The sheet will have been belayed by taking it over the aft edge of the thwart, around the pin under the thwart, and back up to tuck under its standing part and jam in the nip. This will have been secure whilst the sail is drawing, and quick to cast off and belay.

The beams in *Nora* are spaced at between 14 to 16in, close at the mast, and wider at the ends. The main beam at the mooring post was kneed in with lodging knees, although those on *Nora* were not original. The four beams on the ledge were bolted down with coach bolts so that the ledge also acts as lodging knees for each beam. A mast chock is fitted between the aft two beams on the ledge. Conventional mast partners were not fitted (except on the largest nobbies). *Nora*'s mast chock is formed of two athwartships slabs doweled together and bolted thr.ough the two beams by two 1in diameter coach bolts. In addition to the circular mast opening there is a hole cut to port, against the aft beam, to pass the stovepipe. Some trawl boats were not fitted with partners, but had chocks and

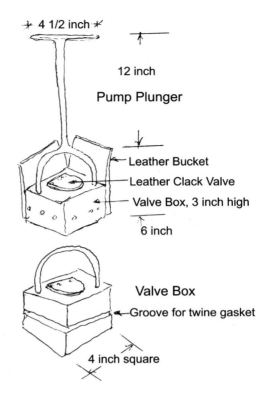

4 1/2 inch

12 inch

Pump Plunger

Leather Bucket

Leather Clack Valve

Valve Box, 3 inch high

6 inch

Valve Box

Groove for twine gasket

4 inch square

Fig. 67. Pump plunger.

a mast gate on the aft face of a heavy sailing beam, this may have been characteristic of the earlier boats. The Bay boats with their long cockpit and short fore deck were different again, being fitted with a heavy sailing thwart kneed in with standing and lodging knees.

All of the deck aft of the mast beams was missing when the author bought *Nora*, but sufficient shelf survived to indicate the position of the remaining beams. All of the earliest photos of *Nora* show the front end of her cockpit rebuilt square for the engine hatch, using the mast beam as foundation for the head ledge. She will be rebuilt, drawing from *Helen III* LL 142, registered on 28/1/1936 and built by William Crossfield & Sons. She is still in original condition. The first piece of reconstruction in this description, and the next piece of structure fitted, is a beam aligned with the for'd face of the frame aft of the mast beam, to which the foc's'le bulkhead is nailed. This beam is not halved into the shelf, and its under side is not cambered, but is fashioned to suit the foc's'le slide. Many nobbies were built without cockpit carlins, relying on the coaming to support the half beams. There is no evidence for carlins in *Nora*. For those with carlins the foc's'le bulkhead must have been worked in a different manner, as the beam fitted to support the bulkhead will not have been capable of supporting the carlins.

When the deck beams, partners, mainstern, shelf and shear are all faired, the nogs, bitts and mooring post are fitted. The bow nogs in William Crossfield nobbies are fitted between the shelf and plank, faying and lying square to the shelf. Although the nog is square above the deck, it is trapezoidal in section with extra material where it is bolted to the aft side of the top timber aft of the lodging knee. In *Helen III*, built in the 1930s, the nog is of heavier scantling, and cuts the beam shelf, so a ledge was worked in spanning three frames for'd and aft of the nog to reconnect the shelf. The bow nogs in the nobby at Harrington are let down into the inboard face of the ledges, and are therefore further inboard than on most nobbies. The mid-nogs are fastened to plank and shelf in the middle of the frame bay aft of the ledges on *Nora*, whilst some nobbies had them fitted for'd of the shrouds. The remaining spaces between the frame heads shelf and plank are filled solid with softwood chocks. The aft nogs are let down into the aft side of the main stern and nailed to a cant in the counter. *Nora*'s were 3½in square. However, photographic evidence indicates that Southport nobbies had their aft nogs fitted at the deck edge. The bowsprit bitts were bolted to the foreside of the mooring post beam to port, and the mooring post to its aft side to starboard. Its heel was stepped in a mortise worked in a chock to the side of the stemson, between the frames and faying the plank. The handing of the bowsprit and mooring post at Morecambe was dependent on the location of the boat's mooring, and whether the approach to it had to be made on the port or starboard bow. The Bay boats did not carry a mooring bit, the mooring or anchor cable was made off to the mast.

With the forward nogs fitted, those boats that were ceiled in the foc's'le could have the ceiling fitted. Some boats were ceiled in the foc's'le only, some in the cockpit, and some throughout. The Arnside Crossfields did not charge for fitting ceiling, as the low cost of the match boarding was offset by the saving in labour due to there being no need to plane up the frame stock and the inside of the topsides planking. The pump will have been built, ready for its installation. The suction was made to fit into the space between the frames at the forward end of the stern knee. With one layer of boards laying on the hull plank, and the other level across the inside of the frames moulding, the suction in a boat with 2¾in by 3¾in frames and 12in room and space will have measured 10in by 1¾in. The pump itself had a square suction, that on *Day Star* having a 4in square plunge hole, built from ⅞in boards. The lower valve box was of elm, with a leather clack valve and an iron staple for a handle to allow its retrieval. It had a groove cut in to hold a twine gasket. The plunger was also wood, with an iron handle and leather clack valve, and four leather flaps nailed on around its top to form the bucket. See Fig. 67 for one example of the arrangement of a pump plunger.

The boat was now ready to receive her deck. On boats with a main stern closing off the counter, the planking in the counter would have been given a good coat of hot gas tar, this is also the best time to sweep out and tar the entire bilge up to the level of the ballast boards and foc's'le locker tops. The caulking would have been completed and the seams paid before the inside will have been tarred.

It is probable that all builders would have fitted the ballast boards and foc's'le sealing (sole) before the deck beams, as Alfie Crossfield described, as they would have provided a level working platform. The foc's'le sealing was supported on for'd and aft risers and lay just clear of the keelson. Those in the Rivers Class yachts had to have pockets cut to clear the nuts and ends of the keel bolts. The ballast boards in later, or perhaps southern nobbies, were set at two levels, at a comfortable height below the cleaning deck, and to provide the steering step. The silver model at Annan had its aft bay set lower, creating three levels. In *Nora* the step was set on the last square frame on the stern knee, its structure is copied from *Helen III*, with a transverse beam and risers supporting carlins that define a hatch, in which the anchor was stowed. The ballast boards in the waist were divided into three zones longitudinally and athwartships. Those under the side decks were left loose and bore directly on the plank and frames, whilst the three mid-line bays were made into hatch covers. They were laid athwartships, and were supported by three beams and two sets of carlins. In some boats the carlins ran right through and the middle pair of beams were in three pieces. The Maxwell Blake drawings published in the books in the Bibliography are misleading in this area.

The deck was laid with 1⅛in spruce, tongued and grooved, with 2½in cover. Being tongued & grooved it was laid parallel, although it was swept aft as it followed the width of the tapering cockpit. The covering board was 1¼in wide, and could not be joggled for the deck plank nibs. This looks poor practice but was founded on sound reasoning. With the spaces between plank, frames and shelf filled in solid, should an accident cause the coaming to go by the board, and rip up the covering board, through which it is spiked, there will be minimal leakage through the deck, even when sailing rail under. The Beach Walk yard continued to use this structure on both trawl boats and yachts until the yard closed. Again the Blake drawing is misleading and self contradictory in this area.

Fitting the coamings completed the deck. There were several styles of inside coaming, varying with time and place. The basic Morecambe pattern had circular cockpit ends, although boats built for an engine, with an engine hatch, would be square forward, set on the mast beam, and round aft. Those with a mast gate on the mast beam had a square forward end. Some Fleetwood half-deckers had a square forward end set on the first beam aft of the mast beams. Some of the Southport boats and the Annan model had round corners on squarish ends. Whatever their plan, they will have been steamed oak one inch thick by eight high, bolted down to the half beams with 'T'-headed bolts.

With the deck complete the top of the rudder case can be completed. On most surviving nobbies the case was cut and faired level with the deck plank, and an oak cap nailed down on top. *Maud Raby*, which still had her original case when seen, had no cap. Her case was carved with a raised circular lip around the rudder stock opening. Careful study of the photograph of *Ailsa* FD 213 suggests that her case was carried up through the deck, without a cap. The nobbies that Alfie Crossfield remembered building were all fitted with caps.

The outside coamings were spiked down into the shear strake. They were 1¼in thick, tapering to 1in at the top, by 3-4in high, running about a ¼in inside the deck edge. Aft, on the counter, the coaming was carved from solid. There was a scupper on the centre line aft, one on the fore side of each of the nogs, and three each side aft of the shrouds.

Even if not carried out before the deck was started the hull will have been caulked and paid by now. Nora was caulked with oakum, and paid with red lead putty. The nail heads were stopped with Portland cement in the bottom, and white lead in the topsides.

The shipwrights not employed on the outside of the hull would have been fitting out the foc's'le. The bulkhead to port ran up to the deck head, but that to starboard was a half bulkhead. They were both tongue-and-grooved match boarding set vertical, nailed to frame, ballast board bearer, and in the case of the port bulkhead to a ground aligned to the frame across the deckhead. The benches were open framed in some boats, but in *Helen III* they are supported on fore and aft boards nailed to the outboard side of the ceiling riser, with their width vertical. The bench was laid with boards running for'd and aft, the middle run being loose and bored with finger holes for locker lids. The space beneath one of these was divided off to form the coal locker for the bogey stove that heated the foc's'le.

The rudder would be hung now, by bilging the hull over. A fashion piece would have been nailed to the sternpost between the heel bit upstand and the rudder case. Older boats had a wooden stocked rudder, whilst Day Star and later boats had a 2in diameter iron stock. Keith Willacy described the older form of rudder hanging that utilised four or five gudgeons on both rudder and sternpost and a long bolt dropped through them all. The upper pair of gudgeons was fitted high enough for the head of the bolt to be accessible from the deck. This arrangement would have required a larger rudder case than the later method. The stock, with two or three straps riveted to it and its top swaged down to a tennon, would be passed up the rudder case and set in its cup bearing. On some of the nobbies and on the Rivers Class yachts the straps were secured to the stock by bolts that were put in place to go through the width of the blade; these were ragged to hold in the wood. The blade was then driven into place and riveted through the pairs of straps. It would probably have required two boards doweled together. Its lower edge was rounded, whilst the top and aft edge was planed to leave a low ridge at the mid-thickness. One or two bands (one on a two strapped rudder, two on one with three straps) would be bolted through the sternpost clasping the stock midway between the straps.

Further items of outfit can now be installed. A second half-bulkhead was fitted to starboard at the aft end of the fore bay, to match the starboard side of the foc's'le bulkhead. One function of these two half-bulkheads was to provide a stowage rack for the topsail and sweeps. The cabin stove was fitted against the bulkhead to port. They were small cast-iron coal stoves, with a double hob. They were probably set in a concrete hearth placed on top of the side locker. The stovepipe went through a deck fitting that was made with an upstand to hold water, intended to keep the fitting and hence the deck cool. A 2ft wide by 10in deep drawer was often fitted aft under the side deck as stowage for netting needles and twine, a knife, and odds and ends. Some Fleetwood cod boats were fitted with stanchions, for pound boards under the side decks. Lytham, Morecambe, and Fleetwood boats were originally fitted with hatch boards; in Fleetwood these were supported on battens fitted inside the inner coamings. Cleats were fitted, to the inside coamings aft for the springers (a rope used to control the trawl), either being horn cleats or cleats bored for belaying pins.

External ironwork and wooden fittings were installed for the sailing rig. The ironwork above the water line was all galvanised, the rest left black. The mooring roller assembly comprised a 1in Whitworth bolt for an axle, with the 4¾ in diameter by 3in by ⅜ in thick gammon iron ring (called the bowsprit iron at Morecambe) on its head. This had a ¾in diameter stay secured with two counter-sunk rivets to the outboard diameter of the ring, coming 1ft 6in down the stem. The bolt went through the stem, the 3¼in wide by 3½in diameter cast-iron roller was slipped on, and a wooden chock was fitted to support the mooring roller outboard. This cheek block was secured by setting up the nut on the roller axle over a square washer, and by driving a coach bolt through the gammon iron stay, the stem, and the lower end of the chock. A knee resembling a Jack Nichols bolted to the shear streak backed up the cheek block. The keel band was finished with the stem faceplate. This was nailed to the face of the stem and the mooring roller chock. It had two nails through the end of the stem bit, which fanned out where the browing off of the stem ran out. The faceplate has a forged eye for the fore stay riveted to its top.

Two pairs of shroud irons were fitted to the hull; some big boats had three pairs. On *Nora* they were bolted to the frame at the mast and the next aft frame, extending down to the strake below the moulding. *Maud Raby*'s irons were made from 3in wide cope iron, shouldered down at the top to make an eye for the bolt of the lower deadeye band. Unlike modern deadeye bands made of flat bar, *Maud Raby*'s were forged from round rod, like large bow shackles. The shroud irons were forged to fit round the moulding, modern replacements are often let down into the moulding for ease of manufacture.

The deck fittings were a hook on a long link in an eyebolt through the mooring post for the mooring strop, and a cross piece bolted to or put through the top of the bowsprit bitts; on some nobbies logs were bolted down on deck and to the bitts to further support them. A cleat was fitted for the jib outhaul. Some nobbies had a transverse chock and staple without bitts, or a ring on the Samson post.

Three pairs of wooden fairleads were nailed down to suit the three jibs. *Ailsa* appears to have eyebolts. Two prism deck lights (called dead lights or t'prism) were fitted to illuminate the foc's'le.

A fife rail or pair of rails is fitted for the array of halyards. On *Nora* the rail is curved, supported on three pillars 2in wide by 3in front to back, and skewed to starboard. There were four pins to port of an eyebolt, and three to starboard. Bigger boats had fife rails at the shrouds. These are visible on the photo of *Ailsa* and of *Onward*.

An iron eye cleat is bolted through the mast partner to starboard aft of the mast for the topsail down haul. A second eye cleat was fitted through the starboard ledge abreast of the mast for the topping lift (see Fig. 68).

A pair of very heavy eyebolts with ⅞in Whitworth threads were fitted through the ledges between the shroud irons, see Fig. 69. These were to take the beaching legs. Some older boats, including *Nora* FD 46, had a pair of irons, similar to shroud irons, fitted amidships for the legs.

Keith Willacy and Dick Woodhouse talked of a small winch, fitted to the inside coaming. Keith positioned it on the round, to port. There is a photo in Horsley and Hirst of a Fleetwood boat trawling off Southport with a top drive hand powered capstan on the centre line between the mast and the coaming.

A pair of foresail sheet fairleads was nailed down abreast of the fore bay of the cockpit. These and the jib fairleads were sawn out of 1in oak board, bored to take the sheet rope, and nailed down with two nails. Some nobbies had a wire sheet horse.

The side decks were left clear, to port for the trawl, and to starboard for cleaning the

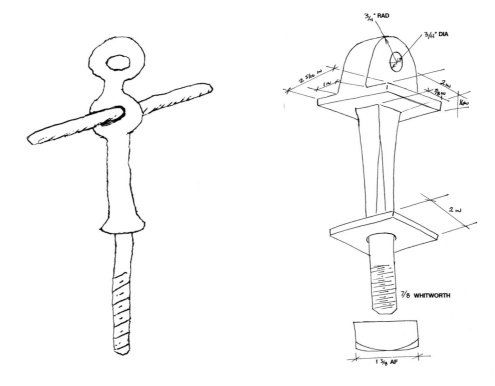

Above left: Fig. 68. Eye-cleat.

Above right: Fig. 69. Beaching leg eyebolt.

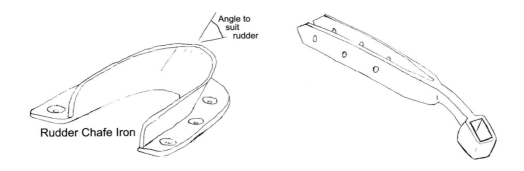

Above left: Fig. 70. Rudder chafe iron.

Above right: Fig. 71. Tiller iron.

catch. The areas of deck were called atop t' foc's'le, trawl deck, cleaning or crab deck, and counter. The counter was fitted with:

One or two strong cleats, for belaying the mainsheet, but strong enough to take the aft (starboard) bridle when shooting and hauling the trawl.

A chafe iron was fastened down on top of the rudder cap. The sketch Fig. 70 illustrates *Day Stars*, to act as an upper bearing for the rudderstock. Fig. 71 illustrates the tiller iron, an iron socket to fit the rudderstock, with straps to clasp the wood of the tiller.

The sheet horse was screwed down with four ⅜in countersunk screws, originally on the centre line, but on many boats moved to starboard to clear the aft trawl head, see Fig. 72. An eyebolt was also fitted for the mainsheet turning block.

The position of all of these items on *Nora's* reconstruction is illustrated by Fig. 73.

The hull is now ready for finishing. The hulls were originally tarred on their bottoms, and black-leaded for speed and ease of scrubbing off. Copper-based antifouling was adopted when it came into the reach of the fishermen, starting a coppery red when new, weathering to a verdigris green. Above water a wide variety of colour schemes were employed. Some of the photos of new nobbies at their builders and Rawstrone and Allunson's records show that black tar varnish was used, this is a very glossy black finish. The Bay boats at Morecambe were always painted white, whilst when colour was applied to the nobbies a wide range of colours was adopted, especially in the latter days of the craft. The colours used included red, blue, yellow, grey, *eau de nil* through lime green to dark green, as well as black, some with a white water cut but rarely a contrasting boot topping, most with either the moulding or the shear strake in a complimentary colour. The cove line would also be picked out in yellow or red, as appropriate. The deck and occasionally the inside of the outside coaming was painted pale green, buff or beige through to mid-tan, and occasionally red lead. Inboard was either varnished, or at Fleetwood painted white between varnished timbers.

The boat's name was carved in the shear just forward of the bow nogs. Her fishing registry number would be painted on the bow below the moulding, and her name and port of registry painted on the stern. The owner normally carried this out after the new boat was registered. The numbers would be black on light hulls, and white on dark. If the main colour of the hull were too light to provide contrast, they would be painted on a black cartouche.

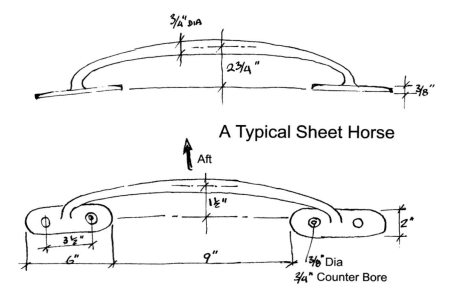

A Typical Sheet Horse

Fig. 72. Mainsheet horse.

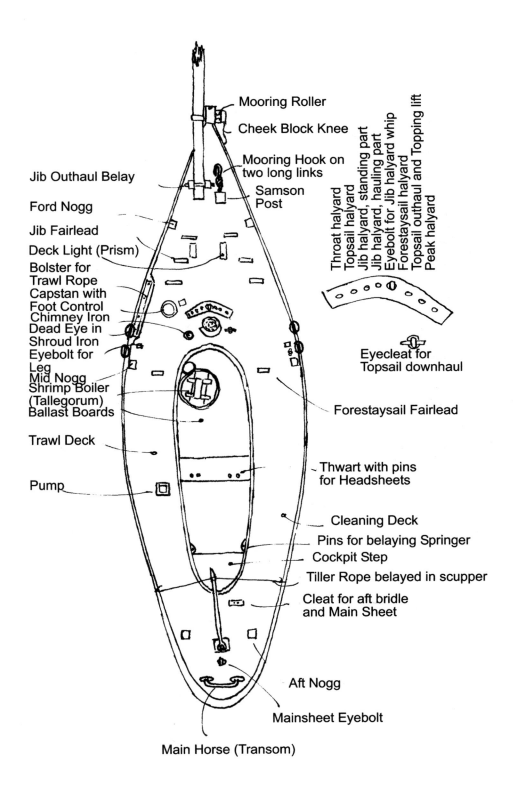

Mooring Roller

Cheek Block Knee

Mooring Hook on two long links

Samson Post

Jib Outhaul Belay

Ford Nogg

Jib Fairlead

Deck Light (Prism)

Bolster for Trawl Rope
Capstan with Foot Control
Chimney Iron
Dead Eye in Shroud Iron
Eyebolt for Leg
Mid Nogg
Shrimp Boiler (Tallegorum)
Ballast Boards

Trawl Deck

Pump

Throat halyard
Topsail halyard
Jib halyard, standing part
Jib halyard, hauling part
Eyebolt for Jib halyard whip
Forestaysail halyard
Topsail outhaul and Topping lift
Peak halyard

Eyecleat for Topsail downhaul

Forestaysail Fairlead

Thwart with pins for Headsheets

Cleaning Deck

Pins for belaying Springer

Cockpit Step

Tiller Rope belayed in scupper

Cleat for aft bridle and Main Sheet

Aft Nogg

Mainsheet Eyebolt

Main Horse (Transom)

Fig. 73. Deck plan.

After 1919 nobbies were allowed engines. Many boats were converted whilst both John and William Crossfield's businesses started building motor nobbies. When *Nora* was converted, a shaft log was bolted over a frame inside, and a boss was bolted on to the external plank. John Crossfield converted his boats by making a square split log, and inserting it through the plank in the quarter. John continued to build his new nobbies in the same fashion, the relevant frame was increased in scantling, the hull was planked, and then the plank was cut to allow the shaft log to be inserted. The nobbies were fitted with a variety of engines, either in the fore bay or under the cleaning deck. The inside coamings were built up to accept the top of the engine hatch and a bulkhead was erected against the foreside of the thoft. A hinged door was made for access. The fuel tank, or tanks on dual fuel engines, and on engines with a dry sump the lubricating oil tank were fitted high under the engine hatch top. It would appear that John Crossfield changed the form of his hulls intended for motors to a greater extent than his brother William. This may be because William's Morecambe customers wanted to retain good sailing properties, so their nobbies still retained some hollow in the garboards. John's nobbies were filled out with both straight floors and shallow sternposts, or in the case of *Lassie*, full floors and a slack bilge on 4ft 11in draft. *Lassie* CH 68 was also built with more freeboard than typical nobbies. This was at the request of her owner, but does make her appear to be floating high, as though without enough ballast.

Nobby spars were of spruce with oak jaws, although there are some reports of the unstayed bowsprit being made from pitch pine, and the mast in *Nance* was reported to be black spruce. The mast in a 31-footer would have been 6½in diameter over the 20ft from deck to hounds, with a 7ft pole head. The hounds were left square, and often had oak bolsters nailed on. The head was tapered to 3½in diameter. There was a sheave fitted for the topsail halyard at the masthead, its slot cut at an angle from the for'd and aft line to allow the topsail yard to hang to the side of the mast and gaff. The angle was about ten degrees allowing the topsail to set to starboard of the main. A mast band (called Truck band at Morecambe) with eyes athwartships will have been driven on above the sheave hole on all but those without cap shrouds. This would have helped to prevent the masthead splitting at the sheave.

Eye bolts or a topmast band would have been fitted for the upper peak halyard and the jib halyard, depending on taste, with the eyes horizontal to allow the hooked blocks to hank correctly. An eyebolt would have taken the lower peak halyard block, an eyebolt was also usually fitted for the topping lift. Next came a light crane for the forestay, to allow the forestaysail block to hang clear of the mast. The throat halyard crane (or iron) was fitted at or just above the hounds. The author has seen examples cut from ¾in plate, and made from round bar. A table was fitted aft on the mast to support the boom at a suitable height above the deck.

When the mast was stepped and wedged, the wedges were cut off flush with the deck, and a wooden mast collar was nailed down into a good bedding of putty to keep the water above deck. The mast hoops, with a couple of spares, were slipped on before the mast was stepped. Most boats had cap shrouds shackled to the mast cap band, but some had paired lowers and no cap shrouds. The lowers had soft eyes to go over the masthead and bed on the hounds. Bigger sprawners and Fleetwood and Southport boats had both paired lower, and cap shrouds. The shrouds on a shrimping nobby were $7/_{16}$in wire, spliced around the deadeyes. When making off the shroud lanyards three racking seizing were used, consuming 2ft of marline each.

In the early days the jib halyard was used as a fish tackle, but latterly, when the jib was given up in the 1930s, a fish tackle pendant went over the hounds to port, underneath the shrouds. The forestay was made from iron rod, with forge-welded eyes for the shackles.

The gaff on a 31-footer was 17ft 6in long, 3½in diameter at the mast, 3¾in in the mid-length and 2⅞in at the outer end. The jaws, which were made from approximately 2in thick oak, were fitted with a tumbler. They were moulded 2¼in where they clasped the mast and 3in in their throat. The only description of the sail's throat attachment we have is from K. Willacy's *Linda*, her halyard block was hooked into an eyebolt that went through the spar to be headed up in the bosom of a clevis fitting. The clevis accepted the throat cringle, whilst the process of heading up the eyebolt was carried out so that the eyebolt could rotate. Thumb cleats were nailed on to fix the position of the peak halyard blocks and span. The final fitting was a small bee nailed to the starboard end of the gaff for the topsail outhaul, and a hole for the peak lashing.

The boom was 20ft 6in long (just long enough to extend over the counter), 3¼in diameter at the mast, 3¼in diameter at mid-length, and 3½in at the outboard end. It had plain wooden jaws, a 'U'-bolt for the tack of the sail, a horn cleat and thumb cleat for the reef tackle, a pair of three hole plain bees for the reef pendants, and a hole for the clew lashing. *Helen III* was more sophisticated, with a short iron horse on the top of the boom end for a clew shackle with a vertical sheave for a clew outhaul. The reef pendant bees will also have been bored for the mainsheet block strop.

The 14ft bowsprit was 6in diameter at the gammon iron, squared at the bitts (some were left round, especially on those without bitts), with several holes for an iron fid to allow the spar to be reefed from its 10ft outboard extent, and a wedge to lock it against the bit's cross piece. The spar usually had no rigging apart from an outhaul sheave, although the Annan model had shrouds to whiskers on the gammon iron, and *Alice Allan* carried a bobstay when racing. The topsail yard was plain with only a hole for the throat and peak lashings. It measured 19ft 6in by 3in diameter over the lower third, tapering to 2in at the peak. The spars were normally painted buff, with the end of the bowsprit and the masthead painted white.

The builders usually supplied all of the blocks and running rigging, and the owners the sails. The iron bound blocks were all provided with solid hooks. This avoided the need for shackles. Keith Willacy's drawings of *Linda*'s rig with Morecambe practice for shrimpers are shown to be the same as Fleetwood practice by the Sankey photographs. The cod and sprawn boats differed, but only in the run of the peak halyard and the belays on boats with pin-rails at the shrouds. The rope used was manila, 1¾in circumference for throat and jib halyards, with the rest one size smaller, as told to E.J. March by F.J. Crossfield. The Morecambe fishermen selected their ropes by the strand count, 1¾in manila has eight yarns per strand, the next size down in the BSI standard of 1953 is given as one inch and five eighths circumference with seven yarns per strand.

Some of the run of rigging on *Nora* can be read off from the photographs taken by *Nora*'s owner Frank Brooks and his friends. The reconstruction of *Nora*'s rigging will use these, along with the holes in her deck from fittings, and will fill the gaps by taking details from *Linda*. The throat halyard will have a single block with a becket hooked into the gaff throat eyebolt, and a double hooked into the halyard crane. *Nora*'s peak halyard had an eye splice slipped over the gaff end, which went through a single hooked into the upper mast band, through a single rope stropped to a thimble on a span on the gaff, and up to a single hooked into the eyebolt in the mast head between the throat halyard crane and the mast band, and down to the deck.

Linda had a single block with a becket hooked into the upper mast band. The halyard rove from the becket through a single rope stropped around the gaff, up to the upper block, down to a second rope stropped single on the gaff, up to a single block hooked into a lower mast band and then down to the deck. The bigger boats such as *Ailsa* had a different run, being in effect that of *Linda* inverted, starting with a single with a becket on the lower mast band, finishing at the upper mast band and then down to the deck.

The boom would have a conventional reef tackle with a single block on a long strop on the boom, and a single block with a solid hook and becket for the pendant, the tackle belays to a cleat on the boom. The sheet was assembled from a single block with becket shackled to the horse. The rope ran from the becket through a single block outboard on the boom, down through the block on the horse, up to a second block on the boom, and down through a turning block in an eye bolt in the deck to belay on the large cleat on the counter. Keith Willacy drew all of these blocks with rope strops, but put eyebolts in the boom, whilst all of the Sankey photos indicate rope strops through holes in the reef bees and round the boom.

There was a single topping lift with an eye splice slipped over the boom end, going through a block hooked into an eyebolt on the pole masthead or into the upper shroud eye. The lift has a single block spliced into the hauling end, this has a line rove that is made off to and belayed to the eye cleat in the starboard scuppers by the after shroud. *Helen III* has a clew outhaul horse with a sheave in the boom end, she was a late built nobby that may have had yacht features.

The mainsail was bent on using a twisted bow shackle to the 'U'-bolt at the tack, and conventional lashings elsewhere. The luff was lashed to the mast hoops by middling the lashing line, cow hitching it to the hoop, and working a square lashing with the two parts. The head was laced on with marling hitches, the eyelets were called lacing eyes at Morecambe. The luff reef pendants were spliced into the reef cringles. In use they were passed around the boom and through the reef cringle twice before being hitched to the reef cringle. There were three rows of reef points in the average mainsail; however, when the nobbies became motor trawlers with auxiliary sail, the mainsail was often cut short in the hoist, the reduction being equivalent to the first reef.

The forestaysail as described by Keith Willacy had some unusual features. Its cut was conventional, with two rows of reef points. It was provided with iron spring hanks to run on the stay. A pigtail hook was permanently fitted directly to the tack cringle. The halyard on shrimpers was a single part, reeving through a single hooked block, whilst the bigger boats had a single whip, a single block with becket at the mast and single block with hook at the sail head, although some men preferred sister hooks. The halyard on shrimpers was simply bent to the head of the shrimpers sail in order to avoid a shackle. As a shackle is dangerous in the clew of a head sail, the sheets were secured by middling the sheet, forming an eye with a round seizing, and securing this to the clew cringle with a wooden toggle and eye. The sheet goes through the fairleads on the side decks, to belay to the pin in the thwart within the cockpit. *Onward* had a different arrangement with a wire horse between her pin-rails, and sheets shackled to the traveller to control the set of the sail.

The jib traveller was a conventional leathered iron ring, with a loose pigtail hook and captive shackle for the outhaul. The gammon iron was woulded with junk rope before the bowsprit was passed outboard, and the traveller put on. The outhaul was spliced to the captive shackle, went through the sheave in the bowsprit end and was belayed on the bowsprit bitts. The jib halyard was double ended; there was a whip with a single block with a becket hooked into an eyebolt in the pin-rail. The other block in the whip tackle was a double block spliced into the halyard end. The halyard went to a double block hooked into the upper mast band, down to a single with a hook for the head of the sail, back to the double on the mast and down to belay. The sheet was the same as the fore staysail going to the fairlead appropriate to the size of the jib, of which there were three: girt jib, middle and lile or spitfire jib.

The topsail completes the suite of sails. Its halyard rove through the sheave in the masthead, to be hitched around the topsail yard. The outhaul went through the bee in the gaff end, through a block hooked into the throat clevis, and down to the deck. When the topsail was set this was hitched to the clew, and belayed on the deck eye cleat that secured the downhaul. When the topsail was stowed the two ends of the outhaul were hitched to a suitable mast hoop. The tack downhaul was of flexible wire, the upper block was a double with becket on a long wire pendant hooked into the tack cringle; the lower was a double with a hook that went into the eye of the eye cleat at the foot of the mast. The wire hauling part started at the becket of the upper block and had a rope tail that turned up on the eye cleat.

The trawl boats dressed their working sails, their jibs and all sails carried by Bay boats being left plain. At Morecambe the recipe started with dressing the dampened sail with tar, followed by boiled oil and red ochre. They must have used a lot of tar, as the colour achieved was very dark, although the damping of the sail with water was intended to prevent its taking up too much tar. At Annan the fishermen dispensed with the red ochre, simply tarring the sails black. The fishing number was painted onto the mainsail above the deepest reef, with white paint.

Conclusions

The introduction stated that the objective of this book is to set down the origins and development of the Lancashire nobby; to describe the way that these vessels were worked, and the communities that used them. In support of the objective to describe their development and how they were worked it is necessary to record and describe the construction of the nobby and its equipment. We are confident that the information and illustrations set out herein will allow a shrimping nobby to be built, rigged, outfitted and fished under sail.

As the author is an engineer by training and experience, the historical record may not be covered to the same level of rigour as the technical descriptions. However, some conclusions may be derived from the preceding chapters. The chapters on the fishing stations set out the environment in which the nobby developed, whilst the chapter 'Origins' sets out the context for this development. The nobby was primarily an inshore trawler, its grounds being within estuarine channels, out to a little over 6fm, say 15m. This generally agreed with the 3-mile limit jurisdiction of the Sea Fisheries committees set up to promote the industry.

Wherries, substantial schooner or shalop-rigged open boats, were used during the eighteenth and early nineteenth centuries around the Irish Sea for a variety of purposes. When based in the Isle of Man they served the herring fleet as carriers bringing the catch ashore, and as fast carriers of high value cargo. At Allonby in Cumberland they were employed as herring drifters, whilst further south they trawled for fish to supply Liverpool. Each of these cases could be classified as 'commercial', most certainly in the case of the herring boats that formed part of an enterprise that cured, packaged, and traded a product. These wherries would have been craft suited to the deeper waters between the British coast and the Isle of Man, having a conventional beam-to draft ratio, not necessarily suited to estuarine waters of Morecambe Bay and the Ribble. Their link to the nobby would have been their use of the trawl on the banks off the mouth of the Mersey and Ribble. They are a possible precursor through their hull form, as many of them sported a square-tuck stern, which was also an attribute of the hull form of nobbies in Morecambe Bay in the mid-nineteenth century.

Set against this in the eighteenth century there existed what we will classify as 'subsistence' fishing. This was pursued by cottagers fishing one tide and hawking the catch around a market within a couple of hours' walk from home. The methods used would have included set nets, baulks, trot lines and shellfish gathering, all of which are worked at low tide on foot or by cart, or by longlining or trawling with a boat. The sources that we have consulted do not talk of trawling in the context of 'subsistence' fishing, although there is a hint that shanking for shrimp was pursued before fish trawling was adopted. The references from Southport all talk of four to six crew at this time, which implies drifting for herring or setting longlines, which can also be referred to as 'trawling'. Improved markets for 'subsistence' fishermen would have arisen with the rise in popularity of sea bathing as discussed around the turn of the eighteenth century at Poulton-le-Sands, Blackpool, Lytham, Southport and Runcorn. This also provided an opportunity to offer amusement in the form of sailing trips at Southport and Blackpool where the schooner rig of the wherry was adapted to pleasure boats working off of the beach. A short counter developed on these Blackpool hulls, which is a common occurrence on beach boats. There were four of these Southport schooners in 1863.

Two newspaper reports of accidents in Morecambe Bay of 1836 and 1840 indicate the use of one- or two-man boats, in one case engaged in shrimping, which we may propose as the prototype of the nobby. Because the term 'shanking' has survived as a name for both the shrimp trawl and shrimping nobby, it may be the case that the nobbies were used as shrimpers before beam trawls for fish were adopted. At Morecambe the shank was given up and beam trawls were used for fish as well as shrimp, whilst in the Ribble the shank was retained. There were also references to the Little London (Southport) trawlers fishing in Cardigan Bay, and occasionally living on their boats at this time. However, as they marketed their catch at Milford Haven or Aberystwyth, they may well have been bigger than the one- or two-man nobbies.

Development of the social context in which the nobbies were employed begins to accelerate with improvements in communications, especially those provided by the railways. This was preceded by the benefits afforded by the passenger coach services and flyboats on the canals, both of which were mentioned in the development of Blackpool and Southport. These facilitated the growth of the resorts, providing bigger markets on the fishermen's doorsteps, whilst the railways arrival from the 1850s both accelerated this change and opened up access to much bigger inland markets. It is now that we find a description of what becomes the nobby at Morecambe and Annan. Although the craft do not have the same elliptical counter as the fully developed form, they are of a similar size and proportion to the later nobbies. It took perhaps thirty years for the evolution to the final form to be completed.

Although it is extremely unlikely that anyone will have thought it necessary to put on record why the hull form was changing, we can postulate two scenarios. The builders on or around the Ribble estuary would have been familiar with the small counters fitted to the schooner-rigged boats used at Blackpool. By fitting a counter, broader in proportion as appropriate for a shallow cutter rigged hull, there would have been twin benefits of increased deck area for stowage of the gear and more powerful aft quarters for stability and lift in a seaway. The square tuck stern of the Morecambe nobby already provided the stowage area aft, so the evolution to an elliptical counter would have been driven by an interest in speed, always of benefit to a fishing station so far up the sand of the Bay. The trigger for this may have been contact with the nobbies from the Ribble, now working from Fleetwood, or from lessons learned from the yachts on Windermere. Comparison of the longer, deeper counters of the earliest examples of the Crossfields' work with the images of the earliest Fleetwood and Lytham boats with their shorter shallower counters tends to suggest that the Windermere alternative is more likely for the Arnside built boats.

Whilst access to new markets was facilitated by the railways, which would have made it worthwhile for nobby fishermen to move to other ports away from the holiday centres where the largest fleets were worked, at Morecambe, and to a lesser extent Southport and Blackpool, the fishing community was closely bound up with the holiday industry. At all of these three towns the fishermen provided the shrimp delicacy demanded by the holidaymakers and operated pleasure boats for sailing trips to entertain the visitors. However, only at Morecambe did the fishing industry form such a large proportion of the town's activities. There were seven landing stages used by pleasure sailing companies at Morecambe. Although Blackpool used purpose-built sloops as tripper boats, they probably only had as many boats as Morecambe had boat companies. The other feature unique to Morecambe was that the fishermen's wives formed a significant portion of the boarding house landlady population. At Lytham St Anne's and Southport the fishing communities lived away from the nucleus of the holiday town. There was a significant nobby fleet at Fleetwood, serving holidaymakers at Blackpool and Fleetwood, but at Fleetwood itself the nobby and holiday industry was always overshadowed by the big trawler industry.

We now come to the final initiative that encouraged development of the nobby and its industry. During the 1880s and 1890s legislation was put in place to regulate and nurture the inshore fishery. Byelaws were put in place to protect trawling, by limiting the kill of fry in the by-catch of shrimping and prawning, to protect shrimping by ensuring free navigation in the vicinity of fixed engines in the channels of the bays and the protection of nursery grounds, and by keeping bigger blue-water trawlers out of the inshore grounds. In addition to regulation the Sea Fisheries committees provided education, and sought out and cleared new fishing grounds to aid the inshore fishermen. As this was happening the nobby increased its range down into Cardigan Bay, to fish grounds from Luce Bay, Galloway, and around to Aberystwyth, driven by a search for new grounds and new markets to be exploited.

The nobbies and the seaside resorts that they served enjoyed their peak during the Edwardian era. The end of the First World War, as in many things, triggered a period of change in the nobby fishery. The most significant change was the adoption of engines. As engines became more reliable and efficient, the sailing rig was cut down or given up, new boats' hull form filled out and often became shallower as sailing ability became redundant. Finally fewer boats and fewer crew were needed due to the ability to supply the markets in spite of a lack of wind, and the benefit of a power take off to drive winches, thereby reducing crew numbers or increasing the size of the gear. All of these reduced the need for new boats, which caused the nobby yards to close as the 'nobby' generation of builders reached retirement age, forcing the fishermen to look elsewhere and purchase different forms of hull.

Now only a few nobbies fish as motorboats working out of Fleetwood and Cumbrian ports, there are hulls in museum collections at Lancaster, Fleetwood and Liverpool, whilst twenty to thirty survive, more or less altered as yachts, on the Mersey and around the UK coast. We had intended to identify builder's traits or idiosyncrasies to help identify the origins of these individual nobbies. This has not been possible, as *Wild Cherry* shows: although built at Southport she is indistinguishable from any of the Crossfields' products. The only builder who went his own way was Stoba, who did not use the 'U'-section keel castings used by all of the other builders, having the keels specifically moulded for the two boats that we have studied.

Conclusions can be drawn from the form of the hulls about their intended service. Yachts are not constrained by draft, so were deeper in proportion than their fishing sisters. The building of the pier out to the deep water of the Bog Hole off Southport allowed for the development of big 40-5ft nobbies of 5-6ft draft, the largest fishing nobbies built. Centre plates were tried in at least one big (36-40ft) nobby built for the Mersey, and in 30ft nobbies at Morecambe and Ulverston. These can be recognised by the way their frame first futtocks and keelsons were worked. The only other distinctive features developed with the use of engines. Motor nobbies are of fuller form, with little or no hollow in the garboards, whilst the Annan motor nobbies were the only fishing nobbies to be built with a centre line propeller aperture.

Appendix I

Sea Fisheries Committee Byelaws and Committees

LANCASHIRE AND WESTERN SEA FISHERIES DISTRICT.
(Cemnaes Head to Haverigg Point.)
BYELAWS.

1. The following Byelaws shall apply to the whole area of the Lancashire and Western Sea Fisheries District, unless otherwise specified, and except in the cases to which the provisions of the 13th Section of 'The Sea Fisheries Regulation Act, 1888,' apply. Provided that nothing in these Byelaws shall apply to any person fishing for sea fish for scientific purposes, or for stocking or breeding purposes, or removing mussels during the close season for use as bait under the written authority in that behalf of the Local Fisheries Committee, signed by their Clerk or Clerks, and in accordance with the conditions set out in that authority.

2. No artifice or device shall be used so as practically to diminish the size of the mesh of any net.

3. No person shall use in fishing for sea fish any net with any trap or pocket, provided that this Byelaw shall not apply to any person using a fish trawl net the mesh of which is in accordance with Byelaw 4.

4. No person shall use in fishing for sea fish, other than shrimps, prawns, mackerel, herring, sparling, or garfish, any net having a mesh through which a square gauge of one and three-quarter inches, measured across each side of the square, or seven inches measured round the four sides, will not pass without pressure when the net is wet, provided that between the 1st day of June and the 15th day of November following, both inclusive, it shall be lawful to use a trawl net having a mesh through which a square gauge of one and a half inches, measured across each side of the square, or six inches measured round the four sides, will pass without pressure when the net is wet, on the seaward side of lines drawn within the following limits:—

(a) A line drawn straight from the south-western extremity of Haverigg Point, in Cumberland, to the north-western extremity of Walney Island,

(b) A line drawn straight from Walney lighthouse to the Wyre lighthouse,

(c) A line drawn straight from the 'Star Inn', South Shore, Blackpool, to the inner northwest seamark on Formby Point,

(d) A line drawn straight from the lifeboat-house at Formby to the Crosby lightship, and then straight to the Leasowe lighthouse, in the County of Chester.

5. No person shall use in fishing for sea fish other than shrimps or prawns, any trawl net except in accordance with the following regulations: —

(a) When the length of beam does not exceed eighteen feet between the trawl heads or irons, the circumference of the net shall be not less than fifty meshes.

(b) When the length of beam, measured as aforesaid, exceeds eighteen feet but does not exceed twenty- five feet, the circumference of the net shall not be less than sixty meshes.

(c) When the length of beam, measured as aforesaid, exceeds twenty-five feet, the circumference of the net shall be not less than eighty meshes.

6. No person shall use in fishing for mackerel, herring, sparling, or garfish, any seine, draft, drift, set, or stake net having a mesh through which a square gauge of one inch, measured across each side of the square, or four inches measured round the four sides, will not pass without pressure when the net is wet.

7. No person shall use in fishing for sea fish any drift net having a depth of more than 200 meshes.

8. No person shall use in fishing for sparling any net or instrument between the first day of April and the thirty-first day of October following, both inclusive.

9. No person shall use, in fishing for shrimps or prawns, any net having a mesh through which a square gauge of three-eighths of an inch measured across each side of the square, or one and a half inches measured round the four sides, will not pass without pressure when the net is wet.

10. No person shall use, in fishing for shrimps or prawns, any trawl net except in accordance with the following regulations: —

(a) When the length of beam between the trawl heads or irons does not exceed twenty feet, the circumference of the net shall be not less than one hundred and twenty meshes.

(b) When the length of beam, measured as aforesaid, exceeds twenty feet, the circumference of the net shall be not less than one hundred and forty meshes.

(c) The length of beam, measured as aforesaid, shall not exceed twenty-five feet.

11. No person shall use, in fishing for shrimps or prawns, any shank or bow net having a less circumference than eighty meshes.

12. No person shall use, in fishing for shrimps or prawns, any hand or hose net having a less circumference than seventy meshes.

13. No person shall use, in fishing for sea fish from any vessel propelled otherwise than by sails or oars, any method or instrument of fishing except hooks and lines.

14. No person shall use, in fishing for sea fish, any stake net, except in accordance with the following regulations: —

(a) The site of the net shall be marked by poles, perches, or buoys, visible above the surface at high water of any tide, and such poles, perches, or buoys shall be maintained so long as the stakes of the net continue in position. All stake nets shall be marked with the owner's name, affixed to the end stakes, so long as the stakes continue in position.

(b) No portion of the net shall he nearer the centre of any stream or channel than the edge of such stream or channel at low water of a tide, the high water line of which stands sixteen feet above the level of the sill of the Old Dock at Liverpool.

(c) No portion of the net shall be nearer than one hundred and fifty yards to any portion of another stake net, not being a hose net.

(d) No mackerel baulk shall exceed 600 yards in length, no other stake net shall exceed 300 yards in length, and no stake net of the description known as a poke net shall exceed 150 yards in length.

15. No person shall use in fishing for mackerel, herring, garfish, sparling, shrimps, or prawns, any method or instrument of fishing, except at the times and places at which and in the manner in which such method or instrument may be reasonably calculated to take such fish respectively.

16. At the times and places at which, and in the manner in which it may be reasonably calculated to take eels or mullet only, an eel or mullet net may be used under the written authority in that behalf of the local Fisheries Committee, signed by their Clerks, Clerk or Superintendent, and in accordance with the conditions set out in that authority.

17. No person shall use, in fishing for sea fish, any seine, draft, trawl, bow, hand, hose, shank, stake, or otter net in that portion of the district which lies between a line drawn true west from the building known as 'Uncle Tom's Cabin,' on the coast, near and north of the Borough of Blackpool, and a line drawn true west from the building known as the 'Star Inn,' on the coast, within the said borough.

18. No person shall fish for cockles except—

By hand or, (b) with a craam, rake, or spade: Provided that between the first day of November and the last day of February following, both inclusive, it shall be lawful to use an instrument locally known as a Jumbo, not exceeding four feet six inches in length, fourteen inches in width, and one inch in thickness, provided that such instrument shall be constructed entirely of wood, and shall not be dragged across the cockle beds or artificially weighted.

19. No person shall remove from a fishery any cockle which will pass through a gauge having a square opening of thirteen-sixteenths of an inch, measured across each side of the square.

20. No person shall fish for mussels, except—

By hand, or with a rake: Provided that on the West Hoyle Bank the rake must not exceed three feet in width, and may only be used from a boat and when the mussel bed is covered with at least four feet of water.

21. No person shall take mussels from the 1st of April to the 31st August following, both inclusive.

22. No person shall remove from a fishery any mussel less than two inches in length: Provided that no mussel shall be removed from the West Hoyle Bank measuring less than two and a quarter inches in length.

23. No person shall remove from a fishery any oyster which will pass through a circular ring of two and a half inches in internal diameter.

24. No person shall remove from a fishery any berried lobster or any berried edible crab.

25. No person shall remove from a fishery—

(a) Any lobster measuring less than nine inches from the tip of the beak to the end of the tail when spread as far as possible flat.

(b) Any edible crab measuring less than five inches across the broadest part of the back.

26. Any person who takes any shell fish, the removal of which from a fishery is prohibited by any of these Byelaws, or the possession of which is prohibited by any Act of Parliament, shall forthwith redeposit the same as nearly as possible in the place from which they were taken, or, under the written authority of the Superintendent, on other suitable ground, and in re-depositing cockles in accordance with this Byelaw, shall spread them thinly and evenly over the beds.

27. No person shall use any method or instrument of fishing for sea fish other than the following—

A method or instrument permitted by these Byelaws.

Hooks and lines.

A pot, hook, or basket, for taking eels, prawns, lobsters, crabs, or whelks.

A hedge baulk in use previous to the 9th of August 1893, the catching parts whereof consist wholly of net having a mesh in conformity with Byelaw 4.

28. The deposit or discharge of any solid or liquid sub- stance detrimental to sea fish or sea fishing is hereby prohibited, provided that this Byelaw shall not apply (1) to the deposit by the Mersey Docks and Harbour Board within the area coloured brown on the Chart marked S. 1568-1895, in the possession of the Board of Trade, of refuse or material dredged or excavated in the course of the execution under statutory power of any work by the said Docks and Harbour Board within the Port of Liverpool, or (2) to the deposit by any person, with the consent in writing of the Committee, given under the hand of their Clerk or Clerks, and confirmed by the Board of Trade, of any such solid or liquid substance on an area shown on a Chart referred to in the consent and in accordance with the conditions laid down in that consent.

29. Any person who shall commit a breach of any of the foregoing Byelaws shall be liable to a Penalty not exceeding for any one offence the sum of Twenty Pounds, and in the case of a continuing offence the additional sum of Ten Pounds for every day during which the offence continues, and in any case to forfeiture of any fishing instrument used or sea fish taken in contravention of or found in possession of a person contravening such Byelaw: Provided that in any case in which a prosecution is instituted for taking sea fish with a net or instrument the use of which for the capture of any particular kind of sea fish would constitute a breach of any of the foregoing Byelaws, not being a Byelaw prescribing a close season, a person shall not be deemed to have committed such breach if he proves to the satisfaction of the Court that he was bond fide fishing only for the particular kind of sea fish permitted to be captured with the net or instrument he was then using, and that

he forthwith returned to the water with the least possible injury all soles, plaice, flukes, flounders, and dabs under 8 inches in length, and all turbot and brill under 10 inches in length, measured respectively from the tip of the snout to the end of the tail, if any such were taken by such net or instrument.

CUMBERLAND SEA FISHERIES DISTRICT.
(Haverigg Point to Sarke Foot.)

1. The following Byelaws shall apply to the whole area of the Cumberland Sea Fisheries District, unless otherwise specified and except in the cases to which the provisions of the 13th Section of 'The Sea Fisheries Regulation Act, 1888,' apply: — Provided that nothing in these Byelaws shall apply to any person fishing for sea fish for scientific purposes, or for stocking or breeding purposes, under the written authority in that behalf of the Local Fisheries Committee, signed by their Clerk, and in accordance with the conditions contained in that authority.

2. No person shall adopt any practice known as hunching or tying round the net, or use any artifice or devise so as practically to diminish the size of the mesh of any net, except the net or trawl used solely for the purpose of taking shrimps or prawns.

3. No person shall use, in fishing for sea fish, any net with any trap or pocket, unless the mesh of such net is in accordance with Byelaw 4.

4. No person shall use, in fishing for sea fish other than shrimps, prawns, mackerel, herring, eels, or sparling (other-wise known as 'smelts'), any net having a mesh through which a square gauge of one-and-three-quarter inches, measured across each side of the square, or seven inches measured round the four sides, will not pass without pressure when the net is wet. Provided that between the 1st day of July and the 15th day of October following, both inclusive, to the west and south of a line drawn from Bow House Point, near Caerlaverock, on the Scotch side of the Firth to Skinburness on the English side, it shall be lawful to use a trawl net having a mesh through which a square gauge of 11 inches measured across each side of the square, or six inches measured round the four sides, will pass without pressure when the net is wet.

5. Between the 1st day of January and the 30th day of June following, both inclusive, no person shall use in fishing for sea fish any trawl net having a beam of greater length than thirty feet between the trawl heads or irons, or any trawl net from any vessel exceeding 15 tons gross register.

6. No person shall use, in fishing for sea fish from any vessel propelled otherwise than by sails or oars, any method or instrument of fishing except hooks and lines.

7. No person shall use, in fishing for sea fish other than shrimps or prawns, any trawl net except in accordance with the following regulations: —

(a) When the length of beam does not exceed eighteen feet, measured between the trawl heads or irons, the circumference of the net shall be not less than fifty meshes.

(b) When the length of beam, measured as aforesaid, exceeds eighteen feet but does not exceed twenty- five feet, the circumference of the net shall not be less than sixty meshes.

(c) When the length of beam, measured as aforesaid, exceeds twenty-five feet, the circumference of the net shall not be less than eighty meshes.

8. No person shall use, in fishing for shrimps or prawns, any net having a mesh through which a square gauge of three-eighths of an inch, measured across each side of the square, or one-and-a-half inches measured round the four sides, will not pass without pressure when the net is wet.

9. No person shall use, in fishing for shrimps or prawns, any trawl net except in accordance with the following regulations: —

(a) When the length of beam, measured between the trawl heads or irons, does not exceed twenty feet, the circumference of the net shall be not less than one hundred and twenty meshes.

(b) When the length of beam, measured as aforesaid exceeds twenty feet, the circumference of the net shall not be less than one hundred and forty meshes.

(c) The length of beam, measured as aforesaid, shall not exceed twenty-five feet.

10. No person shall use in fishing for shrimps or prawns, any shank or bow net having a less circumference than eighty meshes.

11. No person shall use, in fishing for shrimps or prawns, any hand or hose net having a less circumference than seventy meshes.

12. No person shall use, in fishing for mackerel or herring: —

Any seine, draft, drift, or stake net having a mesh through which a square gauge of one inch, measured across each side of the square, or four inches measured round the four sides, will not pass without pressure when the net is wet, or

Any stake net except at the time and places at which, and in the manner in which, such nets have been heretofore commonly used for the capture of such fish respectively.

13. No person shall use, in fishing for sparling (otherwise known as 'smelts'), any instrument between the first day of February and the first day of September following, both inclusive.

14. No person shall use, in fishing for sea fish, any stake net except in accordance with the following regulations: —

(a) The site of the net shall be marked by poles, perches, or buoys, visible above the surface at high water of spring tides, and such poles, perches, or buoys shall be maintained so long as the stakes of the net continue in position.

(b) No portion of the net shall be nearer the centre of any stream or channel than the edge of such stream or channel at low water of a tide, the high water line of which stands sixteen feet above the level of the sill of the Old Dock at Liverpool.

(c) No portion of the net shall be nearer than one hundred and fifty yards to any portion of another stake net, not being a hose net.

15. No person shall fish for mussels except—

(a) By hand, or

(b) With a rake not exceeding three feet in width, and used only from a boat, and when the mussel bed is covered with at least four feet of water, provided that the use of a dredge shall be allowed when the mussel bed is covered with at least 20 feet of water.

16. No person shall take mussels during the months of May, June, July, or August in any year.

17. No person shall remove from a fishery any mussel less than two inches in length.

18. No person shall fish for cockles except—

By hand, or

With an instrument locally known as the 'craam' having not more than three teeth: Provided that between the first day of November and the last day of March following both inclusive, it shall be lawful to use an instrument locally known as the 'Jumbo,' not exceeding four feet six inches in length, fourteen inches in width, and one inch in thickness, constructed entirely of wood, and not dragged across the cockle beds or artificially weighted.

19. No person shall remove from a fishery any cockle, which will pass through a gauge having an oblong opening of three-quarters of an inch in breadth and not less than two inches in length.

20. No person shall remove from a fishery any oyster, which will pass through a circular ring of two-and-a-half inches in internal diameter.

21. No person shall remove from a fishery any berried lobster or any berried edible crab.

22. No person shall remove from a fishery—

(a) Any lobster measuring less than nine inches from the tip of the beak to the end of the tail when spread as far as possible flat.

(b) Any edible crab measuring less than four-and-a- quarter inches across the broadest part of the back.

23. Any person who takes any shell fish, the removal of which from a fishery is prohibited by any Byelaw in force in the District, or the possession of which is prohibited

by any Act of Parliament, shall forthwith re-deposit the same without injury as nearly as possible in the place from which they were taken, and, in re-depositing cockles in accordance with this Byelaw, shall spread them thinly and evenly over the beds.

24. No person shall use any method or instrument of fishing for sea fish other than the following:

(a) A method or instrument specified in and not otherwise prohibited by any of these Byelaws.

(b) A hook and line.

(c) A pot or basket for taking eels, prawns, shrimps, lobsters, crabs, or whelks.

(d) A hedge baulk in use previous to the 27th July, 1896, the catching parts whereof consist only of net having a mesh in conformity with Byelaw 4.

25. No person shall use in fishing for mackerel, herring, eels, sparling (otherwise known as 'smelts'), shrimps, or prawns any mode or instrument of fishing except at the times and places at which, and in the manner in which, such mode or instrument may be reasonably calculated to take such fish respectively.

26. The deposit or discharge of any solid or liquid sub-stance detrimental to sea fish or sea fishing is hereby prohibited. Provided that nothing in this Byelaw shall apply to the deposit by any person with the consent in writing of the Committee given under the hand of their Clerk, and confirmed by the Board of Trade, of any such solid or liquid substance in an area shown on a chart referred to in the consent, and in accordance with the conditions laid down in that consent.

27. Any person who shall commit a breach of any of the foregoing Byelaws shall be liable to a penalty not exceeding for any one offence the sum of twenty pounds, and in the case of a continuing offence the additional sum of ten pounds for every day during which the offence continues, and in any case to forfeiture of any fishing instrument used or sea fish taken in contravention of or found in the possession of a person contravening such Byelaw. Provided that in any case in which a prosecution is instituted for taking sea fish with a net or instrument, the use of which for the capture of any particular kind of sea fish would constitute a breach of any of the foregoing Byelaws, not being a Byelaw prescribing a close season, a person shall not be deemed to have committed such breach if he proves to the satisfaction of the court that he was bond fide fishing only for the particular kind of sea fish permitted to be captured with the net or instrument he was then using, and that he forthwith returned to the water with the least possible injury all soles and plaice under 8 inches in length and all turbot and brill under 10 inches in length if any such were taken by such net or instrument.

The representatives nominated by the Board of Trade for service on the Lancashire and Western District committee for 1893 were:

John Leonard Bolden, Esq., Surveyor General of the Duchy of Lancaster.
Cedric Vaughn, Esq. M.D., Hodbarrow Mining Co. Millom.
John Edmondson, Roosbeck Aldingham.
Thomas Tweedale, Over Sands Guide, Ulverston.
Thomas Robinson, Flookborough.
William Wallbank, Flookborough.
John Taylor Jr, Fisherman, Townend, Bolton-le-Sands.
John Bell, 39 Lord St, Morecambe.
John Borrow, Cumberland View, Heysham.
Richard Leadbetter, North Albert Street, Fleetwood.
Robert Wright, North Church Street, Fleetwood.
Robert Bickerstaff, 45 Market Street, Blackpool.
James Parr, 22 South King Street, Blackpool.
Robert Lamb Ashcroft Esq., 11 Park Street, Lytham.
William Wignall, Clifton Street, Lytham.

Charles Scarisbrick Esq., Scarisbrick Lodge, Southport.
William Robinson, 135a Lord, Street Southport.
John Ball, Marshside.
Lawrence Abraham, Banks.
John Formby Esq. Formby Hall, Formby.
William Schofield, 8 Hughes Street, Garston.
Robert Harley, St John's Fish Market, Liverpool.
John Whitehead, 144 Albemarle Street, Ashton-under-Lyne.
Thomas Banks, Great Meols.
Robert Aldred, Market Street, Hoylake.
James Eccles Sr, Lake Place, Hoylake.
Robert Holmes, Market Street, Hoylake.
Alfred Osten Walker, Nant-y-Glynn Hall, Colwyn Bay.

The full list of the Cumberland District committee's members for 1896 included county council appointees:

Mr William Isaac Barratt, Broughton-in-Furness.
Mr William Burnyeat, Millgrove, Moresby.
Mr J.C. Grainger, Whitriglees, Kirkbride, Silloth.
Mr Alfred Hine, Park Hill, Maryport.
Mr John Musgrave, 2 Lowther Street, Whitehaven.
Mr Cedric Vaughan, Leyfield House, Millom, Carnforth.

Representative of Eden Fisheries Board:
Mr T. Hesketh-Hodgson, Newby Grange, Carlisle

Representative of West Cumberland Fisheries Board:
Mr Robert Jefferson, Rothersyke, Egremont, Whitehaven.

Appointed by Derwent Fisheries Board:

Mr Gordon Falcon, Stainburn, Workington.

Appointed by the Board of Trade:

Hamilton Dixon, Whitehaven.
William Little, Hutton Hall, Penrith.
George Holmes, Airey Hill, Bowness-on-Solway.
Quentin Moore, Harbour House, Maryport.

The representatives nominated by the Board of Trade for service on the joint Lancashire and Western District Committee for 1900 were:

John Leonard Bolden, Esq. Surveyor General of the Duchy of Lancaster.
William Isaac Barratt, Broom Hill, Broughton-in-Furness.
John Edmondson, Roosbeck, Aldingham.
Charles Harrison, 39 Storey Square, Barrow-in-Furness.
Thomas Robinson, Flookborough.
William Wallbank, Flookborough.
Victor Christian William Cavendish, Esq. MP, Holker Hall,
John Taylor Jr. Fisherman, Townend, Bolton-le-Sands.
John Bell, 39 Lord Street, Morecambe.
James Allan, 17 Queen's Terrace, Morecambe.

Richard Leadbetter, North Albert Street, Fleetwood.
Robert Wright, North Church Street, Fleetwood.
Robert Bickerstaff, Central Pier, Blackpool.
James Parr, Hardhorn, Poulton-le-Fylde.
Robert Lamb Ashcroft Esq., 11 Park Street, Lytham.
A R Rogerson, St Anne's Road West, St Anne's-on-Sea.
Robert Houldsworth, Threllfall's Lane, Southport.
John Ball, Marshside.
Geoffrey Aughton, Glebe Lane, Banks.
John Formby, Esq., Formby Hall, Formby.
Thomas Bevington Garnett, 37 Langdale Road, Sefton Park, Liverpool.
Robert Harley, 74 Bedford Street South, Liverpool.
Bancroft Cooke, Esq., Shortwood, Hoylake.
Robert A. Aldred, Market Street, Hoylake.
Thomas Jones, Marmion Road, Hoylake.
Rev. Alfred Hamilton King, The Parsonage, Prenton, Birkenhead.
John Whitehead, 144 Albemarle Terrace, Henrietta Street, Ashton-under-Lynne.
William Horton, Bryn Dinarth, Colwyn Bay.
William Hugh Edwards, Rose Mount, Holyhead.
Jonathan Williams, 2 Little Lane, Beaumaris.
Thomas Ellis, Stanley Crescent, Holyhead.
Charles Freeman, Bangor.
John Williams, 4 Amanda Terrace, Borthy Gest, Porthmadog.
Griffith Davies, 16 High Street, Caernarfon.
Evan Jones, Henblas, Pwlhelli
Thomas Lee Manchester, Westfield, Pwlhelli.
William Thomas, Penrhudliliog, Pwlhelli.
William Harris, 19 Penlan Street, Pwlhelli.
John Morris, Broygraig, Barmouth.
Owen Jones, 4 Aelydon Buildings, Barmouth.
Dr J.H. Lister, Barmouth.
Humphrey Rowlands, Evan Terrace, Aberdovey.
Edward Lewis Rowlands, Liverpool House, Aberdovey.
Francis Bennison, 29 Terrace Road, Aberystwyth.
Richard Saycell, Warwick House, Great Darkgate Street, Aberystwyth.
Albert John Volk, 17 Quay Street, Cardigan.
David Davies, Royal Oak Inn, Quay Street, Cardigan.
Philip J. White, University College of North Wales, Bangor.

The nominees to the Lancashire and Western Joint Committee of 1901 were:
John Leonard Bolden, Esq., Surveyor General of the Duchy of Lancaster.
Charles Harrison, 39 Storey Square, Barrow-in-Furness.
Victor Christian William Cavendish, Esq. MP, Holker Hall.
Daniel Hardman, Flookborough.
John Bell, 39 Lord Street, Morecambe.
James Allan, 17 Queen's Terrace, Morecambe.
Richard Leadbetter, North Albert Street, Fleetwood.
Robert Lamb Ashcroft Esq., 11 Park Street, Lytham.
Robert Houldsworth, Threllfall's Lane, Southport.
John Ball, Marshside.
Geoffrey Aughton, Glebe Lane, Banks.
John Formby Esq., Formby Hall, Formby.
Thomas Bevington Garnett, 37 Langdale Road, Sefton Park, Liverpool.
Robert Harley, 74 Bedford Street South, Liverpool.

Bancroft Cooke Esq., Shortwood, Hoylake.
Robert A. Aldred, Market Street, Hoylake.
Thomas Jones, Marmion Road, Hoylake.
Rev. Alfred Hamilton King, The Parsonage, Prenton, Birkenhead.
John Whitehead, 144 Albemarle Terrace, Henrietta Street, Ashton-under-Lynne.
William Hugh Edwards, Rose Mount, Holyhead.
John Williams, 4 Amanda Terrace, Borthy Gest, Porthmadog.
Thomas Lee Manchester, Westfield, Pwlhelli.
Owen Jones, 4 Aelydon Buildings, Barmouth.
Dr J H Lister, Barmouth.
Enoch Lewis, Aberdovey.
Richard Saycell, Warwick House, Great Darkgate Street, Aberystwyth.
Albert John Volk, 17 Quay Street, Cardigan.
Philip J. White, University College of North Wales, Bangor.

Appendix II
Nicknames at Southport

Nickname	Name	Forename	Nickname	Name	Forename
B.J.	Ball	John	Kendrick	Wright	Richard
Squire	Blundell	John	Lucky	Wright	Thomas
Captain	Caldwell	James	Manty	Wright	John
John Henry	Halsall	John	Manty	Wright	Nicholas
Fag	Johnson	William	Manty	Wright	Peter
Tag	Johnson	Richard	Manty	Wright	Thomas
William's	Johnson	John	Manty	Wright	William
Bold	Rimmer	Robert	Margery's	Wright	Thomas
Manty	Rimmer	John	Olek	Wright	R.
Pluck	Rimmer	Thomas	Orchards	Wright	Richard
Willocks	Rimmer	J.	Pen	Wright	John
Willocks	Rimmer	William	Penn	Wright	R.
Handy	Sutton	Thomas	Peters Dick	Wright	Richard
Rigby	Sutton	Thomas	Pop	Wright	R.
Stitch	Waring	Thomas	Roberts	Wright	Robert
Clogger	Wright	Thomas	Sharpeye	Wright	John
Cotty	Wright	John	Sims	Wright	T.
Cotty	Wright	Peter	Stem	Wright	Henry
Cotty	Wright	Robert	Stem	Wright	Richard
Curly	Wright	Thomas	Stick	Wright	Thomas
Dubby	Wright	R.	Toffy	Wright	John
Henry's	Wright	John	Wheel	Wright	William
Hugh	Wright	Richard	Williams Bob	Wright	T.
Hutch	Wright	Richard	Boozer		
John's	Wright	Robert	Sail		
John's	Wright	William	Tute		

Appendix III
Nicknames at Morecambe

Nickname	Family Name	Forename	Reason	T = Trawler crew, P = Pleasure Co	Nobby
Jack Alex	Alexander	John		T	
Lile Neb	Allan	Harry	Both Lile and Neb mean small	T	
Paily	Allan	James		T	
Dick Bath	Bartholomew	Richard		P	
Just Ted	Baxter	Edward	Third hand	T	
Blowney	Baxter	Jack		T	*May Baxter* LR 33
Frigger	Baxter	Jack		T	*Star of Hope* LR 39
Hard-hat Jack	Baxter	Jack		T	
Mormon Jack	Baxter	Jack		T	
Tatty Jack	Baxter	Jack		T	*Connie Baxter* LR 22
Titeram	Baxter	James		T	Peggy
Pop	Baxter	Percy		T	*Gypsy Queen* LR 62
Graham St Dick	Baxter	Richard	From Graham Street Third hand	T	
Old Dick	Baxter	Richard		T	
Polly's Dick	Baxter	Richard	Polly's son, Third hand	T	
Young Dick	Baxter	Richard		T	
Noisy	Baxter	Robert	Bass soloist in the choir	T	
Old Bob	Baxter	Robert		P	Pleasure boat
Parson Bob	Baxter	Robert		T	Sunbeam
Father	Baxter	Sam		T	*Eleanor* LR 100
Lile Tom	Baxter	Thomas		T	*Nance* LR 181
Old Walt	Baxter	Walter		T	*Crusader* LR 12
Young Casey	Baxter	Walter		T	Speedwell
Black Duck	Baxter	William		T	Isobel
Dolly	Baxter	William		T	
Granny	Baxter	William		T	
Knocker	Baxter	William		T	*Florence Baxter* LR 29
Lile Bill	Baxter	William	Skippered other owners' boats	T	
Old William	Baxter	William		T	
Ringsand	Baxter	William		T	

Nickname	Surname	First name	Description		
Young Knocker	Baxter	William	Knocker's son	T	
Pot-ash	Baxter			T	
Scant	Baxter			T	
Gurt Dan	Bell	Daniel		T	
Lang Dan	Bell	Daniel	Very tall	T	
Young Dan	Bell	Daniel		T	
Manser	Bell	Jack		P	Princess Royal
Manser	Bell	John		T	
Gentleman Joe	Bell	Joseph	A member of the Liberal Club	T	
Young Joe	Bell	Joseph		T	
Bon	Bell	Robert		T	
Young Bob	Bell	Robert		T	
Scrimmer	Bell	Thomas		T	
Mad Ike	Bell	Walter		T	
Doggy	Bell			T	
Royal	Bond	Albert Edward		T	
Bonnye	Bond	Percy		T	
Long Dick	Bond	Richard		P	
Shelly Dick	Bond	Richard		P	
Sambo	Bond	Samuel		P	
Flyer	Bond			T	
Turnip	Braid	James		T	
Calf-sen	Braid	Richard		T	
Duckanoo	Brown	William	Substituted 'duckanoo' for 'double-u' when spelling a word	T	
Tommy and Billy	Brown	Thomas		T	
Billy and Tommy	Brown	William		T	
Shadow	Cocking	Jack		T	
Jim	Cocking	James		T	
Chirp	Cocking	John		T	
Old General	Dobson	James		T	
Sniggy Bill	Douglas	Robert	Third hand	T	
Duggie	Dugdale	Harold		T	*Falcon* LR 45
Danny Boy	Gardner	Daniel		T	Peggy
Humbler	Gardner	James		T	*Edith Nora* LR 129, LR 17
Dicky do nowt	Gardner	Richard	Third hand	T	
Old Dicky	Gardner	Richard		T	Peggy
Old Rafty	Gardner	Richard		T	Zilpha
Robbie	Gardner	Robert		T	Sunbeam
Lively	Gardner	Wilfred		T	Ellen
Billy Rafty	Gardner	William		T	
Old G	Gerrard	Simon		T	

Tatchin	Gerrard	Thomas		T	
Gurt Bill	Gerrard	William		T	
Corny	Hodgson	Cornelius	Third hand	T	
Bert	Hodgson	Herbert		T	Hannah
Holmee	Holmes	John		P	
Kenny	Mayor	Kenneth	Rower	P	
Chronic	Mount	George		T	*Wahine* LR 57
Somebody	Mount	George		T	*Jane*
Young George	Mount	George	Third hand	T	
Old Harry	Mount	Harold		T	*Mascot* LR 1
Cinders	Mount	John		T	*Cricket* LR 20
See Me	Mount	John	Prefaces statements with 'See me. I was....'	T	*Invincible* LR 19
Shiney	Mount	John		T	*Volunteer, Nora*
Geordie	Parkinson	George		T	Ann
Red Hill	Parkinson	Joseph		T	Annie
Young Joe	Parkinson	Joseph	Third hand	T	
Colonel	Raby	Walter		T	
Glasshammer	Rigby	Thomas		T	
Clocky	Swain	Thomas	Top man	P	
Geggie	Swain	Thomas	Back o Dock	P	
Old Ridley	Swain	Richard		T	*Teutonic* LR 85
Ridley Dick	Threlfall	Richard	Third hand	T	
Spaudy	Threlfall	Thomas	Rower	P	
Showy	Threlfall			T	
Old David	Threlfall	David		T	
Ned Russian	Willacy	Edward	'Russian' usually denotes a foul temper	T	
Judd	Willacy	George		T	
Gilly	Willacy	Gilbert		T	
Nibbler	Willacy	Herbert		T	
The Monk	Willacy	Jack		T	
Seaweed	Willacy	James	Recited a weather rhyme about seaweed	T	
Rube	Willacy	Ruben		T	
Jerkem	Willacy	Herbert	Mackerel fisher, cried 'Jerkem in'	T	Jane
Roddin	Wilson	Robert		T	*Nora* LR 59
Fanny Adam	Wilson	Adam	Third hand	T	
Me-Me	Woodhouse	Adam		T	Me-Me
Gurt Hamper	Woodhouse	Arthur	Talked of a 'gurt hamper' full of shrimp	T	*Snowdrop* LR 117
Big Ted	Woodhouse	Edward	Rower	P	
Neger	Woodhouse	Edward	Top man	P	

Kewley	Woodhouse	Eli	Third hand	T	
Corbet	Woodhouse	Fred		T	
Ferdie	Woodhouse	Fred	Rower	P	
Bonny Lile Harry	Woodhouse	Harold	Third hand	T	
Wilt's Harry	Woodhouse	Harold	Third hand	T	
Dick's Harry	Woodhouse	Harry		T	*Blanche* LR 193
Shy	Woodhouse	Harry		T	
Beasley Jack	Woodhouse	Jack	Third hand	T	Mary
Berry Tree Jack	Woodhouse	Jack	Third hand	T	
Happy Jack	Woodhouse	Jack		T	
Christie Jimmy	Woodhouse	James		T	
Lame Jim	Woodhouse	James		T	*Seagull* LR 44
Widgey	Woodhouse	James		T	*Midnight* LR 16
Lile John Thomas	Woodhouse	John Thomas		T	*Sisters, Viking*
Fish John Thomas	Woodhouse	John Thomas	Boss	P	
Old Shut	Woodhouse	Martin		T	Edith
Gentlemen	Woodhouse	Richard		T	
Old Dick	Woodhouse	Richard		T	*Rotha* LR 125
Young Dick	Woodhouse	Richard		T	*Annie Bell* LR 192
Luggy	Woodhouse	Robert		T	
Berry Tree	Woodhouse	Thomas		T	*Topsy* LR 179
Walt	Woodhouse	Walter	Third hand	T	
Old Wilt	Woodhouse	Wilfred		T	*Clara Mount* LR 29
Prodder	Woodhouse	Wilfred	Third hand	T	
Billy Ned	Woodhouse	William	Third hand	T	
Billy Traveller	Woodhouse	William		T	
Old Willy	Woodhouse	William		T	*De Wet* LR 131

Appendix IV
Extract from *Rawstrone's Ledger*, 1870-92

Boat Name	Type	Customer	Address
Town of Preston	Schooner	Mr Jackson & Co.	
Lilla	Schooner	Mr Robert Wright & Co.	
Spencer	Schooner	Mr Robert Wright & Co.	
Mary	Bay Boat	J. Rimmer	
Jane	Schooner	Mr Jas Hargreaves & Co	
Esther Ellen	Bay Boat	Mr Robert Rimmer	Little London
Monarch		Mr John Rimmer	Hesketh Bank
	Bay Boat	Mr Jas Robinson	Southport
Anne Jane	Bay Boat	Mr Hutch (Johns) Wright	Southport
Morning Star		Jas Spencer	Southport
	Bay Boat		Southport
Excelsior	Trawl Boat	Richard Roskall	
	Trawl Boat		
Marco Polo		P. Jackson	Southport
Clipper	Bay Boat	Mr Richard (Henry Cotty) Wright & John (Bull) Rigby	Southport
		Robert Jackson	Southport
		Richard Wright	Marshside
Union		Peter Rigby	
Nimble	Trawl Boat		
	Trawl Boat	Nicholas Leadbetter	
Kathleen	Trawl Boat	Joseph Croft	
Mary Anne	Shanking boat	J. Parker & R. Wright	
Union		Peter Rigby	
Mary Ellen	Trawl Boat		
John	Shanking boat	Peter (Cotty's) Wright	
Bee	Flat		
Mary	Shanking boat	John Rimmer	Southport
Polly	Shanking boat	Cookson	
Prosperity	Trawl Boat	Richard Leadbetter	
Anne Williams	Yacht?	James Spencer	Southport
	Yacht	Mr Hays	Southport
Mary Ellen	Shanking boat	J. Jackson	Lytham
Clipper	Shanking boat	Richard (Henrys) Wright	
New boat	Shanking boat		
New boat	Shanking boat		
	Shanking boat	Mr Hankison	Lytham
Morning Star			
Ivanhoe	Yacht		Southport
Maud	Yacht	Capt Baldwin	Southport
	Shanking boat	Peter (Cotty) Wright	

Surprise	Smack		
Snowdrop		John Keen	
Mistress of the Banks	Shanking boat	Peter Brookfield	
Wonder	Shanking boat		
Isabella	Shanking boat		
Northern Light		J. Spencer	Southport
New boat	Shanking boat	Thos Richardson	
Snowdrop		John Keen	
Mary Alice	Shanking boat		Lytham
Gratitude	Smack		
Snowdrop	Smack		
Onward	Shanking boat	P. Brookfield	
Merlin	Fishing boat		
Maggie	Pleasure boat	Howard	Southport
Polly	Shanking boat	Lawrence Abram	Banks
Onward	Shanking boat		Long Lane Banks
High Flyer	Smack	Robert Dawson	Lytham
Little Nellie	Fishing boat		
Clipper	Shanking boat		
New boat	Shanking boat	Benjamin Ball	Southport
Clipper	Shanking boat	Richard (Henry) Wright	Banks
Lizzie	Shanking boat		Southport
Little Willie			Southport
Beaver	Smack		
	Shanking boat	Richard Abram	
Chester	Shanking boat		Southport
New boat	Shanking boat		
	Shanking boat	Edward Holding	
Prosperity	Shanking boat		
Mary	Shanking boat	John Rimmer	Southport
Little Willie	Shanking boat		Southport
Lark	Shanking boat		
	Shanking boat	John Johnson	3 Shellfield Rd Marshside
Alice Ann	Shanking boat		
	Shanking boat		Southport
Northern Light	Shanking boat		
Alexandra Eccles	Shanking boat		
Merlin	Yacht	J. Richardson	
	Shanking boat	B. Ball	90 Virginny St Southport
Shrimp Girl			
New boat	Shanking boat	John Ball	Marshside
Golden Arrow	Shanking boat	R.L. Ashcroft	
Welcome	Shanking boat	John Rimmer	
Garside	Smack		
Lark	Shanking boat		
New boat	Shanking boat	Dawson	
Little Willie			Southport
Northern Light	Shanking boat	J. Spencer	Southport
Moon Light	Shanking boat	Lawson	Southport
Nightingale	Shanking boat	Dawson	Lytham
Christina		N. Leadbetter	

	Shanking boat	B. Ball	90 Virginny St Southport
New boat	Shanking boat	W. Watkinson	Marshside
Golden Arrow	Shanking boat	T.R. Ascroft	
	Shanking boat	Chas Rigby	Southport
May	Shanking boat	T.R. Ascroft	
	Shanking boat	Wilsons	Lytham
Lamb	Shanking boat	R.L. Ashcroft	Lytham
	Shanking boat		Preston
Bertha	Shanking boat		
May	Shanking boat	R.L. Ashcroft	
	Shanking boat	Peter Kellett	
Teapot	Shanking boat		
Annie	Shanking boat	John Melling	Church Road St Anne's
Mayflower	Smack		

Both trawl boats and smacks were big ketch-rigged first-class trawlers. The yard also did repair work on the dredgers' boats and on two pleasure steamers, and prepared timber products for the local landowners and businessmen.

Appendix V

Scantlings

The parts are numbered to provide a parts list to the ¾inch to 1ft drawings of *Nora*, Figs 74 to 81. In addition to the conventional parts' names, those used at Morecambe are also listed.

No.	Part	Scantlings	Material	Notes
1	Keel Plate	3in x ¾in	Iron	
2	Stem Piece	1¼in x ½in	Iron	Fastened with square boat nails
3	Facing Plate	¼in thick	Iron plate	With forestay lug
4	Keel	4in x 9in	Oak	
5	Filling Chocks		Softwood	
6	Stern post	3in x 8in	Elm	
7	Deadwoods	3½in	Elm and oak	In three parts
8	Forefoot	4in	Oak	Siding reduces to 3¾in
9	Stem	3¾in	Elm	
10	Stemson	3in x 3in	Elm	Apron at Morecambe
11	Stopwaters	¼in diameter	Softwood	Driven clear of rebate
12	Floors	1⅞in	Oak	See also 18
13	Timbers	1⅞in x 2¾in	Oak	See also 14, 20, 27, 29
15	Keelson	9in x 2½in	Softwood	Tapers to 5 in. Inbrest at Morecambe
19	Chocks	1⅞in	Oak	Extend floors to rebate
21	Bulkhead	1¾in	Oak	Three pieces, Mainstern at Morecambe, Tuck elsewhere
22	Rudder case			**Two** pieces, loose tongues
23	Strong-back	2¾in x 1¾in		Clamps rudder case to Mainstern
24	Filling piece	3in x 1in		Hollowed to suit rudder nailed to back of sternpost between case and heel-bit upstand.
25	Horn timber	1½in	Oak	Nailed to centre piece
26	Centre piece	2in	Larch	Nailed to item 23
28	Stern nog	3½in square	Oak	Housed in main stern
30	Bow nog	2¾in square	Oak	Bolted to top timber
31	Riding strip	1in x 2¾in	Larch	Thwart riser
32	Shelf	1in x 4½in	Larch	
33	Counter frame	2in x 4in	The only original part is larch	
34	Quarter knee	2in	Missing	Skew-nailed to mainstern
35	Thwart	9in x 3in		Thoft at Morecambe
36	Plank	1in	Larch	
37	Bilge plank	1½in	Oak	Sand clog by J. Crossfield
38	Rubbing bend	1½in x 2¾in	Oak	Moulding at Morecambe
40	Iron Breasthook	2in x ¼in	Fitted externally as a reinforcement late in *Nora's* life	
41	Ledge	2in x 5½in	Larch	
42	Beams	2¾in x 3in	Larch	½in to foot round up
43	Mast chock	2½in	Larch	In two pieces
45	Deck plank	1⅛in x 2½in	Spruce	Tongue and grooved
46	Covering board	1⅛in x 1¼in	Spruce	

47	Beaching leg Eyebolt		$^7/_8$ Whitworth	
48	Pin Rail	2in x 3in pillars	Three pillars	
49	Eye Cleat		For Topsail Tack on CL, for topping lift to port	
50	Gammon iron			Bowsprit iron at Morecambe
51	Mooring roller	3¼in x 3½in Diameter	Cast iron	
52	Cheek block		Oak	Supported by knee
53	Outside coaming	1½in	Oak	Spiked down
55	Rudder stock	2in diameter	Iron	New, squared top, originally would have been narrower at the square top.
56	Rudder band	2in x ¼in	Iron	Cope iron
57	Rudder band	2in x ¼in	Iron	Flat bar, not original
59	Clip	3in x ¼in	Iron	
60	Beds	3in x 6in	Oak	To suit Kelvin 6-7 engine
62	Bearer	3in x 2in	Oak	
65	Shaft log	6in x 6in	Oak	
67	Shroud iron	3in x ¼in	Iron	Cope with forged lug
68	Mid nog	2¾in sq.		
69	Coaming	1in x 6in		Round ended
70	Hatch top		Made flat	Also "atop t' hatch"
72	Capstan			
73	Samson Post	4in x 4in	Oak	With Hook bolt or hook on long link
74	Forestay lug	$^5/_8$in	Iron	½ in diameter hole, riveted to item 3
75	Mast wedges	$^5/_8$in at deck		
76	Hounds		Left square on mast or oak chocks	
77	Throat halyard crane	Iron	with through bolt and spike, called iron at Morecambe	
78	Forestay crane			
79	Peak halyard eyebolt			
80	Topsail halyard sheave		Set 10 deg. to port forward	
81	Mast bands	3½in & 4in diameter	Iron	With 2 lugs, upper lugs vertical, lower horizontal
82	Reef tackle cleats	Oak	One thumb, one horn	
83	Reef bees	1⅞in thick	Oak	With three holes
84	Main sheet eyebolt			
85	Tumbler			
86	Parrel			
87	Peak halyard span cleat			
88	Topsail outhaul bee	1in x 2in x 10in		
89	Bowsprit fid holes			Three to suit the three jibs.
90	Jib outhaul sheave			
91	Rudder case cap	8in x 20in	Oak	With chafe iron
92	Capstan foot pedal			
93	Staysail fairlead	Oak	1in x 2in x 10in nailed down	
94	Jib sheet fairleads	ditto	ditto	
95	Deck lights		Glass Prism	Also t' prism or dead light at Morecambe
96	Half beams	23¼in x 3in	Larch	1in housing in beam shelf
97	Booby hatch beam			

98	Bowsprit heel wedge			
99	Bowsprit stop pin or fid			
100	Mooring beam	2¾in x 4in	Larch	With lodging knees
101	Deck hook	6in thick	Oak	Grain vertical
102	Limit of cockpit		Built without carlings	
103	Bulkheads	½in	Softwood	Tongue & groove
104	Benches		Softwood	With lockers under
105	Bench support	1in board	Softwood	Nailed to Foc's'le ceiling riser, item 116
106	Foc's'le sole	1in boards	Softwood	Laid athwartships. ceiling at Morecambe
107	Tee headed bolt	¼in diameter		Driven down through coaming
108	Cockpit step	1in boards	Softwood	Laid athwartships, made with centre panel.
109	Cockpit sole	1in boards	Softwood	Laid athwartships, made with three centre panels, ballast boards at Morecambe
110	Shaft centreline			
111	Engine beds	3in x 5in		Deduced from fays and bolt holes
112	Bearer	2in x 3in		Deduced from fay mark
113	Stove chimney			In builders location
114	Pump	4in sq plunge hole	Wood,	fitted to port
115	Capstan drive			
116	Foc's'le sole riser	Softwood	Let down over frames	

Inventory of Blocks

Type	Quantity
Single – rope stropped	Six
Single -solid hook	Seven
Single -hook & becket	Three
Double -rope stropped	Two
Double -solid hook	Three

List of material put in before rebuild commenced.

117	New deck laid on top of new rudder case *c.*1953			
118	Damage to centre piece (26) when removing clamp (23)			
119	Rot in sternpost			
120	Engine Beds	4in x 6in x 9ft	Oregon pine	
121	Cross bearers	4in x 6in	Oak	To support 120
122	Laminated futtock			Fitted after wreck of 1976
123	Pipe tripod feet			For fish tackle
124	Cleat		Oak	Spiked down
125	Capstan pad	2in thick		
126	Location of Capstan foot control			
127	Plywood patch over mast and stove pipe holes			
128	Break in height of coaming			
129	Bow Nogs	3in square	Oak	
130	Deck beams and shelf			
131	Lodging Knee	2½in thick	Oak	
132	Mooring Beam	4in x 4in	Softwood	
133	Samson Post	4in x 4in	Oak	Heel nailed to frame
134	Breast hook	2in	Mahogany	
135	Bow Cants	2in x 2¾in	Oak	

136	Apron	Oak	
137	Stem	Oak	Repaired 1962, and later
138	Stove chimney opening under patch		
139	Capstan drive through patch		
140	Capstan Drive hole under		
141	Bolster with cope for trawl rope		

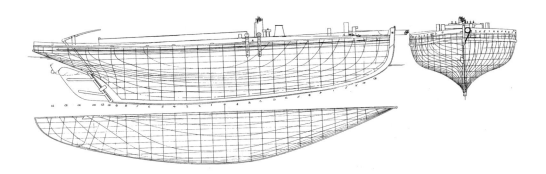

Fig. 74. *Nora* LR 59 lines.

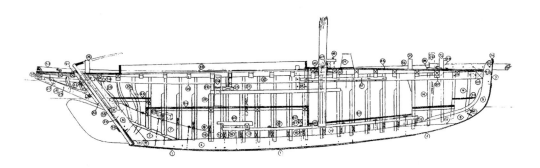

Fig. 75. *Nora* LR 59 construction profile.

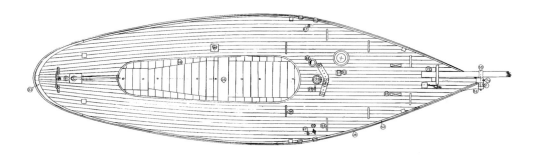

Fig. 76. *Nora* LR 59 deck plan.

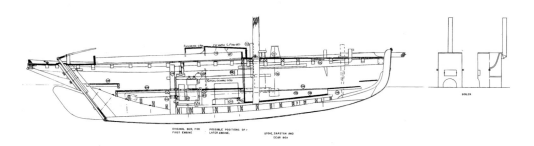

Fig. 77. *Nora* LR 59 outfit profile.

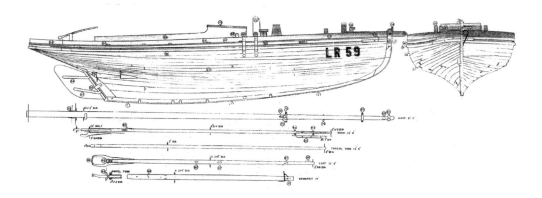

Fig. 78. *Nora* LR 59 profile, run of plank.

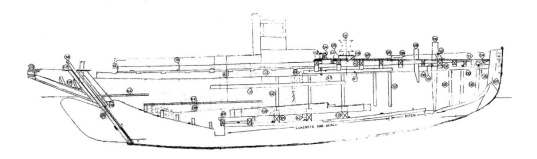

Fig. 79. *Nora* LR 59 rigging list.

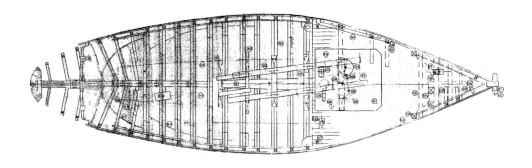

Fig. 80. *Nora* LR 59 profile as found.

Fig. 81. *Nora* LR 59 deck as found.

References

Aflalo F.G.   1904, *The Sea Fishing Industry of England and Wales*, London, Edward Stanford.

Ashton W.   1920, *The Evolution of a Coast Line*, London, Edward Stanford & Wm Ashton & Sons Ltd

Aughton P.   1988, *North Meols and Southport*, Preston, Carnegie Publishing Ltd.

Ayton R. & Daniell W.   1814, *Sailing on Horseback*, Ed. Innes MacLeod, Dumfries, T.C. Fames & Co,

Bailey F.A.   1955, *A History of Southport*, Southport, Angus Downey.

Benham H.   1977, *The Stowboaters*, Colchester, Essex County Newspapers Ltd.

Bingham R.K.   1990, *Lost Resort? The Flow and Ebb of Morecambe*, Milnthorpe, Cicerone Press.

Blake B.   1955, *The Solway Firth*, The Regional Books Series, Clerkenwell, Robert Hale Ltd.

Census returns, *Bulmers, Kellys, Mannex,* and *Steels* directories, *Lancaster Gazette* (edited by Linda Moorhouse, Elsinore House), Morecambe Visitor, Public record Office collections.

Chapelle H.I.   1950, *American Small Sailing Craft*, New York, W.W. Norton

Cumberland Sea Fisheries Committee   1889 et seq., *Quarterly Reports and Minutes*, Unpublished, Cumbria Record Office, Carlisle Castle

Davis F.M.   1958, *An Account of the Fishing Gear of England and Wales*, 4th edition, HMSO.

Elmer W.   1973, *The Terminology of Fishing*, The Cooper Monographs, Ed R Stamm University of Basle.

Glazebrook T.K.   1826, *A Guide to Southport, North Meols in the County of Lancaster*, 2nd ed., London, C. & J. Rivington.

Haley R.   1995, *Lytham St Anne's a Pictorial History*, Chichester, Phillimore & Co. Ltd.

Hatch J. et al, Ed.   1909, *Morecambe Lancaster & District Souvenir of the Conference of the National Union of Teachers*, Pub Henry Frowde, Hodder & Stoughton.

Holdsworth E.W.H.   1874, *Deep Sea Fishing and Fishing Boats*, London, Edward Stanford.

Horsley P. & Hirst A.   1991, *Fleetwood's Fishing Industry*, Beverley, Hutton Press.

Jenkins J.G.   1991, *The Inshore Fishermen of Wales*, Cardiff, University of Wales Press.

Kemp D.   1988, *Manual of Yacht and Boat Sailing*, 8th

Kennerley E.   edition, Southampton, Ashford Press Publishing. 1982, *The Old Fishing Community of Polton le Sands*, Lancaster, Lancaster Museum.

Lancashire and Western Sea Fisheries Committee   1891 et seq., *Report on the Fisheries of the District*, Preston, Lancashire and Western Sea Fisheries Committee.

Lawson Booth, J.H.   1949, *The North Meols Fishermen's Provident Association Minute Book*, Typed Transcript, collection of Botanic Gardens Museum, Churchtown.

Leach A.   1991, *Our Barrow, Barrow Village*, Ulverston, Furness Heritage Press.

Lloyd L.J.   2000, *Botanic Gardens Museum Maritime Collection*, Southport, Sefton Council.

Mannering Julian et al.   1997, *The Chatham Directory of Inshore Craft*, London, Chatham Publishing.

March E.J.   1970, *Inshore Craft*, Newton Abbot, David & Charles.

Mariner's Mirror   1951, *Shipbuilding at Annan*, vol. XXXVII, p 128.

Marshall J.D.   1974, *Lancashire* City and County History series, Newton Abbot, David & Charles.

Mayes G.I. & J.E.   2000, *On a Broad Reach*, Bristol, Bernard McCall.

McKee E   1983, *Working Boats of Great Britain*, London, Conway Maritime Press.

Pearson J.   1990, *Nobby News*, No 7, September, the newsletter of the Nobby Owners Association.

Potter T.   1994, *Reflections on Blackpool*, Wilmslow, Sigma Press.

Quick R.C.   1962, *The History of Morecambe and Heysham*, Morecambe, Morecambe Times

Richardson J.   1880, *Furness Past & Present*, Barrow-in-Furness, Richardson.

Roberts S.J.   1992, *Hoylake & Meols Past*, Chichester, Phillimore & Co.

Rollinson W. & Harrison B.   1986, *The Diary of William Fisher of Barrow, 1811 -1859*, Centre for N W Regional Studies, University of Lancaster, Occasional Paper No 15.

Rothwell C.   1983, *Shipwrecks of the North West*, Chorley, Countryside Publications Ltd.

Scott-Hindson, B.   1994, *Whitehaven Harbour*, Chichester, Phillimore & Co.

Simper R.   1979, *Gaff Sail*, Watford, Argus Books.

Troughton W.   1997, *Aberystwyth Harbour, an Illustrated History*, Aberystwyth, The National Library of Wales.

Twigger R.   23 Feb 1999, *Research Paper 99/20*, House of Commons Library, Westminster.

Walton, J.K.   1978, *The Blackpool Landlady: A Social History*, Manchester University Press.

Woodhouse R.   1979, *Log book/Diary of Dick Woodhouse*, Unpublished, Lancaster Maritime Museum Collection.

Glossary

Ballast Boards	A platform built in the nobby's cockpit, the local name for the cockpit sole.
Barratry	Any fraudulent or knowingly illegal act of the master or crew of a vessel, to the prejudice of the vessel or its owner.
Baulk	A fish trap built from wattle fencing, with a net chamber and cobble walls to retain the fish as the tide ebbed.
Bay Boat	A Morecambe nobby with a large cockpit fitted with bench seating, for the holiday trade.
Bearding	The surface of the rebate that the plank lays against and into which the fastenings are driven.
Birds-nest Model	A half model assembled from a backboard cut to the profile, with five or seven frames cut from board fastened in place in shallow housings. Thin ribbands are then nailed round from stem to stern to define the shape of the hull, these create the birds-nest appearance. Also called Bracket model.
Bobbins	Rollers threaded onto the ground rope of the trawl, like a string of beads.
Bogey	Both the ironic name for the stownet, and for the small double hob coal stove used to heat the foc's'le.
Boomer	A spar, secured to the deck of the nobby and extending outboard, to hold the shank trawl rope away from the hull of the nobby to allow the shanks to cover more ground.
Bracket Model	A half model assembled from a backboard cut to the profile, with five or seven frames cut from board fastened in place in shallow housings. Thin ribbands are then nailed round from stem to stern to define the shape of the hull. The frames resemble brackets. Also called Birds-nest model.
Braiding	The process of hand making nets, with twine held and passed on a shuttle like needle.
Bridles	A pair of ropes each attached to each end of the shank beam or to each trawl head at one end, and to the trawl rope at the other.
Broadsiding	Towing one or two nets over the ground using the power of the tide to drive the nobby, which lays broadside to the tide.
Bunt	The middle part of a seine or draw net, often deeper than the rest. The last part to come ashore, where most of the catch will be found.
By-catch	Unwanted fish caught in the same trawl as the target fish, usually of no value.
Cants	Frames that are not perpendicular to the centre line.
Carlin	A beam running for'd and aft under a deck, to support half beams, either between main beams or bounding a hatch or cockpit.
Cart shanking	Trawling for shrimp in about three to five feet of water, using a two-wheeled horse drawn cart to tow one or two shank nets.
Cod	A bag, the tail end of the trawl, into which the fish are gathered.
Cop	A bank or earthwork, applied to flood defence embankments, from the Old English *copp*, a hill or crest.

Craam	A short-handled three tined rake used to pick cockles out of the sand and flick them into the fisherman's basket.
Cutch	A tanning agent properly called catechu, imported from Spain or the Far East.
Cutting in	Dividing the contents of the stow net cod end into manageable quantities.
Deadwood	Middle line timber, either the knee that ties the sternpost to the keel, or timber fitted beneath the keel to extend it down to the desired profile.
Depth	The register dimension from the crown of the deck beam to the top of the keel or keelson.
Dogger	A large stem punt at Morecambe and in the Lune, strong and burdensome enough to stand being loaded with mussels. They were fitted with a drop keel, and rigged with a standing lug and jib.
Dragging	A term borrowed from North America for the purposes of this book, to identify trawling under the power of the sail, rather than the power of the tide.
Draw net	A curtain of net, worked from the shore, by carrying one end out into the stream, and circling back to the shore, when both ends are pulled in, bringing in any fish encircled by the net.
Dutch pot	The coal-fired portable boiler in which the shrimp was boiled.
Fall	The part of a rope that is hauled on and belayed.
Fay mark	The imprint in the surface of timber caused by wear or crushing inflicted by another component to which it is fastened.
Fid	Wood or iron bar made to fit a hole in a spar, and rest against timbers that constrain the spar, to take the trust of the rig, that may be withdrawn to allow that spar to be reefed.
Fixed engine	The official designation for any net not attached to a boat.
Flapper	A net non-return valve fitted at the start of the cod end, to prevent fish from swimming forward out of the trawl.
Flat knot	The name applied to the reef knot used when braiding net, usually used for shrimp net.
Floor	Transverse framing component that ties the two sides of the boats bottom together and to the keel.
Fluke	Alternative name for the flounder, a fish similar in size and habit to the plaice.
Grape barrel	Grapes used to be imported packed in slack coopered barrels packed in granulated cork.
Haws	Area of sand hills and rough grass or scrubland.
Head ledge	The for'd and after end of a hatch or cockpit coaming, set athwartships.
Hood end	The end of a plank that is fitted into a rebate, at the end of the run, rather than a butt end where two planks join to make up a strake or run.
Horned	Horning in is the process of setting up frames square to the centre line, or for cants so that both sides are symmetrical.
Horn timber	The centre line timber or keel of the counter.
Joggle	A step in the face of a component to fit against overlapping components, or to accept a nib end.
Kebbing	The local term for hand line fishing with baited hooks.
Kentledge	Pig iron ingots when used as ballast.
Kettle	A fixed fish trap, of nets hung on posts, that retained fish as the tide ebbed.
King plank	A thicker deck plank laid along the mid-line of the deck.
Knightheads	Timbers fastened to the sides of the stem or apron, extended above the deck to locate and support the bowsprit.
Leap	A wickerwork fish basket, carried on the back, with a stave that goes across the chest, attached to the basket by short rope straps.

Let Down	The boat building term for a joint, where a component is fitted into a recess cut in a piece of greater dimension, e.g. where a half beam is fitted into a halving in a deeper carling.
Lifts	Boards cut to the shape of horizontal slices through a boats hull, assembled into a block and carved to represent the boats shape.
Lines	A drawing that defines the shape of a boats hull. The abbreviation for Lines Plan.
Longline	A method of catching bottom-feeding fish, comprising halted hooks on lines called snoods, attached at intervals to a stout cord. It is set from a boat, anchored at each end, and marked with buoys. Called a trawl in the USA, and a trotline when set on the beach.
Mollinger	An enamelled quart mug, a quart equals 1.136 litres.
Moulding	Either the dimension across the parallel sides of a piece of framing timber of a boat, or the Morecambe term for a rubbing strake in the topsides of a nobby.
Mousing	A seizing tied across the bow of a hook to prevent it falling out of the eye into which it is placed.
Nib	The practice of cutting a tapering component off square, before it becomes too narrow to accept a fastening, and fitting it into a joggle in its neighbour or in a rebate.
Nog	A timberhead, fitted into the nobby's deck, to which the trawl ropes were belayed.
Oddfellows	An earlier form of self help social security association, whereby the members all paid in a regular subscription, and received financial support when ill or injured.
Offal	The by catch of low value fish.
Pigtail Hook	A self-mousing hook, made by coiling the point like the tail of a pig.
Pitching	Masonry slope erected at the head of the beach to prevent erosion, usually steep and built of rubble masonry.
Potted shrimp	A dish of shrimp preserved in spiced clarified butter.
Pound boards	Boards used to create partitioned stowage's for ice and iced fish.
Power net	A six to seven foot wide net bag, held open by a wooden frame, pushed over the sand in about two feet of water by a fisherman in search of shrimp.
Provident Association	A later form of self help social security, whereby the members all paid in a regular subscription, and received financial support when ill or injured.
Punt	A full-bodied open rowing boat, with a stem and usually a transom stern.
Quarter	A boat has forward and aft quarters, describing the part between the bow and the middle, and between the middle and the stern.
Room and Space	The distance between a boats frame and the same part of the next frame. Literally the 'room' occupied by one frame and the 'space' between it and its neighbour.
Rope walk	A rope manufactory, often a long straight path, but also a roofed building, often 400yd long. The table wheel and spinning wheels are fixed at one end and the sledge and drags work at the other.
Rough	Shrimp sold in its shell, or a rocky bottom where sprawn are found.
Sarn	A shingle or cobble bank, running out perpendicular to the Cardigan Bay coast, from 'a raised road or embankment' in Welsh.
Set net	A relatively simple form of fixed net, set from a row of stakes driven perpendicular to the edge of a river channel, to trap or entangle fish going out with the tide.
Shank	A shrimp trawl, with the main beam at the foot of the net, the head of which was held open by a lighter beam or withy hoop.

Shoot or shout	A nett braiding knot, a sheet bend tied so as to invert the knot, or possibly an alternative name for the flat knot.
Sideing	The dimension between flat sides of a piece of a boats framing.
Skottle	A hatch in the foredeck of a nobby, to give access to and from the foc's'le, or in other craft to allow the mast to lower backwards.
Slack	An ephemeral pool found between established sand dunes.
Slape	A term to describe a smooth fluid sand bottom, with out ripples, on which no shrimp will be caught.
Snood	The cord that attaches the hook to the main line on a hand line or longline.
Springer	A rope, usually weaker than the trawl rope, used to control the direction that the trawl runs away from the boat. It is passed around the trawl rope with both ends secured inboard. It is adjusted to steer the smack.
Standing part	The part of a rope that is secured more or less permanently, that is not adjusted in use.
Stealer	A length of plank in carvel practice, used to either reduce the width of a wide plank, or to combine two narrow streaks into one.
Stopwater	A softwood dowel, driven into a tight hole bored along a joint face to prevent leakage through the joint.
Tallegoram	The Morecambe name for the coal fired boiler in which the shrimp was boiled aboard the nobby.
Tee line	A form of trot or longline set to take flatfish using pin or thorn hooks. These are straight and sharp at both ends, made from brass wire or black-thorn, with the snood tied at their mid length. They work by jamming across the fish's mouth or throat.
Tide edge	The slower running water at the shallower edge of a channel.
Ton, tonnage	The measure of the earning capacity of a vessel based on the number of tuns of wine that she could carry. One ton was a nominal equivalent to one hundred cubic feet (2.83 m³). From about 1780 to 1836 tonnage was calculated as follows, let L = the length from stem to sternpost on deck, and B = the beam outside the planking at the broadest part of the ship, above or below the wales. Then Tonnage = $((L - 3/5 B) \times B \times \frac{1}{2}B)/94$, in tons and hundredths.
Training walls	Rock walls erected along a river channel to confine the flow of the tide with the intention of using the scour of the flow to maintain the channels depth.
Trawl	A bag shaped net dragged through the water, with a rope or chain across the bottom of the mouth, held open by either a beam across its top, or by paravanes called doors or otter boards. Not to be confused with the American term for a long line.
Trot	A longline set on the beach at low tide, to fish the rise and ebb.
Veil	A net curtain fitted to trawls and shanks, to direct fish out through the bottom of a shrimp or prawn trawl, to reduce the bye-catch.
Vivier tanks	Tanks fitted to keep fish alive on their way to market.
Wherry	A fast sailing vessel, used for river or coastal passages carrying high value cargoes and passengers.
Whammel	A form of drift net designed specifically for salmon fishing, and the boat developed to work the net.
Whiskers	Iron bar, or light spars used to spread the bowsprit shrouds, fitted to the stem head or occasionally to the deck edge or to a band on the bowsprit.
Whisket	A wickerwork basket, smaller than a hamper, used when cleaning (sorting) shrimp on the nobby.
White smith	A metal worker making zinc products.

Bibliography

Starkey, D.L. et al., England's Sea Fisheries, Chatham Publishing, 2000.

Millward & Robinson, *Cumbria, Landscapes of Britain*, Macmillan Education Ltd, 1972.

Marshal & Sparham, *Fishing, the coastal tradition*, B.T. Batsford 1987.

Norton, Peter, *End of the Voyage*, Persival Marshall, 1959.

Simper, Robert, *Beach Boats of Britain*, The Boydell Press, 1984.

Walton, John K. *Lancashire – A Social History 1558-1939*, Manchester University Press, 1987.

Index